John Adams Dix

Speeches and Occasional Addresses

John Adams Dix

Speeches and Occasional Addresses

ISBN/EAN: 9783744649179

Printed in Europe, USA, Canada, Australia, Japan

Cover: Foto ©ninafisch / pixelio.de

More available books at **www.hansebooks.com**

SPEECHES

AND

OCCASIONAL ADDRESSES.

BY

JOHN A. DIX.

VOL. II.

NEW YORK:
D. APPLETON AND COMPANY,
443 AND 445 BROADWAY.
1864.

Entered according to Act of Congress, in the year 1864, by
D. APPLETON AND COMPANY,
in the Clerk's Office of the District Court of the Southern District of New York.

RIVERSIDE, CAMBRIDGE:
STEREOTYPED AND PRINTED BY H. O. HOUGHTON.

CONTENTS OF VOLUME II.

SPEECHES IN THE SENATE.

THE PILOT LAWS 1
    A speech on the bill to repeal the Act of Congress, of March 2d, 1802, regulating Pilots.

THE PILOT LAWS 12
    Second speech on the same subject.

ON HON. DIXON H. LEWIS 31
    Remarks on the Resolutions of the Senate on the occasion of the death of HON. DIXON H. LEWIS.

MEMORIALS OF OFFICERS IN MEXICO 35
    Remarks on presenting two Memorials of Officers of the Army serving in Mexico.

ADDRESSES AND REPORTS.

AFRICAN COLONIZATION 41
    Remarks addressed to the New York State Colonization Society.

OPINION ON TWO QUESTIONS OF ALIENISM 56

EDUCATION OF TEACHERS 72
    Report to the Regents of the University on the education of teachers.

REPORT ON THE MILITIA SYSTEM 116

GEOLOGICAL REPORT 181
    Report to the Legislature of New York, on a Geological Survey.

PROGRESS OF SCIENCE 242
    Lecture on the Progress of Science, delivered before the Alpha Phi Delta and Euglossian Societies of Geneva College.

APPORTIONMENT OF MEMBERS OF CONGRESS 279
    Speech on the apportionment of Members of Congress, delivered in the Assembly of New York.

CONTENTS.

RURAL LIFE AND EMBELLISHMENT 318
    An address before the Queen's County Agricultural Society.

GROWTH OF NEW YORK CITY 337
    Lecture on the Growth, Destinies, and Duties of the City of New York, delivered before the New York Historical Society.

AGRICULTURE OF NEW YORK 360
    Address on the Agriculture of New York, before the New York State Agricultural Society.

WAR WITH TRIPOLI 383
    Lecture on the War with Tripoli.

THE REBELLION IN LOUISIANA 410
    Letter from the Secretary of the Treasury on the Rebellion in Louisiana.

PROCLAMATION TO THE PEOPLE OF NEW YORK . . . 452

SPEECHES IN THE SENATE.

THE PILOT LAWS.

FEBRUARY, 1847.

The bill to repeal the act of Congress of 2d March, 1837, regulating pilots, being under consideration, Mr. Dix said:—

Mr. President: The bill under consideration provides for the repeal of the act of Congress of the 2d March, 1837, entitled "An act concerning pilots." Before I show what the act thus proposed to be repealed is, it may be proper to state what was the existing system in relation to pilotage before Congress had any authority to legislate on the subject. Before the adoption of the Constitution of the United States, each State regulated its own pilots. It prescribed the mode of their appointment, their duties, and their liabilities. The Colony of New York, as early as 1694, passed a law providing for their appointment by the Governor and Council, and prohibited all other persons from piloting any vessel into or out of the port of New York, under a pecuniary penalty. From that time to the adoption of the Constitution, the State legislated exclusively on the subject. The regulation of pilotage within its own jurisdiction was a State right. The Articles of Confederation found and left it so. The Constitution of the United States gives to Congress the power "to regulate commerce with foreign nations and among the several States, and with the Indian tribes." Under this delegation of authority, Congress assumed to legislate on the subject of pilotage. I do not stop to inquire now whether this power is fairly incidental to the express authority given to it to regulate commerce. But I desire to call the attention of the Senate to the fact, that, while asserting incidentally its right, it left the whole subject where it found it. For all practical purposes, it left the right as it was before the adoption of the Constitution — a State right. It recognized and confirmed the legislation of the States existing at the time in respect to pilotage, thus pronouncing it to be a fit subject for State regulation. The act of Congress referred to was passed on the 7th August 1789,[1] and the provision relating to the subject is as follows: —

"SEC. 4. That all pilots in the bays, inlets, rivers, harbors, and ports of the United States, shall continue to be regulated in conformity with the existing laws of the States, respectively, wherein such pilots may be, or with such laws as the States may, respectively, hereafter enact for the purpose, until further legislative provision shall be made by Congress."

By this act, it will be perceived that the laws of the States in relation to pilotage were recognized by Congress at its first session after the Constitution was adopted, and that, by referring to the future as well as the existing legislation of the States, it designed to place the whole subject prospectively under State regulation. Congress undoubtedly saw that this was one of those cases in which each State would be best capable of judging for itself what regulations the subject would require within its own limits, and that in providing for its own interest, that of the public would be most likely to be secured. From 1789 to 1837 this was the established system in respect to the regulation of all that relates to pilotage. Though the section I have read contemplated the possibility of future legislation by Congress, no further act was passed during a period of forty-eight years. I have not been able to find any other act referring to pilots in any manner, except the act of 1792, establishing a uniform militia, by which they were exempted from militia duty.

In the year 1837, two disastrous shipwrecks occurred on Long Island; and in the excitement of the moment, the pilots

[1] Laws of 1789, c. 9.

of New York were regarded as responsible for them. The clamor raised in New York extended to this city; and on the day preceding the close of the session of Congress, (March 2d, 1837,) an act[1] was passed providing, " that it shall and may be lawful for the master or commander of any vessel coming into or going out of any port situate upon waters which are the boundary between two States, to employ any pilot duly licensed or authorized by the laws of either of the States bounded on the said waters, to pilot said vessel to or from said port, any law, usage, or custom to the contrary notwithstanding."

The object of this act was to open the pilotage for the city of New York to competition between the pilots of the States of New York and New Jersey, from the idea, which prevailed, that the pilot system of New York had grown into a monopoly, and that the shipwrecks I have referred to were a consequence of it. I believe I may safely say that subsequent examinations before the judicial tribunals of New York resulted in an exoneration of the New York pilots from all censure in respect to those disasters. All the testimony I have seen confirms this statement. It was clearly shown that the loss of the two vessels, the Bristol and the Mexico, was not occasioned by their negligence or unskilfulness. Thus the New York pilots not only suffered for a time in the public estimation, on account of calamities for which they were in no manner responsible, but they have, since 1837, been suffering from an act of Congress passed under a misapprehension of the facts, and under the influence of an unjust judgment in respect to them.

The excitement against the New York pilots was undoubtedly aggravated by a prejudice against them, arising from the fact that under the laws existing at the time the shipwrecks referred to occurred, agreements had been formed among them for an apportionment of the duty of pilotage and a division of their profits, in such a manner as to destroy competition, and

[1] Laws of 1837, c. 22.

that it had led to a dangerous relaxation of vigilance in looking out for vessels and boarding them. There is no doubt that there was some ground for this complaint. But the defects of the existing laws were remedied by an act passed by the legislature of New York on the 12th of April, 1837. A board of commissioners was appointed to license pilots; their number was increased; they were subjected to rigid regulations in respect to training and licensing; the exclusive features of the old system were abandoned, and the freest competition between individuals was introduced by regulations which effectually precluded combination. Under these new provisions it may be confidently asserted that old defects would have been cured, and all the benefits to be anticipated from the most judicious system of regulations would have been secured, if they had been left to operate without any conflicting or contravening legislation by Congress.

The New York pilots, in skill, experience, enterprise, and fidelity, are not surpassed by any similar body of men in any country. They have been trained to their business; they have invested most of their property in it; they are the owners of their own boats, which are equal to any craft in the world, and which are worth in the aggregate about a hundred thousand dollars. The effect of the act of Congress was to introduce the New Jersey pilots into competition with them, under great disadvantages to the latter. This disadvantage to the New York pilots was so apparent, that the legislature, in 1845, deemed it an act of justice to repeal the State law of 1837, in order to place them on a fair footing with the pilots of New Jersey. The whole subject of pilotage in the State of New York has, by this repeal, ceased to be controlled by legal regulation, excepting so far as the laws of New Jersey may have been extended by the act of Congress of 1837 to the waters within the jurisdiction of New York. To this result the legislature considered itself forced by the operation of the act of Congress on a most meritorious and valuable class of its citizens.

Under these circumstances, we ask that the act of Congress may be repealed, in order that the State may be left to regulate pilotage for its own ports for itself. We ask it, because we believe the interposition of Congress to have been wholly unnecessary, and because it was founded upon a misapprehension of the facts. At the very time the act was passed, the legislature of New York had been nearly two months engaged in the investigation of this subject before committees, and on the floor of the two Houses. No act of equal interest ever received a more careful examination; and I have no hesitation in saying, that all the benefits derived from the freer competition which has existed in the business of pilotage in New York, since 1837, would have been secured under the laws of the State, if Congress had not interposed.

But the act of Congress is obnoxious to still weightier objections. It has brought States into conflict, — New York with New Jersey, Maryland with Virginia, and Louisiana with Mississippi. Two of these States (New York and Maryland) have, by legislative resolutions, asked for the repeal of the act. Litigation between individuals in different States, for the assertion of supposed rights under the act, has grown up, and classes have been arrayed against each other, not only in the courts, but as suitors to Congress for relief from grievances caused by its own legislation, or for protection in the enjoyment of privileges acquired under it.

For these reasons, and for the further one, that the act of Congress is unjust in its operation upon a meritorious and valuable class of citizens, who should be left to the regulation of our own laws, we ask for its repeal. Should the application prevail, the State of New York will probably place the subject under such regulations as the mercantile interest of the city of New York, and the commercial wants of the country, require; and the whole subject will be left where it was before the Constitution of the United States was framed, and where it remained for half a century afterwards, under the control of each State within its own jurisdiction. I ought to add, that the first effect of the repeal of the act of Congress will be to leave the business of pilotage wholly open to competition, — a condition which a portion of the commercial community deem preferable to any system of regulation.

Having given this brief history of the pilot laws of New York, and stated the present condition of the pilot system there, I proceed to some considerations of a graver character.

As we have seen, the only act of Congress passed for nearly half a century after the adoption of the Constitution, was to declare that the subject of pilotage should be, where it had been from time immemorial, under State regulation. It is true, the act provided it should remain so until further provision should be made by Congress, thus asserting incidentally the power of Congress to regulate it. The first question which arises is, whether this assumption can be maintained? Does the Constitution, under the authority given to Congress to regulate commerce, confer on it the power of appointing pilots, prescribing their duties, and assigning the limits within which those duties shall be performed? Is the assumption of such a power in accordance with the rules of strict construction, which some of us deem essential to the maintenance of the rights of the States, and the restriction of the powers of the general government to their constitutional boundaries? Sir, I do not propose to discuss this question, for the reason, that, if the affirmative were to be made out, it would not follow that the act of Congress of March 2, 1837, was in accordance with the provisions of the Constitution. Congress has not, by that act, exercised the power of appointing pilots. It has granted no commission, under its own authority, to perform the duties of pilots. But it has assumed to authorize pilots appointed by the State of New Jersey to exercise their functions within the jurisdiction of the State of New York. From this exercise of power we dissent, wholly and emphatically. We deny that Congress can with propriety, under the power to regulate commerce, authorize officers appointed by one' State to come within the jurisdiction of another and perform their appropriate duties. In providing for executing the laws of the Union, and enforcing the authority of the Federal courts, Congress has authorized the appointment of marshals, and given them the same powers, in executing the laws of the United States, as sheriffs and their deputies in the several States have by law in executing the laws of the respective States. But would it be tolerated for a moment, that Congress should authorize a sheriff of Georgia, for instance, to come within the jurisdiction of the State of South Carolina and execute precepts issued under the authority of the United States,—an officer neither appointed or commissioned by the Federal government, nor by the State within which his official act were to be performed? Certainly this would be a great abuse of power, if not a positive usurpation. The authority given to pilots licensed by New Jersey to pilot vessels into New York, through waters wholly within the jurisdiction of the latter, is equally offensive. It is authorizing the officers of one State to exercise their functions within the territorial confines of another. It is stripping the State of New York of a portion of her sovereignty, and conferring it on the State of New Jersey. It is one of those encroachments on the rights of the States which, from small and almost imperceptible beginnings, grow into gigantic assumptions of authority, and lead to the most dangerous abuses.

Independently of these constitutional objections, there are practical inconveniences in the existing system, which are of themselves sufficient to condemn it. The New Jersey pilot, who is faithless to his trust in New York, violates no law of New York. It is true, our State laws are repealed; but from 1837 to 1845 they were in operation, and the New Jersey pilot was in no manner amenable to them. He violates no law of the United States: they have prescribed no regulations for his government: they have merely authorized him to exercise his functions beyond the limits of the State from which he derives his authority. He is amenable only to the laws of New Jersey. By the decisions of the Supreme Court of the United States, " suits for pilotage on the high seas and on waters navigable from the sea, as far as the tide ebbs and flows, are within the admiralty and maritime jurisdiction of the United States." The act of Congress of 1789 virtually adopted the State laws in respect to pilotage; but this recognition or adoption of the laws of the States was not construed to oust the jurisdiction of the courts of the United States in cases of admiralty and maritime jurisdiction. A concurrent jurisdiction was left in the State courts. Thus a New Jersey pilot, commissioned or licensed under the laws of that State, and giving bonds under those laws for a faithful performance of his duties, must either be pursued into a foreign jurisdiction for the purpose of holding him answerable for acts or delinquencies committed beyond and out of it, or be prosecuted in the courts of the United States. The courts of the State of New York have no jurisdiction in such cases; and the State is therefore divested of all control over the subject of pilotage in the chief commercial port of the whole Union, the waters leading to which are almost wholly within its own boundaries, so far as the New Jersey pilots participate in the business of piloting.

But there are other objections of a graver character. The Constitution provides that no preference shall be given, by any regulation of commerce, to the ports of one State over those of another. We insist that such a preference is given by the act of Congress. Massachusetts is left to the exclusive regulation of pilotage for the ports of Boston, Salem, Marblehead, New Bedford, &c.; South Carolina for Charleston; and so of other States. On the other hand, the State of New York is divested, by the act of Congress, of the exclusive regulation of pilotage for the city of New York. The business of pilotage for that port is subject to the concurrent regulation of the laws of New York and New Jersey. New York and Boston, by this act, stand upon a totally different footing. In the one case the regulation of pilotage is exclusive in a single State; in the other, it is concurrent in two States. We insist that a decided preference is given to Boston. We insist that Congress might, with equal propriety, provide that all the ports north of a certain parallel of latitude should be open to the pilots of the adjoining States, as to provide that a port situate on waters which are the common boundary between two States should be open to the pilots of both. The preference is just as palpable in one case as in the other. I speak of the absolute right of Congress. If we look at the reason of the thing, and the operation of the act of Congress, we shall find as little justification for it. New Jersey and New York are apparently put on the same footing. The New Jersey pilots may pilot vessels into the ports of New York, and the New York pilots may pilot vessels into the ports of New Jersey; but practically the advantage is all on one side. New Jersey has no foreign commerce. Her trade is all carried on in coasting-vessels; and these are not, by her own laws, required to employ pilots at all, unless they exceed one hundred tons burden. No New York pilot ever takes a vessel to New Jersey. On the other hand, the commerce of New York is chiefly carried on in vessels of a tonnage requiring pilots; and the New Jersey pilots participate largely in the business of piloting. New Jersey has no real interest in maintaining the act of Congress; New York, on the other hand, has a direct interest in its repeal. It concerns herself alone. The act of Congress, though general in its terms, is, from the nature of the circumstances, partial in its operation, and gives a decided preference to one State over another in regard to their respective ports.

But, independently of all the objections referred to, we had a right to insist, that, if Congress legislated on this subject, it should have legislated directly and efficiently. It should have provided for the appointment of pilots in all the States in the Union, prescribed their qualifications, their duties, their liabilities, and made effectual provision by law for enforcing the performance of their functions, and securing adequate remedies for faithlessness and incompetence. We complain, that, instead of executing this authority, Congress has delegated it to others, and in such a manner as virtually to give effect to the laws of one State within the territorial boundaries of another. To any such delegation of authority we never can yield our assent. I do not wish to be understood as admitting the right of Congress to make such provision for the appointment of pilots throughout the Union. But I wish to say, that, if it can legislate on the subject at all, it is its duty to legislate directly, and for all the States, without making an unjust and invidious distinction between them.

There is another consideration — the only other I shall present to the Senate — in favor of the repeal of this law. Whether it is unauthorized by the Constitution or not, the experience of nine years has shown that it is, at least, in the highest degree impolitic. It has brought the authority of the general government into conflict with that of the States; it has led to collisions between different States; and has produced litigation and unkindness of feeling among different classes of citizens. No act of Federal legislation which leads to such consequences can be justifiable, unless it is demanded by some imperious exigency. The legislation of the central government should be liberal and forbearing, and designed only to effect objects of indispensable necessity. When it departs from this fundamental principle, and encroaches on rights or even on privileges long exercised, it becomes alien to the parental character which every government should possess, and without which it cannot command the approbation of those who are subject to its jurisdiction. I repeat, then, we ask for the repeal of this act, because it is of questionable constitutionality; because it was procured by misrepresentation; because it is unnecessary; because it is unjust to a meritorious class of citizens; because it has led to collision and litigation; and because it encroaches, if not on positive rights, on privileges long enjoyed, and which there is no cause for alienating.

I have discussed this question almost exclusively on legal grounds ; and I trust the Senate will see, in what I have said, sufficient cause for the repeal of the act of Congress, of which the legislatures of New York and Maryland have, by their resolutions, complained. I have purposely abstained from all reference to difficulties of a local character between different classes of the citizens of New York, which have grown out of this unnecessary, and, as I believe, this unauthorized, act of legislation. I shall not enter into an examination of those difficulties, unless compelled to do so; but I rest the application for the repeal of the act on the legal and constitutional grounds I have stated, and leave the question in the hands of the Senate.

THE PILOT LAWS.

JUNE, 1848.

On motion of Mr. DIX, the Senate took up the bill to repeal the act of March 2, 1837, entitled "An act concerning pilots."

MR. PRESIDENT: On a former occasion I said to the Senate all I desire to say in relation to the legal questions involved in this bill. I shall not therefore repeat what I said then, or enter into any new assignment or discussion of objections arising out of the powers of Congress over the subject of regulating pilotage in the States. But I am constrained by the remarks which were made by the Senator from Massachusetts,[1] and the Senator from New Jersey,[2] to enter into a somewhat detailed history of the pilot question in New York. I regret that I am compelled to do so, because it has become, in some degree, a dissension between classes, involving private interests; and these are always subjects which I wish to avoid, when I can do so consistently with my duty to the public.

I have stated heretofore that the pilots of New York, in 1836, had entered into an agreement to share equally their joint receipts, and that this combination had led to a relaxation of their accustomed vigilance in looking out for vessels and taking them into port. In consequence of some disasters which occurred, the public attention was called to the defects of the system of pilotage existing in New York. In the annual message of the Governor of the State, on the 3d January, 1837, he brought the subject before the legislature. On the following day select committees were appointed

[1] Mr. Davis.   [2] Mr. Miller.

in both branches. On the 11th of February, a bill was reported by the chairman of the select committee in the House of Assembly; and after a very thorough discussion in committee of the whole, the bill was reported to the House by a vote of 91 to 7, on the 8th of March. It was subsequently read a third time, and passed by a vote of 85 to 5. In the Senate the bill was received on the 14th of March, referred to the select committee of that body, and reported with amendments which were concurred in; but in consequence of the pressure of important business, it was not passed until the 6th of April. I state these facts to show the deliberation with which the legislature of the State of New York acted on this important question. The number of pilots was increased, a careful system of examination was established, combinations were guarded against, and all the known and alleged evils of the system were provided for by appropriate remedies, or remedies at least which were considered appropriate and effectual.

The Senator from Massachusetts,[1] in his remarks, seemed to assume that the New York pilots of 1848 are answerable for the acts of those of 1835 and 1836; and the Senator from New Jersey,[2] who followed him, made some allusion to them which appears to warrant the same inference. But if those gentlemen will consider how rapidly the lapse of years is thinning the ranks of their own friends and associates, they will not be surprised to learn that the great enemy has been busy with the pilots also. Of the sixty pilots following the business in 1837, there are but twenty-nine now engaged in piloting. More than half have perished at sea, died on shore, or become disqualified by age for the arduous service in which they were engaged. The number of New York pilots holding branches under the laws of the State, is eighty; and of these, fifty-one have been appointed since the State law of 1837 was passed. Whatever responsibility, therefore, belongs to the pilots of 1836, has, for the most part,

[1] Mr. Davis.   [2] Mr. Miller.

gone with them to be met at a higher tribunal than this. I state these facts that the Senate may understand why it will be proper to deal with systems and not with men.

The haste manifested in passing the act of Congress of 1837, of which we ask for the repeal, stands in strong contrast with the legislation of New York. Let me recite the facts as briefly as possible.

By the Senate Journal of 1836-7, it will be seen that a resolution was introduced on the 12th of January, by Mr. Tallmadge, of New York, instructing the Committee on Commerce to inquire into the expediency of legislating on the subject of pilots on the sea-coast, with power to report by bill or otherwise. This resolution was adopted. The Committee on Commerce consisted of the following distinguished gentlemen: Mr. King of Alabama, chairman, Mr. Davis of Massachusetts, Mr. Linn of Missouri, Mr. Brown of North Carolina, and Mr. Ruggles of Maine. The committee, though they had ample time for deliberation, never made a report on the resolution.

On the 28th day of February, the last day of the month, Mr. Wall, of New Jersey, introduced a bill on notice. It was instantly read the first and second time, reported to the Senate, and immediately read a third time,— the work probably of as much time as I take to give the details.

But, sir, it is necessary that we should accompany the bill through all the stages of its course. It was received in the House on the 28th of February, the day it passed the Senate,[1] and on the next day received its proper number of readings, and passed. On the 2d of March it received the President's signature, and became the law of the land.

Nor is this all. The subject had been referred to a committee in the House early in that session. The committee made an elaborate report on the 22d of February, and asked to be discharged from the further consideration of the sub-

[1] House Journal, p. 552.

ject. In the face of this proceeding, the bill was passed, and in the summary way I have stated.

It is as remarkable a specimen of the dispatch of business — business involving a question of constitutional power, and bringing in its train collisions between individuals, and classes, and States — as can be met with. It was hurried, or rather rushed, through Congress, almost at the last hour of its session, — indeed, almost at the last hour of its existence.

I have heretofore told the Senate that the legislature of New York, after becoming satisfied that the act of Congress operated injuriously on the pilots of that State, and after waiting eight years for its repeal, came to the conclusion to repeal her own laws regulating pilotage by way of Sandy Hook, the great outlet and inlet for the foreign commerce of the country, providing only that the pilots then licensed should continue to be pilots. It has been alleged that the New York pilots were applicants to the legislature for repeal. This is a mistake. They appealed to the legislature of the State, to

"Try and determine whether the aforesaid act of Congress does or does not transcend the legislative power of the Federal government, and whether the acts exercised under its sanction and under the authority of the laws of the State of New Jersey by the citizens of that State are or are not in violation of the sovereignty of the State of New York, and in contempt of her laws."

It is true, they acquiesced in the repeal of the State laws, and desired it as an alternative, if they could not procure the repeal of the act of Congress. The latter object was always what they sought. Failing in it, they consented to the repeal of the State laws — a measure proposed by the mercantile interest. The pilots believed it would place them on an equal footing with the pilots of New Jersey. It was under this view of the subject, that the New York pilots, on consultation with the mercantile interest, the Chamber of Commerce and Board of Underwriters, consented to it. Such appears to be the fact from the petition to the legislature, and the debate on the bill. It was supposed that it would open a fair field of competition to them and the New Jersey pilots, and that their fitness and industry would be the measure of their success.

As soon, however, as the State laws were repealed, the Chamber of Commerce and the Board of Underwriters organized a board of commissioners to examine pilots and give them certificates. Nor was this all. They published a notice, which I will read, calling on the ship-masters not to receive a pilot unless he could produce a certificate from them or the State of New Jersey:—

"It is recommended that no vessel receive a person as pilot except on his producing a certificate signed by the above board, or those issued under authority of the State of New Jersey."

This measure was a virtual proscription of the New York pilots, unless they would consent to receive the certificates of this irresponsible board, and acknowledge its authority. It was not to be supposed that they would discredit the licenses they held under the laws of the State by receiving the certificates of a board organized without any legal authority whatever,— certificates which could confer no authority on those to whom they were given. Was it reasonable to expect them to do so? Certainly not. They possessed in the State licenses the highest warrants of authority. They required nothing more: they should not have been asked to take less.

Though the Chamber of Commerce and the Board of Underwriters have no legal control over the subject of pilotage, their actual control is very great. They represent, and indeed wield, the commercial influence of the city of New York. The ship-masters are subject, in a great degree, to that influence, and hence the recommendation had in many cases the efficacy of a command. It was literally warning the public against employing the New York pilots, though trained from their youth to their vocation, unless they, holding the State authority in their hands, would consent to receive certificates from an irresponsible board, having no legal power to grant them. What was the effect? Was it to break up a monopoly — the great evil of which the public complained? The New York pilots were eighty-two in number; the New Jersey pilots seventeen; and the merchants' board, as it is called, soon after these regulations were published, granted certificates to sixteen persons. If the recommendation had been acted on, the whole pilotage of the city would have been given to thirty-three persons, and eighty-two persons would have been excluded from all participation in it. But it was not generally acted on. With all the weight it carried with it, the New York pilots continued to be, and are still extensively employed, though, as I shall show, they have felt severely the effect of the invidious distinction which has been made between them and others.

I will now proceed to state in detail the consequences which have resulted from the act of Congress; for it is to this act that all the difficulty which exists is to be traced.

1. There has not been a fair competition. The ship-owners, who represent a considerable portion of the active commercial capital of the city, have contributed to make it unequal. In the first place, the regulation I have quoted has had its influence. The New York pilots are passed by, and the New Jersey and merchants' pilots, as they are called, are employed in preference; not because the latter are more competent, but because they are considered as preferred by the mercantile classes, on whom the ship-masters are often dependent for employment. The injustice of the regulation is more distinctly seen in a practice which has grown up under it, and become very extensive, of taking a vessel brought in by a New York pilot out of his hands, and giving her to a New Jersey or merchants' pilot to take out.

It may be proper to say that in every State, of which I have been able to examine the laws, and in which those laws are passed with a view to equality, a pilot bringing in a vessel, or a pilot belonging to the same boat, has the privilege of taking the vessel out. The reason is obvious. The inward pilotage is often hazardous and laborious. Vessels are sometimes boarded two hundred miles at sea. Pilots are often out a week or ten days in pursuit of them. They are to be brought into port in all weathers. But the outward pilotage is always easy. Vessels go to sea in fair weather only. The pilot takes his charge a few miles from shore, and leaves her. There is no labor, no hazard, and but little responsibility in it. Nothing can be more unjust, more repugnant to every principle of fairness and liberality, than to take from a pilot a vessel he has brought in, and give her to another to take out. It is in fact only by taking a vessel out, that a pilot can be compensated for the labor of bringing her in. Accordingly, this privilege is usually secured by law. The laws of Massachusetts, for instance, provide that the pilot who brought in a vessel (or one belonging to the same boat) is entitled to take her out. In like manner, the laws of South Carolina provide, that "every pilot taking a vessel in, has the exclusive right to take her out," except in case of misbehavior, &c.

Let us see what has been the operation of the system in New York since the act of Congress passed. That act authorizes a pilot from New York or New Jersey to be employed to pilot a vessel to or from New York. It leaves it optional with the master of a vessel to employ the same pilot who brought in a vessel, to take her out, or to employ another pilot; and here the regulations of the Chamber of Commerce and the Board of Underwriters come in, recommending him to employ no pilot not certified by their board or licensed by New Jersey, excluding the eighty New York pilots. The consequence may be readily seen. I hold in my hand several lists of vessels brought in by New York pilots and given to New Jersey or merchants' pilots to take out again. The names of the vessels are given, as well as the time of the transactions. There is also a list of vessels taken out by the merchants' pilots, which they did not bring in. This list is furnished by the secretary of the board of commissioners, and is under his own hand. The pilotage on these vessels amounted to $3038.53, and must have been taken from the New York pilots. There are, in addition, lists of 148 vessels taken from the New York pilots during a portion of the years 1846 and 1847, and given to other pilots to take out again. Even these lists are not complete. There were numerous cases which were omitted for want of precise information. The average pilot fees for each vessel are estimated at $25. They are probably a little more — certainly not less. At this rate, the amount taken from the New York pilots on the vessels above mentioned, and by violating a rule of universal justice, is $6688.

These facts are proved by unquestionable evidence. In the year 1844, before the merchants' pilots were appointed, it appears by a "remonstrance of the underwriters of the port of New York,"[1] that the New York pilots brought in 1992 vessels, and took out 1610, — a difference of 382, the pilotage on which must have amounted to $9550. By the same return it appears that the New York pilots, 81 in number, piloted in and out 3602 vessels, or $44\frac{1}{2}$ vessels each pilot, giving them, at $25 per vessel, $1112.50 each, to pay the expenses of their boats, and maintain their families on shore. It also appears that the New Jersey pilots, 17 in number, piloted in and out 1131 vessels, giving them, at $25 per vessel, $1663.23 each, or $550.73 each more than the New York pilots. A very considerable portion of this difference is owing to the open manner in which the New York pilots have been discouraged by the board of commissioners.

I have stated these facts, Mr. President, in justice to the New York pilots, who have been charged by the Senator from Massachusetts,[2] and the Senator from New Jersey,[3]

---

[1] Doc. No. 60, House of Representatives, 1st Session, 25th Congress.
[2] Mr. Davis.   [3] Mr. Miller.

with sinister motives in coming to Congress to ask for a repeal of the act of 2d March, 1837. I have felt it due to them to show that they are laboring under a serious disability, and are the objects of a most invidious distinction under the operation of this act.

But I proceed to other considerations.

2. One of the great complaints against the system in force previous to 1837, was, that pilots would not go to sea in search of vessels, but waited at Sandy Hook to receive them. This evil has been remedied; but it has been followed both by inconveniences and injustice, which, perhaps, fully counterbalance it. I will first state the inconvenience. Pilots now go far out to sea in quest of vessels. It is not an uncommon thing for a pilot to present himself two hundred miles from New York. Now, there is no particular advantage in this. It may be safely said that no vessel requires or wishes a pilot at a greater distance than twenty or twenty-five miles from Sandy Hook. If a pilot gets on board a vessel one or two hundred miles from New York, he does not take charge of her. She is ordinarily given to him when she comes in sight of land. It is not every pilot who is capable of taking charge of a vessel out of sight of land, and carrying her into port. The consequence of the present over-active competition is, that the pilot-boats go to sea, vessels constantly pass them, and on reaching Sandy Hook they find no pilots. At the very place where they are most wanted, they are often not to be found. I shall refer to an honorable Senator from Maryland,[1] to know whether, on arriving at Sandy Hook in the Great Western, that vessel was not detained because no pilot could be found. I will read some notes from the log-book of the United States light-ship off Sandy Hook, showing that it is a very common occurrence for vessels to arrive there and be detained for want of pilots. There are over seventy cases on the abstract of the log-book, which I hold in my hand; and in addition, the captain of the

[1] Mr. Johnson.

ship states on one occasion that there was "a large number of vessels in sight wanting pilots"; on another, that "several vessels near us want pilots"; and that there were many other cases which he saw himself, and of which no entry was made in the log-book. While, therefore, the active competition in piloting has corrected one evil, it has produced another.

And now, sir, I will state the injustice of the system. Under the laws of New York and New Jersey, and I believe under the laws of most other States, if a pilot boards a vessel beyond a certain distance from the land, he is entitled to 25 per cent. in addition to his established fees. In New York this distance is some fifteen miles outside of the Sandy Hook light. This is called off-shore pilotage, and was intended as a compensation for the extra labor and inconvenience of the pilot. When there was a legally established system, it could be exacted. Now it cannot; and ship-owners and masters, knowing this, refuse to pay it. This remark is not of universal application, but the practice is becoming very general. It is believed that four fifths of the vessels refuse to pay the off-shore pilotage. They are willing the pilot should go one or two hundred miles to sea, but they are unwilling to pay him the customary addition to his fees. If he presents himself, the first question is, "Do you charge off-shore pilotage?" And if he refuses to give it up, the ship refuses to take him. Or if no bargain is made with him, he is required to deduct it when the vessel goes out, or she is given to another person. Under such a system he has no legal security either for just or liberal treatment.

3. The active competition which has grown out of the existing system, and which would have grown up without the act of Congress under the State law of New York, has not had the effect of securing commerce against shipwrecks and other disasters. I very much doubt whether they have been at all diminished in number. The cases of the Mexico and the Bristol were extraordinary occurrences. They happened

at an inclement season, and even if the old system had been continued, such disasters might not have occurred again in half a century. Since that time there have been shipwrecks equally disastrous, except in the loss of life. Some of the property in the Bristol and Mexico was saved, and the deaths which occurred in the Mexico were not from drowning, but from frost, the passengers, who were emigrants, having been driven to the deck in a winter's night of unparalleled severity.

I hold in my hand a list of 220 vessels stranded, run aground, or wrecked, from April 1839 to March 1846, — seven years, — all under the new system. Of this number, over 30 were a total loss, and 22 were engaged in foreign commerce. Some of these shipwrecks were of a most distressing character on account of the loss of life with which they were attended. The ship John Minturn, for instance, went ashore on Squam Beach, about fifteen miles from Sandy Hook — the captain and his family, the pilot, and thirty-eight others, having perished together, and the ship and cargo were totally lost. On the score of property, it was probably a heavier loss than that of the Bristol or Mexico.

I have another list of 111 vessels stranded, run aground, or wrecked, from February, 1846, commencing where the other list terminated, to the 14th January, 1848, — say two years. Of this number, 24 were a total loss, — a large increase in the ratio compared with former years, — and nine were engaged in foreign commerce. In the first seven years above named, the vessels totally lost amounted to nearly five per annum. During the last two years they have been twelve per annum, — more than doubled, though the increase of the commerce of the city has been in a much larger proportion.

I state these facts to show that security to property and life has not increased under the existing system, whatever opinions may be expressed to the contrary. It is true, I have not been able to make comparisons with the period preceding 1837 for want of data. There is, however, an account by Captain Earl, who was adduced as a witness against the New York pilots, and who stated, in 1835, that he had enumerated, from memory, 39 vessels totally lost within a "few years." The number of years is left to conjecture; but, upon the most unfavorable supposition, the loss could not have exceeded that of the last two years.

I have also felt myself called on to make this statement to meet the declaration of the honorable Senator from Massachusetts,[1] that "shipwrecks in the neighborhood of that harbor are almost unknown," — a declaration which he would not have ventured to make, if he had taken time to investigate the facts with his usual care and discrimination.

From what I have said it will be apparent that the whole control of the subject of pilotage is in the hands of the ship-owners and ship-masters, without legal regulation. The master of a vessel may take any pilot he pleases; he may bargain for the amount of pilot fees; he may, after having taken a pilot two hundred miles at sea, when coming in, give his vessel to another pilot to take out. The pilot himself has no security, either that the customary fees will be paid him, or that he will have the preference in taking out a vessel he has brought in. He is, in fact, wholy dependent on the ship-owner or ship-master. Is this right?

I believe, Mr. President, that the best systems of pilotage are those which are under the most rigid regulation. The defect of the system in New York is, that there is no law, no systematic government or rules. Nor can there be, while a master of a vessel is allowed to take a pilot from two different States. It is impossible to enforce prohibitions or commands in one State, when there is a competition between different classes holding warrants or licenses from two separate authorities, neither of which is responsible to the other.

[1] Mr. Davis.

The Chamber of Commerce and the Board of Underwriters have, by establishing rules themselves, confessed the necessity of legal regulation. They have no authority to enforce the rules they have adopted, and those rules are not enforced. They fixed the rates of pilotage according to the standard established by the law of New York, which had been repealed; but these rates are not uniformly paid. The pilots are constantly obliged to take less in order to obtain employment. Pilots are required to board the nearest vessel under a penalty of $50; but there is no power to enforce the penalty. The commissioners are authorized by the regulations to impose fines; but it is a perfectly nominal authority. Off-shore pilotage is allowed by their regulations; but vessels, as has been seen, in most instances refuse or evade the payment, because there is no legal authority to exact it.

If a pilot offers his services to the eastward of the white buoy, about three miles from Sandy Hook, and is refused, he is entitled to half-pilotage; but it is never paid, because the commissioners had no power to make such a regulation. They have no authority whatever. Their regulations are a dead letter. All the control there is rests upon the commercial influence wielded by the commissioners and the ship-owners.

I believe this state of things to be radically wrong. The reasons for subjecting the business of pilotage to legal regulation seem to me urgent and unanswerable. Let me advert to a single one. The entries and clearances of foreign vessels at New York exceed 1100 per annum. They are entirely dependent on a judicious system of pilotage for their safety. The regular traders may know the pilot-boats, and sometimes may make selections; but foreign vessels, without this knowledge, will naturally take the first pilot that presents himself. They can have no knowledge of his qualifications; they are entirely at his mercy; and it is only by a proper system of regulation, under an undivided authority, that we can do justice to the vast foreign commerce which centres in the city of New York. The act of Congress is the only obstacle to the establishment of such a system. If it were repealed, I am entirely satisfied that a system could be adopted, in concurrence with the mercantile classes, which would meet the views and interests of all, and secure every public object.

But, to pursue this point a little further, the New York merchants are not the only parties in interest. New York is the centre of commerce of the whole Union. Foreign countries, as I have already shown, have also a deep interest in the matter, — an interest which we have no right to subject to the control, without law, of a single class. It is due to the country that the system of pilotage for the great emporium of the Union should be made efficient by judicious regulation, instead of being thrown open to unrestrained competition. The interests at stake are too important: not property alone, but human life is concerned. I am not aware that there is any commercial country which intrusts the business of piloting to open competition. It is one of the few matters in which regulation has always been deemed indispensable. Strongly impressed as I am with the importance of freeing commerce and navigation, as far as possible, from all shackles and restrictions, I cannot, on the fullest reflection, bring my mind to the conclusion that pilotage should be without law.

But there is another consideration. Those who now control pilotage in New York to a great extent, have an interest adverse to the pilots. Their interest is to have piloting done cheap. Bargains are frequently made, and the pilot is compelled to take less than the customary rates, less than the rates fixed as reasonable and just by the Chamber of Commerce and the Board of Underwriters. The tendency of this state of things is to drive the best pilots into other employments, and to introduce an inferior class of men in their place. And from the best judgment I have been able to form, I cannot but think that if this state of things continues until the present stock of well-trained pilots pass off the stage, New York, instead of having pilots equal to the best in any country, will have the worst.[1]

I am not quite certain, Mr. President, that the interest of insurers is so very decidedly in favor of the highest degree of security to property afloat as the Senator from Massachusetts supposes. Insurance is regulated by the hazards. The rates are high when the hazard is great, and they are low when the hazard is small. Now, I believe it may be said with safety that the rates of insurance rise in a ratio higher than that of the increase of hazard, and that the profits of insurance are greatest when the security is least. I speak in respect to the operation of principles, and not in respect to motives of action, and only for the purpose of explaining why a very defective system of pilotage might exist without prejudice to insurers.

The Senator from Massachusetts has said that the mercantile interest generally is in favor of the present system, and he intimates pretty strongly that there is not a merchant in New York who is not opposed to the repeal. Now, I can assure the Senator that the memorials from New York asking for the repeal of the act of Congress, signed by some five thousand persons, contain the names of several highly respectable merchants, besides a large number of ship-masters and ship-owners. I can also assure him that I have conversed

---

[1] Since making this speech, I have seen a notice in the New York papers, which is annexed: —

"*Notice to Ship-masters.* — The Board of Underwriters of this city have resolved to revive the practice of examining the conduct of the masters of vessels wrecked or meeting with serious disasters without extraordinary cause, occasioning loss to the members of the Board; and that pending each examination and suspension, no risks are to be taken on vessels in charge of such masters.

"Notice is also given, that information has been communicated to the Board that several ship-masters have recently entered this port without pilots, and others with persons pretending to be pilots, who were incompetent. The Board requests masters to act with greater care for the future, as the insurance companies will hold parties to a strict accountability for omitting to take a pilot, and also for taking an incompetent pilot.

"JNO. S. TAPPAN,
"*Secretary Board of Underwriters of New York.*"

Nothing can more clearly show the defectiveness of the existing system than this notice, or prove more conclusively the truth of what I have said.

with some of the most respectable ship-masters who sail from New York, and who believe the present system tends to degrade the pilots and to render life and property insecure. It is no doubt true that the merchants generally are opposed to the repeal: 1st, for reasons I have stated; and 2d, because it has been industriously circulated by interested persons that the object of the repeal is to establish the old monopoly. The Senator from Massachusetts twice said so, and I regretted to hear it. He has been deceived. There is not a shadow of foundation for the charge. It is this belief which has produced so much hostility to the repeal, and I regret that my honorable friend from Massachusetts should have fallen into so great an error. Let me state a few facts.

The New York pilots assented in 1846 to the creation of a board of commissioners of three persons, one to be chosen by the Board of Underwriters, one by the Chamber of Commerce, and one by themselves, to regulate the whole business of pilotage. They offered to take into the association of pilots all those now licensed by New Jersey and the merchants' pilots, if found qualified on examination. This proposition contemplated a repeal of the act of Congress, and the establishment of a system of pilotage by State legislation. The agent of those two bodies was understood to give his assent to it in this city, and I supposed the matter would be satisfactorily adjusted. But on his return to New York they refused to accede to it. The pilots agreed that the mercantile interest should have two to one of the commissioners, a complete control, provided they could have legal regulation. Under the existing system this interest has the control without legal regulation. This is the issue joined between the parties. The New York pilots desire no monopoly. They do not ask even for control. They ask only legal protection for rights universally acknowledged to be just.

The Senator from Massachusetts also stated as his belief, that the papers in his possession showed that no persons connected with the shipping interest of the country, except the pilots, desired the repeal of the act of Congress. I have shown this to be a mistake. I might go on and say that two sovereign States have complained of it.as injurious to great public interests. But if it were true that none but the pilots desired the repeal of the law, would it be a reason why Congress should turn a deaf ear to their appeal? May not any individual, or any class of individuals, fairly appeal to Congress for protection against the operation of its own enactments, when they are oppressive or injurious to the party appealing? I have always supposed it to be the peculiar duty of Congress to see that, in the enactment of laws, individual rights were not injuriously affected. The only question is, how far those rights shall give way to great public interests. And, sir, I insist that, on the application of the pilots alone, asking for the repeal of an act which has proved oppressive to them, it would have been the duty of Congress to look into the facts, and to grant the prayer of the petitioners, unless high public considerations rendered it improper. But, as I have already said, the pilots are not the only complainants. Numerous and respectable classes of citizens unite with them; and the legislatures of two States remonstrate against the act of Congress, either as oppressive or as injurious to the public interest which it is designed to secure.

I cannot dismiss this part of the subject without saying that I entertain for the merchants of the city of New York the highest respect. In enterprise, intelligence in commercial matters, and in an honorable discharge of their pecuniary obligations, they are unsurpassed by any class of men in this country or any other. When I took my seat in this body, it was with an earnest desire to contribute my humble efforts to the promotion of the commercial interest of the country, which I thought had not received all the notice to which it was entitled; and it is to this subject, more than any other, that I have devoted myself. I shall continue to do so.

But in this matter of the pilots, I am constrained to differ from what seems to be the general opinion among the merchants of New York. And yet I am entirely satisfied that if we understood each other, there would be little difference between us. I do not think the great body of the merchants have looked into the subject critically. I have inquired of many of them why they were opposed to the repeal of the act of Congress, and I have received the same answer in every case,—because we are opposed to the reestablishment of the old monopoly. And when I have rejoined, that I was equally opposed to such a measure, that I was in favor of placing the whole subject of pilotage for the city of New York under legal regulation, and leaving the administration of the system in the hands of the Chamber of Commerce and the Board of Underwriters, their representatives, I do not recollect an instance in which they have not acquiesced in the propriety of the suggestion. What I have insisted on is legal control, to be exercised by those who have a practical knowledge of the subject. But I am unwilling to leave it even in their hands without legal control,—if for no other reason, because there is no power to enforce proper regulations, or punish their infraction. And I do not hesitate to say, if the merchants will look into this question, that there will be a general concurrence in the propriety of the measure I propose. It is possible I may be deceived; but if I am,—if they shall continue to differ with me in opinion,—one assurance I shall still retain, that they will do me the justice to believe I am actuated solely by what I consider the true interests of the city and country at large.

One word in conclusion. My suggestion in respect to a system of pilotage in New York is this: 1. A board of commissioners of three persons, one appointed by the Chamber of Commerce, one by the Board of Underwriters, and one by the pilots, who shall have power to examine and license all persons desirous of acting as pilots, and to superintend the administration of the system generally. 2. A classification of the boats, to include those of New York, New Jersey, and merchants' pilots, with all the persons now belonging to them, who shall be found competent, and an assignment of the boats, in turn, to three descriptions of service, viz: cruising out of sight of Sandy Hook, within sight of the light-house, and in the vicinity of the Hook. This will correspond substantially with the station-system at Liverpool, and will at all times insure to vessels arriving at the city of New York competent pilots, under legal regulation, and under the supervision of the mercantile interest of the city. The first step towards the establishment of such a system is a repeal of the act of Congress, without which it cannot be placed upon such a footing as to insure its efficacy.

ON HON. DIXON H. LEWIS.

DECEMBER, 1848.

Resolved, unanimously, That the Senate, from a sincere desire of showing every mark of respect due to the memory of the Hon. DIXON H. LEWIS, deceased, late a member thereof, will go into mourning by wearing crape on the left arm for thirty days.

Resolved, unanimously, That, as an additional mark of respect for the memory of the Hon. DIXON H. LEWIS, the Senate do now adjourn.

The resolutions being under consideration, Mr. Dix said: —

I RISE, Mr. President, to second the resolutions offered by the honorable Senator from Alabama.[1] When the career of his lamented colleague was suddenly terminated in the city of New York, I chanced to be there, and I was the only one of his associates on this floor who had the opportunity of following him to his final resting-place. It seemed to me for this reason that I might appropriately speak of his last illness; of the honors paid to his memory; and, for the satisfaction of distant friends, of the spot where his remains repose. Of his talents, his patriotism, his public services, the kindly feeling which he carried into his intercourse with others, the purity of his private character, his stern integrity, and his fidelity to all the obligations of life, I need say nothing. On this subject the honorable Senator who moved the resolutions has left little to be said. But I cannot forbear to add, that all my intercourse with him in this body strongly impressed me with his liberality as a gentleman, his uprightness as a man, and his conscientiousness as a legislator.

Mr. Lewis arrived at New York on the 9th of October, unwell, though not, as was supposed, seriously so. He ac-

[1] Mr. King.

companied a friend, shortly after his arrival, on an excursion through the city, and passed nearly an entire day in the examination of various objects of interest. On several succeeding days he was out again. But he soon afterwards became indisposed a second time; from this moment his strength rapidly declined, and on the 25th of October his connection with the things of earth was dissolved forever.

The Mayor of the city, on receiving the mournful intelligence, called the Common Council together, and it was immediately resolved, with one accord, to give his remains a public burial. I will not dwell on the funeral ceremonies performed at the City Hall, the words of eloquence spoken over him, or the extended procession moving through streets thronged with the population of the city. Suffice to say, the former Mayors of New York, members of Congress, State and city authorities, public societies, citizens, all united in paying the honors due to him as one of the representatives of a sovereign State in this body, cut off at a distance from those by whom these tributes of respect would otherwise have been rendered.

Thus attended, his remains were consigned to the earth, in one of the rural cemeteries, which the principal cities of New York and some of the neighboring States have, within a few years, set apart for the reception of their dead,—places selected for their natural beauty, and adorned with all that art could devise or taste suggest. Greenwood, where our departed associate lies, is one of the most beautiful of these receptacles for the dead. It is on Long Island, four miles from New York, and contains near two hundred acres, covered with forest-trees, and in its season with luxuriant vegetation, swelling into hills and sinking into valleys and dells, where all that could offend the eye has given way to embellishments in harmony with "the religion of the place." There is nothing in which the spirit of improvement has manifested itself in a purer sentiment and taste. Our ancient burying-grounds were too often bare and unsheltered fields, on which settlement had encroached and robbed them of their only fitness — solitude. Sometimes they had become unsightly enclosures, in the heart of busy towns, with the tide of population sweeping by, and the noisy conflict of life perpetually breaking the silence of the scene.

Turning from these exposed and neglected repositories to the rural cemeteries, the mind is relieved and elevated by the contrast. It was a noble conception — worthy of our endowments and our destinies — to make the cities of the dead more attractive in their external aspect than the cities of the living.

Among the surest of our instincts is the desire that our own remains, and those of our kindred, may rest amid scenes of rural beauty in undisturbed repose. Nature herself associates quietude and stillness with sleep, whether it be the sleep of life or of death. It is her voice which speaks within us, when we ask that our last resting-place may be chosen apart from the turbulent haunts of men. It is said (with what truth I do not know) that Mr. Lewis, when he first visited Greenwood, intimated a wish, if he should die in the neighborhood, that his remains might be deposited there. I have before me a letter from one of his most intimate friends in New York, who says: "A year ago he visited Greenwood, and was enchanted with it. He often referred to this visit, and spoke of the cemetery as above all others suited to be the last resting-place of men. It was, therefore, with melancholy pleasure that we selected it for him." It is satisfactory to reflect that he rests in the spot which so often called forth expressions of his admiration, and to believe that his own wishes in this respect could not have been better fulfilled. Near the principal entrance into these consecrated grounds, on a slight elevation, overlooking some of the most varied and beautiful scenery they contain, reposes all that was mortal of our deceased associate and friend. And if I might express the feeling of the community by whom his remains were given back to the dust from which they came, it would be responsive to his own,—that they may rest where, in the order of Providence, the thread of his life was severed, among those whose mournful privilege it was to enshrine them with the ashes of their own kindred. If this feeling shall be gratified, his family, his friends, the State he represented here, may be assured that he will lie among us, not as a stranger, but as one of ourselves, children alike of a common Union, and heirs of a common prosperity and fame.

MEMORIALS OF OFFICERS IN MEXICO.

DECEMBER, 1849.

Mr. Dix presented the memorial of officers of the army, now serving in Mexico, praying the passage of an act granting pensions to the widows and orphans of such as may die in service.

Mr. D. also presented a memorial of officers of the army, now serving in Mexico, praying the passage of a law authorizing the retirement of officers of the army from active service on certain conditions.

On presenting these memorials, Mr. Dix said: —

I RISE to present two petitions, to which I desire to invoke the attention of the Senate. It was not until yesterday that I was apprised of their contents, or I should have brought them here at an earlier day. They were left on my table in the city a week or ten days ago, when I was absent, sealed and addressed to an honorable Senator from Missouri,[1] not now in his place, who served for many years as chairman of the Committee on Military Affairs, with distinguished honor to himself and advantage to the country ; and I greatly regret that he is not here to take charge of them. I am not in the habit, sir, as you know, of accompanying the presentation of papers with introductory remarks. In ordinary cases, it is doubtless more proper to await the action of appropriate committees on the subjects to which they refer. But I trust the nature of these may be deemed by the Senate to justify a departure from the usual practice.

They are petitions signed by the officers of the army at Puebla, on the 1st day of August last, just before it commenced its march towards the city of Mexico. The first is styled "A petition for a retiring list." It contains two hun-

[1] Mr. Benton.

dred and thirty-three signatures, and prays for certain legislative provisions in respect to aged and disabled officers, which, without casting any new burden on the public treasury, would, in the opinion of the petitioners, add greatly to the efficiency of the army, and at the same time do justice to those who perform the drudgery, and encounter the perils of military service in the field. I will only say further in reference to this petition, that the plan suggested corresponds, to some extent though not fully, with one proposed by a late commander of the army, (General Macomb,) and I believe recently recommended by the present Adjutant-General, with a view to the same objects.

The second is styled "A petition for widows and orphans." It is signed by two hundred and twenty-two officers, and I believe the names, as far as they go, are identical with those borne on the first. It is also dated at Puebla, on the 1st day of August last, almost at the moment the army took up its march for the valley of Mexico; and when considered in connection with the surrounding circumstances and the brilliant events which followed with a rapidity of succession scarcely exceeded by those which signalized the first entrance of Buonaparte into Italy, it addresses itself with great force to the feelings, as well as the justice, of Congress and the country.

I will not detain the Senate by entering into any detailed review of these events, with a view to enforce the appeal contained in the petition on the attention. I hope, however, I may be indulged in saying, in justice to those who bore a part in them, that the first conquest of Mexico cannot, as it appears to me, be compared with the second, either as to the obstacles overcome or as to the relative strength of the invaders. The triumphs of Cortez were achieved by policy and by superiority in discipline and in the implements of warfare. The use of fire-arms, until then unknown to the inhabitants of Mexico, was sufficient in itself to make his force, small as it was, irresistible. In the eyes of that simple and superstitious people, he seemed armed with superhuman power. Other circumstances combined to facilitate his success. The native tribes by which the country was possessed were distinct communities, not always acknowledging the same head, and often divided among themselves by implacable hostility and resentments. Cortez, by his consummate prudence and art, turned these dissensions to his own account; he lured the parties to them into his own service, and when he presented himself at the gates of the city of Mexico, he was at the head of four thousand of the most warlike of the natives, as auxiliaries to the band of Spaniards with which he commenced his march from Vera Cruz. Thus, his early successes were as much the triumph of policy as of arms. General Scott, and the gallant band he led, had no such advantages. The whole population of the country, from Vera Cruz to Mexico, was united as one man against him, and animated by the fiercest animosity. He was opposed by military forces armed like his own, often better disciplined, occupying positions chosen by themselves, strong by nature, and fortified according to the strictest rules of art. These obstacles were overcome by his skill as a tactician, aided by a corps of officers unsurpassed for their knowledge of the art of attack and defence, and by the indomitable courage of their followers. With half his force left on the battle-field or in the hospital, and with less than six thousand men, after a series of desperate contests, he took possession of the city of Mexico, containing nearly two hundred thousand inhabitants, and defended by the remnant of an army of more than thirty thousand soldiers. I confess I know nothing in modern warfare which exceeds in brilliancy the movements of the American army from the Gulf to the city of Mexico. I shall not attempt to speak of them in the language of eulogium—they are not a fit theme for such a comment. Like the achievements of General Taylor and his brave men on the Rio Grande, at Monterey, and Buena-Vista, the highest and most appropriate praise is contained in the simplest statement of facts.

Mr. President, the gallant achievements in the valley of Mexico, to which I have briefly referred, were due to the chivalrous men whose names are signed to this petition, and to their gallant associates in the field. The names of the volunteer officers who so nobly distinguished themselves are not borne on the petition. The subject concerns the regular army only, and the petitioners belong exclusively to that arm of the service. At the head of the list I find Winfield Scott, William J. Worth, John A. Quitman, Gideon J. Pillow, David E. Twiggs, James Shields, George Cadwalader, and Persifer F. Smith, all general officers; Harney, Clark, Riley, and Garland, among the colonels; and among the field and staff and lower commissioned grades, other names, too numerous to mention, which those who bear them have, by their gallantry, made familiar to their countrymen. I have already said that this petition was signed at Puebla, almost at the moment the army commenced its march from that city for the valley of Mexico. Sir, it is more than probable that the last time many of these gallant men held a pen was to inscribe their names upon this petition; and when this appeal to their countrymen was made, in full confidence, doubtless, that their prayer would be heard, their hands thenceforth dealt only with the weapons with which they were vindicating their country's honor in the field, and which none but Death, the conqueror of us all, could wrest from their grasp.

Mr. President, I will not undertake to give a summary of the contents of this petition. It is very brief. Preparing, as the petitioners were, for the unequal contest which awaited them, and of which, perhaps, they alone did not doubt the issue, they had no words to waste even on the subject nearest to their hearts. I will read it, with the Senate's permission, in their own language:—

" *To the Senate and House of Representatives of the United States of America:*

" We, the undersigned, officers of the United States Army, beg leave, most respectfully, to represent to your honorable bodies, that many of us are married and have left wives and children at home dependent upon us; that we are constantly exposed to danger and sudden death, not only on the field of battle, but by exposure to unhealthy and deadly climates; and that in going to the fight many of us have our hearts depressed by the melancholy conviction that, if we fall, our wives and children will be helplessly thrown on the cold charities of the world.

"We most respectfully ask our country to give us the assurance, if we offer up our lives in her service, that she will provide for our destitute widows and orphans: and that she may do so, we humbly petition your honorable bodies to pass such a law as you in your wisdom shall deem just — as shall give to the wives and children of officers and soldiers dying in the service of their country, pensions during the natural lives or widowhood of the wife, and during the minority of the children; and your petitioners, as in duty bound, will ever gratefully pray.

"PUEBLA, MEXICO, *August* 1, 1847."

It is due to General Scott to say, that in signing the petition he added these words: "Without any desire of procuring for my own family any contingent benefit from the proposed change in the pension laws of the army, I entirely concur in the reasonableness of the foregoing petition, and can see no military or other objection to its being signed and presented."

General Quitman also signs with the following addition: "I approve the measure of placing the regular army on the same footing with the navy and volunteers."

This remark of General Quitman explains all. The army is not on an equally favorable footing in respect to widows and orphans with the navy or volunteers. Without complaining of the inequality, the petitioners respectfully ask that it may be rectified.

Mr. President, I have no doubt that, in reading and signing this petition, the recollection of wives and children thousands of miles away, many of whom were to become widows and orphans before this last missive could reach the capital, was to the signers far more trying than the scenes of danger and death, on which they were about to enter. If it was to them a moment of weakness, — the only weakness pardonable to gallant men, — the memory of a dozen battle-fields attests that it was the last. Some of them sleep in honorable graves; some are lying on beds of sickness in Mexico; many are still in the field, ready, as ever, to peril all in their country's cause; and others,—I am sorry to say not a few,—restored to their homes, are dragging about their scarred and mangled limbs, in the face of their friends and kindred, with lives held by the frailest tenure.

But, sir, I have said enough. It would be to distrust the right feeling of the Senate to say more. Less I could not say, in justice to myself, with this paper before me, on which I recognize the names of numerous friends and former associates, many of whom we shall see no more. It gives me pleasure, not unmixed with pain, to present their petition; and if the presentation has been accompanied with the manifestation of more feeling than becomes the performance of a public duty on this floor, I am sure it will be ascribed to a right cause. I will conclude, sir, by reading to the Senate an extract of a letter enclosed with the petition, with the single remark that it was written, in behalf of the army, by Major Harvey Brown, a gallant officer, with whom I had the pleasure of being associated many years ago in the staff of a former commanding general of the army. It is dated at the National Palace, in the city of Mexico, on the 1st of October, two months after the petition was signed.

"I would also call to your notice the melancholy fact, that many of the officers who have signed this petition have since gloriously fallen in the service of their country, leaving destitute widows and helpless orphans. And being dead, they now emphatically speak, saying, 'We have offered up our lives to our country, and we now call upon her to provide a decent competence for our bereaved widows and fatherless children.'"

Is it too much, Mr. President, to ask that these petitions, with the names attached to them, may be printed? I know it is not the practice of the Senate to print petitions. But these are something more. As far as they go, they are lists of the gallant living and the honored dead in Mexico. I make the motion to print.

ADDRESSES AND REPORTS.

AFRICAN COLONIZATION.

The New York State Colonization Society held its first anniversary meeting at the Capitol, in the city of Albany, on the 2d of April, 1830.

The following resolution, offered by John A. Dix, Esq., of Cooperstown, Otsego county, and seconded by Alonzo F. Paige, Esq., of Schenectady, was unanimously adopted: —

"*Resolved*, That the Board of Managers be requested to cause such information to be disseminated in relation to the plan of colonizing the free blacks of the United States in Africa, and to adopt such measures as they may deem best calculated to promote the formation of auxiliary societies in the different counties in this State."

In support of this resolution, Mr. Dix addressed to the society the following remarks: —

IN advocating the adoption of this resolution, it is not my intention to enter into a regular discussion of the great subject of African colonization, but merely to touch upon particular questions relating to it. The able and eloquent examination which the whole subject received at the organization of this society, has left scarcely a leading topic to be illustrated or an argument to be supplied. In enlarging, however, upon some of the considerations presented at that time, the occasion seems to me a suitable one for entering into a brief review of the efforts and progress of the American Colonization Society; and in doing so, I cannot forbear to congratulate this assembly, that a preliminary question — the practicability of settlement upon the African coast by emigration from the United States — can no longer be drawn into controversy. In the settlement of this question, the most formidable obstacle to the accomplishment of the objects of the society has been removed. It has united to us many, who, under different circumstances, would now be contending against us; and it has doubly augmented our strength by breaking the force of prejudice, and by narrowing the field of argument, which it is our business and our duty to maintain.

It may be said, without exaggeration, that the plan of colonization thus far has not only been successful, but that its success has been triumphant. Only seven years have elapsed since the first band of emigrants (about eighty in number) landed on the African coast. They were without shelter and protection, and almost without the supplies of subsistence necessary to sustain them until they could draw their nourishment from the earth by the labor of their own hands. Disease, the constant enemy of that enterprise which ventures upon new and untried climates; the hostility of the native possessors of the soil, who, as it almost always happens, looked upon them with distrust and suspicion; the scarcity of the means of subsistence; and the innumerable difficulties in reducing to culture a soil which human industry had never attempted, have all been encountered and overcome. A population of 1500 souls is now sustained by its own industry; and in the year 1828 a surplus production, equal in value to $90,000, was exported for foreign consumption. A system of laws, administered, with the assistance of three or four whites, by the colonists themselves, secures to them the same rights of person and property, and the same impartial distribution of justice, which we ourselves enjoy. Schools have been established at various points throughout the colony; and the children of the surrounding tribes of natives, who have been buried for centuries in unmitigated darkness, are seen mingling with the colonists for the acquisition of moral and intellectual lights.

Compared with the British colony at Sierra Leone, the progress of Liberia is still more strongly marked. It has, after seven years, a population which the former did not possess after twenty years from the date of its establishment; and in all its moral and intellectual acquisitions it is far superior to the condition of that colony at the period to which I refer. In the capacity for extension by force of its own possessions, Liberia may be said to be almost without limit. The society has obtained from the actual occupants of the soil the cession of a territory unbounded in extent.

From the condition of the colony at Liberia, the transition is not an ungrateful one to the state of the society at home. More than half the States in the Union have formed societies auxiliary to the parent institution; and the subordinate associations are exceedingly numerous. The current of opinion is with the institution; and it will be borne on to the fulfilment of its objects, — gradually it may be, but they are destined, nevertheless, to be fulfilled. If any one shall venture to draw into controversy the practicability of the scheme, it is sufficient for our purpose to insist on what we have actually accomplished. If any one shall suggest that our free blacks will not be disposed to emigrate to Liberia, it is a sufficient reply, that, from the first establishment of the colony, the applications for passages have constantly exceeded the means of the society; that there are, at this moment, more than a thousand applications by free blacks for passages, which the society is unable to supply; that there are two thousand slaves ready to be liberated by their masters, whenever the means of their removal shall be provided; that there are, doubtless, thousands who are restrained from applying by the known inability of the society to accomplish its purposes.

In promoting the emigration of the African race, whether bond or free, every State in this Union has a separate interest, as well as an interest in common with all the others; for there is no section of the country which does not participate in some degree in the burden of its presence. In the Northern and Middle States, indeed, the pressure of the evil is at this moment more severe than in the South. We have no restraint upon free blacks, except that which is contained in the general denunciations of the law against offenders. But in the South the system of domestic servitude is a system of incessant care and vigilance, which is maintained by a coöperation of private interest with municipal regulation: it is a system, not merely of retributive, but also of preventive justice, which it is difficult either to overpower by force or to elude by artifice. The mass of crime committed by Africans is greater, in proportion to numbers, in the non-slaveholding States; and, as a general rule, the degree of comfort enjoyed by them is inferior. This is not an argument in favor of slavery; but it is an unanswerable argument in favor of rendering emancipation and colonization coextensive with each other. It presents to every State in the Union a powerful motive to promote the objects of the institution, of which we are an auxiliary. The South has as deep an interest in the removal of our free blacks as we have in the manumission and removal of their slaves. The different members of this confederacy are bound to each other by ties of which we ourselves are incapable of properly estimating the force. Whatever augments or diminishes the strength of one is so much added to or drawn from the strength of all the others. In modern times the numbers of a nation do not constitute its greatest strength, but the moral force which it is capable of putting forth for the multiplication of its resources in peace, and for their protection in seasons of public danger. Sir, it is impossible to estimate the increase of moral power which we should acquire, if the place of the two millions of Africans, who embarrass the operations of the body politic, could be supplied by as many free citizens, sharing our intelligence, bearing our blood, and nurtured with us in the enjoyment of a common liberty.

In everything but the removal of our free blacks, we are but the followers of the South in a career which they themselves have opened to us; and it is, indeed, a career in which we could not well have led the way. For, although the first effect of colonization is to provide a refuge for blacks who have been emancipated, another is to promote emancipation, and a still more remote effect to hasten the extinction of slavery itself. This, therefore, is a measure which, in some of its leading tendencies, relates peculiarly to the South, and our coöperation can only be lent as far as it is invited. The American Society has disclaimed, from the first moment of its institution, all intention of interfering with rights of property recognized by the Federal compact to which the States are parties. It contemplates no purpose of abolition; it touches no slave until his fetters have been voluntarily stricken off by the hand of his own master; it removes no free black but upon his own solicitation; all its purposes are subordinate to the rules of public law and the suggestions of private justice and humanity. But it is to the South — to VIRGINIA — that we are indebted for the origin of this great plan; and we are indebted to that State at least for a coöperation in every plan which has tended to elevate the human character or to promote the interests and honor of the Republic. Her voice was raised against the intrusion of slaves upon her during her colonial subjection; and, faithful to her principles, she was the first among the Southern States in endeavoring to free herself from the incumbrance when she had risen to independence.

The subject of African colonization is full of powerful appeals to sympathy; but it is not my intention to advert to any topics of this description. Considered as a mere measure of political economy, it has as strong a claim upon us in its tendency to hasten the extinction of slavery as any measure which can be devised for the promotion of the productive industry of the United States. It is an opinion as ancient as slavery itself, that the labor of bondmen is gradually destructive of the soil to which it is applied: it is only where the cultivator has an actual interest in the soil, that the care and attention necessary to perpetuate its productiveness will be bestowed upon it. There is an account by

Columella of the condition of Roman agriculture, when it had passed from the hands of the citizens into those of slaves, which is applicable to every country in which slave labor has been employed for a length of time. Pliny refers the decline of the agriculture of Rome to the same cause, — to its transfer from freemen to slaves, wearing upon their very countenances the badges of servitude, —

"Vincti pedes, damnatæ manus, inscripti vultus exercent."

And Tacitus, in referring to the same causes, says that Italy could not be subsisted but for the supplies derived from the provinces.

"Nisi provinciarum copiæ et dominis, et servitiis et agris subvenerint."

Yet the territories of Rome were remarkable for their fertility and productiveness as long as they were cultivated by her own citizens. When agriculture had become degraded from an honorable pursuit to a mere menial occupation; when the implements of husbandry had passed from the hands of Cato and Cincinnatus into those of the captives of Phrygia and Thrace; and when, to translate the words of a Roman author, the fields of Italy resounded with the clattering of innumerable chains, Rome became dependent for the sustenance of her own citizens upon the productions of distant provinces; and, in the language of Tacitus, the daily subsistence of the Roman people was at the mercy of winds and waves.

The authority of antiquity is confirmed by the opinion of our own times. With a single exception,[1] every modern writer upon political economy asserts the superior productiveness of free labor, and the tendency of slave labor to waste and consume the fertility of the soil to which it is applied. It has been shown conclusively that wherever free labor can be found, it is most profitable to employ it. And it would be contrary to all the deductions of reason if it were not so. The industry, which is not protected in the enjoyment of a

[1] Say.

portion of its own proceeds, cannot be so productive as that which is recompensed in proportion to its exertions. In the agricultural operations of the slave, nature is the principal laborer, and her power soon becomes exhausted without the renovating care and providence of man. Whether industrious or indolent, the slave must be clothed and subsisted; let him produce as much as you will, and he is entitled to nothing more at the hands of his master. His impulses are all derived from physical causes, and these of the weakest class; he is not even stimulated by physical necessity or suffering, for these it is the interest and care of the master to relieve. So much has the mind to do with the operations of human industry, that even in countries where, by oppressive taxation, all the proceeds of man's labor, excepting a bare subsistence, are absorbed by his government, the labor of the freeman is far more productive than that of the slave. His condition may be no better; his supplies of clothing and subsistence may not be more abundant; he may be equally restricted in his comforts: but he ministers to his own wants; he does not receive his daily subsistence at the hands of a task-master; his little surplus, whatever it be, is his own; and he is not controlled in the application of it to his own uses.

The results of our own experience on this subject concur with the united testimony of ancient and modern times. It is impossible to pass from a State in which slavery exists to one in which it is prohibited, without perceiving a marked difference in the condition of the soil, and in the structures which human art has reared upon its surface. But it is not by ocular observation alone that the fact of the difference is attested. In contiguous sections, lands of the same quality bear a different price, and the disparity is constantly increasing with the duration of the cause. It seems to be a law of slavery, that it gradually consumes and dissipates the resources of those to whom it is tributary. There are exceptions to the observation, but not in sufficient number to affect its accuracy as a general principle.

If the place of every slave in the United States could be supplied by a free laborer, the augmentation of our productive industry would be immense, and it would totally renovate the face of the country in which the exchange should take place. At the lowest calculation, there is a difference of one third in the productiveness of free and slave labor in favor of the former, independently of the gradual destruction of the powers of the soil by the latter. Free and slave labor move in opposite directions from the same point of departure; and while one is regularly diminishing the capacity of the earth for production, the other is constantly nourishing and invigorating its powers. It is one of the consequences of this tendency of slave labor to deteriorate the properties of the earth, that it cannot reclaim what it has once exhausted. There are lands in the Northern and Middle States now exceedingly productive, which were formerly exhausted by slave labor; and so they would have continued to this day, if they had not been reclaimed by free labor. Some of the most beautiful sections of Virginia, under the operation of injudicious systems of husbandry by slaves, wear the aspect of wastes and barrens; and so they will remain until they shall be renovated by the hands of freemen. That this result is not a distant one may readily be shown. The influence of great moral causes, which are working far more momentous changes than this, would alone be sufficient to produce it. But it is destined to attend upon particular causes now in operation within our own limits, — causes peculiar to the condition of the country and the state of society. Slave labor, from its inferior productiveness, cannot compete with free labor: wherever the latter appears, the former must give place to it. This principle is visible throughout the North in the abolition of slavery: the progress of emancipation has been regular towards the South; peculiarities of soil and climate have retarded its progress, but it is retarded only. In several sections of Maryland and Virginia, emigration from the Middle States has introduced a laboring class of whites; and wherever they have appeared, slaves have given place to them. The masters find it more profitable to sell their slaves and hire free laborers. It is in this manner that freedom is constantly encroaching upon the dominion of servitude.

But there are other and mightier causes in operation, which are rapidly approaching this result. Recent examinations have shown that, with the exception of the States of Missouri and Louisiana, we have only sufficient territory beyond the Mississippi river for four more States of the dimensions of Missouri. Farther on lies a barren waste, extending to the base of the Rocky Mountains, without wood, water, or stone, and therefore unfit for the habitation of an agricultural people. This fact is not, perhaps, understood, but it has been satisfactorily ascertained by philosophical observers. The region referred to is as distinctive in its character as the desert of Siberia, to the descriptions of which it is said to bear a general resemblance; and it is, probably, destined at a future day to constitute a boundary between us and our dependencies, or between us and another people, as flourishing and powerful as ourselves. At our past rate of increase, settlement will soon press upon these limits: the vacant places within them will be filled up; and the current of emigration, which has so long been flowing across the Alleghanies, will be poured back upon the region in which it has its source. The surplus population of the Northern and Middle States will find its way to the vacant spots in Virginia, which slavery has exhausted and abandoned; it will penetrate to the very seat of its strength, and it will gradually uproot and destroy it. In every contest, the inferior must yield to the superior power; and who can doubt the issue, sir, when the contest shall be between brute force and the moral force of opinion? — between a class whose impulses are all derived from physical causes, and another class whose incentives to exertion are derived from the mind itself? Slavery will cease to be profitable; and, when this shall happen, slaves will cease to be cherished by their possessors. They may be emancipated; but emancipation cannot elevate their condition or augment their capacity for self-preservation. Want and suffering will gradually diminish their numbers, and they will disappear, as the inferior has always disappeared, before the superior race. The fate of the African is as certain as that of the original possessors of the soil upon which we stand; but there will be no heroism or dignity in his fall: his struggles will be with the arts, not the arms, of his oppressors: he will leave nothing behind him but the history of his sufferings and his degradation to challenge the remembrance or the sympathy of after-times.

Colonization is the only expedient by which these evils can even be mitigated. We may prevent the increase of the African race within our limits: we may provide for them a refuge to which they may flee when their presence shall be useless to us and their condition here intolerable to themselves: we may substitute removal for extinction; and by our own providence we may enable many, perhaps the mass, to escape what would otherwise be their inevitable fate.

But it is not merely because slavery is an impediment to the development of our national resources that its presence among us is to be deplored. It is an impediment also to an assertion of the rank which we claim to hold among the advocates of the rights of man. It may not put at hazard the success of the great experiment which we are carrying on of the competency of mankind to self-government; for it is not inconsistent with its success that he who is fitted for freedom should hold in bondage his fellow-man. But it involves, unquestionably, a denial of the fundamental doctrine of our political institutions, that life, liberty, and the pursuit of happiness are natural and inalienable rights. It is a degradation of the tenure of freedom from a principle above all human law to the principle of brute force — the principle from which despotism itself derives its title. It may not impair the stability of our free institutions; but it impairs our influence in promoting the diffusion of their principles. For who shall be bound to attend to the assertion of rights by us, which we refuse to recognize in others? With what effect can we pronounce the eulogium of free institutions when our utterance is mingled and confounded with the accents of oppression and servitude? We have, unquestionably, a justification in the fact that slavery was imposed upon us against our wishes during our dependence upon a foreign state; but this circumstance will cease to be a justification the moment we falter in our exertions to redress the injury.

In speaking these sentiments, I say nothing to which the sentiments of every liberal gentleman in the South will not respond. Nor do I fear, sir, that their utterance here will be misapprehended. I believe the universal feeling of this assembly will bear me out in saying, that the slaveholding States themselves would not be more ready than we to resist any attempt to exterminate the unquestionable evil of slavery by measures not warranted by the Constitution under which we live. That it has been abolished with us, is the happiness of our accidental position: that it still exists in other sections of the Union, is the misfortune of theirs. When and in what manner it shall be abolished within the limits of individual States, must be left to their own voluntary deliberations. The Federal government has no control over this subject: it concerns rights of property secured by the Federal compact, upon which our civil liberties mainly depend; it is a part of the same collection of political rights, and any invasion of it would impair the tenure by which every other is held. For this reason alone, if for no other, we would discountenance and oppose any attempt to control it by unconstitutional interference. We can only hope, in advocating the plan of colonization, that the theatre of its operations may be extended at a future day in subordination to the wishes and arrangements of the slaveholding States.

There is a higher object in the contemplation, and I trust

within the compass of this institution,—the civilization of the African continent by means of our colonial establishments along the coast. With the exception of a few points along the Mediterranean, hardly extending into the interior sufficiently to indent it, this continent has been buried throughout all the changes of human society in perpetual darkness. Whatever civilization may have done for other portions of the earth, it has done nothing for Africa. Ignorance and barbarism, opposing an impenetrable cloud to the lights of religion and science, which have at different eras risen upon the world, have spread a vast, unbroken shadow over the whole face of that continent. Civilization has indeed visited Africa — not to elevate and enlighten, but to corrupt and debase — to convert simplicity into error, and darkness into depravity. Sir, we are accustomed to shrink with horror and indignation from a recital of the cruelties inflicted upon modern Greece by her barbarous oppressors. But all the miseries which that classical region has endured during century after century of Ottoman domination would not fill up the measure of suffering which Africa is every year sustaining through the seductions of her Christian spoilers. The massacre of Scio may present a sublimity of suffering, an acuteness of distress, a fulness of desolation, which carry their appeals to the sympathies with greater boldness and intensity of solicitation. But they do not all compose an aggregate like that which a single slave-ship presents in the history of its miserable tenants, if we follow them out from the forcible separation to the prolonged, the boundless career of servitude which opens on them at the hour of their captivity. Civilization alone can heal the wounds and assuage the sufferings of Western Africa. Wherever her influence is felt, the slave-trade has ceased; and it is in the most benighted regions of that continent that she can most effectually plant those beacons of intelligence from which her lights are to be reflected to the interior. Egypt and Barbary are shut out from the approaches of civilization in the direction of the European continent by an intervening sea: they lie over against portions of Europe in which knowledge and truth have made the least progress; and these barriers between the two continents are rendered almost insurmountable by false systems of religion and government which hold in bondage the African states. Colonization, on the other hand, has fixed her very seat in the empire of ignorance: she is surrounded on all sides by a surface of extended, unbroken, unmitigated darkness. The mind of Western and Central Africa is a vast blank, upon which no inscription of falsehood or bigotry has ever been traced: civilization, in asserting her dominion over it, has no error to eradicate or prejudice to subdue: there is no obstacle to stay the progress of knowledge; Nigritia, Ethiopia, and Abyssinia are all open to its approaches; and the time may not be far distant when the lights of civilization, issuing from the beacons of Montserrado, shall be diffused over the whole face of the African continent — to change it, as they have changed every region which their influence has overspread.

These anticipations may seem sanguine, and they are, doubtless, to be contemplated rather in a spirit of distant hope than of present expectation. They look, however, to changes inferior, if possible, to those which the same causes have wrought upon this continent. If any one had ventured a century ago to extend his view to the present moment, and had foretold what this age has accomplished, he would have incurred the reproach of visionary speculation. Nay, sir, what credit would he have obtained who had ventured to foretell, twenty years ago, the changes that have been wrought within our own limits? — who had predicted, that, in this short period, the Western wilderness would be penetrated and subdued; that the boundaries of the Republic would be borne onward to extremities which were not even explored; and that a line of civilization would be extended around us, which can never be broken by a hostile force? Sir, the opinion of mankind has always followed the march of improvement; and it is rarely even that individual opinion has preceded it. The civilization of Africa may be frustrated by unforeseen contingencies; but a moral power is in operation there, which no obstacle has ever yet been able to resist. The stores of knowledge, unlike all others, can neither be wasted nor consumed: no further deluge of vandalism can overwhelm the places of her dominion to destroy her treasures or extinguish her lights. The physical annihilation of three quarters of the globe would be necessary to blot out the evidences of her moral conquests and arrest their extension to the other. Since the invention of the press, the movement of society has been uniformly a forward movement, and there is not an instance of retrogression with any people to whom the influence of knowledge has extended. Her empire is fixed in Africa, and it will soon be beyond the reach of human force. Our anticipations may not all be realized; our hopes may not all be fulfilled; but if we err, we shall err with the spirit of the age, not in opposition to it. If the objects in view of the plan of colonization were to be attempted by a public sacrifice, we should not, perhaps, be justifiable in seeking to accomplish them. But every step we take is in coincidence with the public interest and the public reputation. Every liberated African, who is withdrawn from us, diminishes the general mass of ignorance, vice, and degradation by which our social operations are embarrassed and oppressed. We are fulfilling also a duty which we owe to the unfortunate race for whose benefit this institution was originally designed. Whatever we have done, whatever we may do, to ameliorate their condition among us, they are destined to be forever proscribed and debased by our prejudices. Emancipation cannot liberate us from the responsibility which rests upon us. The free black, whom prejudice consigns to a moral debasement in the North, is as deeply injured as the slave, who in the South is held by physical bondage. We cannot insist on the plea of necessity to mitigate the odium which attaches to us as the authors of his degradation until we shall have employed every expedient to relieve him from it. The hopelessness in which his crimes and his depravation have their origin is in its turn a fruit of our prejudices; and we shall not have done what is incumbent on us, unless our coöperation is lent to remove him from the theatre of their influence. We are bound by every principle of justice and humanity to provide the means of removal for all who ask a removal at our hands. We are bound by every motive of patriotism to promote the emigration of a caste whose presence among us is an impediment to the development of our national resources, to the progress of our social improvements, and to the fulfilment of our destinies as a great people. And we are bound by our devotion to the cause of liberal government to UNITE in the execution of a plan of which the most distant result may be the extinction of an institution which stands alone and isolated among the other institutions of society — A SOLITARY MONUMENT OF A BARBAROUS AGE.

OPINION ON TWO QUESTIONS OF ALIENISM.

The question of alienism is one of great interest in the United States by reason of the flood of immigration and the doubts which have existed in regard to the true construction of the naturalization laws passed by Congress. The doctrine laid down in the following opinion in the case of Zule was afterwards held by Chancellor Walworth in the case of West v. West, which was decided in 1840.[1]

STATE OF NEW YORK,
ADJUTANT-GENERAL'S OFFICE.
January 14, 1833.

SIR: I received, some time ago, your letter of the 25th October, submitting two cases for my decision, with a view to an amicable disposition of them. I now proceed to comply with your request; and as there appears to have been some disagreement between the court and the counsel employed by the delinquents on trial, I shall state, in detail, for their information as well as yours, the grounds on which my opinion rests.

1. In the year 1803, James Titcomb arrived in this State from England, aged five or six years, and, some time during the spring of 1832, purchased a lot of land in the town of Mayfield, in the county of Montgomery, for which he took a common warranty deed.

The question submitted is, whether Titcomb is exempt from military duty on account of alienism?

Although it is not expressly stated, I take it for granted that he has not only not been naturalized, but that he has never taken any of the incipient steps specified in sec. 15, art. 2, title 1, chap. 1, part 2, Revised Statutes. If he has purchased lands without taking such steps, it is at his own

[1] 8 Paige's Reports, 433.

OPINION ON TWO QUESTIONS OF ALIENISM. 57

peril, and he cannot hold them against the State, after an inquest of office found. But his liability to military duty depends upon other considerations: to incur such a liability he must either have been naturalized, or at all events he must have complied with the provisions of the article above referred to.

There is a principle connected with this question, which from its importance deserves to be stated and briefly examined. There was a provision in the militia law of 1823,[1] directing the captain of each company of infantry to enroll "every able bodied alien, who shall at any time have been *seized of any real estate within this State*, and the sons of every such alien," &c.; but this provision is repealed by the Revised Statutes. It is, however, provided, by the 20th section of art. 2, title 1, chap. 1, part 2, Rev. Sts., that every alien holding any real estate by virtue of any of the provisions of that article, " shall be subject to duties, assessments, taxes and burthens, as if he were a citizen of this State." It would appear that Chancellor Kent[2] considers this liability as extending to the performance of military duty. It is true, he not only refers to it in such a manner as to convey the impression that it depends upon a distinct provision of law, but from the employment of the same terms it would almost appear that he considered the provision of the militia act of 1823 still in force. For instance, he says : " In New York, resident aliens are liable to be enrolled in the militia, provided they are lawfully *seized of any real estate within the State, and* they are *in that case* declared to be subject to duties, assessments, taxes and burthens as if they were citizens." If he considered the liability to military duty, referred to in the first part of this sentence, as depending upon the words which he quotes from the statute in the latter part, (and this is most probable, as he makes but a single reference to the statute,) there is, to say the least, great want of precision

---
[1] Laws of New York, Sess. 46, ch. 144, sec. 8.
[2] Kent's Commentaries, 2d ed. Vol. II. p. 64.

in the manner of stating it. It is also a little remarkable that it did not occur to him to inquire, whether this provision is consistent with the Constitution and laws of the United States, — a question which may fairly be raised; for if it be not so, the liability which he considers it as creating, cannot have a lawful existence.

The Constitution of the United States (art. 1, sec. 8, part 15) gives to Congress the power "to provide for organizing, arming and disciplining the militia," &c.; and in pursuance of this grant of authority, the act of Congress of May 8, 1792, provides that "every able bodied, free, white, male citizen" shall be enrolled, &c. Under the provisions of this act, the militia of this State must be organized; and any provisions in our laws inconsistent with them would be null and void, as Congress has exclusive jurisdiction over the subject-matter regulated. It seems proper that the power of providing for the organization of the militia should reside where the Constitution has placed it — with the general government. The latter is charged with the public defence; and it is but reasonable that it should possess the power of designating the nature and extent of the enrolment, for these are necessarily regulated by the public exigencies. The act of Congress referred to intends that none but "free, white, male citizens" shall be enrolled; and it is worthy of reflection, whether the designation of a particular class of persons from which the enrolment is to be made by the authority having exclusive jurisdiction in the case, does not render illegal the enrolment of any other class. An express prohibition can hardly be necessary; for, if under the laws of this State aliens may be enrolled, because the act of Congress prescribing the organization of the militia contains no express prohibition as to them, females and blacks may also be enrolled for the same reason, or even slaves in a slaveholding State. But in any of these cases, it seems to me that the militia would not constitute such a force as was contemplated by the act of Congress.

I am, therefore, inclined to the opinion, that an alien, although holding real estate and coming within the provisions of art. 2, title 1, chap. 1, part 2, Rev. Sts., might, before a court-martial, maintain his claim to exemption, by setting up the provisions of the act of Congress of 8th May, 1792; and, consequently, that the provisions of section 20 of the article of the Revised Statutes last referred to, if that section is to be construed to extend to the performance of military duty, are inconsistent with the Constitution and laws of the United States. But admitting that the provisions of that section are of binding force, still they do not reach the case in point; they subject to the "duties, assessments, taxes and burthens" of citizens such aliens only as hold real estate by virtue of the provisions of the article of which that section is a part, one of which provisions is, that a deposition, duly certified, shall be filed in the office of the Secretary of State; and with these it does not appear that Titcomb has complied.

I am, therefore, of the opinion that he is not liable to military duty; and that a fine, imposed on him for disregarding a warning to attend a company or regimental training, would be unlawfully imposed.

2. A Mr. Zule arrived in this country from Scotland a number of years ago, and soon after his arrival was naturalized according to our laws on that subject, and now possesses property. His son came over with him at the same time, being three or four years old. He has now passed the age of eighteen years, and refuses to train because he is an alien.

The question submitted is, whether the naturalization of the father, in this case, carries with it the naturalization of the child, so that the latter is to be considered as a citizen of the United States?

This is a question of some difficulty. The only existing law under which he can be claimed as a citizen, is the act of Congress of 14th April, 1802; and to comprehend more clearly the intention of this act, it may not be improper to glance at the laws previously passed on the same subject.

The act of Congress of March 26, 1790,[1] provided, "That any alien, being a free white person, who shall have resided within the limits and under the jurisdiction of the United States for the term of two years, may be admitted to become a citizen thereof, on application to any common-law court of record in any one of the States wherein he shall have resided for the term of one year at least, and making proof to the satisfaction of such court that he is a person of good character, and taking the oath or affirmation prescribed by law to support the Constitution of the United States, which oath or affirmation such court shall administer; and the clerk of such court shall record such application, and the proceedings thereon; and thereupon such person shall be considered as a citizen of the United States. And the children of such persons so naturalized, dwelling within the United States, being under the age of twenty-one years at the time of such naturalization, shall also be considered as citizens of the United States. And the children of citizens of the United States that may be born beyond sea, or out of the limits of the United States, shall be considered as natural born citizens," &c.

The foregoing provision was the earliest adopted after the government had gone into operation under the Constitution of the United States; and it shows manifestly the intention of Congress to have been to confer the right of citizenship on the minor children of persons naturalized in pursuance of the rule therein contained, provided they were dwelling in the United States at the time of the naturalization of their parents. Under this provision, the political condition of the child, while laboring under the disability of nonage, was to follow the condition of the parent. With regard to the minor children of aliens, the qualification of residence

[1] Laws U. S. Vol. II. p. 82. Bioren's edition.

in the United States at some period would be indispensable to the application of the rule to those whom it was intended to reach; and by this act it appears to have been referred, as seems most proper, to the period when the change in the political condition of the parent was effected, — the period of his admission to the rights of citizenship. If the children were resident in a foreign country at that period, their citizenship would not have been affected by the naturalization of the parent in the United States.

The provisions of this act were highly favorable to aliens. The general government had but recently gone into operation upon the liberal basis of amity and mutual concession between the parties to the compact from which it derived its existence. It was, indeed, less than a year after the first act of Congress under the Constitution of the United States was passed; and it was natural that every facility should be extended, in the spirit of the times, to those who, without the ties of native citizens, were nevertheless disposed to unite their fortunes to the new Republic.

The act of Congress of 29th January, 1795,[1] repealed the act of 26th March, 1790, and prescribed other requisites for admission to the rights of citizenship. The alien was required to make a declaration of his intention to become a citizen three years at least before his admission, and to renounce his native allegiance, &c. But it was also provided that any alien, residing within the limits and under the jurisdiction of the United States, might be admitted upon declaring on oath, &c. that he had resided two years within and under the jurisdiction of the same, &c.

It was further provided, (sec. 3,) "That the children of persons duly naturalized, dwelling within the United States, and being under the age of twenty-one years at the time of such naturalization; and the children of citizens of the United States, born out of the limits and jurisdiction of the United States, shall be considered as citizens of the United States," &c.

[1] Laws U. S. Vol. II. p. 466. Bioren's edition.

The provisions of this act, though less liberal than those of the act of 26th March, 1790, in relation to aliens who should come to reside in the United States after its enactment, make no change in the requisites for the admission of their children to the rights of citizenship. The only difference in the provisions of the two acts in relation to the children of persons naturalized, is in the addition of the word "and" between the two qualifications of residence in the United States and minority, — an addition which does not vary the effect.

The act of Congress of 18th June, 1798,[1] provided that no alien should become a citizen of the United States, except in the manner prescribed in the act of 29th January, 1795. Every alien was required to make a declaration of his intention to become a citizen five years before his admission, and to prove that he had resided fourteen years in the United States. It was also made the duty of the clerk of the court before which the declaration was made, to transmit an abstract, duly certified, to the office of the Secretary of State.

The act (sec. 4) provided that all aliens, who thereafter should continue to reside, who should arrive, or who should come to reside, in any port or place within the territory of the United States, should be reported, if free and of the age of twenty-one years, by themselves, or being under the age of twenty-one years, or holden in service, by their parent, guardian, master, or mistress, for registry. This report was required to be made in all cases of residence, within six months after the passing of the act; and in all subsequent cases, within forty-eight hours after the first arrival or coming into the territory of the United States. In case the alien refused to make report, he might be required to give surety of good behavior; and, in failure of such surety, he was liable to be committed to jail.

The provisions of the 4th section of this act were made, not with a view to the admission of aliens to the rights of citizenship, but as a precaution against them; and they are

[1] Laws U. S. Vol. III. p. 61. Bioren's edition.

cited with a view to illustrate the prevailing spirit of that epoch in our political history. They originated in the same feeling of jealousy, which produced the act of the 25th of the same month, (same volume, page 66,) commonly called the alien law, — by virtue of which the President of the United States was authorized to order all such aliens as he should judge dangerous to the peace and safety of the country, to depart out of the territory of the United States, — an act which, though it expired by its own limitation, was condemned as arbitrary and unconstitutional by the judgment of the people of the United States; for it was one of the questions put at rest by the political revolution of 1800. All the provisions of the act of 18th June, 1798, were exceedingly illiberal and onerous. Yet it is worthy of particular observation that it did not repeal or in any manner amend the provisions of the act of 29th May, 1795, in relation to the children of aliens, excepting so far as it rendered their registry necessary; but this, as has been seen, was not with a view to their naturalization: it was designed as a precaution against fancied hostility. The children of aliens, duly naturalized, would, notwithstanding the act of 18th June, 1798, still have been citizens without performing any act themselves, if they were minors and residents in the United States at the time of the naturalization of their parents.

The act of Congress of 14th April, 1802,[1] repeals the act of 29th January, 1795, and the act of 18th June, 1798, and prescribes a new mode of naturalization. It reduces the residence necessary to gain a title to citizenship from fourteen years to five, and confines its provisions to those aliens who were desirous of becoming citizens of the United States. All others were left at liberty to come within and depart from the territory of the United States, without being subjected to the odious forms of examination and registry. The first section prescribes various acts (which it is unnecessary to

[1] Laws U. S. Vol. III. p. 475. Bioren's edition.

the present purpose to detail) to be performed by aliens, in order to become citizens. The second section provides, "That, in addition to the directions aforesaid, all free white persons, being aliens, who may arrive in the United States after the passing of this act, shall, in order to become citizens of the United States, make registry and obtain certificates in the following manner, to wit: Every person desirous of being naturalized, shall, if of the age of twenty-one years, make report of himself; or, if under the age of twenty-one years, or held in service, shall be reported by his parent, guardian, master, or mistress," &c.

It might be supposed from the language of the above provision, that it was designed to apply to the minor children of all aliens, even of those who had, with a view to their own naturalization, complied with the requisites prescribed by this act. But if this construction were to be adopted, it would render the act, compared with that of 29th January, 1795, exceedingly illiberal; whereas it is manifest, from an examination of all its other provisions, as well as from a recurrence to the history of the times, that it was intended to be a liberal act. It was passed a little more than a year after Mr. Jefferson came into office by virtue of a reaction in public opinion, which was influenced in no inconsiderable degree by the unfriendly policy of the preceding administration in relation to aliens. It was intended to rescind the obnoxious provisions of the act of 18th June, 1798; and it is difficult to suppose that it intended to substitute for the liberal provisions of the act of 29th January, 1795, relating to the children of aliens, which were continued in force during the whole of the seven preceding years, a rule which, in comparison with them, would have been in the highest degree onerous and illiberal. It is more probable that the second section above quoted, so far as it relates to alien minors, was intended to reach those cases not provided for by previous acts, in which such aliens could not by possibility become citizens by virtue of the naturalization of their parents. For instance, an alien parent might bring with him into the United States children above the age of sixteen years. In this case, the naturalization of the parent could not carry with it the naturalization of the children, because by virtue of the same act he must have resided five years in the United States before he could become a citizen, and his children must have been under age at the time of his naturalization; whereas they would have become of age before he could be admitted to the rights of citizenship. The case might also frequently happen of an alien minor coming to the United States after the naturalization of his parent, and, according to the construction which I put upon a subsequent section, not entitled to the rights of citizenship by virtue of such naturalization, because not a resident in the United States, either at that time, or at the time the act was passed. An alien parent might also wish to procure the naturalization of his children, though unwilling, for substantial reasons, to renounce his native allegiance himself. Other cases analogous to these might be cited, which could only be reached by the provisions in question.

Section 4 provides, "That the children of persons duly naturalized under any of the laws of the United States, or who, previous to the passing of any law on that subject by the government of the United States, may have become citizens of the United States under the laws thereof, being under the age of twenty-one years at the time of their parents being so naturalized or admitted to the right of citizenship, shall, if dwelling in the United States, be considered as citizens of the United States; and the children of persons who now are or have been citizens of the United States, shall, though born out of the limits and jurisdiction of the United States, be considered as citizens of the United States."

That part of the above provision which relates to the children of aliens is susceptible of two constructions: 1st, That it was intended to apply to children under age, and dwelling in the United States at the time of the naturalization of their parents; and, 2d, to children under age at the time of the naturalization of their parents, and dwelling in the United States at the time of the passing of the act.

The first construction would make the act both prospective and retroactive in its operation, applying as well to the children of alien parents already naturalized, as to the children of alien parents who should be thereafter naturalized; it would make it conform to the provisions of the acts of 1790 and 1795, which were in force up to that period, which were not repealed by the illiberal acts of 1798; and it would make it correspond with its general scope, which was to be liberal and corrective.

The second construction would make the act retroactive merely, applying to children then dwelling in the United States, of parents who had already been naturalized; it would make it a virtual abandonment of the liberal provisions of the acts of 1790 and 1795, in relation to the children of aliens duly naturalized; and it would make it conflict with the general scope of the act, by engrafting a highly illiberal provision upon an act of a highly liberal character.

The only adjudication I can find at all favoring the latter construction, is a decision of the Supreme Court of the United States, in the case of Campbell *v.* Gordon *et ux.* 6 Cranch. 176. By that decision, an alien female under age, but not in the United States at the time of her father's naturalization, was considered a citizen, because she was in the United States at the time of the passing of the act. Thus it would appear that the court deemed a residence in the United States, at the time of the passing of the act, to have been intended, and not at the time of the parent's naturalization. It is worthy of observation, however, that the court entered into no argument to show the reason of this construction, that their decision was obviously founded upon an examination of a single section of the act of 1802, and that they passed no comment upon the repugnance of their construction to preëxisting rules, or to the tenor of the act, upon the intention of which they thus pronounced judgment. The court do not say that the words "dwelling in the United States" were not intended to be applied to the time of the parent's naturalization; yet, by applying it to the time of the passing of the act, they would seem to have indirectly renounced that application; as the female, whose case they decided, was not in the United States at the time of the naturalization of her father. The question will then occur, whether the decision of the Supreme Court, pronounced as it was upon an examination of a single provision of the act of 1802, without any reasonings, or references to previous legislation upon the same matter, calculated to illustrate its intention, should not be regarded as the result of a desire to construe the act in the most liberal manner with regard to the particular case before them, without designing to confine its operation within the narrow limits to which that construction would restrain it; whether, under all the circumstances, that decision is to be taken as a precedent of overruling authority to pervert the whole tenor of the act, and frustrate the liberal and beneficent purposes which it would otherwise be suited to accomplish.

In support of the construction that the act was intended to be prospective in its operation, is the authority of Chancellor Kent,[1] although he gives with great caution the construction to which he leans. He says, "there is color for the construction that it may have been intended to be prospective." He adds, (page 52,) "in the supplementary act of the 26th March, 1804, it was declared, that if any alien, who should have complied with the preliminary steps made requisite by the act of 1802, dies before he is actually naturalized, his widow and children shall be considered as citizens. This provision shows that the naturalization of the father was to have the efficient force of conferring the right on his children."

[1] Kent's Commentaries, 2d edit. Vol. II. p. 51.

Although I concur in the correctness of the Chancellor's construction, I am constrained to say, that I consider the grounds he assigns to be exceedingly inaccurate. For instance, the act of Congress of 26th March, 1804,[1] to which he refers, does not provide, as would seem from his references to it,[2] that the widow and children of an alien, who dies after making his declaration, shall be considered as citizens without doing any act themselves; but it requires them, in order to become entitled to all the rights and privileges of citizens, to take the oaths prescribed by the act of 1802, which are to support the Constitution of the United States, and to renounce and abjure, absolutely and entirely, all allegiance and fidelity to every foreign prince, &c. And yet it would not appear from the Chancellor's references to it, that this very essential step was required. The inference of the Chancellor from the provisions of the act of 1804, that the naturalization of the *parent* was to have the efficient force of conferring the right on his *children*, is altogether unsupported by the reasoning on which he relies, unless the naturalization of the *husband* was also to have the efficient force of conferring the right on his *wife*; for the widow and children are included in the same provision. But this inference as to the intention of the act is inadmissible with regard to the widow, since it would come in direct contravention of the rule of law, that the naturalization of the husband does not naturalize the wife. The Supreme Court of this State, in the case of Sutliffe *v.* Forgey,[3] say, "If a man seized of lands take an alien to wife and die, the widow cannot be endowed. And as the laws authorizing the naturalization of aliens give no greater privileges to the naturalized alien than the natural born citizen enjoys, it seems to follow that the alien widow of a naturalized husband cannot be endowed." But it is questionable whether this is strictly a just mode of stating

[1] Laws U. S. Vol. III. p. 614. Bioren's edition.
[2] Kent's Commentaries, Vol. II. pp. 52, 66.   [3] 1 Cowen, 89.

the principle. The denial of the rights of citizenship to the wife by force of the naturalization of the husband, it is conceived, rests upon other grounds than that assigned by the court. It is not because the laws providing for the naturalization of aliens give no greater privileges to the naturalized alien than the natural-born citizen enjoys, that the alien widow of the former cannot be endowed, but because those laws have not conferred the specific right on the wife. The rights of citizenship and the disabilities of alienism at common law depend upon the birth of the party within or without the jurisdiction of a particular sovereignty. The cases provided for by acts of Congress in the United States, as well as by acts of Parliament in Great Britain, in contravention of this principle, are so many exceptions to a general rule. No British statute, which I can find, provides for the admission of the wife to the rights of a British subject by virtue of the naturalization of the husband: nor has any provision been made by act of Congress by which the rights of citizenship are conferred on the wife in this manner. The nearest approach to such a provision is the act of 1804, by virtue of which, in case of the death of the husband after making his declaration, the law interposes and extends both to the alien widow and children, upon a formal renunciation of their native allegiance, all the benefits which can accrue to them from the relation of citizenship.

It will be perceived, by an examination of the 3d section of the act of 29th January, 1795, and the 4th section of the act of 14th April, 1802, that, although the identical words are retained in the latter, ground for a different construction in the two cases has been furnished by the introduction of a new member of the sentence, and a consequent transposition of terms. The act of 1795 was found not to reach the cases of aliens who had become citizens under the laws of individual States before the enactment of any law by Congress; and in providing for them, the words " dwelling in the United States " were, in the act of 1802, probably without the intention of changing the effect of the provision, separated from the members of the sentence with which they were in juxtaposition in the act of 1795. This conclusion is the more reasonable, as a still more remarkable change was made in relation to the children of citizens born out of the limits and jurisdiction of the United States; and it could hardly have been intended to increase their disabilities. The acts of 1790 and 1795 adopted the British statutory rule, that the children of subjects [citizens] born out of the jurisdiction of their government, should nevertheless be considered subjects [citizens]. But it will be perceived that the language of the act of 1802 is so changed that only the children of persons who had been citizens before, or were citizens at the time of the passing of the act, are, if born out of the limits and jurisdiction of the United States, to be considered citizens; and, as is justly observed by Chancellor Kent, "the benefit of this provision narrows so rapidly by lapse of time," that it will soon be wholly unavailing. It seems impossible to account on any rational ground for these changes in the language of the act of 1802, when compared with the act of 1795, except by the supposition that they were made without a distinct perception of their illiberal and oppressive consequences. It cannot be admitted that the effect of the provisions of the act of 1795 was intended to be changed, without doing violence to the whole scope and tenor of the act of 1802. In the case last mentioned, the language is clear, and its sense cannot be disputed: the latter must therefore prevail. But in the other, the language is plainly susceptible of such a construction as to render the whole act consistent with itself, with previous legislation, and with the liberal intentions of the Congress which passed it. This construction, therefore, I adopt; and I feel the more confidence in doing so, as the uniform practice in this State, so far as I can ascertain, is in conformity to it.

I regret that I can find no adjudications upon this important question, calculated to shed light upon it. But, upon the whole, I am of the opinion, after a careful examination of all the laws in relation to the naturalization of aliens, that the act of 14th April, 1802, was intended to be prospective, and to apply to the minor children of aliens, who should arrive in the United States and become citizens after the passing of that act. If this construction is correct, the son of Mr. Zule, is not an alien, but has become a citizen by virtue of his father's naturalization, having been under age and dwelling in the United States at that time. He is, of course, liable to be enrolled at the age of 18 years.

There have been many changes in the provisions of the act of 1802 by laws passed since that time, but none which affect this case.

I am, sir, very respectfully,
Your obedient servant,
JOHN A. DIX, *Adjt. Gen.*

Lieut. Col. JOHN I. SHEW,
122d *Regt. Infantry.*

EDUCATION OF TEACHERS.

The following Report is the basis of the system of education adopted by the State of New York for common-school teachers. It was prepared by Mr. Dix as chairman of a committee appointed by the Regents of the University, and presented to that body at their annual meeting at the Capitol, in the city of Albany, on the 8th day of January, 1835.

To THE REGENTS OF THE UNIVERSITY. — "At a meeting of the Regents of the University of the State of New York, held on the 22d day of May, 1834, a certified copy of an act of the legislature, entitled 'An Act concerning the Literature Fund,' passed May 2d, 1834, was presented to the Board and read; and it appearing that the subject-matter of the said act related to the application of part of the income of the Literature Fund to the education of teachers of common schools, under the direction of the Regents of the University, it was thereupon

"*Ordered*, That it be referred to Messrs. Dix, Buel, and Graham, to prepare and report to the Regents, at some future meeting, a plan for carrying into practical operation the provisions of the said act."

IN discharging the duty confided to them under the foregoing resolution, the committee have become deeply impressed with the importance of the subject. They are satisfied that it will depend much on the measures which may be adopted by the Regents in pursuance of the authority conferred on them by the act of the 2d May last, whether the leading and acknowledged defect in our common schools — the want of competent teachers — shall be remedied, or whether it shall continue to embarrass, as it long has done, the efforts of the legislature and of individuals to carry out our system of popular instruction to the great results which it is capable of producing. In its organization, and in the annual contributions which are made to its support, the liberality of the legislature, and of the people on whom the burden principally falls, is in the highest degree creditable to the State; and if the effects of a large expenditure of money, continued for a series of years, have not been as beneficial as might have been anticipated from the amount of the expenditure, the causes are to be found in some defects of the system, for which an early remedy should be provided.

The committee have already said that the principal defect is the want of competent teachers; and the position is indisputable, that, without able and well-trained teachers, no system of instruction can be considered complete. Much may be accomplished by a judicious choice of the subjects of study, and by plans of instruction divested of everything which is superfluous; but to carry these plans into successful execution, talent and experience are indispensable, and if they are wanting, both time and money are misapplied, and the effort which is put forth falls short of its proper and legitimate effects.

In other countries, seminaries for the education of teachers have been deemed an essential part of the system of primary instruction. Mr. Cousin, in the year 1832, in his report "on the condition of public instruction in some of the provinces of Germany," asserts that "primary instruction is wholly dependent on the primary normal schools," or schools for the education of teachers; and he observes that in France thirty have been established, "of which twenty are in full operation, forming in each department a great focus of illumination for the people."

In Prussia, the system of public instruction had an earlier origin, and results far more extensive and beneficial have been obtained. It is more complete in its organization, and more efficient in its practical operation than any similar system of which we have any knowledge. In the year 1833, that kingdom had forty-two seminaries for teachers, with more than two thousand students, from eight to nine hundred of whom were annually furnished for the primary schools. The vocation of instructor is a public office, as well as a profession. He receives his education almost wholly at the expense of the state; his qualifications to teach are determined by a board deriving its authority from the government; his salary cannot be less than a certain sum, which is augmented as occasion requires, and the local authorities are enjoined to raise it as high as possible above the prescribed minimum. Finally, when through age or infirmity he becomes incapable of discharging his duties, he is allowed to retire with a pension for his support. These provisions of law have made the business of teaching highly respectable, and have secured for the primary schools of Prussia a body of men eminently qualified to fulfil the elevated trust confided to them.

It must be confessed that the efficiency of these measures is derived in a great degree from their compulsory character, and that they could only be carried into complete execution by a government having the entire control of the system of public instruction. It was apprehended that the subjection of the system to the discretion of the persons on whose contributions the schools depend for their support might frequently thwart the government in its measures, and sometimes wholly defeat them. For this reason, parents are required by law to send their children to school, and they are punishable by fine, if they refuse or neglect to do so. For the same reason, the principal part of the expenditures necessary to comply with the law in maintaining the primary schools, paying the salaries of teachers, providing schoolhouses, with their appurtenances, furniture, books, maps, and apparatus, is paid by property and income in proportion respectively to the amount of each in value; and those on whose contributions the maintenance of the schools depends are neither allowed to judge of the extent of the provision required for the objects referred to, nor to have any voice in the selection of their teachers, those provided by the state being employed under the direction of an authority independent of them. These features of the system are in a great degree irreconcilable with the spirit of our political institutions; but the committee believe that public opinion may be stimulated to a just conception of the importance of making more ample provision for teachers, and thus supplying a deficiency, apart from which our system of popular instruction would be equal in efficiency, as it is now superior in extent, in proportion to our population, to any other in the world.

Common-school instruction in this State existed a long time upon the foundation of voluntary private contribution before it was recognized and reduced to a system by public law. The result was to put in requisition the services of large numbers of persons who by long practice had become familiar with the business of teaching; and it is doubtless to be ascribed, in no inconsiderable degree, to this circumstance, that the necessity of making some provision for the education of teachers was not felt at the time the common-school system was established.

Although this important subject had been repeatedly recommended to the attention of the legislature by several of the governors of this State, no provision was made by law, in conformity to these recommendations, until the year 1827, when an act was passed adding to the capital of the Literature Fund the sum of one hundred and fifty thousand dollars, for the avowed object of promoting the education of teachers. But as the annual income of the Literature Fund has been heretofore distributed among the academies in the State, without any restriction as to its application, it has in very few instances been devoted to the object in view of the law. To this remark there are, however, several exceptions. The St. Lawrence, Oxford, and Canandaigua academies have each established a course of lectures and exercises for the preparation of teachers; and such has been their success with a very limited contribution from the public treasury, that an augmentation of the means of some of the academies is obviously all that is necessary to render such a course of instruction of inestimable value to the common schools of the State. In the neighborhood of the St. Lawrence Academy, the school districts are almost entirely supplied with teachers educated at that institution; and so beneficial has been the effect of introducing into the schools a better class of instructors, and more efficient plans of instruction, that the compensation of teachers is already, on an average, from thirty to forty dollars per annum more than it was before the academy had established a department for training them. The influence of these measures upon the public opinion of a small section of the country furnishes the strongest ground of assurance that it is necessary only to extend them in order to produce the same results on a more extensive scale.

It may not be improper to remark that the question of creating separate seminaries for the education of teachers has been repeatedly before the legislature, but after full examination it was deemed more advantageous to engraft upon the existing academies departments of instruction for the purpose.

This may now be considered the settled policy of the State; and it will, therefore, be necessary only to inquire in what manner it can best be carried out to its results.

The act of the 2d May, 1834, authorizes the Regents of the University to distribute the excess of the annual revenue of the Literature Fund, or portions of it, over the sum of twelve thousand dollars, " if they shall deem it expedient, to the academies subject to their visitation, or a portion of them," to be expended in educating teachers of common schools; and it is made the duty of the trustees of academies, to which any distribution of money shall be so made, to apply it to the purpose specified " in such manner and under such regulations as said Regents shall prescribe."

The Regents are, therefore, intrusted with an unlimited control over such portion of the excess of the revenue of the Literature Fund as they may think proper to appropriate to the purposes of the law last quoted; and as this is the first

EDUCATION OF TEACHERS.

instance in which the contributions of the State to this great object have been accompanied with such a delegation of authority as is necessary to insure its execution, it appears to the committee that a most important and delicate duty is devolved on them. The first step towards the execution of the plan adopted by the legislature, for the education of common-school teachers, is now to be taken. We are to lay the foundations of a system which may become an essential part of our plan of common-school instruction, and which, if properly organized, may be the means of remedying existing deficiencies, and elevating the standard of education to a grade in some degree commensurate with the high responsibilities which the Constitution of this State has cast upon its citizens as incidents of the condition of citizenship. If we are successful, the foundations, which will now be laid, may hereafter be made to sustain a system adequate to the wants of all the common schools in the State. The point, therefore, which of all others the committee deem it indispensable to secure, is efficiency in the departments to be created. The funds at the disposal of the Regents being limited in amount, the aim of the committee has been to devise such measures as, on a limited scale, would be most efficient. The sum in the treasury applicable to the object expressed in the resolution is ten thousand and forty dollars and seventy-six cents; and the annual excess of the revenue of the Literature Fund, after distributing twelve thousand dollars to the academies, as required by the act of the 22d April, 1834, will amount to about three thousand five hundred dollars. The sum first mentioned is now applicable to the establishment of departments of instruction for common-school teachers in the existing academies; but it is obviously too small to admit of a general distribution among them; and if it were adequate to the establishment of a department in each, the annual surplus of revenue applicable to the support of those departments would be too small, when divided among so great a number, to be of any practical utility. It has appeared indispensable to the committee, therefore, that the academies selected for the purpose should be limited in number. If departments can be established in which even a small number of teachers can be well prepared for the business of instruction, the good effects which would result from the improvements they would introduce into the common schools would be likely to become so manifest as to lead to more enlarged provisions for the purpose of extending the benefits of the system. The committee, therefore, as they have already observed, deem it of the utmost importance that the departments to be organized should be put on such a footing as to insure efficiency to the extent of the means at the disposal of the Regents; that the end proposed should be to prepare a limited number of well educated teachers, rather than a large number with inferior qualifications. This end must necessarily be attained by selecting for the purpose a limited number of academies. At the same time the public convenience would demand that the number should not be too limited, but that one should be within the reach of every county in the State; although it is manifest that the efficiency of the departments will be in the ratio of the sum expended on their organization, and the amount annually contributed to their support. The least number which could perhaps be selected, consistently with the general convenience, would be eight, or one in each Senate district; and the committee are of the opinion that eight might be maintained without putting at hazard the great object of rendering them equal to the preparation of well-instructed and competent teachers.

The committee are aware that the establishment of these departments on the most favorable footing will not remove every difficulty; that there are others inherent in our system of common-school instruction which may not be so easily obviated. The inhabitants of school districts have, through the trustees, who are elected by their suffrages, the selection of their teacher and the regulation of his wages; and if the

State were to prepare a sufficient number of teachers to supply all the districts, there would be no absolute certainty that they would find employment. There would be no probability that they would find, after devoting the best part of their lives to the business of teaching, a provision for them in their old age.

With regard to the first difficulty referred to, it may be safely calculated that the people will, when the good effects of improved modes of teaching are brought directly under their observation, make more liberal contributions to the support of competent teachers.

With regard to the second, there is good reason to doubt, so far as the public is concerned, whether in the end a provision of law which holds out to any class of men the assurance that they will, at all events, be employed or supported for life, would be salutary in its effects. The greatest stimulus to improvement is, unquestionably, the necessity of arduous and unceasing exertion. Places of trust in which the incumbents are permanent, are not, as a general rule, those which are best administered. The efforts of the incumbents are most likely to be fresh and vigorous when they are in danger of being displaced by other individuals of superior qualifications, and when the tenure of office is made to depend on the ability with which its duties are discharged. If, therefore, the compensation of teachers were equal to that of other employments, the public end would probably be as well answered as by securing to them an unfailing provision for life.

It would be extremely difficult, even if it were desirable, under our institutions, to make the system of public instruction compulsory by subjecting it wholly to the regulation of the government; and it must be admitted that this is the feature of the Prussian system, from which it derives its principal efficiency. The occupation of teachers must, therefore, necessarily be with us somewhat less certain; and it will require stronger persuasives to induce individuals of competent abilities to enter into and pursue it as a permanent vocation. This is an inconvenience for which there is not, perhaps, a perfect remedy, although it is conceived that it may be, in a great degree, obviated by the adoption of measures which will secure to them a better compensation for their services.

Much may undoubtedly be done by providing for the education of a certain number of individuals, and by sending them abroad among the common schools, to raise, by the exhibition of the improved methods which they have gained, the standard of education to the level of their own superiority over the great mass of common-school teachers. In this manner the inhabitants of school districts may, and doubtless will, in most cases, be led to make more enlarged and permanent provision for those to whom the instruction of their children is intrusted; and to the adequacy of these provisions the standard of education will acquire and maintain a uniform and certain relation.

The committee, then, would recommend that one academy in each Senate district be selected for the purpose in view, and that the selection be made from those which, from their endowments and literary character, are most capable of accomplishing it. The object to be attained is public, and the interest of one academy or another cannot properly be taken into consideration, with a view to influence the choice which may be made from among them.

Should this recommendation be adopted by the Regents, it will remain only to consider: —

1st. On what principle the funds applicable to the establishment or organization of the departments shall be apportioned to the academies which may be selected for the purpose.

2d. On what principle and to what extent the annual excess of the revenue of the Literature Fund, applicable to the support of the departments, shall be apportioned to the academies in which they may be established.

EDUCATION OF TEACHERS. 81

3d. What shall be the organization of the departments. I. As to the course (or subjects) of study; II. As to the duration of the course; III. As to the necessary books and apparatus.

4th. What evidence of qualification to teach shall be given to the individuals who may be trained in the departments.

These subjects will now be considered in the order in which they are stated.

1st. On what principle the funds applicable to the establishment or organization of the departments shall be apportioned to the academies which may be selected for the purpose.

As a general remark it may be observed in this case, as it has been already said in relation to the selection of the academies, that the object in view is public, and that the only legitimate consideration is, in what manner it can best be attained. Under this view of the subject, no embarrassment can arise as to the question of allowing the academies which may be selected to participate, in ratio of their respective wants, in the funds to be applied. The departments should all be placed in their organization on the same footing: they should have the same apparatus, and be provided, in all respects, with equal facilities for commencing the contemplated course of instruction. It may, and doubtless will, happen that some of the academies will be found in better condition than others for commencing such a course; and to render the departments equally efficient, it may be necessary to apportion the funds applicable to their establishment in unequal sums among the academies selected. It will, therefore, be advisable, after fixing upon the apparatus, maps, &c. which may be required, to ascertain how far the academies are provided with them, and to distribute the funds with reference to the deficiencies which may be found to exist.

The funds now in the treasury applicable to the object, amount to $10,040.76; but of this sum the committee are of the opinion that not more than $4000 should be applied to the establishment of the departments. The sum of $500 for each, will, it is believed, be adequate to the object in most cases; and as some of the academies may not require so large an amount, a surplus may remain and be applied to deficiencies in others, or carried to the fund applicable to the annual support of the departments.

If the sum of $4000 only be appropriated to the establishment of the departments, a surplus of about $6000 will be left for future uses; and for reasons which will be hereafter explained, it may be important to keep on hand an annual surplus to meet any deficiency in the revenue of the Literature Fund in succeeding years.

2d. On what principle and to what extent the annual excess of the revenue of the Literature Fund, applicable to the support of the departments, shall be apportioned to the academies in which they may be established.

If the departments are to be maintained at all, it is necessary that there should be apportioned annually to each of the academies in which they shall be established, in addition to the amount to which these academies will be entitled under the general annual apportionment, a sum as nearly adequate as possible to the support of a competent instructor. The largest sum which can be regularly apportioned to each, is four hundred dollars; and it is conceived that each of the academies referred to should receive that sum annually, without reference to the number of pupils in training.

With such a permanent provision, the object of the academies will be to render the department efficient, rather than to secure the greatest possible number of pupils. The rule suggested ought not to be carried to an extreme; and if, in the course of time, any academy should be found, without good cause, to have failed in promoting the object in view to a reasonable extent, another should be selected and substituted for it, so that the public munificence may not be expended in vain. If, after appropriating to each of the academies the sum above mentioned, a further sum could in any year be safely apportioned to them, the most equitable rule would seem to be, to distribute it in proportion to the whole number of pupils in training for common-school teachers, and to the aggregate length of time in such year during which they shall have been so trained according to the prescribed plan. It is on a similar principle that the greater part of the revenue of the Literature Fund is now distributed under the general law; and, after securing a proper degree of efficiency in the departments to be created, there can be no reason to apprehend inconvenience from stimulating the efforts of those who have the direction of the academies to augment the number of their pupils, and thus to extend, as widely as possible, the benefits of the system.

The proposed sum, to be apportioned annually as above suggested for the support of instructors in the eight departments, is three thousand two hundred dollars; and this is about as much as can be regularly applied to the object. The capital of the Literature Fund amounts to $262,573.-10; and the annual income will not fall short of $15,500. Of the last-mentioned sum, $12,000 must be apportioned to all the academies subject to the visitation of the Regents pursuant to the act of 22d April, 1834, to be expended under the direction of the trustees, towards paying the salaries of tutors.

Only $3500 will, therefore, remain to be applied annually to the support of the departments for the instruction of common-school teachers.

It is true that there will be on hand, after applying $4000 to the organization of those departments, about $6000 applicable to their support. But it is to be considered that a large portion of the capital of the Literature Fund consists of bonds and mortgages, on which the interest is not always regularly paid, and it is desirable to keep in the treasury a surplus of a few thousand dollars, to meet in future years any deficiency which may grow out of such irregular payment of interest; for it is of the greatest importance that the academies in which the departments are established should never be disappointed in the anticipated annual contribution to the support of the instructors of those departments. By the arrangement suggested, the contribution will be rendered certain; and should it be deemed safe at any future time to distribute a portion of the surplus on hand, after paying out three thousand two hundred dollars for the support of instructors, such distribution might be made on the principle before suggested, and the amount so distributed applied to the purchase of books, or to such other objects as the Regents might designate.

It is also to be observed that under the act of 22d April, 1834, applications may be made from other academies for a portion of the excess of the revenue of the fund, for the purchase of philosophical and chemical apparatus, &c.; and although the Regents have by that act a discretion as to making any application of such excess to the object referred to, it may be desirable in some cases to have funds at command for the purpose. For this reason, also, it is important that the whole surplus on hand should not be expended.

3d. What shall be the organization of the departments.

I. *As to the course (or subjects) of study.*

In determining the course of study, the committee have thought it proper to designate as subjects to be taught, all which they deemed indispensable to be known by a first-rate teacher of a common school.

In fixing a standard of requirement in any pursuit, it is always desirable to raise it as high as possible; for the qualifications of those who follow it will incline to range below and not above the prescribed standard. In this case, as the principal object is to influence public opinion by exhibiting the advantages of that practical skill which may be gained by proper training, care should be taken that those who are relied on to exert the influence referred to should be made fully adequate to the task.

EDUCATION OF TEACHERS. 85

In select schools, in our cities and large towns, qualifications of a still higher grade than those in contemplation for common-school teachers, may be required; but as it is not intended, with regard to the latter, to dispense with any essential branch, so it is not intended to exact anything which is not indispensable. If the subjects, which they will now proceed to state in their proper order, be taught in such a manner and to such an extent as to be thoroughly understood by the pupils, the committee feel confident that the course will be found equal to the object to be obtained.

It is proper to premise, however, that no individual should be admitted to the teachers' department until he shall have passed such an examination as is required by the following extract from the ordinance of the Regents of the University to entitle students to be considered scholars in the higher branches of English education : —

"No students, in any such academy, shall be considered scholars in the higher branches of English education, within the meaning of this ordinance, until they shall, on examination duly made, be found to have attained to such proficiency in the arts of reading and writing, and to have acquired such knowledge of the elementary rules or operations of arithmetic, commonly called notation, addition, subtraction, multiplication, and division, as well in their compound as in their simple forms, and as well in vulgar and decimal fractions as in whole numbers, together with such knowledge of the parts of arithmetic commonly called reduction, practice, the single rule of three direct, and simple interest, as is usually acquired in the medium or average grade of common schools in this State; and until they shall also, on such examination, be found to have studied so much of English grammar as to be able to parse correctly any common prose sentence in the English language, and to render into good English the common examples of bad grammar given in Murray's or some other like grammatical exercises; and shall also have studied, in the ordinary way, some book or treatise in geography, equal in extent to the duodecimo edition of Morse's, Cumming's, Woodbridge's, or Willet's geography, as now in ordinary use."

Subjects of study.
1. The English Language.
2. Writing and Drawing.
3. Arithmetic, Mental and Written; and Book-keeping.
4. Geography, and General History, combined.
5. The History of the United States.
6. Geometry, Trigonometry, Mensuration, and Surveying.
7. Natural Philosophy and the Elements of Astronomy.
8. Chemistry and Mineralogy.
9. The Constitution of the United States and the Constitution of the State of New York.
10. Select parts of the Revised Statutes, and the duties of Public Officers.
11. Moral and Intellectual Philosophy.
12. The Principles of Teaching.

These subjects are not intended to exclude others, should the academies think proper to introduce them. The Regents should, however, insist that the foregoing be thoroughly studied, and that they be not allowed to give way, in any degree, to others; nor should any others be required in order to entitle the pupils to the prescribed evidence of qualification.

The committee will now proceed to state some of the most important suggestions which occur to them in relation to the several subjects of study enumerated, — not for the purpose of pointing out in every case the whole extent to which the course is expected to be carried, but to designate certain particulars, which they deem most worthy of attention.

THE ENGLISH LANGUAGE. This branch constitutes the most extensive, and perhaps the most important field of instruction for a teacher. Unless the pupil is thoroughly master of his own language, he cannot be a competent instructor.

The utmost pains should therefore be taken to give him an accurate knowledge of it; and the proper process of instruction is that which it will be his business to employ in giving instruction to others.

He should be made familiar with the best methods of teaching the alphabet, and the steps by which children can be conducted, with the greatest facility, through the first lessons which they receive. Rules for spelling should also be learned, and their application shown, particularly in the orthography of compound and derivative words, the plurals of nouns, the inflections of verbs, and the comparison of adjectives; and in these exercises black boards or slates should be used, so that the eye as well as the ear may be made instrumental to the correction of errors.

In reading, the lessons should embrace a just enunciation of sounds as well as words, and a careful regard to distinctness of pronunciation, as well as a proper fulness and modulation of the voice. A clear and correct enunciation is of the highest importance to a teacher, whose defects are almost certain to be communicated to his pupils; and it is, therefore, indispensable that reading, with criticisms in orthoepy, accent, emphasis, cadence, and punctuation, should constitute a part of the exercises in this branch of study.

The pupil should not only be practised in reading the English language with accuracy and distinctness, but he should be taught to write it correctly. He should be made thoroughly acquainted with its structure and its idiomatic peculiarities. In addition to the ordinary routine of parsing, the principles of universal grammar should be critically discussed; the structure and philosophy of language should be made the subject of a minute investigation; the offices which are performed by the different words of a sentence, and the rules by which their relations to each other are governed, should be explained, until the whole subject is thoroughly understood.

Original composition, and declamation from the writings

of standard authors, are also an essential part of the course; the first for the purpose of facilitating a correct understanding of the laws of language, and the acquisition of a correct style, and the second for the purpose of cultivating a distinct articulation as well as a refined taste. In both, the utmost care should be taken to select subjects on a level with the capacity of the pupil, so that his interest may be kept alive and the mind not tasked beyond its powers; and he should be continually cautioned against the error of an affected or artificial manner. Nature is always simple, and for that reason always effective.

In the Kinderhook Academy, in which a department for the education of teachers has been recently introduced, a complete course of instruction in the English language has been adopted, embracing the following details: —

1. Orthography. Sounds of Letters. Rules for Spelling. Spelling. Words of doubtful or various Orthography.
2. Pronunciation.
3. Etymology. Prefixes. Terminations. Derivation and Definitions. Synonymes. Inflections.
4. Syntax.
5. Prosody, in all its parts.
6. Punctuation. Use of Capitals. Abbreviations.
7. Reading.
8. Composition. Weekly exercises, — topics selected with reference to the business of teaching.
9. Extemporaneous Speaking, — subjects connected with the business of teaching.
10. Rhetoric. So much of Blair's Rhetoric (Mills's edition) as treats of language.
11. History of the Language, as contained in Johnson's and Walker's prefaces to their large dictionaries.

Although the committee have not, in the course of study, designated Rhetoric as a distinct branch, they consider it advisable that all the academies in which departments are established should introduce so much as is contained in the above synopsis of the course in the Kinderhook Academy.

WRITING AND DRAWING. Every pupil must be able, before he leaves the institution, to write a good hand. For this purpose he should be made to practise from the beginning of the course, under the personal direction of the tutors, with the best writing-materials, and with proper attention to the positions of the body, arm, and hand.

For beginners, slates may be used with great advantage, as suggested in Taylor's "District School."

Much may be gained by reducing to writing parts of the prescribed course, if done with attention to the manner in which it is executed; but in all these exercises the tutors should take care to check any appearance of negligence or haste. By a careful attention from the outset to the correct formation of the letters, and to those circumstances which must concur to enable one to write with freedom, a good style of writing may be acquired without the least difficulty; but it will be almost a hopeless attempt, if bad habits are contracted before the handwriting is completely formed.

Drawing is only expected to be taught so far as it may be necessary for the purpose of mapping. In learning geography, the pupils should be required to delineate on the black board the outlines of the general divisions of the earth, the different countries, oceans, rivers, &c., and they should afterwards be practised in similar delineations, executed with care, on paper. In geometry, trigonometry, mensuration, and surveying, linear drawing will be indispensable, and the tutors should study to convert these exercises to the best use.

ARITHMETIC. In this branch the pupil must be thoroughly instructed in the four ground-rules of arithmetic, as well in their compound as in their simple forms, and as well in vulgar and in decimal fractions as in whole numbers; the single rule of three, together with reduction, practice, interest, fellowship, barter, &c., so that the course shall be at least equal in extent to that contained in Daboll's "Arithmetic."

In all the operations performed by the pupils, black boards should be used for demonstrations and illustrations, and every lesson should be explained until the pupil comprehends it thoroughly. In nothing is the dependence of one step on another so complete as in the science of numbers; and if the pupil leaves behind him anything, which he does not distinctly understand, his progress must always be difficult, and the result of his calculations uncertain. In facilitating a clear perception of abstract numbers and quantities, visible illustrations should be liberally employed. Mental arithmetic may also be advantageously resorted to, and, indeed, may be deemed indispensable, as a discipline to the mind. To all these exercises a practical direction should, as far as possible, be given, by selecting as subjects for practice those familiar operations of business with which the pupils must become conversant in after-life. Thus the mind may be strengthened by the same process which is storing it with useful information.

A knowledge of arithmetic enters into so many of the common operations of life that it is not only an essential part of the most ordinary education, but it should be so thorough that an application of the rules of the science may be made with ease and certainty. As a mental discipline, also, the study is of great value; and it should be so conducted as to secure all the benefits which it is capable of producing. The aim should be to make it an exercise of the reasoning faculty, and not, as it has usually been, a mere exertion of memory. A facility in performing the operations of arithmetic may be acquired without a distinct understanding of its principles; but to render sure and easy an advance into the branches of mathematics, for which it is a necessary preparation, a clear and familiar knowledge of principles is indispensable.

BOOK-KEEPING. A simple course of book-keeping should be taught in every common school, and it is, therefore, an essential part of the course of instruction for a teacher.

The method pursued in the St. Lawrence Academy is, perhaps, as concise and as likely to be successful as any that could be devised. The system contained in the first part of Preston's "Book-keeping" is taken as a guide. "The pupil is first taught to rule his book, and is then required to carry his slate to the recitation-room ruled in the same manner. For several of the first lessons, examples of accounts are taken where the articles delivered are charged directly in the individual's account. The teacher then reads the several charges, which the scholar copies on his slate; and the scholar is required, as an exercise in writing, to transfer the account to his book. The teacher then proceeds with the charges in the short specimen of day-book entries, giving as many at one lesson as the scholar will be able to transfer with care, in the allotted time, to his day-book. When the several charges are copied into the scholar's day-book, he is required to post his book."

In this manner a sufficient knowledge of book-keeping for ordinary purposes may be readily acquired, and the student may improve as much in penmanship as though he had passed his whole time in writing after a copy.

GEOGRAPHY AND GENERAL HISTORY. Geography, to be profitably studied, must be continually explained by maps and the globe. Neither the artificial nor the natural divisions of the earth, nor the proportions which its several parts bear to each other and to its whole surface, can be readily comprehended without having recourse to visible demonstrations. To young pupils there is a difficulty, even with the aid of maps and globes, in communicating a distinct conception of the positive or relative magnitude of different countries, or the remoteness of different places from each other. Much depends on minute and patient explanation, especially in that part of geography which treats of the physical divisions of the earth, including continents, peninsulas, islands, oceans, lakes, rivers, mountains, &c.

Physical geography, or that part of the description of the

earth which treats of its natural features, is of great interest and importance; the more so, as with it are necessarily interwoven matters which in strictness belong to the department of astronomy. The figure and motions of the earth; the causes of the variation in the length of the days; the seasons; the principles upon which the tropics and polar circles are drawn at their respective distances from the equator; the general features of the earth's surface, embracing a knowledge of the influence of elevation above the sea upon temperature, climate, productions, &c.; a description of volcanoes and earthquakes; the various theories relative to the causes of eruptions and shocks; the atmosphere, winds and their agency in the distribution of heat and moisture, embracing the subject of rain, fogs, dew, hail, &c.; the theories relative to tides; a description of the most remarkable currents in the ocean; and all those natural causes by which the condition of the various parts of the earth are influenced, should be briefly, but clearly and carefully, explained.

In this branch will also be included a general knowledge of the geological structure of particular regions and their most remarkable productions, animal, mineral, and vegetable. In the St. Lawrence Academy the whole subject of physical geography is systematically and critically discussed, commencing with the " history of the science and the adaptation of the objects it embraces to awaken interest by their endless diversity," and running through the details of the science in a complete course of seventeen lectures.

With a description of the different countries of the earth, some account of their inhabitants, forms of government and religion, and their general statistics, must also be united. Nor will this suffice to render the view complete. We must not be content to see the earth and its possessors as they are. We must look also at what they have been, through the lights of history. A general idea of the progress of each country from infancy to age, from weakness to power, or from dominion to servitude, should be acquired; their most distinguished men and some of the most remarkable events which have accompanied their growth and decay, should be pointed out, and a cursory survey of the whole earth, in its relations both of time and space, should be taken by the pupil. The undertaking may seem arduous, but it may be executed, under judicious direction, with much less time than would be supposed necessary to accomplish it. The course of history should be equal to that contained in Tytler's "Elements of General History, ancient and modern."

The course in geography should not be less in extent than that contained in Woodbridge and Willard, the volume in general use in the common schools. The course should be accompanied with copious illustrations by lectures, and by reference to larger works, so that the pupils may be made familiar with the sources from which they may be able to enrich the instruction they may themselves give when they become teachers.

HISTORY OF THE UNITED STATES. The history of the United States is so essential, that it may justly be treated as a distinct branch of study. In this, a mere outline is not sufficient. The pupil should understand, in all its details, the history of his own country. He should begin with its discovery and first settlement, and trace it through the various stages of its colonial dependence to its emancipation from the control of the mother-country. In the character of the men who stood foremost in the contest for independence, the measures of provocation by which they were roused to resistance, the trials through which they passed, the reverses which they sustained, the triumphs which they achieved, and the great political principles which were vindicated by them, there are lessons of instruction not inferior in value to any which can be drawn from the history of any other age or people; and if the mind of every youth can be made familiar with them, and his feelings imbued with the moral which they contain, no better security can be provided against the degeneracy of that unconquerable spirit in which the foundations of our freedom were laid.

GEOMETRY, TRIGONOMETRY, MENSURATION, AND SURVEYING. The committee regret that they cannot refer to any single work which contains such a course on all these subjects as they deem necessary. The works on each separate subject are in general too extensive for the purpose in view. The course should be altogether practical in its character, and should be divested of everything superfluous. The principles of geometry and trigonometry should be so thoroughly understood, that their application may be made with facility. The pupils should be able to measure solids as well as surfaces with ease; and they should be made so well acquainted with the rules of surveying, and the instruments used for the purpose, as to be able to ascertain heights and distances, and determine the contents of a given piece of land, with readiness and precision.

As the committee are unable to refer to any modern work precisely adapted to the course required on all these subjects, they propose to leave the extent of the course, at present, to the academies, with the single remark, that each pupil should have such an acquaintance with each of the specified subjects as is necessary for every practical purpose.

NATURAL PHILOSOPHY AND THE ELEMENTS OF ASTRONOMY. The course in natural philosophy will embrace a clear understanding of the several properties of bodies, gravitation, the laws of motion, simple and compound; the mechanical powers, the mechanical properties of fluids, the mechanical properties of air, the transmission of sound, and optics. Each academy should be furnished with a complete philosophical apparatus, and all the subjects should be taught with full illustrations. A practical direction should, as far as possible, be given to the science, by teaching the proper application of its laws to useful purposes. It is from this course that those who intend to devote themselves to mechanical pursuits may reap the greatest benefits; and it is of the utmost importance to introduce it into the common schools. The first step towards the accomplishment of this object is to prepare instructors competent to teach it; and it is for this reason that it should constitute a particular object of attention.

In connection with natural philosophy there should be a brief course of instruction in the principles of astronomy. The nature and causes of the earth's motions, the planets and their motions, their size and positions in relation to the earth and the sun, their satellites, the cause of eclipses, the variations of the seasons, the length of the days, the causes of heat in summer, &c., should all be made familiar to the pupils. Each academy should be furnished with an orrery, a movable planisphere, a tide-dial, and a set of globes; and nothing which is capable of being illustrated by apparatus should be taught without illustration.

The same apparatus may be employed for the illustration of subjects connected with physical geography, between which and that part of astronomy which treats of the earth's motions and the effects consequent upon them, there is a very close connection. In pointing out some of the subjects which belong to the department of physical geography, some of the foregoing have been already enumerated, as the motions of the earth, the seasons, tides, &c. It is, indeed, not always easy, nor is it always necessary, to assign to each science its exact boundaries: so far as instruction is concerned, the separation of one from another is of no practical importance, so that all the subjects are clearly understood.

CHEMISTRY AND MINERALOGY. The course in mineralogy and chemistry is not expected to be carried far. It is intended that each academy shall have a small cabinet of minerals; and the pupils should be able to distinguish the different specimens, which should be well characterized, and to understand clearly their composition and distinctive properties. Chemistry should be taught in such a manner as to elucidate these distinctions in the mineral kingdom, and to give a correct knowledge of the properties of the various bodies and substances which are in most common use; and its application to agriculture and the useful arts should be made a prominent subject of instruction. Mineralogy is usually a preliminary of the science of geology; but it is not expected that the latter will constitute a subject of study, except so far as it is connected with physical geography, which will necessarily embrace some account of the structure of the earth, with a description of the principal classes of rocks and the mineral and metallic substances with which they are found united. One of the most salutary effects of combining with elementary education some knowledge of the foregoing subjects is to guard against the impositions so frequently practised upon the ignorance of the uninformed in the discovery of some unknown and often worthless substance, to which an imaginary value is assigned. It is exceedingly desirable to spread correct notions concerning limestone, gypsum, and coal, the ores of iron, lead, copper, &c. The modes of verifying their composition should be made familiar; and it should be understood in what proportions quantity should be combined with quality in order to reward labor.

Those experiments in chemistry which are merely calculated to produce brilliant effects, without subserving a useful purpose, should be laid aside, and others of a more practical value substituted for them. The course will necessarily be limited, and it should possess in utility what it lacks in extent.

In the foregoing branches there may, and doubtless will, be felt the want of proper class-books, those in general use not being so directly adapted as is desirable to teach the application of the sciences to practical purposes. The committee trust that the organization of the departments may lead to the preparation of suitable books on all the subjects in respect to which they may be wanting; and, indeed, they are encouraged to believe that a work on chemistry will appear at no distant time, the whole aim of which will be to show the application of the science to the useful arts. Until these deficiencies shall be supplied, the Regents must trust to the academies to extract from the existing works all which they may deem best suited to the objects of the prescribed course. Nothing, perhaps, can be better calculated to accomplish these objects than the preparation of lectures on the different subjects of study, taking care to illustrate everything which is taught, by demonstrations and experiments. So far as instruction is carried, it should be thorough and clearly understood.

THE CONSTITUTION OF THE UNITED STATES, AND THE CONSTITUTION OF THE STATE OF NEW YORK. Every citizen, in order to exercise discreetly and intelligently the right of suffrage, upon which questions of constitutional power are frequently dependent, must understand the provisions of the Constitution of the United States and the constitution of his own State; and there cannot, perhaps, be a better mode of attaining the object than to require each pupil to make a brief analysis of both. With regard to the Constitution of the United States, he should be required to specify the qualifications and disabilities of the members of the Senate and House of Representatives, the rights and privileges of each House, the powers of Congress, the powers prohibited and reserved to the States, the limitations of the legislative, judicial, and executive authorities, and the manner in which the various officers of the government are respectively chosen or appointed. In short, all the provisions of the original instrument and of the successive amendments, which have, by virtue of the proper ratifications by the States, become a part of it, should be thoroughly understood by the pupil. In like manner, he should know the qualifications of the various officers of government in his own State; the several divisions of authority provided by the constitution; the organization of the legislative, judicial, and executive departments; the powers respectively allotted to them; the rights of the citizens; and for the purpose of impressing strongly on the mind these fundamental principles and provisions of law, which every citizen owes it to the public and himself to understand, the pupils should be required to make an analysis of the constitution of New York, which should be carefully examined by the instructor. In pointing out the principal and most important provisions of both instruments, so far as they confer power or restrain its exercise, the reasons on which the grant in the one case or the prohibition in the other is founded, should be clearly explained. Questions of disputed right, growing out of the provisions of either instrument, had better be passed by; but if they are made a subject of comment, the arguments on both sides should be fairly stated. Schools for popular instruction depart from the end of their institution when they are made subservient to the propagation of particular tenets on any subject which is open to a diversity of opinion. In every matter which enters of necessity into the proposed plan, it should be the aim of the instructor to furnish his pupils with all the materials for forming unprejudiced opinions, but to leave their minds free from all bias.

SELECT PARTS OF THE REVISED STATUTES, AND DUTIES OF PUBLIC OFFICERS. A compendious work on the duties of public officers was published a few years since at Utica, and it embraces all that the committee deem necessary under this head. It is hardly necessary to add, that, under a form of government which throws open to all its citizens the avenues to political power, it is important that all should have, in early life, a general knowledge of the duties which they may be called on to discharge, or over the faithful performance of which, by others, it will be their province, in common with their fellow-citizens, to exercise a constant supervision.

Appended to the work referred to, there is a short treatise on the domestic relations, which may properly be considered as an exposition of the eighth chapter of the second part of the Revised Statutes, and is all that is necessary on this particular subject. There is also an article on wills, and another on executors and administrators. It is to be regretted that a work containing the most important principles of civil and criminal jurisprudence cannot now be referred to, as proper to be used for the proposed course. Until such a one shall be prepared, the principals of the academies should be charged with the duty of extracting from the Revised Statutes such portions as will show the particulars necessary to give validity to conveyances, the time limited for commencing suits, the rules relative to fraudulent conveyances and contracts as to goods, chattels, and things in action, and the offences to which penalties are annexed, as contained in chapter 3d of the 2d part; title 3d, chap. 7, of the 2d part; chap. 4th of the 3d part; and chap. 1st of the 4th part. The aim should be to extract only such portions of these chapters as contain some essential fact or principle, without which the responsibilities or the rights of the parties interested in the subject-matter would not be clearly apprehended.

MORAL AND INTELLECTUAL PHILOSOPHY. The laws which should govern all men, both with respect to the investigation of truth and to the discharge of the duties resulting from the relations which they bear to each other, and to the author of their existence, should be familiar to every teacher, particularly as his own moral character is subject to a periodical examination by the inspectors. A knowledge of these laws is indispensable to those whose province it will be to watch over the development of the moral and intellectual faculties, and direct them to their proper objects. The study itself is not only valuable as a discipline to the mind, but as a means of acquiring an influence over the minds of others. Although a facility for distinguishing the shades of character which exist in those with whom we are brought into contact, and thus ascertaining how far and how readily they are likely to be actuated by particular motives, can only be gained by continued experience, our progress may be aided by attending to the principles which enter into the mental constitution of all mankind.

Dr. Abercombie's treatise, entitled " Inquiries concerning the Intellectual Powers, and the Investigation of Truth," is well adapted to give a clear and correct conception of that part of the subject; and the first five books of Paley's "Principles of Moral and Political Philosophy" will suffice for the other part of the course. In general, the subject-matter of the latter is more practical, and better calculated to delineate with accuracy "the offices of domestic life" than most of the popular treatises on the same subject; and it has an advantage over them in giving an explanation of some of the obligations resulting from the rights of property, and from contracts with regard to its transfer and use.

The political part of the work, or the sixth book, should not, for various reasons, be made a part of the course. Of these it is perhaps only necessary to assign a single one, — the obvious objection of making the course too extended.

The family-library edition of the former, and several school editions of the latter, have each appended to them a series of questions upon their respective contents for the examination of students.

THE PRINCIPLES OF TEACHING. In this branch, instruction must be thorough and copious. It must not be confined simply to the art of teaching, or the most successful methods of communicating knowledge, but it must embrace also those rules of moral government which are as necessary for the regulation of the conduct of the teacher as for the formation of the character of those who are committed to his care.

Although this branch of instruction is mentioned last in the order of subjects, it should in fact run through the whole course. All the other branches should be so taught as to be subservient to the great object of creating a facility for communicating instruction to others. In teaching the principles of the art, it would be desirable to make Hall's "Lectures on School-Keeping" a text-book; and Abbot's "Teacher," Taylor's "District School," and the "Annals of Education," should be used as reading-books, for the double purpose of improvement in reading the English language, and for becoming familiar with the most improved modes of instruction and the best rules of school government. From the "Annals" select parts only would be chosen for the purpose.

The pupils in the departments should be practised in all that can devolve on a teacher. It is of the first importance that they should be made, each in turn, to conduct some part of the recitations, to prepare proper questions on the particular subject of study, and to illustrate it by explanations, for the purpose of improving their colloquial powers, and thus giving them a facility for explaining whatever they may be required to teach in the future office of instructor. The tutor should then go over the whole ground after them, pointing out their errors or defects, and giving them credit for whatever may appear to merit commendation. In this manner the future teacher will readily acquire a facility for communicating instruction, which is one of the highest elements of his art.

In all these exercises the language of the pupils should be watched and criticised, every want of perspicuity pointed out, and a rigid conformity to the true standards of etymology and pronunciation insisted on. At the same time everything artificial or affected in tone or manner should be studiously avoided; and the pupils should be taught that elocution is always effective in proportion as it is natural and unconstrained.

It has been customary in the examination of teachers, with a view to determine their qualifications, to ascertain only whether they possess a proper knowledge of the subjects in which they are expected to give instruction. But although this is in general the only object of inquiry, it is in fact a very erroneous criterion of their ability to teach. The possession of knowledge does not necessarily carry with it the faculty of communicating knowledge to others. It is for this reason that the best methods of imparting instruction should be made a subject of instruction to those who are preparing themselves for the business of teaching. They should know how to command the attention of their pupils, to communicate the results of their own researches and experience in the manner best calculated to make a lasting impression on the mind, to lead their pupils into the habit of examining for themselves, instead of being directed at every step of their progress by their instructor, and thus to observe, investigate, and classify objects, to combine the fruits of their observation, and draw conclusions from the facts which they have obtained. Under such a system of instruction and exercise, the mind cannot fail to gain strength, and to acquire that salutary confidence in the result of its own operations which is the best safeguard against the prevalence of error, and against those impositions which are almost necessarily the fruit of imbibing opinions without a rigid scrutiny into the nature of the foundations on which they rest.

In carrying into execution the plan of instruction about to be established, it should not be for a moment forgotten by those who are charged with the important task, that the object of education is, not merely to amass the greatest possible amount of information, but at the same time to develop and discipline the intellectual and moral faculties. It is in vain that the stores of knowledge are enlarged, if the skill to employ them for useful purposes be not also acquired. At every step, the mind should be taught to rely on the exercise of its own powers. The pupils should be required to assign reasons for every position assumed in their various studies, not barely with a view to give them a thorough comprehension of the subject, but for the purpose also of cultivating that habit of critical investigation which is unsatisfied until every part of the subject of inquiry is understood. The result of common-school education in most cases is to burden the memory with facts and rules, of which the proper practical operation is but imperfectly comprehended. This defect is at war with the spirit of the age, which is to probe to its inmost depths every subject of knowledge, and to convert the results of our inquiries to useful purposes. Practical usefulness is the great end of intellectual discipline; it should be kept steadily in view by the teacher, and he will soon learn that his lesson, when its reason and its object are presented to the mind of his pupil, will arouse an interest which, in the absence of this full understanding of the subject, he would have labored in vain to excite.

In the present condition of our common schools, much time is lost and labor misapplied by injudicious systems of instruction: they are fields for collecting facts and details, rather than for disciplining the faculties. This radical error should be corrected. Pupils should be made to think for themselves, instead of treasuring up merely the results of other men's thoughts. The great instrument of reform will be to make demonstration keep pace with knowledge. Nothing should be left unexplained; nor should anything be allowed to rest on mere authority, excepting where, from the nature of the subject, it admits of no other foundation.

Subjects which are susceptible of demonstration must, however, not be studied to the neglect of those which are not. First principles and certain classes of facts are of such a nature that the mind can only take notice of them as such, without being able to assign the reason of their existence. Separately, they are proper subjects for the attention and memory, but not for the reasoning powers, until they are considered in the relations which they bear to others. They are, however, the very materials on which the mind is to be employed. Nor should it be forgotten that there are mental processes depending wholly on an exercise of memory, which constitute a valuable intellectual discipline. In cultivating the reasoning powers, the memory should also be strengthened by habitual exertion, and stored with useful facts. The mind cannot be brought into complete exercise without a systematic discipline of all its faculties.

To almost every species of instruction the inductive method may be applied to great advantage. Nature herself seems to teach that the observation of facts should precede inductions, and that general principles can only be deduced from particular facts. An intelligent instructor will know how to apply the rule and convert it to the most useful purposes.

In determining the proper organization of the departments, the committee have fully considered the question whether the studies and recitations should be distinct from the ordinary academic exercises; and although they are disposed to leave this, in some degree, to the discretion of the academies, yet they are decidedly of the opinion that convenience coincides with good policy in requiring that pupils, who are in a course of training for teachers, should be taught in connection with the other students. So far as mental discipline is concerned, both classes of pupils require the same mode of training, and to a certain extent the same studies will be pursued. Whenever the peculiar duties of teachers are the subject of study and examination, separate recitations will become necessary; and although an instructor is proposed to be maintained in each of the departments to be organized, this provision should not be deemed to preclude a division of labor, or to devolve on the individual thus supported the task of conducting the pupils in a course of preparation for teaching through all the studies required to be pursued. On the contrary, it may be both convenient and profitable to assign recitations in different branches to different teachers, according to their peculiar fitness, and thus bring into the most efficient action the united skill of all. In this respect the Regents must rely on the principal of each academy to make such arrangements as to convert the intellectual force under his control and direction to the best possible use in furthering the great object in view.

The committee cannot forbear to add that the instructors, in the academies with which the proposed departments may be connected, should labor to impress on the minds of those who may be preparing themselves for the vocation of teaching, a deep sense of the responsibility which belongs to it.

There is, in truth, no other in which a conscientious and discreet discharge of its appropriate duties can well produce more beneficial or lasting effects. It is from the conduct and precepts of the teacher that the minds committed to his guidance are destined to receive impressions which may accompany the individuals through life, and give a determining cast to the character. In his demeanor they may read impressive lessons of moderation, forbearance, and self-control; from his rules of government they may learn the value of firmness, justice, and impartiality; or they may find, in exhibitions of petulance, unsteadiness of purpose, and unjust distributions of favor, a license for the indulgence of their own prejudices and passions. Nothing is more vital to the successful government of the teacher, and to the execution of his plans of instruction, than a steady self-command. The most certain mode of bringing his own authority into contempt is to show that he is not his own master. The moral atmosphere of the school-room will be pure or impure according to the conduct and character of him who presides over it. On his example will, in no inconsiderable degree, depend, for good or evil, the destiny of numbers whose influence will, in turn, be felt by the political society in the operations of which they are to take an active part. The teacher should be made to feel so sensibly the importance of his position, that it may be continually present to his thoughts, and become the guide and rule of his actions. He should bear perpetually in mind that he is the centre of a little system, which, as time advances, is destined to spread itself out and carry with it, for the benefit or injury of all which it reaches, the moral influences imparted by himself.

It is equally important that teachers should become acquainted with their own capabilities, and inspired with the feeling that they may, by their own industry, raise their qualifications to any standard. The discipline of their own faculties should not terminate with the close of their course of preparation. The intervals of teaching may be filled up by studies which will not only be a source of constant improvement in their vocation, but which will elevate their own character, enlarge their stock of moral and intellectual power, and render them better qualified for success in any other pursuit in life. In proportion as their ability is increased will be their chances of procuring prominent situations as teachers, with adequate compensation. Their qualifications and the successful results of their labors will stand so strongly in contrast with those of ordinary teachers as to create a competition among districts which are desirous of obtaining their services, and thus secure a competent provision for their support.

It must be confessed that there is much in the present prospects of those who intend to devote themselves to the business of teaching, which is calculated to produce indifference and to damp exertion. The vocation does not now insure constant employment, and therefore is not to be relied on as a certain support; nor does it yield rewards at all adequate to its toils and sacrifices. But it is not improbable that more liberal views will prevail in relation to the remuneration of teachers; and it is certain that the most effectual method of bringing about such a change is a course of conduct and an exhibition of skill on their part, which will elevate the character of their vocation, and, by making the public more sensible of the value of their services, will secure a proportionate increase of compensation. Teachers should feel that, without a deep interest in their occupation, they cannot bring into operation the talent requisite to do themselves justice, and to convince the public of the necessity of a higher standard of education. Time may be necessary to produce upon the public mind the requisite impression, but there is no reason to doubt the result. If in the mean time they lose, through the narrow views of their employers, something of the indemnity to which they are entitled for their labors in a most difficult and responsible sphere of action, let them not superadd to this loss a sacrifice of their own reputation by a careless or imperfect discharge of their duties. Let them resolve to gain in character what they may lose in pecuniary profit; and let them be assured, that, if anything can succeed in obtaining from the public the justice which they seek, it is a course of generous devotion on their part to the great cause of education. If such a course should fail to win from those on whom they are now dependent a corresponding return of benefits, it is to be hoped that the time is not far distant when the value of their labors will be better appreciated, and complete justice awarded to them.

II. *As to the duration of the course.* This is necessarily regulated by the number and extent of the subjects of study. In the Prussian seminaries, in which the requirements for teachers of the first grade are about equal in importance to those which the committee have proposed for the departments in question, the term of study is three years; and they are of the opinion that a shorter period would not be sufficient for a strict compliance with the proposed course. As has already been observed, the object in view is to prepare teachers of the first grade; and every other consideration should give way to this. It should be recommended to the trustees of the academies in which the departments may be established, to make the rate of tuition for those who intend in good faith to devote themselves to the business of teaching as low as possible; and to regulate the terms of instruction in such a manner that the pupils in the teachers' department, who are sufficiently advanced, may have an opportunity of taking schools during the three winter-months. They may, by this means, earn something to enable them to complete their course of instruction, and at the same time improve themselves by making a practical application of the knowledge which they will have gained during the rest of the year. To accomplish this object it may be necessary to have only two terms per annum, of four months each. The pupils must not only be required to comply with the entire course, but they must understand thoroughly every subject of study before they receive diplomas or certificates of qualification. In this respect the Boards, from whom the evidences of qualification are to issue, must practise the greatest caution. Their own and the public interest alike demand it. The system cannot become popular, unless it is made equal to its objects. A single individual, educated in one of the proposed departments, and going forth to teach with a diploma, but without the requisite moral and intellectual qualifications, would do much to bring the whole system into disrepute. The Regents should, therefore, insist strongly on the fidelity of the academies to withhold the necessary evidence of qualification to teach from all who are not entirely worthy of it.

The trustees and officers of the academies, which may be selected, cannot fail to perceive that a most favorable opportunity will be presented to them for elevating the character and extending the reputation of their institutions. Whether they succeed in doing so must depend on the fidelity and zeal with which the prescribed plan of instruction shall be carried into effect. They cannot but perceive, also, that if, through the want of proper exertions, any one of them should fail to give satisfaction, and thus render it incumbent on the Regents to transfer the department to some other institution, a duty would devolve on the latter as disagreeable to themselves as it would be prejudicial to the character of the academy in relation to which its performance would be required.

The committee propose that full reports shall be annually made by the academies with regard to the departments. These reports should contain the name of every person receiving a diploma, and the date on which it was issued, so that a complete register of those who have passed through the prescribed course of training will be on file with the secretary of the Board for any necessary purpose of reference. The reports should also show the condition of the departments, as to the number of pupils, the time each has been in training, the books in use, the extent to which each book has been studied, the state of the libraries and apparatus, and, in short, everything which is contained in the reports now made to the Regents in relation to other students. They should also exhibit everything which may be calculated to point out defects and suggest improvements; and they should be accompanied with such observations as may have occurred to the officers of the academies in carrying into execution the prescribed plan. The form of the report need not differ materially from that now used, except so far as it may be necessary to embrace new items of information. The form, accompanied with the necessary instructions, would, they have supposed, be most properly prepared under the direction of the Secretary of the Regents.

III. *As to the necessary books and apparatus.*

Books. Each academy should be furnished with a library well stored with the best authors on the prescribed subjects of study. The committee propose to leave the selection of the books for further consideration. A list can be made out on consultation with the academies, and presented at a future day for the sanction of the Regents. As these books will be wanted for examination and reference, several copies of the same work will be required.

The committee have had under consideration the expediency of designating all the class-books which shall be used in the departments to be established, or of leaving them to be selected by the academies; and, although they deem it of great importance to reduce the course of study to the greatest possible precision, they have come to the conclusion that it is better at present to adopt the latter course. The principal consideration by which they have been guided, is the belief that the Regents may, by allowing the academies to make the selection in the first instance, and requiring them to state in their annual reports the books which they have used, and their reasons for preferring one author to others in common use, be furnished with the means of making a selection themselves at a future day, should it become necessary, for the purpose of securing entire uniformity.

At the same time they would suggest that it will in general be found most advantageous to use for the instruction of teachers the books from which they will be required to teach in the common schools. Larger and more copious treatises on all the subjects of instruction will, it is true, be necessary for the course of study in the departments; but the principal use of the latter will be for reference, and for the purpose of more full illustrations than are afforded by the smaller works.

APPARATUS. The following list includes all the apparatus and maps which the committee deem necessary at present, with the prices annexed, so far as they can be ascertained: —

No. 1.	Orrery,	$20.00
	Numeral frame and geometrical solids,	2.50
	Globes,	12.00
	Movable planisphere,	1.50
	Tide-dial,	3.00
	Optical apparatus,	10.00
Box No. 2.	Mechanical powers,	12.00
Box No. 3.	Hydrostatic apparatus,	10.00
Box No. 4.	Pneumatic apparatus,	35.00
Box No. 5.	Chemical apparatus,	25.00
	100 specimens of mineralogy,	10.00
	Electrical machine,	12.00
	Instruments to teach surveying,	80.00
	Map of the United States,	8.00
	Map of the State of New York,	8.00
	Atlas,	5.00
	Telescope,	40.00
	Quadrant,	15.00
		$309.00

The price of the entire apparatus, including maps, for each department will not much exceed three hundred dollars, so that about two hundred dollars will remain to be appropriated to the purchase of books for each.

The apparatus in contemplation of the committee, and understood to be the best of the kind, is prepared by Brown &

Peirce of Boston, and may be procured in the city of New York.

4th. What evidence of qualification to teach shall be given to the individuals who may be trained in the departments.

In the Prussian and French seminaries of teachers, different grades of qualification are recognized, and the certificates which the pupils receive on completing their course of preparation are framed according to their respective ability to teach. If the departments about to be established were to be adequate to supply with teachers the districts throughout the State, such a distinction might be desirable. But as the number of teachers will necessarily be limited, and as one of the most important effects to be anticipated and desired from the establishment of these departments is to influence public opinion, and by an exhibition of improved methods of teaching to correct prevailing errors with regard to the necessity of providing such a compensation for teachers as shall be in some degree adequate to the value of their services, all the pupils who are in training should be encouraged to complete the prescribed course of preparation. The only distinction proposed to be taken by the committee for those who have gone through the entire course, is between those who are and those who are not qualified to teach; and they deem it proper to intrust the decision of this question to the principal and trustees of the academies in which the departments may be established. It has been suggested that some evidence of qualification from the Regents of the University would carry with it greater weight. There may be, and doubtless is, some force in the suggestion; but as such evidence of qualification must after all rest upon the representation of the officers of the respective academies, they propose to let it issue from the latter, and purport to be what it must be from the necessity of the case. They have drawn a form for a diploma, which is hereunto annexed, marked A, and which from its terms can only be given to those who have completed the course of instruction prescribed by the Regents, and have passed a satisfactory examination in all the subjects of study.

The examination should be public, and be made in the presence of the principal and a majority of the trustees of the academy.

The diploma will not of course dispense with the necessity of a certificate from the Inspectors of common schools of the town, in order to enable the individual to whom it is given to teach a common school and receive the public money. The existing rule of law in this respect will not be affected. Every individual engaged in instructing a common school must once in each year be examined by the Inspectors, and receive a new certificate of qualification. There would be a difficulty in dispensing with this rule, as one of the objects of such a periodical examination is to pass judgment upon the moral character as well as the ability of the individual, who may, by contracting bad habits, become totally unworthy of being intrusted with the education of children. The only advantage, therefore, which the diploma will give, is the assurance that the individual who holds it has been regularly trained for his vocation.

It may often happen that students will not be disposed or able to go through the whole of the prescribed course of instruction for teachers. In this case the principals of the academies should be at liberty to give them a certificate setting forth the particular studies they have pursued, with such opinion of their moral character and their qualifications to teach the branches which they have studied as they may be considered entitled to. But this certificate should be merely under the signature of the principal and not under the seal of the institution; for the committee deem it of the utmost importance that no evidence of qualification should be given which can be mistaken for the diploma received by those who have completed the prescribed course. To avoid all misapprehension, the committee have prepared and hereunto annexed a form for such a certificate, marked B.

The committee deem it within the scope of the reference to them to designate for the consideration of the Regents the academies with which the proposed departments may, in their opinion, be most advantageously connected. They would, therefore, respectfully suggest the following, viz:—

    1st District, Erasmus Hall, Kings county.
    2d   "   Montgomery, Orange county.
    3d   "   Kinderhook, Columbia county.
    4th   "   St. Lawrence, St. Lawrence county.
    5th   "   Fairfield, Herkimer county.
    6th   "   Oxford, Chenango county.
    7th   "   Canandaigua, Ontario county.
    8th   "   Middlebury, Genesee county.

In making this selection, the committee have been guided, in the preferences they have given, by one of two considerations: 1st, that the value of the philosophical and chemical apparatus and library was superior to that of others in the district; or, 2d, that, by reason of their endowments or their peculiar situation, the course of education in the academies selected would be likely to be least expensive to students. The only instances in which they have departed in any degree from this standard are in the 6th and 7th districts. The Oxford Academy has a small amount invested in apparatus, &c., and the Canandaigua Academy is in a large village, where the expense of board might be supposed to be greater than in places of less importance. But each has already a department for the instruction of teachers in full operation; and the endowments of the latter are so ample that the rate of tuition is extremely low, so much so as to compensate for a somewhat higher standard of expense in the item of board. Upon full consideration, they are of the opinion that neither of these academies could be advantageously exchanged for others in the districts in which they respectively lie.

Should the funds at the disposal of the Regents be so augmented hereafter as to admit of an additional expenditure for the support of the departments, the committee are of the opinion that great benefit might be derived from a course of lectures, accompanied with experiments on Chemistry and Mineralogy, and Natural Philosophy and Astronomy, by an individual who would make it his whole business to lecture on these subjects. The pupils in each department might be prepared by the study of the proper text-books so as to be ready at a specified time for the lecturer, who would carry his apparatus with him, and who, from his familiar knowledge of the subjects, could, in a course of lectures of not more than one month in duration in each of the academies, give more practical information than could be gained in the ordinary way in a much longer period. The services of an individual of competent talents might undoubtedly be secured for $1000 per annum. This sum, with what he would be likely to receive from other students not in training for the business of teaching, who might wish to attend the lectures, would cover his expenses and afford him an adequate compensation for the service rendered. The time occupied would not exceed eight months, and the lectures would be given during such portions of the year as to leave the individual employed the entire winter to lecture in other institutions. Thus, for the sum of $1000 per annum the students in the eight departments would be carried through the entire course in the subjects, which present the greatest difficulty, from the necessity of being taught by individuals familiar with them and with the use of the apparatus by which they require to be illustrated.

With this object might be combined another, not less important. The individual thus employed by the Regents might be required to examine into the entire condition of the departments, and report to them all the information which may be necessary to enable them to determine whether the prescribed plan is carried into complete and efficient execution.

As the Regents have not now the means of making this

addition to the proposed plan, and as it will not be necessary until the departments shall have been organized and put fairly in operation, the committee merely suggest it at this time, as a subject worthy of future consideration.

In concluding their report, the committee beg leave to observe, that, in a matter of so much importance, in which the ground to be occupied is yet untried, many considerations may have escaped their notice, which may be disclosed when the proposed plan is put in operation. They do not present it with the confidence that it is perfect, or that experience may not dictate salutary alterations in it, but as the best which, with the lights before them, they have been able, after full consideration, to devise.

All which is respectfully submitted.

Albany, Jan. 8th, 1835.

REPORT ON THE MILITIA SYSTEM.

JANUARY 5, 1832.

The report of Gen. Dix, as Adjutant-General, was made to the Legislature of New York in 1832. It was called forth by a reference to him for examination of two bills, which were introduced at the previous session. The object of both was to dispense with military parades as useless, and both proceeded upon the assumption that the militia system, beyond a mere formal organization, was an unnecessary burden. The report treats these attempts to diminish in any degree the exercises of the militia as a fatal inroad on the efficiency of the system. The importance of retaining the organization of the militia, of keeping up its drills, inspections, and reviews, is maintained as an indispensable preparation for war, and as the chief security of the country against internal disorder and violence. The attacks upon the system were not confined to the legislature, but were set on foot in the principal cities by mock organizations, which were paraded through the streets in fantastical dresses in derision of the militia. The views presented in the report have found a striking vindication in the existing civil war. Without the aid of the militia regiments, which rushed to the defence of the Capital at the first note of alarm, the government might have been overturned or expelled from its seat by the insurgents.

Congress has passed but one general act for the organization of the militia — that of 1793. It is still in force. The arguments in the following report are, therefore, as applicable to the subject now as they were when they were presented to the Legislature of New York thirty years ago; and the defence of the whole system as an essential ingredient in the political organization of the State, in regard to domestic as well as foreign exigencies, will not be unacceptable at a period in which the public mind is directed with so much solicitude to the true sources of the national order and safety.

STATE OF NEW YORK, }
ADJUTANT-GENERAL'S OFFICE. }
January 5, 1832.

TO THE HONORABLE THE SENATE OF THE STATE OF NEW YORK.

IN obedience to your resolution of the 21st of April last, directing the Adjutant-General to report, at the next session

REPORT ON THE MILITIA SYSTEM. 117

of the legislature, upon a bill entitled "An act to reduce the parades and rendezvous of the militia, and to amend the provisions of chapter ten, part one, of the Revised Statutes, so far as to conform them to this act"; and in obedience to your resolution of the 23d of the same month, referring to him a bill entitled "An act to amend the tenth chapter of the first part of the Revised Statutes, relating to the militia and the public defence," he has the honor to submit the following report:—

In the examination of the bills thus submitted to him, he has endeavored to confine himself as strictly as possible to the specific provisions which they contain; but such is their connection with the government of the militia, and the principles on which the system is founded, that he has considered it within the scope of the reference to present some general views of the whole subject; and he trusts that he will not be deemed to have exceeded the just limits of the duty assigned to him, if those views shall be found to illustrate the matters referred.

In adverting to the origin and uses of the militia of the United States as a military institution, it cannot fail to strike the observation that it is as peculiar in its character as the civil institutions of which it is designed to be the protection and support. In most other countries it is a practical rule of government to limit as much as possible the influence of all, who live under it, over its measures and movements, and to arm and discipline such only as are in its pay and under its control. The spirit of our political organization, on the other hand, is, by extending as far as practicable the right of suffrage, to subject the measures and operations of government to the influence of the greatest possible number, and, by arming and disciplining every citizen, to be prepared to sustain in all emergencies, by the united force of the whole community, a system instituted for the benefit of the whole. The theory of this part of the system is, that every citizen shall be armed, and that he shall be instructed also in the use of arms. The reasonings by which the utility of such a social organization is supported are so unanswerable, that it is doubted by the most sagacious observers whether our civil liberties could be maintained for a length of time without the influence and protection of a militia. The same causes which would render such a force dangerous to the existence of an arbitrary government render it indispensable to the existence of ours. That this was the opinion of the original parties to the Constitution of the United States, is apparent from the second article of the amendments of that instrument, which assumes that "a well-regulated militia" is "necessary to the security of a free state," and declares that "the right of the people to keep and bear arms shall not be infringed"; showing that the militia was designed by those who had the largest share in its institution, not merely as a support to the public authority, but, in the last resort, as a protection to the people against the government itself. The militia system is to be regarded, therefore, not only as a part of the political constitution of the State, but as an eminently republican feature of that constitution, fitted equally with its civil features to maintain and give effect to the principles upon which it is founded. So intimately, indeed, are they all interwoven with each other, that the connection which exists between them could not be dissolved without impairing the strength of the whole fabric.

The particular uses for which the militia is designed are declared by the Constitution of the United States to be "to execute the laws of the Union, suppress insurrections, and repel invasions."

The testimony of all history shows that the best regulated governments are liable to disturbances, which the civil arm alone is incompetent to quell. For the purpose of preserving the public order, therefore, a military force of some description is necessary. In most countries the civil authority is upheld by a regular force; and if the militia system were to be abolished, the army would necessarily be employed for this purpose by the Federal government, and the States would have no agency in maintaining the supremacy of their own laws. But it is a striking illustration of the genius of our institutions, that, although we have at no period been without a standing army, the few insurrections which have interrupted our domestic tranquillity have been suppressed by the citizens themselves. Indeed, the nature of our political system and the spirit of the people are such that the employment of any other than a militia force on these occasions would inevitably have the effect of rendering every contest more protracted and sanguinary. A regular force, in the permanent service of the central government, is apt to be regarded, however unjustly, as an instrument of power without affinity with the mass of citizens; and when employed against any portion of the people, it assumes from that very circumstance the aspect of oppression. But to a body of insurgents the spectacle of a military force depending upon the separate authority of the State, drawn from among themselves, and composed of those who have participated in the very evils which they are seeking to redress, presents a moral example of forbearance, order, and submission to the laws, which must have a powerful influence in allaying the violence of their resolutions. With the established militia system, an overwhelming force may be embodied on the most sudden emergency in any quarter of the country; and it is one of the most salutary consequences of the employment of this species of force, that the military mass is dissolved as readily as it is created, without leaving a vestige behind it to commemorate the disgrace of the vanquished and perpetuate exasperation of feeling. If a portion of the regular army had been employed in suppressing the recent disturbance at Providence, it may justly be questioned whether the public order would have been so promptly reëstablished, or the laws so soon and so silently have resumed their sway.

But the most important relation in which the militia can

be considered, is that which it bears to the public defence. The modern practice in Europe of maintaining large standing armies for defensive purposes in time of peace makes it necessary for countries contiguous to each other to be constantly equipped in the same armor with which they are liable to be assailed. Such a state of martial preparation is highly unfavorable to national wealth, by withdrawing from the productive departments of industry a large number of laborers; it is exceedingly expensive and burdensome to the community from which the means of maintaining it are drawn; and it is in principle unfriendly to popular liberty, by arraying on the side of the government large masses of armed men under its absolute control. Our geographical position happily dispenses in a great degree with this species of military preparation, and enables us to rest our public safety upon the people themselves, withdrawing none permanently from the ordinary pursuits of industry in peace, bringing in time of war the highest possible enthusiasm and spirit to the defence of our possessions, and through all vicissitudes insuring to popular liberty its most certain protection. The policy of the United States is eminently pacific; the genius of our institutions, the divisions of our industry, our habits, and the spirit of society are all averse to external acquisition; our schemes of aggrandizement have a reference only to the development of our own resources upon our own soil, by force of the enterprise and industry of our own citizens. The militia system is peculiarly fitted to cherish this spirit of peace, and to eradicate every other inconsistent with it: it is calculated for defence only, and not for offence or conquest. Standing armies, on the other hand, are calculated for offence as well as protection; and one of the evils of maintaining a large regular force is, that it invites to conquest by inspiring a consciousness of the ability to execute its purposes. It would seem to be unwise, therefore, whether we look to the most profitable employment of our resources, the security of our popular liberties, or the removal of all

REPORT ON THE MILITIA SYSTEM.

temptation to an unnecessary exertion of our strength, to allow the efficiency of the militia to be impaired by negligence or disuse, if by maintaining it all our purposes of defence may be answered. Our whole history proves that it is adequate to these purposes; and if the authority of names were wanting to confirm the testimony of our experience, a higher in any respect than that of President Washington could not be cited. His familiarity with the qualifications and uses of the militia was exceeded by that of no other man; he was made fully sensible of its deficiencies, also, during the long and eventful period of the Revolution. Yet he did not hesitate to declare in his messages to Congress, long after the termination of that struggle, that " a free people ought not only to be armed, but disciplined "; and that the militia might " be trained to a degree of energy equal to every military exigency of the United States."

In enumerating the advantages of the militia as a system of public defence, its effect upon foreign nations ought not to be overlooked, — presenting, as it does, a numerical force which with the least expense is fitted to exercise the greatest restraint upon hostile enterprises against us. A vigorous tone of preparation for war is unquestionably the surest pledge of the duration of peace. A state of weakness invites aggression; and those countries are the most certain to be assailed which are the least able to make resistance. To a country meditating hostilities against another, the spectacle of a whole people well armed, and so far disciplined as to be capable at a moment's warning of arraying at any point a force adequate to repel an invader, would present a much more formidable aspect than a regular force of limited numbers, however perfect its discipline. The opposition of a force of limited numbers may always be calculated; but where a whole people are armed and disciplined, the amount of the efficient population is the only measure of resistance. The truth of these observations may be better illustrated by a single example. If the whole number of days annually consumed for military purposes in the State of New York were to be estimated in money, it would not amount to a sum which would meet the annual expense of paying, clothing, and subsisting a regular force of 2000 men. Yet how much more efficient, as a principle of restraint upon the unfriendliness or cupidity of foreign nations would be our present well-organized militia force of near 200,000 men, capable of further augmentation by extending the enrolment, than a regular corps, however well disciplined, of 2000 men, scattered over our wide-spread territory, or even concentrated at the meditated point of invasion! The expenditure of time, therefore, necessary to discipline the militia, will insure the preparation of a military body infinitely more efficient for all the purposes of national security, in consequence of its vast superiority of numbers, than an equal expenditure in money upon a regular force.

Thus, in all the essential properties of a safe, economical, and extensive system of public defence, suited to our institutions and geographical position, the militia was justly regarded, by the framers of our constitution, as preferable to every other description of force. Any alteration, therefore, in the existing militia system, which should have the effect of rendering it inadequate to the declared objects of its institution, would involve a virtual abandonment of the principles in which it had its origin; and the expediency of the alterations proposed by the two bills under consideration will depend on their consistency with the accomplishment of those objects.

The bill first referred to is entitled,

"An act to reduce the parades and rendezvous of the militia, and to amend the provisions of chapter ten, part one, of the Revised Statutes, so far as to conform them to this act.

"SECTION I. The militia shall rendezvous as follows:

"1. For inspection and martial exercise, by companies, in their respective beats, on the first Monday of June in every year, at ten o'clock in the forenoon.

"2. At such other times and places, either by regiments, battalions, companies, or troops, as the case may require, and as shall be directed in any order of the proper authority, calling into the service of the United States, or of this State, the whole or any part of the militia."

This section proposes to limit the exercises of the militia, excepting uniform corps, to one company parade, on the first Monday of June in each year, at ten o'clock in the forenoon. Under the existing law, the same corps, in the interior of the State, are required to meet once, by companies, on the first Monday of September, at nine o'clock in the forenoon, for the purpose of training, disciplining, and improving in martial exercise; and once by regiments, or separate battalions, for inspection, review, and martial exercise, between the first of September and the fifteenth of October. The proposed alteration is, therefore, to make the company parade on the first Monday of June, instead of September, at ten o'clock in the morning, instead of nine, and to dispense altogether with the regimental or battalion parade.

If the last provision were to be adopted, there would be no objection to the proposed change in the time of holding the company parade, excepting the hour of the day, which is, perhaps, not very material; but if the regimental or battalion parade be detained, the first Monday of September would be preferable, the troops, as a general rule, being better prepared for one in proportion as it approaches the other in point of time. The instruction received at the company training being recent and fresh in their minds, they enter upon their battalion exercises with more spirit, and better qualified to improve by them. But the important question presented by this section is, whether the regimental or battalion parade shall be dispensed with.

The militia law of this State being subordinate, in some respects, to the Constitution and laws of the United States, the question must necessarily be considered under two points of view: 1st. Whether the proposed alteration would be consistent with provisions of higher authority than those of the laws of this State; and, 2d. Whether, if not inconsistent with any such provisions, it would be advisable on the score of expediency.

1st. By the Constitution of the United States,[1] Congress has power "to provide for organizing, arming, and disciplining the militia, and for governing such part of them as may be employed in the service of the United States; reserving to the States, respectively, the appointment of the officers, and the authority of training the militia according to the discipline prescribed by Congress." By the seventeenth paragraph of the same article, Congress has power " to make all laws which shall be necessary and proper for carrying into execution the foregoing powers," &c.

In pursuance of these provisions of the Constitution, the law of Congress of May 8, 1792,[2] requires that the militia shall be organized into divisions, brigades, regiments, &c.; prescribes the proper arms and equipments, and assigns to certain officers the discharge of such duties as are necessary to secure the execution of the law. The principal of these is the duty assigned to the brigade-inspector, who is required to attend the regimental and battalion meetings of the militia, to inspect their arms, ammunition, and accoutrements, &c., and to make returns, once in each year, to the Adjutant-General of the State, reporting the actual condition of the brigade, &c. From these returns of the brigade-inspectors a general return is required to be made by the Adjutant-General to the Commander-in-Chief of the State and to the President of the United States.

It was undoubtedly considered necessary, by the framers of the law of 1792, that there should be some mode of determining whether the provisions of that law, relating to the organization and equipment of the militia, were complied with; and it is probable that this object was intended to be accomplished by requiring periodical inspections and reports of such inspections. Although it would seem to be incident

---

[1] Art. 1, sec. 8, part 15.
[2] U. S. Laws, Vol. II. p. 293. Bioren and Duane's ed.

REPORT ON THE MILITIA SYSTEM.

to the power of passing laws to make such further provisions as are necessary to secure their execution, yet all doubt as to the existence of the right in this case, as with regard to all powers granted by the Constitution of the United States, is removed by the seventeenth paragraph of sec. 8, art. 1, above referred to; and if the periodical inspections required are necessary to secure the organization or equipment of the militia, according to the law of 1792, the provision requiring those inspections would seem to be both "necessary and proper." That they are necessary to the organization of the militia may not seem clear; but that they are necessary to secure the equipment of the militia can hardly be doubted. It is deemed indispensable, in all countries where military forces are maintained, to secure the execution of the laws or ordinances regulating their equipment and discipline by means of periodical examinations, executed by competent officers. It is the only certain method of transmitting to the government the intelligence necessary to enable it to supply their deficiencies and rectify departures from the prescribed standard of discipline, &c. to which they are required to conform. The President of the United States is charged with the duty of taking "care that the laws be faithfully executed." It is his duty also "to give to the Congress information of the state of the Union," from time to time; and of the state of the Union the condition of the public defence is a most essential part. The inspections and returns required by the law of 1792 to be performed and rendered, seem to be absolutely necessary to enable him to determine whether its provisions have been complied with, and to communicate to Congress all useful information with regard to the organization and equipment of the militia, and the preparation of the country for the emergencies of war. It is, indeed, worthy of consideration in this case, whether a construction, which should deprive him of the means of knowing how far the provisions referred to had been complied with, would not be equivalent to a denial of his right to carry them into execution, by wholly defeating its exercise. The inspections required may justly be regarded as a part of the discipline of the militia, for which Congress has power to provide; and being essential to the execution of that part of the law which relates to its equipment, the law requiring them to be performed would seem not only proper but necessary, and therefore within the scope of the seventeenth paragraph of the article of the Constitution referred to. If this position be true, a State would neither have the right to dispense with those inspections, nor to provide for their performance in any other than the manner prescribed.

Although the law of 1792 does not in terms declare that there shall be regimental and battalion parades, it assigns to the brigade-inspectors duties to the performance of which such parades are indispensable. If those parades were to be dispensed with, the prescribed duties could not be performed. To dispense with them, therefore, would be a virtual nullification of the law which prescribes them. It follows that, unless a State can lawfully declare that brigade-inspectors shall not perform the duties prescribed by the law of 1792, it cannot pass a law containing provisions with which the performance of those duties is incompatible; for this would be attaining by indirection that which cannot be directly attained.

2d. But in the absence of any legal impediment to the abolition of regimental or battalion parades, the arguments against it, as a measure of expediency, would appear to be decisive of the question. These meetings furnish the only occasions for bringing the several companies, of which regiments and battalions are composed, into contact with each other, and of exciting among them a salutary spirit of emulation in acquiring a knowledge of their duties. A comparison of attainments is always a stimulus to improvement; and to military corps it is peculiarly so. Their progress in discipline depends in a great degree upon the moral spirit which animates them; and if there were no standard of comparison by which their respective merits could be tested, no adequate incentive to exertion would exist. When different corps of different degrees of proficiency are made to act together, that which has attained the highest becomes a standard of imitation for all the others. When they are made to act separately, those which have attained the greatest proficiency decline, for want of the opportunity to exhibit it; and those which have made less progress fail to improve, for want of a higher standard for imitation. Thus the effect of contact upon military corps is to improve, and of separation to degrade, them. To the rank and file the effect of abolishing regimental and battalion parades would be highly pernicious; but to the spirit and efficiency of the officers there is reason to apprehend that it would be fatal. Field-officers would be so in name only, because they would have no active commands. Without the habit of commanding or exercising regiments, they would soon become unable to command or exercise them. This would be more emphatically true, as the field-officers, who have been formed under the existing system, should retire, and new ones succeed them; and these changes might be expected to occur in rapid succession; for those who are worthy of commissions would find no adequate motive to retain them, when deprived of the opportunity of making such proficiency in a knowledge of their duties as to render the tenure honorable to themselves. The company officers might be expected to decline as rapidly in character and qualifications, from the operation of the causes first referred to, if restricted to separate company exercises. A decline in discipline, instruction, and military knowledge would inevitably follow this deterioration of the commissioned grades; for no military corps can be efficient without well informed and capable officers. The officers' drill would not be calculated to supply the absence of regimental parades. It has its utility in familiarizing the officers with the branches of instruction which they are to communicate to their men. But no officer becomes capable of commanding by merely being exercised as a soldier. The habit of command is as necessary to the officer as the habit of obedience to the rank and file : neither the one nor the other would be prepared for the duties respectively required of them, without the kind of discipline respectively suited to each.

But a still higher objection to the proposed change is, that no two companies would be capable of acting together in any sudden emergency, without waiting to be practised in the necessary evolutions. The State of New York, with a military force of near 200,000 men, would be without a regiment, except in the nominal organization exhibited upon the records of the Adjutant-General's office. This result would be the more to be regretted, as there are now in service many regiments which perform all their appropriate exercises and evolutions with the spirit and precision of regular troops, and which might be led into the field upon the shortest notice, with the assurance of maintaining unimpaired the military reputation of their country.

A general languor in the performance of military duty might, therefore, be expected from the abolition of regimental and battalion parades, and a rapid decline in all that is calculated to qualify the militia to accomplish the objects for which it is maintained.

. . . .

"SECTION IV. The commissioned officers of each regiment and separate battalion, and warrant officers not attached to companies, shall rendezvous within their respective beats, on the first Monday in September in each year, for inspection and martial exercise: the officer in command on that day shall be the inspector. The time and place shall be prescribed by the commanding officer of the regiment or separate battalion."

The existing law requires the officers and non-commissioned officers of each regiment and separate battalion in the interior of the State to rendezvous two successive days in each year, for exercise and discipline ; on the last of which the brigade-inspector is required to attend, for the purpose of instructing them in a knowledge of their duties. The section under examination proposes,

1. To substitute one parade for the two required; 2. To make it an inspection for the persons present; 3. To make the senior officer present the inspector; and, 4. To dispense with the attendance of the non-commissioned officers of companies.

1. *To substitute one parade for the two required.*

The consideration which most naturally suggests itself in the examination of this provision is, that, so far as it relates to the commissioned officers, it proposes to dispense with duties which are voluntarily performed. They are incident to the tenure of a commission, which any individual to whom it is offered is at liberty to decline or accept. If they were absolutely useless, they might be dispensed with as an unnecessary burden. But so obvious is their utility, that it is believed the majority of those who bear the burden would rather be in favor of increasing than diminishing it. As they have not petitioned for relief from any portion of it, it is respectfully recommended that it be continued as it now exists.

There is perhaps no proposition, connected with the organization and discipline of military corps, better settled than the necessity of having a body of intelligent and well-trained officers. If they are without experience or instruction, it is impossible that those whom they command can make any progress in the knowledge of their duties. On the other hand, a body of untrained individuals may in a short time be brought to a high state of improvement in discipline by competent officers. The reverses which our regular forces experienced at the commencement of the late war are, in a great degree, to be traced to the inexperience of the officers by whom they were commanded. They were generally as ignorant of their duties as the men whom they led : when their education should have been complete, the very rudiments were to be acquired. Unskilfulness, misdirection, disaster, and defeat were the necessary consequence of these deficiencies. So obvious was the cause of the reverses which for a time embarrassed our military operations, that the organization of the regular army was radically changed soon after the termination of the war, and its preparation for a future state of hostilities regulated by totally different principles. The system, the theory of which is to dispense with the greatest possible number of rank and file, to retain a large proportion of officers, and to cause them to be thoroughly instructed in all the branches of military science, has been put into operation; and the government has under its control a corps of officers practised in all military exercises, embracing a larger amount of military science than any other body of equal number in any foreign service, and capable of preparing for action in a short period a large body of troops. The same arguments which show the propriety of preparing such a corps of officers for the regular army, are equally applicable to the militia. In case of war, even if a numerous regular force is to be levied, the defence of the country is of necessity intrusted, at the commencement of hostilities, to volunteers or drafts from the militia. The enlistment of regular corps, and their transportation to the vulnerable points on the frontier, are the work of time; and it is, therefore, necessary that the militia should be commanded by officers capable of training the corps intrusted to them to such a state of discipline as to be in a condition to take the field, on a sudden emergency, against an enemy.

The qualifications of officers being of a higher character, and more difficult to be acquired than those of the rank and file, it is indispensable that a greater number of drills should be exacted of them. The additional trainings now required by law bear no more than a fair relation to the greater application and time necessary to make them acquainted with their duties. If it be requisite, then, as a provision against the exigencies of war, that they should be better practised in their particular duties than the rank and file, the proper change to be introduced, if any be necessary, would be to increase rather than diminish the number of their days of exercise and instruction. It is proper to observe that these observations are not intended to apply to the city of New York: the exposed situation of the city, and other sources of danger, which will be considered hereafter, have rendered necessary a higher standard of requirements for the militia within the limits of the county,—a standard fully equal perhaps to any necessity, however sudden or pressing.

2. To make it an inspection for the persons present; and,

3. To make the senior officer the inspector.

It will be perceived that these propositions, so far as they relate to the inspection of the officers, are intended as a substitute, *pro tanto*, for the annual regimental and battalion inspection now executed by the brigade-inspector. The only object of such an inspection as the one proposed would be to ascertain that the uniform and equipments of the officers conform to the established regulation. This duty might very well be executed by the senior officer present, should the propositions contained in this section be adopted: it could not be performed by the brigade-inspector for more than one regiment in each brigade in the interior of the State, as the officers of each are to meet within the beats of their respective regiments on the same day. But it may be urged as a leading objection to this section, as well as to the first section of this bill, by which regimental parades are abandoned, that the attendance of the brigade-inspector is dispensed with. This is the only officer, in the performance of active duties in each brigade, who receives a regular compensation for his services. Though small, it is still sufficient in most cases to enable him to devote his time to the performance of his duties without any sacrifice. The post is one of considerable personal consequence, particularly in the interior of the State; and the incumbents are for this reason more permanent than those of the other officers in the militia. There are now in commission, as brigade-inspectors, several individuals who have held the post more than twenty years, and one who has held it nearly thirty. To the character of the brigade the place is of much more consequence than to the individual.

It is his duty to superintend the exercises of the officers at their second parade, to introduce the established system of discipline, and instruct them in their duties. His instructions constitute in many cases the most valuable part of their discipline; and they are much better qualified, after receiving them, to impart knowledge to their men. If his attendance were to be dispensed with, he would himself, for want of practice, soon become inadequate to the discharge of his duties; the discipline and instruction of the officers would devolve, as provided for by this section, on the senior present, who is frequently now, and would in most cases, if regimental parades were abolished, be, incompetent to the task; and the officers would be subjected to a mere consumption of time, without any adequate benefit. Under such a plan of instruction, the militia system could hardly fail to go rapidly to decay.

4. To dispense with the attendance of non-commissioned officers of companies.

This provision is liable to the same objection which applies to the provision relating to commissioned officers. Efficient and well-trained non-commissioned officers are indispensable to the good government of a company and its improvement in martial discipline. They are entitled to privileges which materially diminish their burdens; and after a limited period they become exempt from military duty, except in case of invasion, &c. Upon the whole, the burden is not much heavier than that borne by the privates; and as their exercises, in conjunction with the commissioned officers, are not only essential to their improvement, but also personally advantageous to them, by rendering them better qualified for the commissioned grades to which they are frequently elected, it would be advisable to require their attendance as now provided for by law.

If the provisions of this section should be adopted, it would be important, in order to mitigate as far as possible their evil effects, to require the attendance of the brigade-inspector at the drill of the officers proposed to be retained, with a view to superintend their exercises and inspect them. For this purpose, it would be necessary that so much of it as requires the officers of each regiment to parade on the same day should be expunged, and the day left to be appointed, as it now is, by the brigadier-general.

. . . .

"SECTION VII. The commandants of the several companies shall inspect their several companies and troops on the first Monday in June in each year, and make inspection returns thereof to the commanding officer of the regiment or separate battalion, on or before the first day of September in each year; to which returns the number of conditional exempts residing within the company beat shall be added. The commanding officers of the several regiments and separate battalions shall make inspection returns of their regiments or separate battalions to the brigadier-general and to the brigade-inspector, on or before the first day of November in each year; and the brigade-inspector shall make an inspection return of the brigade to the major-general of division and to the adjutant-general, on or before the first day of December in each year."

The inspections required by this section to be made by captains of companies are intended as a substitute for the established system of inspection by the brigade-inspectors, and are a necessary consequence of the abolition of regimental and battalion parades. To the considerations already presented, with a view to show the pernicious tendency of that measure as relates to the practical exercises of the militia, may be added the pernicious tendency of the proposed substitute as relates to its equipment. With a lax system of inspections, it could not be expected that the laws regulating arms and equipments would be observed: thorough examinations, regular reports of delinquencies, and a rigorous exaction of the legal penalties, are essential to the proper execution of those laws. All these ends are secured, as far as practicable under the existing law, by the examinations annually performed by the brigade-inspector. Captains of companies, knowing that their commands are to pass this ordeal, and that the discredit of a general deficiency will affect their character as officers, have a motive to carry into effect, as far as depends on them, the requirements of the law. At the parade of the company previous to the general inspection, their attention is directed to the state of its arms and equipment, and deficiencies are often supplied before that inspection occurs. If the captains of companies were to be made the inspectors, no such motive would exist. There would be no supervisory power to secure a faithful, or detect a negligent, discharge of their duties. Deriving their commissions from the suffrages of their companies, there would be too much reason to apprehend, in many cases, that the commander would not be disposed to enforce the law against those to whom he owed his elevation, and that the subordinates would be disposed, in many cases, to place over themselves individuals on whose indulgence they might rely to screen them from the penalties of disobedience. In regular armies, commanding officers of corps, responsible for their condition, are never intrusted solely with the inspection of their commands. The principal business of inspection is confided to officers wholly disinterested, who may be relied on for a punctual and impartial discharge of the duty. To devolve the duty on the responsible person is to make him responsible to himself alone, or, in other words, wholly irresponsible. Laxity in enforcing the law against offenders would very naturally be accompanied by a corresponding laxity in making the returns of inspections. The return of a company deficient in its arms, equipments, &c. would be a record of the delinquency of the captain, who is the responsible officer; and yet, by the provisions of this section, it would depend on him whether the return be made or not. None of the annual returns, required by law to be made to the Adjutant-General's office, are, taken collectively, either correct in themselves, or made at the prescribed periods, excepting the returns of the brigade-inspectors, who are paid for making them. It has been found nearly impossible to procure an annual roster of all the officers of each brigade, above the rank of captain, to enable the Adjutant-

REPORT ON THE MILITIA SYSTEM. 135

General to prepare annually the roster, required by law to be kept in his office; and the present incumbent has adopted the rule of correcting his roster by the election returns, whenever a vacancy is filled and a commission issued. If such is the difficulty of procuring eighty-two simple returns, the difficulty of procuring two thousand nine hundred and thirty-four returns of inspections, which are far more complicated, and which must, in many cases, show upon their face the delinquency of the persons who are required to make them, may readily be conceived. Two thousand four hundred and eighty-eight captains would be required to make returns of their companies, three hundred and forty-five colonels of their regiments, nineteen majors of their separate battalions, and eighty-two inspectors of the brigades to which they belong; and all without compensation for their services. It is not too much to say that the provisions of the law would not be complied with. Both the State and the general government would consequently be but imperfectly informed as to the condition of our military force, and therefore incapable of measuring our capacity for resisting external violence, or maintaining internal tranquillity. That the arms and equipments of the militia would regularly become more deficient seems equally clear. Some corps would doubtless be kept up with regularity and spirit, but it would be through the labors and devotion of individuals, and not by force of law. Such a dependence is, from its nature, exceedingly uncertain, both in duration and degree, and, therefore, unfit to be relied on as the basis of a system, whether of civil order or public defence.

The only modes of enforcing the requirements of this section would be to allow to each officer a compensation for his services, in inspecting and making a return of his command, or to annex a heavy penalty to the non-performance of the service. The first would require a large disbursement of public money, and the second, however effectual in most cases, would sometimes fail, from the great number of persons of whom the service is required. The present mode is more simple, and, by providing an adequate compensation and putting in requisition the services of a much smaller number of individuals, rarely fails to accomplish the object proposed.

. . . .

[This Report contains only the most important portions of the original. Many sections of the bills examined are omitted. Eleven of these sections provided for a total abolition of the established system of imposing and collecting fines, substituting civil for military process.]

It is to be observed that the established system of penalties to secure the execution of the militia law is designed exclusively for a state of peace. In a state of war, the militia, when called into actual service, becomes subject to the martial code, which proceeds upon the principle of enforcing obedience by imprisonment and other personal inflictions. These punishments are awarded to purely military offences, and not to deficiencies in arms or equipments, which are in war provided by the public. But in time of peace there is an additional class of delinquencies growing out of the legal obligation of those who are subject to military duty, to arm and equip themselves; and to these deficiencies a distinct class of penalties is annexed. Purely military offences, such as disobedience of orders, insubordination, &c., may be punished by commanding officers on days of martial exercise, as in time of war, by putting the offender under guard; but as the punishment is limited in this case by the duration of the authority of the officer, which expires with "the setting of the sun," the law provides also that the offender may be returned to a court-martial, to be punished by a pecuniary mulct. For the other class of delinquencies referred to, such as a deficiency in the arms and equipments required by law, or non-attendance at the established parades, a double remedy is not provided: they can only be reached under the existing law by fines imposed by courts-martial and levied upon the property of the delinquent. These delinquencies, as well as the penalties with which they are visited, partake more highly of a civil than a military character; and no reason founded in principle is perceived why the final application of the penalties may not be made by a civil magistrate. If a private appears upon parade without a musket, the law immediately subjects him to a penalty of one dollar. The only question is whether the penalty has been incurred; and this is a mere matter of evidence, which a civil magistrate may investigate and decide without any knowledge of the principles or usages of military service. It is only to be considered, therefore, whether, in reference to this class of delinquencies, the proposed change may be adopted consistently with a proper regard to the interest of the public and the convenience of individuals.

The first objection which suggests itself, is the additional burden it would impose on individuals. Under the existing law a court-martial is organized for the trial of this class of delinquencies as well as all others; and the members being paid for their services by an appropriation of a portion of the fines imposed and collected under their authority, the law allows no costs of process. Under the proposed system, the costs of proceeding would be added to the penalty, and adjudged against the delinquent. Thus in the case of a deficiency in the articles of a bayonet and belt, the delinquent would incur a penalty of twenty-five cents, which under the existing law he might pay into court at the trial without incurring any costs. But under the proposed system he would not only incur this penalty, but would be compelled also to pay the justice his fees, besides the fees of the constable who served the summons. The average amount of these costs would not fall short of seventy-five cents; so that a delinquent who should forfeit twenty-five cents would be compelled to pay costs to three times the amount of the penalty, and four times as much under the proposed as he would under the existing system. And if he were to contest the justice of the imposition, go into an investigation of facts and fail in his justification, he would subject himself to a much heavier burden of costs.

The second objection is, that it would impose a heavy burden of expense on the public. It is presumed that the return required by section tenth to be made to a justice of the peace is in the nature of an information, upon which proceedings are instituted in behalf of the people with a view to the recovery of the penalty incurred. If the delinquent appears and shows cause why the fine imposed should not be collected, as he may under section twelfth, he would become entitled to a discharge, without costs, from all further liability, and the justice and constable would have a claim for their fees upon the State. The sufficiency of the excuse could not appear without an examination of witnesses under oath, and the justice would be entitled to additional fees for this examination. Upon the lowest calculation, fees to the amount of one dollar would accrue upon almost every case in which a delinquent should be excused from the payment of the fine. The number of regiments and separate battalions in service are three hundred and sixty-four; and the average number of delinquents in each annually about sixty. Of these about one half, say one third, are excused for non-appearance at parades, by the court-martial before which they are arraigned for trial, on account of sickness in their families, absence on business of a pressing nature, &c., or for deficiencies in arms, &c. on showing sufficient cause. The number of persons excused from payment of the fines imposed on them would not fall short of seven thousand two hundred and eighty; and the costs annually accumulated against the State would not be less than $7000.

If the nature of this prosecution has been mistaken in the foregoing remarks; if, instead of a public prosecution, it is to be an action brought in the name of the officer imposing the fine, making him a party to it, and liable for costs in all cases where the delinquent is excused, the returns of delinquents would be rarely made. No individual could be

REPORT ON THE MILITIA SYSTEM. 189

expected to subject himself to a certain loss, in many cases, when he could not by possibility be a gainer in any. If this be the intention of the law, it would be necessary, in order to secure its execution, to make provision for the payment of these costs by the State; and this would revive the objection already glanced at, and predicated on the supposition that it is intended to be a prosecution in behalf of the people.

Thus, although there be no objection in principle to the imposition of fines for mere delinquencies by the joint authority of the commander and a civil magistrate, the practical inconveniences would be far superior to those of the existing mode, both as relates to the public and to individuals.

But offences of a purely military character involve other considerations; and to bring them in any manner under the jurisdiction of a civil magistrate, would not only be objectionable in principle, but would be fraught with objections altogether fatal on the score of justice and policy. The inconveniences above mentioned in case of deficiencies would attend upon this class of cases also, the proposed mode of imposing and collecting fines being the same in both. But the leading objection is to giving the civil magistrate jurisdiction of subjects which, to be disposed of in such a manner as to do justice to individuals and maintain military subordination, should be adjudicated by persons familiar with military principles and usage. These, not being a part of the study of civil magistrates, and of a nature not to be properly understood without some study or experience, would be liable to interpretations so lax, and so various from the great number of interpreters, as to be subversive of all discipline in the performance of military duty, and of all uniformity in the punishment of disobedience.

. . . .

But a still more serious objection to the proposed substitute is, that the decision of the justice is final and conclusive. If there is any class of cases which seems entitled to a hearing on an appeal to a higher tribunal, it is this. The change in all its parts is highly unfavorable to those most affected by it, when compared with the present system, but in none more so than in taking away the right of appeal. By the present law, if a fine is imposed by a court-martial upon a delinquent, he has a right of appeal to the officer instituting the court; and if his appeal is dismissed, he has a further right of appeal to the commander-in-chief. If a court, forgetful of its obligations, or misjudging the facts of a case, should not do justice to a party arraigned before it, an appeal to the officer instituting the court rarely fails to procure a redress of the grievance; yet, if the application should fail, justice will always be done by an appeal to the highest military authority of the State. But so little cause is there of complaint with the sentences of regimental and battalion courts-martial, and the decisions of officers instituting them, that not more than twelve or fourteen appeals from them are annually addressed to the commander-in-chief, although fines are annually imposed by more than three hundred of these courts.

. . . .

The provision contained in section twelve is an exemption of all persons from imprisonment for penalties incurred by reason of any deficiency, delinquency, or offence whatsoever. To a certain extent this provision seems proper; but beyond that point it would tend to the utter subversion of military order and discipline. Where a deficiency in arms and equipments exists, and a fine is imposed, it would be agreeable to the provisions of the act passed at the last session of the legislature for the abolition of imprisonment for debt, to limit the liability to the property of the delinquent. If he has no property, and is therefore unable through poverty to provide himself with arms and equipments, it would not only be unjust but barbarous to imprison him. Courts-martial have the power of remitting the penalty in such cases, and it is always exercised where satisfactory evidence of inability to pay it is shown. Still it would be well to rest the exemption from imprisonment, in every such case, upon the more certain and durable basis of law. But to extend the exemption to offences, or to any other class of delinquencies, would have a highly prejudicial effect upon military subordination and obedience. As the section now stands, an individual, fined for the grossest acts of insubordination and disrespect to his officers, could not be imprisoned. It would be a virtual release of all who are without property from the obligations of obedience. To extend the exemption to fines imposed for non-attendance at parades, would in like manner be a virtual release of all who are without property from the obligation of attendance. It is respectfully submitted, therefore, whether the exemption should be extended to any other than fines imposed for deficiencies in arms and equipments. The ground of the proposed exemption is the want of property; and it would be more conformable to the principle on which it is founded to make it a release from those requirements only to the fulfilment of which the possession of property is indispensable.

. . . .

As the result of the foregoing examination, it is recommended that of the act entitled "An act to reduce the parades and rendezvous of the militia, and to amend the provisions of Chapter ten, Part one, of the Revised Statutes so far as conform them to this act," section third with an exception in favor of officers superseded by the election of juniors to command them; so much of section sixth as requires captains of companies to include conditional exempts in their company rolls; and so much of section twelfth as provides that no person shall be imprisoned for non-payment of a fine imposed for deficiencies in arms or equipments, should be adopted; and that all the remaining sections and provisions of that act should be rejected as incompatible with the accomplishment of the objects for which the military establishment is maintained, or as inconsistent with justice to individuals.

The second bill referred to is entitled "An act to amend the tenth Chapter of the first Part of the Revised Statutes relating to the militia and the public defence."

"SECTION I. The sixth section of the first Title of Chapter ten of the first Part of the Revised Statutes is hereby repealed."

The effect of this section is to subject to the performance of military duty the following persons heretofore exempt, except in cases of insurrection and invasion, viz : " Every person actually employed by the year, month, or season, in any blooming-furnace, iron-foundry, glass, woollen, or cotton factory ; and every student in any college or academy within this State."

The section proposed to be repealed operates as a protection of the branches of industry above enumerated by exempting from military duty all persons employed in them. The relief provided is an addition of the value of the time saved and the expense of arming and equipping to the profits of their respective occupations, and may be regarded as a bounty upon the productions of their industry. To render the discrimination in favor of those branches right in principle, they should be of greater public utility than others not protected in the same manner, and the exemption should be necessary to sustain them by securing them from competitions dangerous to their existence. If the necessity, founded upon such a concurrence of circumstances, was apparent at the origin of the law, it is no longer so with regard to the two classes of persons engaged in cotton and woollen factories. Both those branches of industry are amply protected by the laws of the United States ; and it is believed that their profits are fully equal to those of any other. Their operations being carried on in a great degree by females and children, and in many cases by foreigners not naturalized, the males, who would become liable to military duty, are comparatively few, and, as a general rule, are employed at high wages. If the nature of their occupation admits of fewer interruptions than that of the farmer and mechanic, it is from that very circumstance the more productive, and they are, therefore, better able to contribute to the support of the military establishment, by paying a fine for non-performance of military duty. Although the same remarks do not, in all respects, apply to persons employed in blooming-furnaces, iron-foundries, and glass-factories, yet it is believed that these branches of industry are at least as productive as those of the great mass of citizens subject to military duty, and that they are as fully protected by public law, without further discriminations in their favor. All these classes should, therefore, be made to contribute in personal service to the public defence.

But there is a more conclusive argument against the continuance of this exemption. The spirit of the act of Congress, exempting certain classes from the performance of military duty, is to release those only who are engaged in rendering other services to the public, or who, from the nature of their pursuits, are unable to comply with any regular requisition of personal service. The officers of the civil government and persons engaged in the care and conveyance of the United States mail come within the first class of persons exempted, and mariners within the second. None of these persons are exempt as a matter of indulgence, but because the performance of military duty is incompatible with the nature of their occupations. With a few exceptions, the law of this State is framed in the same spirit; and for the sake of the principle involved, it is desirable that the exceptions should be reduced to the smallest possible number.

But with regard to students in colleges and academies, it is worthy of consideration whether a repeal of the present exemption would not be productive of greater inconvenience and evil than utility. It is well understood that this class of persons does not come within the general rule of exemption above stated; but it is conceived that it deserves, from the peculiar circumstances of the case, to be treated as an exception to the rule. If there be any object to the accomplishment of which every proper encouragement should be given, it is that of diffusing, as widely as possible, the advantages of education. A pervading intelligence is the surest support of our free institutions, and any enactment which has the effect of opposing obstacles to its extension is in operation hostile to the principles of those institutions. The consequence of repealing that part of the section relating to students is to subject all above the age of eighteen years to the performance of military duty. It rarely happens that the children of those whose means are abundant are not prepared at the age of eighteen or nineteen to graduate and enter on their professional studies. The children of those whose means are limited are necessarily more retarded in their progress, for want of early advantages; and the result would be that the greater part of the students affected by the repeal of this exemption would belong to that meritorious class who, with no other resources than the unassisted efforts of their own powers, are struggling to qualify themselves for professional distinction. By devoting their vacations to teaching school in villages and country towns, they are enabled to procure the means of continuing their studies during the regular terms; but, with the most rigid frugality and the most industrious habits, their efforts are often unequal to the task. It is to be considered, also, that in many of our collegiate and academic institutions, military corps are already formed by voluntary associations of the students, and almost all who are able to equip themselves, or who are not designed for the profession of divinity, are found in their ranks. With this distinct organization, they have the advantage of being exercised under the supervision and control of their teachers; whereas, if they were compelled to perform duty with the militia, they would be withdrawn from this salutary supervision at an age full of dangers, to be exercised at a distance from their temporary guardians. Being, in most cases, away from their homes, their condition would be far more inconvenient than that of the youth of the country in general, who are enrolled under the roof of their natural protectors, and are often attended by them to the field of exercise. Neither is it to be overlooked that every student above the age of eighteen years, who goes from home, must carry with him his arms and equipments, which would become as indispensable as his books. But the leading objection is, that the repeal of the existing exemption would have the effect of subjecting to a heavy imposition a few, least able to bear the burden they are already sustaining under the impulse of a spirit which deserves to be cherished by every practicable encouragement. It would devolve the burden of arming and equipping upon students without means, who, relying upon themselves alone, have entered into unequal competition with those who are sustained by the patronage and wealth of others. This spirit lies at the very foundation of all improvement in science, as well as the practical business of life; and it deserves to be regarded with favor by the government, as one of the powers through which inequalities of wealth and condition are to be corrected. By continuing the existing exemption, all these objects are promoted, without devolving on the public any additional imposition. It is, therefore, recommended that it should not be disturbed.

"Section II. The privates in the militia of this State, except such as belong to uniform companies or troops, shall not hereafter be required to parade more than once in each year, except when called into the actual service of the United States, or of this State, which parade shall be for inspection and review, at such time and place, between the first day of September and the fifteenth day of October, and either by regiments or battalions, as shall be ordered by the commandant of the brigade."

That part of the foregoing section which gives to commandants of brigades a discretion to direct the parade proposed to be retained either by regiments or battalions, is defective in recognizing a form of organization which has in practice been abandoned. Under the act of Congress of the 12th May, 1820, the system of discipline and field exercise observed by the regular army is established for the government of the militia. By that system, each regiment forms a battalion for manœuvring; and the only known division, either in its exercises or on the records of the Adjutant-General's office, is into companies. The system of discipline and exercise before referred to recognizes no other division of a regiment. Separate battalions are authorized by law, but their organization is totally distinct from that of regiments; a battalion, as part of a regiment, is unknown to the existing organization. To make this section correspond with it, it would be necessary to provide that the parade should be by regiments or separate battalions.

But the main provisions of this section are liable to more serious objections. They abolish all company parades, and, by exacting only one parade by regiments, and that for review and inspection, virtually abandon the established system of instruction and exercise. The change proposed proceeds upon the assumption that this system is under the absolute control of the legislative authority of the State. If this position be improperly assumed, the first question to be considered is, how far the State is competent to legislate upon the subject?

As has been already seen in another part of this report, the Constitution of the United States gives to Congress the power of providing for organizing, arming, and disciplining the militia, reserving to the States respectively the appointment of the officers, and the authority of training the militia according to the system prescribed by Congress. These provisions are to be regarded as the result of a compact between the original parties to the Constitution, dividing between the Federal and State governments, to be exercised by them respectively, certain coördinate powers in relation to the militia, — an institution assumed by those very provisions, independently of express declarations, to be indispensable to the great objects of upholding the authority of the laws, repelling foreign invasions, and maintaining the public tranquillity. It is apparent that a failure on the part of either of the proper authorities to execute the trusts respectively confided to them, would not only be fatal to the system which they were designed to put in operation, but would be an invasion of the rights of the other, by wholly defeating the exercise of its legitimate powers over the subject-matter to be regulated. If Congress had failed to pass a law providing for the organization of the militia, the power of the States to appoint the officers would be defeated. By passing such a law they have devolved on the States the duty of appointing the officers according to the prescribed organization. On the other hand, if the States were to refuse to appoint officers, the power of Congress to prescribe an organization would be wholly annulled. The exercise of the powers respectively allotted to each, is, therefore, a matter of obligation growing out of provisions inherent in the Constitution. Congress has also prescribed a system of discipline for the government of the militia; and, by force of this obligation, the duty of training the militia according to the prescribed system has devolved on the States. They can no more decline, under the constitutional compact, to train the militia according to the prescribed system of discipline, than they can decline to appoint officers in order to make the establishment conform to the prescribed standard of organization. The States are, of necessity, from the nature of their reservations of power over this part of the subject, judges of the extent to which the trainings shall be carried. But it is conceived that this faculty does not imply the right to dispense with trainings altogether, since it would thereby defeat the exercise of the power granted to Congress. This right might, perhaps, be justly asserted, if the militia system had no reference to the general purposes of government. But the maintenance of a militia is not designed exclusively for the benefit of the States. It is also intended to put at the disposition of the Federal government, to which the general defence is intrusted, the force necessary to accomplish that object, reserving to the States such powers over it as to secure its fidelity and guard against its application to purposes of oppression. To refuse to exercise those powers, necessarily takes from the Federal government the ability of executing one of the leading objects contemplated by the Constitution, and has the effect of annulling one of the fundamedtal provisions of that instrument. If the militia were merely designed as a protection in the last resort for the residuary powers of the States, the exercise of those powers might be regarded as a matter of discretion; but the relation which the institution bears to these great ends of government seems to render their exercise a matter of good faith, if not of imperious obligation.

In estimating the extent to which trainings under the established system must be carried, a correct decision will be facilitated by referring to the duties which, in pursuance of its constitutional powers, Congress has required to be performed by the militia. To insure the execution of the law of 1792, prescribing its organization and equipment, the brigade-inspectors are directed to attend the regimental and battalion trainings, to instruct the officers in their duties, to examine into and report upon the condition of arms, equipments, &c., and to enforce the system of discipline prescribed by Congress. That this part of the law may be executed, the several regiments must have their proper number of officers and non-commissioned officers, and they must be divided, according to law, into companies. The company officers must be so far instructed in their duties as to be able to make a proper arrangement of their non-commissioned officers and men, who must, in their turn, know their places, understand the use of the musket, be able to face, wheel, break into sections, and march with some degree of concert. Unless they are familiar with these elementary exercises, they can never be put into form as a company, much less as a regiment. If there were no company trainings, there is no hazard in asserting that they would be incompetent to perform these simple movements; they could have no knowledge of company exercises; they could not be formed and put in motion as such, nor for that very reason as a regiment; for the exercises of regiments are nothing more than the combined movements of companies, regulated by the same principles, depending for their execution upon a knowledge of company exercises, and differing only in the circumstance of being carried out to an extent commensurate with the enlarged sphere and more complex character of the combination. To enable the brigade-inspectors to perform their duties, the officers and men composing each regiment must come together, not as an armed multitude, but with a proper organization, and with sufficient instruction to form as a regiment. Without a knowledge of company exercises, which can only be acquired by means of company trainings, this could not be accomplished. A knowledge of the "school of the soldier," the "school of the company," and the "school of the battalion," or, in general terms, a knowledge of company and regimental exercises, is the least degree of preparation which would insure a proper compliance with the requirements of the law. These exercises are a part of a system of tactics recently published and distributed under an act of Congress for the government and use of the militia; and the very act of prescribing it devolves on the States the duty of training the militia by it, so far as to fulfil the requirements above referred to. To obtain the necessary proficiency, at least one company and one regimental training annually would be indispensable; and, with the exception of the city of New York, the militia not uniformed are relieved from all but these two trainings.

If these views be just, the militia system is, with regard to its exercises, reduced to the lowest standard consistent with a proper observance of the requirements of the laws of the United States. Any further reduction of its exercises would render nugatory the constitutional powers of Congress over the subject, by defeating the execution of arrangements made in pursuance of those powers.

The constitution of the State of New York (art. 7, sec. 5) provides that "the militia of this State shall at all times hereafter be armed, and disciplined, and in readiness for service." The section under consideration, by dispensing altogether with the system of exercises, is in direct contravention of this provision of the constitution. Without a knowledge of company exercises at least, the militia could with no propriety be said to be "disciplined," much less "in readiness for service." It may be considered doubtful whether the requirements of the constitution would be complied with, unless the militia were to be instructed also in battalion exercises, so far as to enable the different companies to act in concert when called into service. But to dispense with all military requisitions excepting an inspection and review, is manifestly repugnant to the spirit and letter of the provision above cited. The difficulty would not be obviated by making the regimental or battalion parade a meeting for exercise as well as inspection and review. Without company trainings, it is believed, for the reasons already assigned, that a regiment would not be able to meet and organize as such; and with a single regimental parade, the time consumed in organizing, reviewing, and inspecting would leave none to be devoted to instruction and discipline. The militia may, therefore, be considered as reduced, with regard to its exercises, to the lowest standard consistent with the provisions of the constitution of this State.

If there be a legal impediment to the adoption of the proposed alteration, any argument drawn from the inexpediency of its adoption would be superfluous. But as much misapprehension has prevailed with regard to the utility of the existing exercises, the legal objections to their abolition will be waived for the purpose of considering them.

It has been urged that the company trainings, proposed by this section to be dispensed with, are necessary to keep up the organization of the militia; and the truth of this position can hardly be called in question by those who understand the difficulty of preserving a regular order and arrangement throughout the State, with the existing exercises. As was said with regard to the abolition of regimental trainings, the State would not possess a single regiment excepting in name, so it may be said, with regard to the abolition of company trainings, that the State would neither possess a regiment nor a company, excepting upon the records of the Adjutant-General's office. The militia would become the mere material, without any of the active properties of a military force. Its principal value is in its ability to act on sudden emergencies. The great objection to the abolition of trainings is, that it would require time for preparation before it would be competent to act. It may, therefore, be considered as reduced, with regard to its exercises, to the lowest standard consistent with the preservation of such a degree of efficiency as will make it equal to the objects of its institution.

With those who are in favor of abolishing the established system of exercises, various theories have been proposed with regard to a substitute. With some it has been a favorite theory, in dispensing with the trainings of the great mass of citizens, and preserving a mere enrolment, to embody annually, for a few weeks, small corps of the militia, for the purpose of making them good soldiers. The section under consideration proposes to dispense with the trainings without substituting a higher degree of discipline in a few corps. The theory in both cases is substantially the same; and it is conceived to be based upon a proposition, which is altogether erroneous in point of fact, viz: that the slight degree of training to which the great body of the militia is subjected is of no value.

This proposition mistakes altogether the proper uses of the militia, which are essentially different from those of a regular force in a state of war. The object of training is not to make every man a good soldier; for to the accomplishment of this object it would be necessary to sacrifice, in some degree, his character as a good citizen, by withdrawing him too long a time from his domestic occupations, and breaking up the habits of life which are best suited to the discharge of his civil duties. As has already been observed, the great object is to instruct every citizen so far in martial exercises in peace as to enable him to act in concert with his fellow-citizens if called on to maintain the authority of the laws, and to be at all times prepared to take the field and resist the shock of invasion until a more permanent force can be created, and a higher degree of military discipline attained. This object is secured, in most cases, by the existing system of exercises, limited as it is: with capable and spirited officers, it answers every purpose. There are several brigades of infantry, not uniformed, in the city of New York, which are in the habit of executing evolutions of the line with great promptitude and accuracy, and which are well prepared for acting with effect upon the most sudden emergency.

Some countenance has been given to the proposition under examination by an observation, which was not uncommon among the officers of the regular army during the late war, that an individual wholly untrained could sooner be brought to the perfection of a soldier than one who had been thoroughly trained in the militia. At that time the remark was, to a very considerable extent, true. The militia was trained according to Steuben's system of exercise, while the regular army was trained according to a modern system, adapted in its principles to the great changes which had been made in military science. A militia-man, thoroughly instructed in the former, had to unlearn what he had acquired before he was qualified for improving by the latter: both time and trouble were necessary to correct bad habits and eradicate erroneous impressions. But this difficulty cannot recur. A uniform system of tactics has been prepared with great care, and prescribed by Congress, both for the regular army and militia; and the books of instruction have been distributed within the

REPORT ON THE MILITIA SYSTEM.

last two years among the several States and territories, for the use of their militia. The exercises, words of command, and all the rules of discipline are precisely the same, so that the utmost degree of uniformity will be secured. A militia corps, brought suddenly into the field to act in conjunction with a regular force, is in no danger of being embarrassed by hearing movements directed which it does not understand, in language with which it is not familiar; but everything is regulated by the principles in which it has been instructed, and ordered in the same words of command by which it has already been trained. Thus, by closing up this fruitful source of embarrassment, the militia is not only rendered capable of executing the prescribed movements so as to accomplish the purposes of the common commander, but the very circumstance of understanding what is required to be performed inspires confidence, and makes the whole body more efficient in action. Every step which the militia-man takes under the established system, is a step towards the perfection of a soldier. Under this change of circumstances, to assert that an untrained individual can be made a good soldier in a shorter time than a militia-man, is as unwarrantable as it would be to say that an individual who has acquired the rudiments of any science requires a longer time to be brought to perfection in its higher branches than one who is totally ignorant of those rudiments; and there can be no better evidence of the utility of military exercises under the established system.

The theory of confiding the public defence to small bodies well trained, or, in other words, to volunteer corps, and of releasing the great body of the militia from all exercises, is liable to the objection of abandoning the fundamental principle of the system, independently of the difficulty of maintaining those corps upon principles consistent with the public safety, and justice to other classes of citizens. The instant a knowledge of military exercises is restricted to a few, the militia system will lose its distinctive character, which is that every citizen is a soldier; and the whole train of reasoning, which led to our present social organization, will by that very act be abandoned as erroneous. As long as the great body of the people are trained to arms, volunteer associations will be kept up; for as all must perform duty, many prefer to perform it by uniting with their friends and intimates, and forming separate corps. The release of the great body of the people from martial exercises will destroy this motive to the formation of volunteer corps. They must be kept up by exemptions or pecuniary rewards. The former are almost always unjust to a portion of the community. An exemption from jury duty, and a deduction from labor on highways, devolve an additional burden of labor and service on those who are left to perform it: the first is a personal tax upon a class, and the last a pecuniary tax upon property. But as personal exemptions are already nearly exhausted, for the encouragement of uniform corps, it would be necessary to have recourse to a direct compensation in money, which would be found to be exceedingly burdensome, or to exemptions from taxes, which are indirectly a compensation in money for the services performed. It can make but little difference in the result, whether a sum of money is paid to an individual for his military service, or whether, by exempting him from a tax, he is enabled to retain an equal sum already in his pocket. The operation of these causes is so modified now by the leading impulse to the formation of volunteer corps, which is to perform duty in bodies distinct from the general enrolment, that their tendencies may not be perceptible. But if the great body of the militia were to be exempt from military duty, the leading impulse would lie in the pecuniary rewards, which in some shape or other it would be necessary to create for the purpose of maintaining them. In times of emergency, private spirit and patriotism may be safely relied on as incentives to the performance of military duty, but it would be unsafe to trust to them in time of peace. All burdens are apt to seem unnecessary when their utility is either remote or contingent; and they will not for that reason, as a general rule, be voluntarily assumed. To expect volunteer corps to assume the whole burden of military duty without rewards, is to expect them to be actuated by a more liberal spirit towards the public than the public towards them. It would be necessary to create rewards, in order to preserve them; and the militia system would instantly cease to be (what was intended) an organization of the whole body of the people, trained to arms for the purpose of maintaining, against external and internal dangers, the public rights and their own. The creation of select bodies, compensated for their services in money, and distinguished from the mass of citizens by the exercise of those important functions which now devolve on all, would establish a precedent, from which the transition would be natural, if not inevitable, to corps more limited in numbers, on a more permanent footing, and with a higher compensation. The first effect of such a change in the established system would be to degrade uniform corps in character, to reduce their numbers, and to fill them with an inferior order of persons, by bringing their services to a pecuniary standard which would in the outset be a mere equivalent for the necessary expense of time and money, and therefore extremely low. A high standard of compensation, it is true, would always insure the proper character and spirit, but it would impose on the public a burden of pecuniary contribution more oppressive than that which is now borne in personal service. But however oppressive it might be, the necessity of such a standard would become apparent as the character and numbers of the volunteer corps should decline (for diminished numbers must be supplied by increased efficiency), and to reduce the burden of contribution so as to render it supportable, it would be necessary still further to diminish their numerical force, and to distribute the same money among a smaller number of persons. Our internal tranquillity and our security from external dangers would, therefore, be dependent on a few corps,

— a change utterly at variance with the fundamental principles of our political system; and the great body of citizens would be released from responsibilities the very sense of which, kept alive as it is by annual exercises, is among the highest conservative principles of our civil liberties.

To suppose that a body of officers, respectable for character or qualifications, could be preserved under such a system as is proposed by this section, supposes the absence of those qualities which lie at the foundation of all military improvement. There is no pursuit to which the spirit of pride is so essential as the military in time of peace, when its burdens are all present, and its rewards and benefits remote and contingent. No individual can be expected to meet the expenses of time, labor, and money incident to the tenure of a commission, without the opportunity of exercising command. The only reward of which he is certain, is the gratification of exhibiting the improvement of his subordinates to those who are able to put a proper estimate upon it. The pride of appearance and the pride of discipline are very nearly related; they have their origin in the same spirit of ambition; and anything which tends to degrade or mortify it is fatal to the improvement of which it is the source. If there were to be no company parades, and consequently no opportunity for company officers to exercise command, even for their own improvement; if the exhibition of their qualifications were to be limited to a regimental parade, when their men, for want of the previous preparation of a company training, would come together without a knowledge of the most simple evolutions, unorganized, and incapable of being reduced to order; in a word, if the officers were to be degraded into mere superintendents of undisciplined multitudes and registers of their delinquencies, it would be but reasonable to expect that the grade of intellect and character which would fill these places, hitherto of honorable trust, would speedily sink down to the level of the occupations annexed to them.

If the provisions of this section should be adopted, there is reason to apprehend that they would have the effect of destroying the uniform corps in the city of New York, as their privileges are not extended, while their exemptions are materially abridged. If their present privileges and exemptions are no more than an equivalent for the additional service required of them, any diminution of those privileges or exemptions, to be consistent with the preservation of the corps, should be attended with a corresponding diminution of their duties. This object does not appear to be attained by the proposed alterations. The parades of the militia not uniformed, in the city and county of New York, are three, — one by companies, and two by regiments or separate battalions. This section proposes to reduce them to one by regiments or battalions, relieving the privates of two thirds of the whole burden. The uniform corps do not participate in any degree in this reduction; and as the inducement to join them partly consists in their exemption from the duties thus reduced, the inducement is diminished in ratio of the reduction. If the inducement is already no more than sufficient to preserve them, any diminution would be fatal. That it is no more than sufficient, is apparent from the impossibility of keeping them up, so that they shall bear a uniform relation to population. Although the population of the city has increased during the last five years at the rate of nearly four and a half per cent. per annum, the increase of the uniform corps has been during the same period less than two per cent. per annum. While the population was increasing at a rate by which it would have doubled in about twenty-two years, the uniform corps were increasing at a rate by which they would not have doubled in less than fifty. Without creating additional inducements to join them, they would, instead of increasing, rapidly decline under the proposed reduction of their exemptions.

From the peculiar local situation of the city of New York, and from circumstances connected with its internal condition, the responsibilities and duties of the military corps, upon which its protection is dependent, are essentially superior to those of the corps in the interior of the State. However remote the chances of war may seem, a state of hostilities is to be guarded against by every possible precaution. The maintenance of a military establishment for the public defence assumes the necessity of employing it to be probable; and of every system of defence, a leading principle is to protect, with that part of its force best prepared to act on a sudden emergency, those points which are most exposed. Looking to external dangers only, the city, from its exposed situation, should be covered by a more numerous and better trained force than would be required if its position were more central. The arguments in favor of maintaining such a force, drawn from a view of its internal condition, are not less powerful and convincing. The continued extension of its commercial operations for a series of years has made it a depot for the productions of a vast interior, which are intended for exportation; and having acquired the character of a general mart, by far the greater part of the productions of foreign countries received in return are imported into the city for general distribution. The extent of these operations, and the vast accumulation of wealth attendant upon them, may be estimated from the fact that two thirds of the whole impost revenue of the United States is collected at its custom-house. If a sudden blow should ever be struck by an enemy, it would naturally be directed to that point where it would fall with the most destructive effects. But the danger from abroad is not the only one which is incident to this ascendency in commerce. Wherever great wealth is accumulated, are sure to be found those vices which seek an unlawful sustenance by preying upon it. It is well known that great numbers of persons without visible occupations have their habitations within the city; and the detection of crimes has more than once led to the exposure of organized bands of marauders, depredating under the cover of secrecy upon the property of the citizens. The dangers to be apprehended from riots and resistance of the public authorities are much increased by the presence of such an abandoned class of transient persons. That these elements of disorder have not led ere this to far more serious evils, is perhaps to be ascribed to the restraint of a numerous and well-trained volunteer force, capable of being arrayed at a moment's warning in defence of the lives and property of the citizens. If the city of Providence, with comparatively few sources of disorder, should be disturbed by a riot, which was not quelled without a military force and a loss of lives, how much greater cause is there for apprehension in the city of New York, where the temptations and facilities exist in a much higher proportion! That it would be dangerous to trust to the municipal police to maintain the public tranquillity, is apparent from the fact that portions of the volunteer force have several times within a few years been held in readiness to quell anticipated disorders, to the suppression of which the police was avowedly incompetent. In this view, indeed, the uniform corps of the city may be regarded as a part of the municipal police, and in times of emergency by far the most efficient part. The destruction of these corps, therefore, would expose the vast wealth of the city to depredation, and the public order to scenes of violence and confusion; and it is to be apprehended that they would not only rapidly decline, but in the end be totally disorganized under the proposed reduction of the duties of the ununiformed militia, unless further privileges are extended to them. The difficulty of creating such privileges, consistently with a proper regard for the rights of other classes, and with the preservation of the spirit of those corps, has already been glanced at; but a wise policy would suggest that an additional inducement to join them should in some manner be provided simultaneously with the reduction, in order to guard against its consequences.

There is another consideration connected with the proposed

reduction of trainings under this section, which ought not to be overlooked. One of the privileges of the members of the city fire companies is an exemption from the performance of military duty; and it has had its share in keeping up their complement of high-spirited and adventurous members. It is not contended that militia trainings, if they are unnecessary, should be continued for the purpose of preserving these companies, however important their services to the possessors of property. Their maintenance being exclusively for the benefit of property, property should in strictness pay the expense of their maintenance. If the existing burden of militia duty were useless, therefore, the argument in favor of continuing it for the preservation of the fire companies would have no force. But as the burden is necessary for the higher purposes of the public defence and the civil order, the argument against discontinuing it derives additional force from its influence upon those companies. The performance of military duty being exacted during a certain period of time from all classes with a few exceptions, without a reference to numbers, the exemption of firemen devolves no additional burden upon any other class. In this respect it differs materially in principle and in operation from their exemption from jury duty. A certain number of jurymen being required annually, and being selected from a certain class of citizens, the exemption of firemen from that duty diminishes the number from which the selection is made, and thereby devolves an additional burden on the diminished number. This exemption is a privilege, which is purchased by a poll-tax paid by a certain class of citizens for the protection of property. It is possible that the increased burden may be so light that the pressure is not very perceptible; but the lightness of the burden does not affect the principle. If the performance of militia duty were useless, it would come within the same principle, and with a force proportioned to the greater number of those who perform the service; but being necessary, it is not liable to the same objection. The ques-

REPORT ON THE MILITIA SYSTEM. 161

tion presented in the proposition to reduce military parades is, whether a necessary burden shall be discontinued, with the effect, among others, of disorganizing a body of men upon whose exertions the safety of an immense property depends. It might be added, also, with the further effect of rendering necessary a resort to measures objectionable in principle; for if the proposed reduction of the number of parades be adopted, some further personal exemption would be necessary to countervail its operation. It is believed that a pecuniary compensation would not accomplish the object; that the spirit, which constantly leads the members of those companies to encounter the most imminent dangers and sometimes to sacrifice their lives in the performance of their duties, is not to be purchased by pecuniary rewards; that their places would be filled, as has been said of uniform corps, by an inferior order of persons the moment their services were to be estimated by a mercenary standard; that the companies would become less efficient, property be less secure, and the rates of insurance rise in proportion. To guard against these evils, it would be necessary to create additional personal exemptions, and the burden of these would fall unequally upon certain classes of the community. While the present parades of the militia are continued, such a resort will probably be unnecessary, although there is some difficulty now in keeping up the requisite number. If this section should be adopted, it would be necessary that some provision should be made at the same time for the preservation of these vigilant and enterprising guardians of the public wealth.

It is one of the consequences of the compactness of a city population, although its condition is such as to require a more efficient force for its protection from internal, and sometimes from external dangers, that such a force may be prepared without devolving on it a greater burden than that which is sustained by a country population in preparing a less efficient force. In the interior the beat of a company often includes several square miles, and a regiment frequently comprises several towns within its beat. To attend the company parade, its members are therefore compelled to travel three or four miles; and to attend the regimental parade, six and eight miles, and sometimes fifteen or twenty. The members of city corps, on the other hand, meet almost at their own doors both for company and regimental trainings. Their attendance is required during fewer hours; they lose no time in travelling; and they incur no expense in procuring meals away from home. The three parades of the city corps are for these reasons far less burdensome than the two parades in the country. The higher responsibilities which devolve on them, and the greater necessity of maintaining a vigorous tone of preparation, are all met with less sacrifice of time, money, and personal service.

The parades in the country, although comparatively more burdensome than in the city, are not essentially so much so as at first glance might be supposed. For the privates, with the exception of a few counties, in which population is thin and considerable distances are to be travelled to the place of rendezvous, only two days are required for martial exercises. The great body of the people are liable to the performance of military duty during the term of twenty-seven years, (from eighteen to forty-five years of age,) making in all fifty-four days consumed in preparing them for the discharge of the highest duties that can devolve on freemen, — the protection of their lives and property from external dangers, the preservation of the public order, and the maintenance of a system of government which they have themselves constituted and which they are constantly directing, through the control exercised over it by the right of suffrage, to the promotion of the general good. There is no other people on whom so slight a burden of military contribution is imposed for the public defence alone; nor is there any other who are charged with the execution of such elevated civil functions. The days devoted to martial exercises have their advantages in other respects also: they afford relaxations from the labors and business of life,—relaxations which, if those exercises were abandoned, might be sought for by a considerable portion of those who perform military duty in occasions of less utility to themselves. The regimental meetings in the country are, by a great many of those who are required to attend them, made subservient to the purposes of business and of social communications with their acquaintances and friends in adjacent towns, so that they are looked upon, as a general rule, without vexation or regret.

It has been common, with a view to show the oppressive character of the militia parades, to estimate in money the value of the days consumed in them, and exhibit the aggregate amount as a public loss. This is obviously an unfair method of computation. In the country, most persons by timely arrangement, which the legal notice of the trainings enables them to make, may so dispose of their business as to spare a day or two annually without any considerable sacrifice. There are few occasions of public festivity that would not be likely to be as numerously attended as a militia training. Indeed, the trainings themselves are generally attended by large numbers of those who have become exempt by serving out the prescribed period in the ununiformed militia or in volunteer corps. But even admitting that a pecuniary estimate of the value of the days consumed in military exercises is a proper criterion of the pressure of the service on those who perform it, the question will still recur whether the service is necessary. If it be, any argument drawn from the pressure of the system will be overruled by the necessity of maintaining it. Otherwise, a similar estimate would be fatal to every institution connected with the performance of our civil duties. The number of days lost in attendance upon juries for the purpose of distributing justice between man and man, and the time consumed in exercising the right of suffrage, might be made the subject of pecuniary computation to prove, in one case, the utility of confiding the decision of disputed questions of right to the judges without the intervention of a jury and of electing public officers, in the other, for a longer period of time, in order to guard against the frequent recurrence of days of election. The objects of maintaining a military establishment are not less important than these; for what would avail an impartial administration of justice or a careful delegation of political power, if that security from external invasion and internal disorders, which is the very essence of our public prosperity, were not provided for by an efficient system of military preparation, upon principles consistent with the preservation of our civil liberties? After all, the necessity of the burden is the only standard by which the performance of military duty should be settled; and this has already been sufficiently considered in other parts of this report.

"SECTION III. Every non-commissioned officer, musician, and private of any uniformed company or troop, who shall uniform and equip himself, and whose term of service in any such company or troop shall amount to ten years from the time of his enrolment therein, shall be exempt from military duty, except in case of insurrection or invasion."

With the exception of the members of certain corps specially provided for, the present law exempts from military duty non-commissioned officers, musicians, and privates, who have served in uniform companies during the term of fifteen years. This section proposes to reduce the term of service to ten years. If the provisions of section second were to be adopted, and the parades of the militia not uniformed were to be reduced to one, such a reduction in the term of service of uniform corps would be necessary to their preservation. But if the provisions of section second should not be adopted, section third ought not to be, as the inducements to the formation of uniform corps are sufficient under the existing law with the present term of service. It is presumed that this was the view of the framers of the bill, as the duties of uniform corps are voluntary, and therefore that the proposed

REPORT ON THE MILITIA SYSTEM. 165

reduction was not intended to relieve them of a burden, but to provide for their preservation.

"SECTION IV. So much of the second section of the tenth Title of Chapter ten of the first part of the Revised Statutes as requires the commissioned and non-commissioned officers of any company or troop which is not uniformed, to meet for military improvement more than four times in any year is hereby repealed, and they shall hereafter be required to meet only four times in each year."

This section reduces the number of meetings from eight to four, and is applicable only to the officers and non-commissioned officers of infantry in the city of New York. If the parades of the privates should be reduced to one, the parades of the officers and non-commissioned officers should be reduced as proposed. With regard to the latter it would be no more than just; and with regard to the former it could not be expected, otherwise, that there would be any candidates for commissions, when the inducements to accept them are so much diminished. Indeed, it is doubtful whether, with the proposed reduction, there would be any respectable candidates for commissions if section second should be adopted, for the reasons already assigned in the examination of that section. If section second should not be adopted, this section should not be. Although the duties of officers may seem onerous, there is no complaint from them. They are not compelled to accept commissions: their service is perfectly voluntary; and it is but just to them to say that their duties are, as a general rule, performed with spirit and with a proper sense of their responsibility.

"SECTION V. All persons residing in this State, who may be averse to bearing arms from conscientious scruples, not otherwise exempt by law, may be free from all military requisitions in time of peace, by complying with the following terms: every such person, on paying the sum of two dollars to the trustees of common schools in the district in which he may reside, for the benefit of common schools, in lieu of all other military requisitions and commutations in time of peace: *Provided*, That, on or before the first Monday of June, in each and every year, he produces to the commanding officer of companies, in whose beat he may reside, a certificate, signed by two of the trustees of common schools in his district, that he has actually complied with the provisions of this act."

The constitution of the State of New York (art. 7, sec. 5) provides that "all such inhabitants of this State, of any religious denomination whatever, as from scruples of conscience may be averse to bearing arms, shall be excused therefrom by paying to the State an equivalent in money; and the legislature shall provide by law for the collection of such equivalent, to be estimated according to the expense, in time and money, of an able-bodied militia-man."

The existing militia law has already provided for these cases, and the only points in which the 5th section of the bill under consideration differs from it, are: 1st. In requiring a certificate to be produced by the person commuting to the captain of the company within the beat of which he resides, on or before the first Monday of June, that the contribution has actually been paid to the trustees of common schools. Under the existing law, a notice of an intention to commute is required to be given to the captain of the company, on or before the first day of April, and a list of all such notices is furnished by him, through an assessor, to the supervisor of the town, and the money is collected of the persons by whom the notices are given. 2d. It fixes the commutation at two dollars instead of four; and 3d. It applies the proceeds to a specific object, instead of being paid into the county treasury for general purposes.

1st. No reason is perceived why the change in the mode of payment should be made. In one case the commutation is paid to the assessor, on application to the individual who has given notice of his intention to commute, and in the other it is the duty of the individual himself to seek the trustees of common schools, and make the payment. The proposed mode would be more inconvenient to those who are affected by it, and it is not perceived that anything would be gained by the public. If a person having conscientious scruples fails to give notice of his intention to commute under the existing law, he is summoned before a court-martial, and a fine is imposed on him to the amount of the commutation. With the proposed change, the result would be the same, if he should fail to make payment and produce a certificate from the trustees of common schools, as that part of the militia law is not repealed by this section. It is recommended, therefore, that the mode of payment should be the same.

2d. In fixing the commutation, the only question is, what is an equivalent for the annual expense, in time and money, of attending the established parades according to law. The estimate being once made, and the amount fixed by the legislature, the constitution leaves no power to augment it from considerations of policy, or to diminish it from motives of indulgence.

It is to be observed that the relief provided by this section for persons having conscientious scruples is not only an exemption from the parades required by law, but from the expense of arming and equipping. In this view, the proposed contribution does not appear commensurate with the exemption for which it is exchanged. The parades of the infantry not uniformed, in the interior of the State, are two, and the fine usually imposed for non-appearance without excuse, seven dollars. Fines are not intended as a commutation for the service for the non-performance of which they are imposed. The object in imposing them is to secure the performance of the service, and not to secure to the public an equivalent. They are, therefore, as a general rule, more than equivalent: if they were not so, they would not accomplish the purpose for which they are intended. Seven dollars per annum is obviously more than an equivalent for the two days' service, and that portion of the expense of arming and equipping which would fall to each year of enrolment. But the sum to be paid by the persons proposed to be relieved by this section should, in the absence of any constitutional provision, be as nearly as possible an equivalent, the very foundation of the relief being an equal contribution to some other object of public utility. The expense of arming and equipping is not far from twelve dollars; and during the twenty-seven years' service required by law there would be, on an average, a deterioration of fifty per cent. in the arms and equipments.

The two days' service required annually may be estimated at..	$1.50
Interest on twelve dollars, the expense of arming and equipping, ...	84
Deterioration of arms and equipments, ...	22
Expense of attending two parades, (average 25 cents each,)...	50
	$3.06

Three dollars would, if this estimate be correct, not be far from a fair equivalent for the exemption.

3d. To render the exemption complete, the application of commutation moneys should have no reference to objects connected with the performance of military duty; under the existing law they are not so applied. They are paid into the county treasury for general purposes, excepting particular cases, in which they go to the benefit of the poor of the county. Under the proposed alteration they would be applied to the use of common schools, thereby affording to persons having conscientious scruples a perfect security against a possible appropriation of any portion of their contribution to military objects. No reason is perceived why this indulgence may not with propriety be extended to them. It is conceived, however, that the appropriation of commutation moneys to the use of the common schools of the district within which the persons paying them reside is objectionable on the score of its inequality, as those districts which comprise within their limits societies having conscientious scruples would be unduly benefited by such a provision. The exemption is from a burden which is borne by the whole community; and it would be proper that the equivalent should be distributed as equally as possible for the general benefit. It is, therefore, recommended that commutation moneys shall be collected as they are under the existing law, and paid into the treasury of the State, to be passed to the credit of the common-school fund. If this proposition be accepted, the only change required in the existing law would be a reduction of the amount of the equivalent to be paid from four dollars to three.

"SECTION VI. No person shall hereafter be imprisoned for the non-payment of any military fine imposed for not appearing at any parade, or for not being equipped according to law."

For the reasons assigned in the examination of section twelfth of the first bill under consideration, it is recommended that the exemption from imprisonment for non-payment of military fines should be limited to those cases in which fines are imposed "for not being equipped occording to law."

As the result of the foregoing examination of the bill entitled "An act to amend the tenth chapter of the first part of the Revised Statutes relating to the militia and the public defence," it is recommended that section first should be adopted, excepting so far as it proposes to subject students at colleges and academies to military duty; that, instead of section fifth, the existing law, with regard to persons having conscientious scruples against bearing arms, should be amended so as to fix the equivalent in money at three dollars instead of four, and to require it to be paid into the treasury of the State, to the credit of the common-school fund; that section sixth should be adopted with the exception of that part which relates to fines imposed for non-appearance at parades; and that all the remaining sections and provisions should be rejected as incompatible with the objects for which the militia system is maintained.

Having thus discharged the duty assigned to him by examining the specific provisions of the bills referred, any further examination of the subject by the Adjutant-General may possibly be considered as an unauthorized interference with matters not submitted for his opinion. He ventures, however, to trust to the indulgence of the Senate, for suggesting what he understands to be the true causes of discontent in relation to the existing militia law, and for pointing out what he conceives to be the proper remedies. He has been the more strongly incited to this course, as he has felt it his duty to report unfavorably upon the main provisions of the two bills referred to him, and is therefore anxious to guard against the inference, which his silence might authorize, that he considers the militia system susceptible of no improvement. His objection to those bills is, that, without reaching the real defects of the system, they provide for alterations which would be altogether destructive of its usefulness. He regards the militia law of this State, setting aside a few inconsiderable defects, as superior to any other which he has examined; and he is not aware of any very material alterations, with one exception, which can be introduced without exceeding the just limits of the authority of the State over the subject. At the same time, he conceives that material improvements of the system, under the powers of Congress, are not only practicable, but necessary.

If the views presented in the foregoing examination be just, the exercises of the militia are reduced to the lowest standard consistent with the preservation of a proper degree of efficiency. But, although a less efficient militia might not answer the purposes of its institution, it is conceived that a less numerous force would be fully adequate to those purposes; that the burden of military duty may be lightened consistently with all the ends which the system is intended to secure, by an abridgment of the period during which military duty is required to be performed, and consequently by a reduction of the number of persons liable to perform it. The power of Congress to provide for the organization of the militia includes the right to specify the extent of the enrolment; and by the law of 1792, all free able-bodied white male citizens, between the ages of eighteen and forty-five years, are required to be enrolled. Although the condition of the country at that period rendered it indispensable to carry the enrolment to so great an extent, no such necessity is apparent in its present condition. At the period referred to, the Federal government had hardly gone into operation, and it was difficult to foresee, in the unsettled state of the Union during the ten or twelve years subsequent to the acknowledgment of our independence, what degree of preparation might not be necessary against internal commotions. Our western frontiers were exposed to the incursions of numerous tribes of Indians, who had been stirred up by recent contests to the most fierce and vindictive animosities. Some of our fortresses were still in the possession of Great Britain, who, under the pretence of securing the adjustment of disputed questions, refused to surrender them. All these circumstances rendered not only an efficient force necessary, but a general enrolment for the purpose of securing, as far as possible, at every point a proper preparation against the dangers to which it was exposed. The scarcity of population in proportion to territorial extent would alone have required so extensive a preparation. Even with the prescribed organization, an adequate protection could not be secured, excepting at a few points along the coast, without resorting to the military force of remote districts. All these sources of danger are partially, and some of them entirely, closed up. The harmonious action of the Federal and State authorities, the extension of our settlements in the west, the vast increase of our physical power in population, wealth, and facilities of internal communication, the construction of extensive fortresses upon the vulnerable points along our coast, and the moral influence of all these causes combined upon other countries, have obviously diminished the necessity of maintaining a force regularly increasing in ratio of our increasing numbers. The rule of enrolment under the law of 1792 being founded upon age, the numerical force of the militia must always bear nearly the same relation to population. An estimate of our dangers, founded upon a careful survey of our condition, makes no longer a part of the standard by which the numerical force of the militia is determined; whereas the only true criterion is conceived to consist in such an estimate. It is our change of condition which has rendered false and oppressive in its application a standard which was just when it was originally assumed. The cause of the difficulty has not been generally perceived; and it is for this reason that the authority of the State has been arraigned for the existence, and appealed to for the redress, of evils which have their origin in the laws of Congress, and which must derive their remedies from the same source. It is due to the State that the responsibility should be made to rest where it belongs, and the just claim which the public has to be relieved from so much of the burden as is unnecessary should be addressed to the authority which is alone competent to provide the required relief. If, as has been supposed, the true ground of discontent is, that a numerous class is subjected to military duty who might be exempt without diminishing the general strength or security, and without casting an additional burden upon the remaining classes, the true remedy for the evil is in a modification of the law of 1792, which Congress alone can alter or annul.

One of the advantages of this mode of relieving the people of a portion of the burden is, that it would maintain unimpaired all the principles upon which the militia system is founded. If the period of liability to the performance of military duty were reduced from twenty-seven years to fourteen, by taking its commencement at the age of twenty-one instead of eighteen, and its termination at thirty-five instead of forty-five, the result would still be to put every citizen through fourteen years of military exercise and discipline, which would be sufficient to prepare him for usefulness in case of insurrection or invasion, while the burden of military duty would be diminished nearly one half, and a force sufficiently numerous for all the purposes of the government would still be maintained. By exempting the whole body of the militia, as proposed by the bills which have been examined, from a portion of their burden, the efficiency of the system would be destroyed; whereas, by exempting a portion of the militia from the whole burden, we may preserve its efficiency, and maintain a force fully adequate to our necessities. In either case the aggregate relief is nearly the same.

By maintaining the present organization in all other respects, a larger force, should it be required, might be prepared at once by merely extending the enrolment to ages either above or below, or both above and below, the existing limitation. Thus, in case of hostilities, there would be nothing to create anew, and the transition from peace to war would be accomplished without the confusion and delay inseparable from the necessity of organizing a system at the very moment when it should be put in operation. In the Southern States, where, from the nature of their population, the sources of internal danger are more numerous, the necessary provision against them might be made by keeping up, at their discretion, in time of peace, a more extended enrolment.

It will be observed that the enrolment above suggested proposes to exempt all minors from the performance of military duty in time of peace, by limiting the commencement of the enrolment to the age of twenty-one years; and it is believed that the rule is founded upon principles the justice of which cannot be drawn into controversy. The personal service which a government may properly demand in all cases of those who live under its protection, is conceived to be due from such only as are admitted to a full participation in its benefits. Minors are excluded from some of the highest functions and privileges of citizenship, particularly from the exercise of the right of suffrage, and from eligibility to office; and by reason of this exclusion they are denied all influence over the measures of government. The law treats them as infants with regard to the most important franchises of citizens; and it is worthy of reflection whether it should treat them as citizens with regard to services. If it be a principle that burdens and benefits shall be proportioned to each other, it would seem proper that the exclusion in this case should be attended by the exemption suggested. Occasions of extraordinary emergency may properly be considered as exceptions to the rule. In times of public danger, when the lives and property of all are in some degree at hazard, the country has a right to the services of all who are capable of rendering service. It is conceived, too, that the relations of parent and child, guardian and ward, and master and apprentice, should be disturbed only in extreme cases. The effect of subjecting minors to military duty, is to withdraw them, for the time being, from the control of those whom the law holds responsible for them. This is to insist on a responsibility, and at the same time to deprive the responsible person of the power of providing against its consequences. Nothing can well be fancied which is more oppressive than to levy upon the property of a master a fine imposed upon an apprentice for insubordinate and disorderly conduct on a day of martial exercise, when the latter is withdrawn from his control. Another oppressive effect of the liability of minors to military duty is the unequal burden which it imposes. A master, with half a dozen apprentices between the ages of eighteen and twenty-one years, bears the burden of seven persons, while he only enjoys the political privileges of a single one. It is not uncommon for a farmer in the country to have two sons between the ages of eighteen and twenty-one years, before he has himself attained the age of forty-five. He is consequently compelled to equip and perform the duty of three persons. Independently, therefore, of the principle involved, the practical inconveniences of this part of the system are too burdensome and unequal to be continued in time of peace.

It may be suggested that an exemption from military duty at that period of life when the stimulus to perform it is greatest, would seriously impair the spirit of the militia. Without insisting upon the principle of the exemption, it is to be considered that the greater part of the young men of military spirit, who become liable to perform duty, immediately unite themselves to uniform corps, and in a great many instances, under the present law, before they have attained the age of eighteen years. This early commencement of their military service is to be traced to the provision of the existing law, which exempts them after fifteen years' service. To them it can be of no consequence whether their term of service commences at an earlier or later period. By continuing this provision, with such a reduction of the term as to preserve the same relation which it now bears to the general enrolment, the same object will be secured, as far as it can be without injustice. Young men will commence their service at the period when the impulse is strongest, if they can procure the consent of their natural or legal protectors; so that many of those who are fitted to add to the spirit of the military establishment may still be preserved. Those only will be excluded who cannot obtain the requisite consent; and without it military service, for the reasons assigned, ought not to be exacted by the government.

The relief which would be afforded by the suggested diminution of the period of enrolment will appear from the following estimate. According to the census of this State for the year 1820, the males between the ages of eighteen and forty-five years were about one fifth of the whole population, and of these about one half were enrolled. About one fourteenth part of the whole population were males between the ages of eighteen and twenty-one, and thirty-five and forty-five; and it is estimated, for exact certainty is not to be attained, that the same proportion of these were enrolled. Assuming this as the basis of the estimate, the military force of the State in the year 1830 should have been 191,000, (which is about the real number,) the population according to the late census being 1,919,404 souls. Of this number about one fourteenth part would be within the ages proposed to be excluded by the new enrolment, and, assuming that one half only are enrolled, this would be a deduction of about 70,000 persons from the aggregate military force, which would be reduced to 120,000. This estimate is not, perhaps, strictly accurate, but the result will not differ materially from it. Seventy thousand persons, therefore, would be relieved of the burden of military duty, by adopting the proposed alteration in the established period of enrolment, and more than one third of the whole burden would be removed.

There is another burden imposed by the law of 1792, which is far more onerous than the burden of personal service, and it is the more oppressive, as it is conceived to be wrong in principle. By the provisions of that law, every person liable to do military duty is required to provide himself with a musket and equipments, the price of which is not less than twelve dollars. The effect of these provisions is to impose on all who perform military duty, in addition to the personal service required of them, a capitation tax to that amount. The inequality of this requisition is exceedingly oppressive, falling as it does without distinction upon those who are worth but one hundred dollars, and those who are worth one hundred thousand; and so generally has it been evaded by borrowing and hiring arms and equipments, that probably not one half of the militia of this State is armed and equipped in good faith, according to law. This fact alone shows the propriety of a different provision. The services which citizens owe to their government are twofold, personal and pecuniary. The first is, from its nature, not susceptible of apportionment between individuals, but must be rendered equally by all. The second is apportioned upon the basis of property, and is, therefore, paid unequally by those on whom it is imposed, by reason of the unequal value of their respective possessions. The military duty required of all within certain ages, comes within the rule of the first; and the right to exact it on principles of justice cannot be disputed. But when an individual is called on to provide

REPORT ON THE MILITIA SYSTEM. 177

instruments of offence, he is required to render a pecuniary service, which, to be just, should be in ratio of his property. There is a violation of one of the first principles of political justice in imposing the burden, without discrimination, upon all. The right of the government to compel a portion of the militia to organize as artillery is as perfect as the right to require them to organize as infantry. Nor is any reason perceived why it may not, with the same propriety, compel each company of artillery to provide a piece of cannon, without which its services would be of no avail, as to compel each company of infantry to provide the muskets and equipments, without which its services would be unavailing. The injustice of the imposition lies in the circumstance of founding it upon the basis of personal service, instead of pecuniary contribution. The truth of this position is conceded by an act of Congress, passed the 23d April, 1808, entitled "An act to provide for arming and equipping the whole body of the militia of the United States," and intended to remedy the unequal operation of the law of 1792. But although the injustice of the requisitions of this law is admitted, the provisions of the law of 1808 are altogether inadequate to the object intended to be accomplished, and further legislation by Congress is necessary to provide a remedy for the former. Congress alone has power, under the Constitution of the United States, to provide for arming the militia, and it is a step towards its execution to admit, as the law of 1808 does, that it is not executed by requiring every citizen liable to military duty to arm himself. The accomplishment of the object will require time, and there may be some difficulty in arranging the details of the system; but it is considered both practicable and within the compass of our public resources. The difficulty attending it, however great it may be, is no argument against its adoption, if the present mode is wrong in principle and oppressive in its application.

Bills providing substantially for the improvements in the militia system above suggested, have heretofore been submitted to Congress; and to secure their adoption, it is believed only to be necessary that it should be urged by the united efforts of some of the principal States. A more favorable period than the present has, perhaps, never before been presented. The subject has already attracted the attention of the able and enlightened chief of the War Department, and has been recommended to the consideration of Congress. The legislature of Massachusetts, at their last session, declined acting upon a bill providing for essential alterations in the militia system of that State, under the expectation that it would be acted on by Congress, and that the necessary remedies would be provided for its prevailing defects throughout the Union; having become convinced, after mature consideration, that the paramount powers of Congress over it opposed an insuperable barrier to the action of State legislation upon it to such an extent as to accomplish the desired objects; that it was difficult even to break down the system, much more to remedy its deficiencies, so long as the law of 1792 continues in force. It is understood that the State of Virginia, under the impulse of a recent disturbance, has also turned her attention to the subject, and with an earnestness proportioned to the extent of that calamity. The coöperation of the State of New York with those two States, the earliest and the most efficient agents in organizing and putting in operation the political institutions of which the militia is an essential part, could hardly fail to secure the introduction of the proposed amendments.

The acknowledged defects of the present militia system, and the dissatisfaction which they have produced, indicate the propriety of providing a remedy for them at the earliest possible day, independently of the injustice of continuing burdens which may be dispensed with consistently with the public good. It is one of the ill effects of all abuse, that the just discontent which it creates is apt to degenerate into a prejudice against the institutions with which the abuse is connected, by confounding that which is useful with that which is unnecessary and oppressive. The most ready and effectual mode of reëstablishing the system in the public confidence, is to correct its defects, and thus insure a general assent to its importance in its amended form. It is, therefore, earnestly to be hoped that an application may be addressed to the proper authority, under such circumstances as to render its success speedy and certain. Nothing could be more animating to the enemies of liberal government than to behold the people of the United States, under the influence of inconsiderable evils, voluntarily laying aside their arms, and declining to prepare themselves by exercise and discipline for the preservation of social institutions and privileges which their ancestors purchased with years of suffering and a profuse expenditure of treasure and blood. No other event, it is conceived, would furnish evidence so conclusive of the decline of that moral spirit in the people upon which our public liberties are dependent.

As a final observation, it may be remarked, that, by impairing the efficiency of the militia, the strongest argument is furnished in favor of increasing the regular army. Whenever it shall become apparent that the former is inadequate to the public defence, — a period which may be indefinitely postponed by a continuance of martial exercises, — the whole responsibility of maintaining the public order must be confided to regular troops, in the pay and under the control of the central government. Under such circumstances, the close of a war would no longer be a signal for disbanding the army employed in carrying it on; but it would be kept up as a provision both against internal and external dangers. Without reference to the incompatibility of this order of things with the great principles of our political system, the vast expense of such a military preparation would be a constant drain upon our public wealth, and impair our ability to meet future exigencies, by diverting our resources from the higher and more beneficial purposes of improving our internal condition. In a word, it is only under the protection of the militia system that the country is enabled, at the termination of every contest, to lay aside the more massive and burdensome parts of its armor, and to become prepared, with energies renewed by that very capacity, for succeeding scenes of danger.

Respectfully submitted,

JOHN A. DIX,
Adjt. Gen.

GEOLOGICAL REPORT.

The following Report was the basis of the examination which has given to the State of New York the full account of its natural history contained in the series of publications commenced in the year 1837 and continued through a period of nearly a quarter of a century. The results of this examination are embodied in the final report known as the "Natural History of New York."

STATE OF NEW YORK,
SECRETARY'S OFFICE.
Albany, January 6, 1836.

TO THE LEGISLATURE. — By a resolution of the Assembly, bearing date the 18th of April, 1835, the Secretary of State was "requested to report to the Legislature, at its next session, the most expedient method of obtaining a complete geological survey of the State, which shall furnish a scientific and perfect account of its rocks, soils, and minerals, and of their localities; a list of all its mineralogical, botanical, and zoölogical productions, and provide for procuring and preserving specimens of the same; together with an estimate of the expenses which may attend the prosecution of the design, and of the cost of publication of an edition of three thousand copies of the report, drawings, and geological map of its results."

In pursuance of the request contained in the foregoing resolution, the Secretary of State has the honor to present the following Report: —

In submitting to the Legislature a plan for the execution of the work contemplated by the resolution, he has not considered himself called on to enter into a detail of the advantages to be anticipated from its accomplishment, excepting so far as they may be incidentally discussed in delineating the plan referred to. Although the undertaking has not been authorized by law, the passage of the resolution presupposes the adoption, at a proper time, of the necessary legislative provision to that effect. His duty is, therefore, plainly limited to the suggestion of the measures best adapted to secure the objects of the survey; but in the performance of this duty, a reference to the importance of the various subjects of investigation will be indispensable.

In presenting to the Legislature such suggestions as occur to him, he will have frequent occasion to refer to opinions and statements of facts connected with the geological formations of this State and of other countries. In doing so, it is his intention to specify, in every case, the authority on which such statement or opinion is advanced; and for greater convenience, the authority will be named at the bottom of the page on which the reference is made. This course seems proper, not only for the purpose of doing justice to the individuals themselves, by pointing to the sources where their views are to be found in a more extended shape, but for the convenience of those who may be selected to execute the survey, should the Legislature direct its execution.

It is proper to state, that, soon after the adjournment of the Legislature, the Secretary of State addressed a circular letter containing a copy of the resolution of the Assembly, to a large number of scientific gentlemen in different parts of the country, requesting the communication of their views in relation to the proposed survey. From seven of those gentlemen answers were received, containing many valuable suggestions. But as in most of the cases their answers were not designed for publication, he has been constrained to resist the desire which he felt to annex copies of them to this report; being unwilling, on the one hand, to communicate to the Legislature a part of them only, and feeling not at liberty, on the other hand, to make that disposition of the rest. Should the survey be authorized by the Legislature, these answers will be put into the hands of the gentlemen who shall be appointed to execute it, that they may have the benefit of such of the suggestions contained in them as have not been adopted in this report.

At the end of the report will be found a list of publications, containing articles on the geology, mineralogy, zoölogy, and botany of this State, with the numbers of the volumes and the pages in which they occur. For this list, which has been of great service to him, the Secretary of State is indebted to a gentleman distinguished for scientific acquirements, who has devoted much attention to the subjects referred to.

The objects in contemplation of the proposed survey are economical, or such as relate to practical purposes; and scientific, or such as concern the interests of science.

That part of the survey which proposes to furnish a scientific and perfect account of the rocks, soils, and minerals of the State, embraces within its scope both the classes of objects referred to. A scientific and perfect account of our rocks, by explaining the nature of the substances of which they are composed, their distinguishing qualities, and the changes to which they are liable from the action of natural or artificial agents, will indicate the uses for which they are respectively fitted. A similar account of our soils may come strongly in aid of the agricultural experience of the State, and form, in combination with the latter, the basis of a system of husbandry adapted to all their varieties, and thus add in an eminent degree to their productiveness. In the same manner the mineral treasures of the State may become better known, their uses understood, and their value appreciated.

So far as it is proposed to furnish a list of the mineralogical, botanical, and zoölogical productions of the State, and to preserve specimens of each, the objects in view are principally scientific, although in this case, as in the other, substances hitherto unobserved in this State may, in the effort to make this list complete, be discovered and brought into profitable use. Nor ought it to be overlooked that these specimens, properly arranged, where they shall be open to the inspection of all the citizens, and indicating at all times the objects to which their labor and capital may be advantageously applied, cannot be without some practical benefits.

Under whatever aspect the work may be regarded, it is certainly one of great importance; and if it be executed in a manner corresponding with the magnitude of the design, it cannot fail to be in a high degree beneficial to the productive industry, and in an equal degree creditable to the liberal and enlightened character of the State. In the practical utility of the work, however, lies the principal motive to undertake it. It deserves, therefore, to be considered in what manner it may be made to minister to the general wealth, and thus compensate for the large expenditure which will be necessarily involved in its execution. For this purpose, the various subjects of examination will be taken up in the order in which they are presented in the resolution, and some suggestions with regard to each will be made, with a view to indicate, as far as practicable, the objects to be kept in view by those who may be chosen to execute the work. In attempting to discharge this duty, the Secretary of State cannot forbear to express his regret that it had not been assigned by the Assembly to some one more capable than himself of performing it in a manner commensurate with its importance.

ROCKS.

Although the entire mineralogical constitution of the State has never been systematically investigated, enough has been ascertained to show that no section of the country of equal extent contains a greater variety of valuable rocks. The marbles of Westchester county, and the limestones of Onondaga, Cayuga, Jefferson, and many other counties are extensively employed for various objects; and it is believed that nothing is wanting to bring into use others of equal value but to point out their localities, and subject them to such tests as may indicate the purposes for which they are best fitted. The researches which have been made into the geological formation of particular sections of the State have been few and partial, and any idea of the nature or extent of our mineral resources, founded upon those researches, must be very imperfect. At the same time it may be well to advert briefly to some of the observations which have been made with respect to such of our rocks as would, if on a more critical examination they should be found of the proper quality, be most valuable.

Granite. — The geological formation of the State precludes the idea of finding this rock, excepting in districts of very limited areas. For architectural purposes it is of great value; it is extensively used in the city of New York, and constitutes the principal material of more than one of the most beautiful edifices in that city. As it is brought from a great distance at a heavy expense, it is important, if we have within our own limits the means of supplying our own demands, that the fact should be ascertained and known. New York Island, and the region embraced within the western line of the State of Connecticut and the Hudson river, as far up as the Highlands, are of primitive formation.[1] This tract of country has not been so carefully surveyed as to show with precision the peculiar character of all its minor localities; but its leading characteristics are found to be identical, so far as they have been observed, with those of the great range of primitive rocks running through it. The products of the marble quarries at Sing-Sing and Eastchester do not differ essentially from those at Stockbridge; they are a part of the same range of granular limestone,[2] and a part of the great primitive formation extending from the State of Mississippi to the northeastern boundary of the

[1] McClure, on the Geology of the United States. Trans. Am. Phil. Soc. (New Series) Vol. I. p. 68.   [2] Ibid. p. 22.

United States. The Highlands (a part of the same formation) are a branch of the Green Mountain range, and have their central beds of gneiss in alternating layers with granite.[1] Dr. Akerly, in his essay on the geology of the Hudson river,[2] considers granite as entering into the formation of the Highlands, though gneiss and micaceous schistus predominate. According to Mr. James Pierce, granite, often containing black mica, is the predominant rock in the interior ranges of the Highlands.[3]

Granite is also found in the northwestern part of Saratoga county,[4] but it lies at a distance from the navigable communications of the State, and as it is of a very coarse structure, it is highly improbable that it will ever enter into competition with the finer granites of New England.

The value of granite for architectural or useful purposes depends on its structure, and on the predominance of some one of the materials of which it is composed. The New-England granites are usually finely granulated, easily wrought, and often almost indestructible.

Should we be so fortunate as to secure within the State a supply of this stone, to meet the demands of our rapidly increasing cities, it will doubtless be found on the banks of the Hudson river, where, from the convenience of transportation, its presence is most desirable. The difference of cost, where an active competition in furnishing it exists, may be estimated from the fact, that in Boston rough blocks of granite have been sold at less than fourteen cents the superficial foot, whereas but six years since the same stone cost two dollars per foot.[5]

Gneiss. — This rock is often equal, both in beauty and usefulness, to granite. It consists of the same materials;

---

[1] Eaton, Survey of Canal Dist. p. 23, Sill. Jour. Vol. V. p. 234, and Vol. XIV. p. 145.
[2] Ibid. p. 39. [3] Sill. Jour. Vol. V. p. 27.
[4] Steel's Geology of Saratoga County. Memoirs Board of Agriculture, Vol. II. p. 48.
[5] Hitchcock's Geology of Massachusetts, p. 28.

but from the arrangement of the mica in laminæ, it may often be split into parallel planes. Thus, much of the labor and expense of preparing it for use is saved. It is extensively used for building in Massachusetts, and is considered in no respect inferior to granite, from which it is sometimes not readily distinguished.[1]

The Highlands are principally of gneiss; it enters largely into the composition of the primitive ranges along the Hudson river, and it would be remarkable if localities could not be found in which it may be quarried and prepared for building. If, as is said, it resembles the New-England ranges,[2] it may prove equally valuable for architectural purposes, though it is undoubtedly true that the real value of a rock for such purposes cannot always be determined, until it has been worked and brought into use.

The primitive granitical rock, which appears at the surface in the northern part of the island of New York, is gneiss. It occurs in strata of limited thickness, but is extensively used for building and for curb-stones.

The tract of country bounded by the St. Lawrence and Lake Champlain, and a line drawn from the Thousand Islands in the river St. Lawrence to the southern point of Lake George, is of primitive formation, and has been denominated the northern primitive district. It consists of mountain ridges of gneiss, with intervening valleys of transition sandstone and limestone.[3] The distance of this body of gneiss from the city of New York would probably interpose an insuperable obstacle to any attempt to bring it into use there, if it were of a suitable quality for building. From the examinations of this rock, made by Mr. Eaton at Little Falls, where the canal severs a spur of the mountain ridges of the northern district, he considers it "a more recent variety" than that of the New-England ranges, and subject to rapid

---

[1] Hitchcock's Survey of Massachusetts, p. 30.
[2] Eaton's Index to the Geology of the Eastern States, p. 131.
[3] Eaton's Survey of the Canal District, p. 43.

disintegration.[1] Should this opinion prove, upon a more critical investigation, to be well founded, it will doubtless yield, for all economical uses, to the secondary limestone with which the adjacent country abounds. Attempts have been made to introduce it into the structures on the Erie Canal, but it has not been much used in consequence of the difficulty of splitting and working it. It is found to be exceedingly hard, and as the laminæ are irregular and contorted, it will not cleave advantageously, excepting into small blocks. So far, however, as it has been used, it has not proved to be deficient in durability.

Limestone. — This is, beyond all comparison, the most valuable stone in the State of New York. If the granular limestone of Westchester alone were considered, the remark would be just. But limestone, in some of its varieties, enters into the composition of nearly, if not quite, two thirds of the entire surface of the State. From the Hudson to Lake Erie on the west, and Lake Ontario on the northwest, there is hardly a district of the narrowest dimensions in which this stone is not devoted to some valuable purpose.

In the survey of the county of Albany, by Mr. Eaton and Dr. T. R. Beck, executed at the expense of Gen. Stephen Van Rensselaer, large masses of secondary limestone were discovered. The calcareous ingredient is intermixed with grains of silex, and it is difficult to work it down to a smooth surface. It has, however, been brought into general use in the city of Albany, for flagging and doorstones. For these purposes it requires but little dressing, and is a valuable stone. Some specimens have received a polish, and the gentlemen who executed the survey are of the opinion that strata of a finer texture, and more free from impurities, might be found in the same locality.

The same variety of compact limestone, which is used as a water-cement, abounds in the Helderburgh mountains, which run through the western part of Albany county. It

[1] Eaton's Survey of the Canal District, p. 52.

has less carbonate of lime, and more quartz than that used in the western district, but is not, perhaps, for that reason less durable and firm as a cement.

The district in which the water limestone is most abundant, includes Madison, Onondaga, Cayuga, and some of the adjacent counties. It abounds also in Ulster county. The value of the cement which it yields cannot be too highly appreciated. The mason-work of the locks on the Erie Canal is laid in it, and whenever the stone is of a quality to resist the action of water and the work is properly executed, the structure may be said to be proof against dilapidation. In all parts of the State this cement is used for cisterns, and for masonry which is to be permanently immersed in water.

Throughout the western counties there is an abundance of limestone suitable for burning for the manufacture of quicklime. The principal varieties are known as the blue and gray. The former is more pure as a carbonate, and when burnt yields the largest quantity of lime. The latter contains a larger proportion of silex, which, when burnt, becomes a sharp sand, and for this reason requires less sand when made into mortar. In this extensive district, lime is often procured at twelve and a half cents per bushel. Fuel is cheap, and the expense of burning the stone is trifling. But as settlement extends, the cost must be enhanced from the diminished supply of wood. The discovery of coal in this region is therefore an object of great importance, and it will become more so as the forests give place to agricultural improvements. A great deal of quick-lime is also made in Ulster and other counties on the Hudson river.

The gray limestone is one of the very best materials for architectural purposes, and indeed for every species of structure. It is firm in its texture, has a good color, and is exceedingly durable. Many of the locks on the Erie Canal, and the abutments of the bridges, are built of this stone. The blue limestone is of a more brilliant color, and is also an admirable building-stone. The gray limestone of Cayuga county is wrought at the State Prison at Auburn, for dwellings and public edifices. It breaks with an uneven fracture, and is exceedingly tough, so much so that it will show indentations without breaking. In this last property it resembles some of the limestones of Berkshire county, Massachusetts, as described by Mr. Hitchcock.[1]

The granular limestone or marble at Sing-Sing is one of the most beautiful materials for ornamental architecture in the United States. It may be seen in the Lagrange terrace in Lafayette Place, in the city of New York; in the City Hall, at Albany; and in the new State Hall now erecting in the latter city. One of the objects of establishing the State Prison at Mount Pleasant, Sing-Sing, was to employ the convicts in quarrying the marble which had been found in great abundance on the grounds now known as the State farm at that place. Since the quarries were opened they have at times presented discouraging indications; but the Inspectors of the prison during the last two years represent their condition to be as favorable as it has ever been. When the stone fails at one point, or ceases to be of a proper quality, a new quarry is opened. Sometimes the stone proves good when appearances are most unfavorable; and at others it proves to be of an inferior quality when it presents the best indications.[2] On the extent of these quarries depends the permanence of a branch of business at the prison, which it is on many accounts extremely desirable to continue. Of 843 convicts at the prison in 1834, about 200 were engaged in quarrying and dressing marble. The amount received during the same year for stone quarried and dressed by the convicts, and sold for the support of the prison, exceeded thirty-four thousand dollars. The advantage of having near at hand, and at a reasonable price, an abundant supply of so fine a material for public edifices cannot be too highly appreciated, and it is desirable to know how far it may be relied on hereafter. Some estimate of the extent of the beds may

[1] Survey of Mass. p. 800.   [2] Senate Doc. No. 8, 1835, p. 8.

be formed by ascertaining the direction of the range of which they are a part; and by uncovering them at different points the quality of the marble may be learned with an approach to certainty.

In addition to the quarry on the State farm at Sing-Sing, there are others in Westchester county, belonging to individuals, which have been worked, containing marble of the finest quality. Two of them are now worked for the New-York custom-house. There is every reason to believe that the county of Westchester contains a sufficient quantity of marble to furnish the city of New York with an inexhaustible supply of building-stone, inferior to no other for beauty or durability. As new quarries are opened, the price may be still further reduced, although it is now afforded at reasonable rates; more reasonable, indeed, than some of the granites which are brought from New England.

The marble at Kingsbridge is mixed with iron pyrites, which, on exposure to the weather, stains and hastens the decomposition of the stone. Unless it is found in a purer state on further examination, it cannot be advantageously used for architectural purposes.

In the lower parts of the counties of Jefferson and St. Lawrence, bordering upon the St. Lawrence river, there is an abundance of excellent limestone for building, as many of the dwelling-houses and barns in these counties sufficiently attest. While the wooden buildings of other counties are hastening to decay, these will be lasting monuments of the wise economy which has led to the selection of more durable materials for structures which constitute so large an item in the expense of agricultural improvements. The strata running through this district are believed to be secondary, and lie along the confines of the great primitive formation between Lake George and the river St. Lawrence.

To explore the vast calcareous formations of this State, to trace out their varieties, to ascertain with precision their components, to point out their proper uses, to show where they lie, and in what manner they are most readily accessible, are among the most important objects of the proposed survey. Next to the salt springs, the limestones of New York may be regarded as her greatest treasure. In comparison with it, the richest mine of gold would be of small account. That fountain of wealth is unquestionably the most precious, as well as the most sure, which stimulates human industry to exertion in the most useful channels, and furnishes it with the direct aids which it requires.

There are various other rocks in the State, which are of great value for ordinary purposes, but in what quantities they may be procured, or of what quality, is not often well ascertained.

Thus, there is a variety of freestone in Rockland county, which has the property of resisting heat. It is extensively used for furnaces in the city of New York, and commands a great price.

In Rensselaer county, there are found considerable quantities of the very best slate for roofs; and the same stone is found in various other localities.

Sandstone of the finest quality for building abounds at Potsdam and other localities in St. Lawrence county.[1] It is quarried with great ease, is almost indestructible, and requires nothing but facilities of transportation to bring it into use at distant places.

Steatite, or soapstone, is also found in different parts of the State; but it is suggested by a scientific gentleman, who has paid much attention to our geological formations, that, if it exists in place, it must be sought on the southeastern face of the Highlands, in Rockland and Westchester counties; and that the occurrence of boulders in those counties seems to indicate that the native stone is not far distant.

The city of New York is indebted to other States for most of the important stone, of nearly every description, which it employs. Its freestone is brought from New Jersey

[1] Sill. Jour. Vol. XIX. pp. 220, 227.

and Connecticut, its soapstone from Pennsylvania, and much of its building-stone consists of the New-England granites, principally of the variety known as sienite. For the latter, it is believed that the Westchester marbles might be advantageously substituted. It is neither a narrow nor an unsocial view of the subject, which regards as extremely desirable the discovery within our own limits of such materials as we require for our own use. If for no other reasons, it would be important for the purpose of saving the expense of transportation from remote places, and opening new sources of supply to meet the increased demands of our augmenting population.

The importance of ascertaining the mineralogical composition of rocks employed for building may be readily understood by a reference to some of the circumstances attending the construction of the Rochester aqueduct, by which the Erie Canal is carried over the waters of the Genesee river. When this work was in progress, a stone in the neighborhood was quarried and dressed for some part of the exterior of the structure; but after being exposed to the action of the atmosphere for a short time, it was found to have literally crumbled to atoms. Another stone, somewhat different, was obtained, and after being subjected to some partial trials, it was selected for the arches and other parts of the work, in which a firm and durable material was indispensable. This structure is now so nearly in ruins in consequence of the disintegration of the stone, that contracts have already been made for reconstructing it. The material referred to is a porous sandstone; and it would not have been difficult to foresee, if its mineralogical structure had been critically investigated, the consequences which have ensued. In so severe a climate, water, insinuating itself into the interstices of the stone, must freeze and force its particles asunder. As the capacity of the Erie Canal is to be increased, the Rochester aqueduct, which would be altogether insufficient for the transmission of the quantity of water required for navigating the enlarged channel, must have been partially rebuilt within a short time. Its decay, from the cause referred to, is, therefore, not to be deemed a total loss. But it illustrates the necessity of ascertaining, as far as possible, before a material is used for a given work, whether it possesses the requisite durability.

It is true, it is not always easy to appreciate the effects of atmospheric influence upon a particular rock, by a mere examination of its structure. It is often necessary, and always desirable, to learn what effects have followed its exposure to the action of air or water, for a length of time. But with respect to certain classes of rocks, a simple knowledge of their composition is sufficient. Thus it must be manifest that an extremely porous sandstone will not long withstand the action of frost, and that slate highly argillaceous is liable to rapid disintegration by the alternate action of rain and sun. But care should be taken, wherever a building-stone of any description abounds, to ascertain not only its mineralogical character, but as far as possible to learn what changes have been caused in its structure or its external appearance by continued exposure to frost, heat, and moisture. This knowledge may generally be acquired without difficulty, unless the stone is recently discovered or brought into use, by an examination of structures into which it has been introduced.

SOILS.

As one of the objects of the proposed survey is to procure a scientific and perfect account of the soils of the State, it becomes important to consider how minute the examination and report in reference to them shall be. To enter into all the minutiæ of the changes which are visible in passing from one locality to another, where the general character of the soil remains the same, would involve great expense and consume more time than could reasonably be devoted to this part of the survey. Such was not, it is presumed, the intention of the Assembly. On the contrary, it is supposed that the design was to describe those soils only which are distinguished from each other by such characteristic differences as would, in the case of rocks, require a distinct description. Natural soils are the result of the disintegration of the contiguous rocks, and of the decomposition of vegetable and animal substances which have decayed upon them. When the subjacent rock is slow of disintegration, the soil is usually thin, but composed of a larger proportion of vegetable matter, and is generally exceedingly fertile. When the subjacent rock disintegrates rapidly, the soil will be found deep, and to be fertile or otherwise according to the nature of the ingredients which enter into the composition of the rock beneath it. In the geological investigations to be made in this branch of the survey, the observers will of course be careful, whenever the mineralogical character of the rocks in a particular district changes in passing from one locality to another, to ascertain whether a corresponding change has not taken place in the character of the soil also. Everything, in short, which affects the nature or quality of the soil, in such cases, should be carefully examined. Instances will doubtless be found in which masses of earth have been brought to particular localities by the transporting power of water, or by other causes, and which do not partake in any considerable degree of the quality of the rocks beneath them. All such cases have an interest independent of that which enters into the examination of soils resulting from the disintegration of the rocks on which they rest. The nature of the power by which the soil was displaced, the distance from which it was probably brought, the time when the occurrence took place, and the contemporaneous effects produced, so far as any such effects are visible, are all interesting inquiries in a philosophical point of view, and deserve attention.

But, with respect to soils, the great object is to learn, by a careful investigation of their distinctive properties, what kind of vegetation they are best calculated to support, how far they contain within themselves the elements of amelioration, by what processes of cultivation, and by what admixtures of foreign substances, their productiveness may be increased. In all cases, the most intelligent farmers should be consulted as to the qualities of the soil, the vegetation best suited to it, their modes of cultivation, the practical difficulties they have encountered, and the effects which they have observed from the application of particular manures. These observations should be reduced to writing on the spot, and specimens of the soil should be taken and marked for the purpose of analyzing them at a future time. With a knowledge of the mineral constitution of the particular soil, and of the practical observations of those who have cultivated it, erroneous systems of culture may be reformed, and a far greater degree of productiveness attained. In this way every man's farm may become more valuable to him, and the general wealth can hardly fail to be greatly increased.

There is another consideration of importance connected with this branch of the survey. A knowledge of the nature of the soil and of the neighboring rocks may be made instrumental to the improvement of roads and highways, by indicating in what manner they may be constructed and repaired, so as to secure the greatest practicable durability. Our roads are generally bad, and yet an immense amount of money and labor is annually expended on them for repairs. Much of this expenditure might doubtless be avoided by attending more to the materials of which they are composed. Being designed to connect one point with another, in the most direct line practicable, a choice of direction cannot always be controlled. But it may, and doubtless will, sometimes happen that by a slight deviation in the proposed direction, a road may be conducted through a soil better adapted to durability than that through which it would have run if a direct line had been pursued. So, when a road is to be repaired, the earth or stone taken for the purpose should be of the proper quality. If they are hard and durable, the road will be so; but if they are of a different character, the expense of repairing must be again incurred. A very great misapplication of time and money might unquestionably be avoided by attending to principles which too rarely, it is feared, enter into the consideration of questions of this sort, and a due regard to which would conduce as much to the convenience of the public as to the interest of those more immediately concerned in them.

In Onondaga, Albany, and Rensselaer counties, deep beds of shell-marl have been found. In the two latter they occur in connection with gravelly soils, to which they may be most advantageously applied.[1] Similar beds are doubtless to be found in other parts of the State, and probably in situations where they may be profitably used as a manure. To soils deficient in calcareous ingredients they are of great value.

The geological and topographical survey of the State of Maryland, now in progress under the direction of Messrs. Ducatel & Alexander, has already produced a very able and valuable account by the gentleman first named of the marl beds in that State, and the mode of rendering them beneficial to its agriculture. By this account, it appears that of the several species of shells found in marl beds, some decompose more readily than others, and that the utility of the marl, as a fertilizer of the soil, depends not only upon the species of shells contained in it, but also on the nature of the cement by which the shells are often held together.[2] Sometimes they are united by an argillo-ferruginous cement, and in such cases the marl is considered useless, and to some soils positively injurious. Whether the observations of Mr. Ducatel on the marl beds of Maryland are applicable, in their full extent, to the beds which occur in this State, may be questionable. The marl beds of the eastern shore of Maryland contain marine shells only. Those which have been discovered in this State contain only land and fresh-water shells.

[1] Eaton's Survey of Rensselaer County, p. 26. This survey, together with the survey of the district adjoining the Erie Canal, was executed at the expense of Gen. Stephen Van Rensselaer.
[2] Report, American Journal of Science and Arts, No. 1, Vol. XXVII.

Whether with us marl may in general be as advantageously applied as a manure, may also admit of some question. In our soils throughout the greater part of the State, calcareous ingredients may be expected to predominate. To soils of this description, marl (itself a calcareous ingredient) cannot always be beneficially applied. But it may, as in Albany and Rensselaer counties, often occur in localities where the nature of the soil is such as to need its presence.

Specimens of the soils are, under the resolution of the Assembly, to be preserved. They will be kept in phials, which may be of moderate size, and will not require a case exceeding fifteen feet in height, twenty in width, and one foot in depth.

MINERALS.

Salt. — The Salt Springs of Onondaga county have for many years constituted one of the most fruitful of our internal resources. They are indeed of greater value than any other. They provide our citizens with one of the first necessaries of life, at a very moderate expense, and they are a perpetual source of revenue to the State.

The springs from which the salt is manufactured penetrate the whole district of country around the Onondaga lake. Those at Salina are the most strongly impregnated with saline ingredients. The grounds on which the manufactories are erected belong to the State, and are leased for a term of years to individuals, on the sole condition that they shall be devoted to the manufacture of salt.

For the purpose of raising the brine to the surface of the ground and conducting it to the various manufactories, three pumps, with the necessary machinery, have been erected, at an expense to the State of about forty thousand dollars. One, at Geddes, supplies that village; and the other two, at Salina, supply the three villages of Salina, Syracuse, and Liverpool. The brine is conveyed in logs to Liverpool, a distance of three miles, and a mile and a half to Syracuse.

In the year 1831 there were 153 manufactories of fine

salt, and six of coarse salt. The latter occupy about 200 acres of ground, and are almost wholly dependent on solar evaporation. The fine salt is produced by boiling. In 1831 there were manufactured 1,441,559 bushels of salt. Of this quantity, 189,000 bushels were of coarse salt, of which 161,753 bushels were produced by solar evaporation, and the remainder by artificial and solar heat combined.

The manufacturers of salt pay to the State a duty of six cents on every bushel manufactured, and two mills per bushel for the brine supplied by the State pumps. Yet the price of salt at the works, during the year 1835, did not exceed fifteen cents per bushel, including those charges.

The quantity of salt manufactured, and the amount of revenue derived from it by the State, from 1831 to 1835 inclusive, after deducting the expense of superintending the works, will be seen by the following table : —

	Bushels of Salt.	Amount of Duty.
1831	1,441,559	$122,769.86
1832	1,652,986	179,096.46
1833	1,838,646	227,860.05
1834	1,943,252	160,782.98
1835	2,222,694	118,364.92

Previous to the year 1834, the duty or excise on each bushel of salt manufactured was twelve and a half cents. It was reduced, in consequence of the reduction of the impost on foreign salt by Congress, for the purpose of enabling the domestic manufacture to compete with the other in our own markets. This change in the rate of duty will account for the diminished revenue in 1834, on the increased production of that year, as compared with the preceding year. The law providing for the reduction of the duty went into operation in April, 1834. The fiscal year 1834 commenced on the 1st October, 1833, and ended on the 30th September, 1834. Part of the salt manufactured in that year, therefore, paid a duty of twelve and a half cents, and part of it a duty of six cents.

By the amended constitution of this State, as adopted in 1822, the salt duties were pledged to the payment of the debt contracted for the construction of the Erie and Champlain canals. The revenues of those canals from tolls on property transported on them having become so great as to render any auxiliary resource unnecessary, and an amount of surplus revenue almost equal to the outstanding debt having already been accumulated, an amendment to the constitution has been submitted to the people, and ratified by them, providing for a restoration of the salt duties (together with the duties on goods sold at auction, which were similarly pledged) to the General Fund. The salt duties will soon be applicable to the payment of the ordinary expenses of the government. Indeed, they constitute, together with the auction duties, the only revenues of the State which can be so applied.

These facts have been briefly presented with a view to exhibit the value of the salt springs as a source of revenue to the State, and the importance of giving the greatest practicable extent to their productiveness. To our own citizens it is an object of the greatest interest. To an extensive region beyond our own limits, but within the circle supplied with this necessary of life from our manufactories, it is scarcely less an object of interest. This circle has been regularly extending with the progress of settlement westward. The reduction of the duty on the manufacture has given an additional impulse to production. The effect of such a reduction is to enlarge the boundaries of the circle in ordinary cases as far as the manufacture can be transported for a sum equal to the amount so reduced. But where the circle is bounded by rival articles, the enlargement will be only half as great as in the cases last mentioned, if the facilities of transportation are equal in both directions. In 1831, about 50,000 bushels of salt were sent into Upper Canada for consumption. The amount is now doubtless increased. In 1833, about 4000 bushels were sent to Chicago, near the southern extremity of Lake Michigan; in 1834, about 16,000 bushels; and during the last year, in consequence of the extraordinary influx of population, the amount must have been much greater. A very extensive region of country is, therefore, interested in this manufacture — interested in procuring it at the lowest price. Facilities of transportation give it an advantage, in many portions of the northwestern States, over the salt manufactured in those States. In Missouri, Illinois, Kentucky, and Ohio, salt springs have been worked, but at an expense far exceeding that of manufacturing salt at the Onondaga springs. On the Kenhaway river in Virginia and in the neighborhood of Pittsburgh in Pennsylvania, the cost of manufacture is much less than in the States referred to; but the products of the works at these two points cannot come in competition with the Onondaga salt within the circle now supplied by the latter. If, however, from any change of circumstances the cost of production shall be enhanced, the rival productions of other works will press upon the boundaries of this circle, and narrow it. Such an enhancement can only be expected to arise from the increasing cost of fuel, and this may possibly be counterbalanced by introducing greater economy into the process of manufacture. About 100,000 cords of wood are annually consumed at the Onondaga works, at an expense of about $1.50 per cord, equal to an annual expenditure of one hundred and fifty thousand dollars for this object. As population increases, fuel must become dearer, and the cost of manufacture will be augmented. The discovery of coal in the vicinity of the springs, or of beds of rock-salt beneath them, would counterbalance the inevitable increase of the cost of production, from the cause referred to. A critical examination of the strata through which the water percolates, the rock on which it appears to rest, and the geology of the surrounding localities, might lead to conclusions on both these points, which would at least put an end to conjecture.

The existence of beds of rock-salt in the vicinity of the springs has been the subject of great diversity of opinion.

Mr. Eaton supposes the brine to be produced by combinations perpetually in progress between the elementary materials furnished by the subjacent rock and some of the superincumbent strata.[1] In another place the same opinion is expressed, and maintained by reference to a case in which crystals of muriate of soda had appeared on a piece of the rock taken from the floor of a salt spring, and exposed in a humid atmosphere.[2] Dr. Lewis C. Beck, who examined the springs and analyzed the various kinds of salt manufactured at the works, dissents from this opinion.[3] Others have also called it in question.[4] Indeed the common opinion seems to be, that beds of rock-salt exist in the vicinity, and that the brine is formed by the passage of water over their surface. This opinion derives strength from the fact, that the geological character of the strata, through which the brine is drawn to the surface, bears a strong resemblance to that of the strata overlaying the beds of rock-salt near Northwich in Cheshire, England,[5] as well as to that of the strata in the immediate vicinity of the salt mines of Cardona in Spain.[6] Borings have been made at the springs in Onondaga, at several points, in one instance to the depth of 250 feet, without finding fossil salt. The beds of salt in Cheshire were discovered about 160 years ago, in boring for coal, at 125 feet below the surface of the ground; but they have now been penetrated to a much greater depth. The solution of this question with respect to the origin of the Onondaga salt springs, is a matter of no inconsiderable interest for the reasons already assigned. For scientific purposes, the discovery of beds of rock-salt would determine nothing, unless the discovery were accompanied by circumstances calculated to shed light on the origin of such beds. Fossil salt has not always been found in the vicinity of salt springs. In France, though there are

[1] Survey of the Canal District, p. 108.
[2] Silliman's Journal, Vol. VI. p. 242.
[3] Medical and Physical Journal, Vol. V. p. 182.
[4] Silliman's Journal, Vol. XIX. p. 141.
[5] Transactions of the Geological Society, Vol. I. p. 62.   [6] Ibid. p. 404.

many salt springs, no beds of rock-salt have been discovered.[1] On the other hand, fossil salt has been found in localities widely different. In Cheshire, it lies below the level of the sea. In Spain, Poland, and in South America, it is found at the summit of the loftiest mountains. But, in an economical point of view, the discovery of rock-salt in Onondaga would be of the greatest importance. The salt beds near Northwich yield more than 150,000 tons of salt per annum, nearly three times as much as the whole annual product of the Onondaga springs. What an addition would such an increased production make to the wealth of this State!

The salt district does not terminate in Onondaga county. It commences in Oneida and extends two hundred and fifty miles farther west, carrying with it an average breadth of twenty miles.[2] At Montezuma, about thirty miles west of Salina, salt springs were worked several years, but they are not now wholly discontinued. The brine is, however, much weaker than that at Salina, and the product has never been so considerable. More than fifty springs had been discovered in the salt district when Mr. Eaton's survey of the district adjoining the canal was made, and many more have been found since. This district should be carefully examined throughout its whole extent. There is good reason for supposing that it may contain in its bosom other treasures not inferior in value to those which have already been disclosed.

Coal. — Some of the features of the salt district bear a close resemblance to those of the coal district, of which Newcastle-upon-Tyne constitutes a part, as described by Mr. Winch in his observations on the geology of Northumberland and Durham.[3] According to Mr. Eaton, the floor of the salt springs consists of a rock, which, on the authority of Conybeare and Phillips, he denominates saliferous rock, and which is subdivided into red sand rock and red slate.[4] Its

[1] Silliman's Journal, Vol. XV. p. 2.
[2] Eaton's Survey of the Canal District, p. 103.
[3] Trans. of the Geol. Society, Vol. VI. part 1.
[4] Survey of the Canal District, pp. 19, 23, 35, 102.

thickness varies in different places, and, as must be supposed in an extent of 250 miles, it approaches much nearer the surface at some points than at others. Below this rock lies what has been denominated by English geologists the millstone grit, or a coarse grained sandstone, — the same rock, as Mr. Eaton confidently believes, which " accompanies the most important coal measures of the eastern continent." This stone is deemed an essential feature of the coal district of Northumberland; and when it is seen cropping out with the limestone on which it rests, the coal formation is considered as terminating.[1] At the Madeley colliery in Shropshire, England, a stratum of coarse sandstone or grit is found at the depth of 430 feet. Below this stratum are two distinct strata of sandstone differing in their geological character, and separated by beds of coal. In 1811, the whole depth of the pit was 729 feet.[2] The sandstone at the Onondaga salt springs has been bored through, and a conglomerate of rounded pebbles penetrated to the depth of eight feet. The whole depth of the boring in this case was but about 250 feet. No traces of coal have been discovered, and nothing to raise the expectation of finding it, but the nature of the formation, which has been described. In treating of the principal coal formations of England, the following series of rocks are considered in connection with the coal measures: 1. Coal measures; 2. Millstone grit and shale; 3. Carboniferous or mountain limestone; 4. Old red sandstone.[3] Sometimes the last two members of the series are wanting, and the coal is found resting upon transition rocks, forming what has been denominated independent coal formations.[4] The strata at Salina have never been examined to the termination of the second rock in the series; and to that extent a strong similarity is found between them and the upper strata of some of the coal fields in England. The whole

---

[1] Trans. Geol. Society, Vol. VI. part 1, p. 11.   [2] Ibid. Vol. I. p. 195.
[3] Conybeare and Phillips's Geology of England and Wales, p. 335.
[4] Ibid. p. 334.

matter is however left in great uncertainty; but if in this widely extended district, characterized, so far as it has been examined, by the geological features which everywhere else afford to the man of science the strongest assurance of the presence of this valuable mineral, it is not to be found, the case will constitute a singular instance of the failure of indications hitherto regarded as nearly infallible.

The probabilities of finding coal within this State are briefly presented in an article to be found in "Silliman's Journal."[1] If the view therein presented is correct, the salt district is the only one in which such a probability exists. Examinations have been made in several of the central southern counties with the hope of finding a continuation of the coal formation in the neighboring counties of Pennsylvania, but without success. More critical investigations may possibly lead to more satisfactory results, although the writer of the article above referred to, who has examined the country from the coal mines in Pennsylvania to the Seneca and Cayuga lakes, deems all such expectations hopeless.[2] This position is questioned by a writer in "Silliman's Journal,"[3] and there may still be reason to anticipate better success in further investigations. The district of country bordering on the Susquehannah from the Pennsylvania line to its source, the Otsego lake, has not, it is believed, been systematically examined. In this section anthracite coal has been found, and in a recent instance an inconsiderable expenditure of money has been made to ascertain the extent of the bed. Between the geological character of parts of Orange, Ulster, and Greene counties, and that of the coal fields of Pennsylvania, there is a strong resemblance; and in this district, also, coal might be sought for with reasonable expectations of finding it.

If bituminous coal should be found in the neighborhood of the salt springs, it will doubtless be at a depth of several hundred feet below the surface. The cost of boring to such a depth would be more than an individual would be willing

[1] Vol. XIX. p. 21.   [2] Mr. Eaton.   [3] Vol. XIX. p. 236.

to incur for an uncertainty. The State has a deeper interest in the discovery than any individual can have. The salt springs are the property of the people. They are one of the principal sources of the public revenue; but as time advances, their productiveness may, and doubtless will, be impaired to a greater or less extent by the increasing cost of fuel. The salt works on the Kenhaway river in Virginia would ere this time have been embarrassed for want of fuel but for the discovery of coal in the vicinity of the Salines. The neighboring hills were completely divested of their woods before coal came into use; but these works must now continue to be among the most productive in the Union.[1] Should the proposed geological survey of this State be executed, and should the result of the examination of the Onondaga district be such as to justify the expectation of finding coal in the vicinity of the salt works, the time must come when the public interest will so strongly indicate the importance of realizing that expectation as to require some provision by law for making the necessary experiments by boring.

Gypsum. — The association of gypsum and rock-salt is so common, that it has almost been regarded as invariable. It is found in abundance in several of the counties in the salt district; but not, as is said, in immediate contact with the strata through which the brine is drawn at Salina. It abounds, however, in the immediate vicinity of the springs at that place. In digging wells it is always met with, but at a greater elevation than the salt marshes. Mr. Eaton[2] asserts that all the gypsum of the salt district exists in limited beds in the contiguous strata of calc slate, which extend without interruption from the Oneida creek to the Niagara river, a distance of more than two hundred miles; and that there are three distinct strata between those which contain the gypsum and those which contain the salt. Dr. Lewis C. Beck concurs in the opinion that gypsum is not associated with the

---

[1] Silliman's Journal, Vol. XXIX. p. 119.
[2] Survey of the Canal District, p. 124.

salt formation of the canal district.[1] Other writers, however, assert that gypsum and salt are associated in this district in the same manner as in Europe;[2] and in boring for salt water at Montezuma, about thirty miles west of Salina, the gentlemen engaged in the experiment penetrated several layers of gypsum before reaching the brine, and in immediate contact with the strata containing the latter. In a philosophical point of view, the question is worthy of investigation ; and should it prove, as Messrs. Eaton and Beck suppose, the case will be an uncommon one. Although the association of the two minerals is nearly constant, more particularly when the salt occurs in a solid state, it was for a time supposed that the "usual concomitant, gypsum," was wanting in the immediate vicinity of the salt mines of Cardona in Spain,[3] which are among the most remarkable deposits of rock-salt in Europe. But on a subsequent examination gypsum was found to enter very largely into the formation of the mountain of salt.[4] The gypsum found in association with rock-salt is believed to be almost universally anhydrous, though sometimes mixed with common gypsum. That which is found in the salt district in this State is believed to be the common gypsum, containing a due proportion of water of crystallization. This fact may possibly furnish ground for inferences unfavorable to the existence of beds of rock-salt in this vicinity ; but such inferences ought not to be drawn without considering whether the gypsum of this district may not have been originally anhydrous. The latter, when exposed to the action of moisture, readily absorbs water, and is converted into common gypsum.[5]

The region in which gypsum is most abundant includes Madison and some portion of the adjacent counties. It is

[1] Med. and Phys. Journal, Vol. V. p. 180.
[2] Dr. Van Rensselaer's Essay on Salt, p. 81, and Silliman's Journal, Vol. XIX. p. 141.
[3] Account by Dr. Traill, Trans. of the Geol. Society, Vol. III. p. 412.
[4] De la Beche, Selections from Annales des Mines, p. 55.
[5] Bakewell's Introduction to Geology, pp. 171, 176.

also found in Ancram, Columbia county, and in numerous other localities. But it is to the salt district that we must look for such supplies of this mineral as are necessary for the various uses to which it is applied. Its localities should all be particularly noted, together with the extent of its beds, and the geographical relation which it bears, in all cases, to the salt springs.

Iron. — No State in the Union is richer in iron ores than New York. In the northern primitive district it is most abundant. The valley of the Ausable river has about eighty forge-fires constantly in operation in smelting the ore and converting it into pig iron. The estimated value of the iron manufactured in and exported from this valley in 1831 was about $280,000. There are two beds of ore (in one of them a steam-engine is employed) which annually furnish ore to be worked in the neighborhood of the value of from $30,-000 to $40,000. St. Lawrence, Jefferson, Franklin, Clinton, and Essex counties are full of the richest ores of iron, and in all these counties it is manufactured into pigs, bars, bolts, or castings. This district, still almost entirely unexplored as to its mineralogical character, probably contains a larger amount of valuable metals than all the other counties of the State combined. It is stated as a very interesting fact, that, so far as it has been examined, it bears a striking analogy in its formation to that of the iron districts in Sweden.[1] The tract of country which separates Montgomery and St. Lawrence counties may prove not less valuable with respect to its metallic contents than the section before referred to. Broken and sterile, presenting in its external features an aspect which appears to set every effort of enterprise and industry at defiance, it may yet be found to contain, under this forbidding exterior, substances which may be made subservient to the amelioration and embellishment of more favored districts, and reclaim the region in which they now lie concealed, from neglect and solitude.

[1] Dr. T. R. Beck's Address, 1 vol. Trans. Albany Institute, p. 143.

GEOLOGICAL REPORT.

In the towns of Watervliet, Guilderland, and Bethlehem, in Albany county, bog iron ore has been found, sometimes in very large quantities.[1] It is now worked, and the iron is manufactured in Philadelphia. Deposits of the same ore are found in various parts of the State. The processes by which the deposits of this ore are formed may be expected to continue until they are interrupted by the introduction of disturbing agents into them. These deposits may, therefore, be considered inexhaustible; but as the beds are liable to be temporarily drained, they cannot be worked again until a renewal of the deposit takes place. The time required for the completion of these processes is variously stated, and probably varies in fact in different localities.[2]

Oxyde of iron, in some of its varieties, is found in Columbia county; in Rome, Oneida county; in Ontario, and in the town of Williamson, in Wayne county; in Queens, Saratoga, New-York, Rensselaer, and St. Lawrence counties; and throughout the northern primitive district it occurs in almost every variety. In the neighborhood of the Ausable river there is said to be an extensive bed of carbonate of iron which is converted into steel by a single process.

A critical examination of the localities in which these ores occur would doubtless lead to larger investments of capital in their manufacture, and extend in no inconsiderable degree this branch of our industry.

Sulphuret of iron, or iron pyrites, is of common occurrence. It is found in the Helderberg mountains, in several towns in Schoharie county, in Moreau, Saratoga county, and in Wawarsing, Ulster county, in considerable quantities.

In Canton, St. Lawrence county, there is an immense amount of sulphuret of iron, from which, during the last three years, a considerable quantity of copperas has been manufactured. The ore is found imbedded in a hard rough stone, which is blasted, and afterwards broken with hammers

---

[1] Geol. Surv. of Albany County, p. 41.
[2] Hitchcock's Surv. of Mass. p. 67.

into very small fragments. These fragments are collected in large piles, with a small quantity of wood under them, and in this manner the mass, which is readily ignited, burns by force of the sulphur contained in it with great freedom and often with violence. After the process of decomposition has been carried on for some time, water is thrown on the pile, and the lixivium is conducted into boilers, in which about thirty-three per cent. is evaporated by boiling, when it is drawn off into vats, where, on cooling, the copperas is formed by crystallization.

This establishment is yet in its infancy, but is likely to become one of the most interesting and valuable in the United States. The ore is composed principally of iron pyrites and alumina. In Stafford, Vermont, where there is an extensive establishment for the manufacture of copperas, the ore is composed of sulphuret of iron, with a slight admixture of copper pyrites. At Canton, the attention of the proprietors of the establishment was first directed to the manufacture of sulphate of iron, or copperas; and during the process it was found that in the decomposition of the pyrites a portion of the sulphuric acid united with the alumina and formed a sulphate of alumina. The presence of this salt proved to be an inconvenience in the manufacture of copperas, and during the year 1835 the proprietors have turned their attention to the manufacture of alum. The establishment was formed in the year 1833, and during a portion of the year fifty tons of copperas were manufactured. In 1834 the quantity was increased to 200 tons. During the year 1835 the quantity manufactured was but fifty tons, the proprietors having, as already stated, directed their labor to the manufacture of alum. Of the latter, fifteen tons were made.

During the last year, these works, and an adjacent district of country of several miles in extent, have been examined by Mr. James Hall, at the expense of Gen. Stephen Van Rensselaer, the proprietor. From Mr. Hall, the facts above stated have been principally obtained, though some of them were previously furnished by a gentleman of St. Lawrence county. The rock containing the ore "occupies," to use the language of Mr. Hall, "an extensive range of country." It was traced by him to a distance of ten miles from the works in one direction, and a mile and a half in the other. This district is destined, beyond doubt, to become celebrated for the manufacture of copperas and alum. The difficulties hitherto encountered are in separating the sulphate of alumina from the copperas during the process of manufacturing the copperas, and in separating the iron from the alum in manufacturing the latter. Mr. Hall has suggested methods of obviating these difficulties; and it is hardly possible, in the present advanced state of chemical science, that the object should not be effectually attained. At all events, the manufacture of copperas can always be carried on to an unlimited extent.

Graphite or plumbago is found at Ticonderoga, in Essex county, in large quantities, and of excellent quality; and it occurs in various other localities.

Lead. — Galena, or sulphuret of lead, occurs in Ancram and Hudson, Columbia county; Amenia, Dutchess county; Salisbury, Herkimer county; Westmoreland, Oneida county; Carlisle, Schoharie county; Wawarsing, Ulster county; and Greenbush, Rensselaer county. In White Creek, Washington county, a vein has been discovered, which yields seventy-five per cent. Descriptions of the mine at Ancram have been frequently published in "Silliman's Journal."

During the last year lead has been brought into this State from Galena, near the Upper Mississippi. After reaching Chicago by land, it was sent through Lakes Michigan, Huron, and Erie, to Buffalo, by trading vessels, and thence to Albany by the Erie canal, and to New York by the Hudson river. This route is expensive by reason of the land transportation to Michigan. If a canal or railroad should be constructed, as is contemplated, from Chicago to the

Upper Mississippi, the product of the lead mines destined for consumption in this State and in New England would doubtless come in this direction. But until such an improvement shall be made, it will probably descend the Mississippi to New Orleans, and thence reach us by sea, unless an amendment of the constitution should be made, as suggested by the Commissioners of the Canal Fund in the year 1834, in order to admit of its transportation on the Erie canal at a lower rate of toll. From the superiority of the western ores of lead as respects richness and abundance, the demand in this State may be expected to be supplied for many years from those sources, until geological examinations shall disclose more abundant veins of this metal than have yet been discovered within our boundaries.

There is a tradition with respect to the existence of a very rich lead mine in the southern part of St. Lawrence county, and it is quite certain that the Indians were, down to a late period, abundantly supplied with that metal from the interior of the northern district.

Since this report was commenced, the Secretary of State has received a very fine specimen of lead ore from a mine in Rossie, St. Lawrence county, which has just been opened. The ore is said to yield eighty per cent. and to be very abundant in quantity. Should this prove to be true, a large portion of our demands may be supplied from this source.

Copper, Zinc, Manganese, &c. — These and many other valuable metals occur in different parts of the State ; but the extent or value of the veins has hardly been, in a single instance, satisfactorily ascertained.

Gold and Silver. — Of the precious metals, no traces have been discovered in this State of such a decided character as to furnish any well-grounded expectation of finding them in sufficient quantities or in such proportions, in reference to the soil in which they are contained, as to repay the labor of working. Yet individuals in various parts of the State have been beset with idle hopes of finding them where there were no manifestations of their presence, — sometimes imposed on by ignorant and mercenary adventurers, and at others misled by the deceptive lustre of sulphuret of iron, or some other shining substance. The same career of credulity and fanaticism, which is described by Professor Hitchcock in his report on the geology of Massachusetts,[1] has been run by individuals in this State, in the pursuit of gold and silver mines, characterized by the same self-delusion and the same distrust of the efforts of the better informed to convince them of the fallacy of their expectations. Mines of gold and silver are the property of the people of this State. By our laws, every person who shall discover a gold or silver mine becomes, by filing a notice of such discovery in the office of the Secretary of State, exempted from paying to the State any part of the ore, produce, or profit for twenty-one years. Under this provision, which was enacted in 1789, eighty-one notices have been given, most of them within the last fifteen years, of the discovery of mines of gold or silver. In most of these cases, if not all, considerable sums of money have been expended in digging. In every one of them the visions of the fancied discoverers have been disappointed — oftentimes after involving themselves in irretrievable embarrassment. A scientific account of the localities in which the supposed fountains of treasure were discovered would have exposed the fallacy of the supposition, and spared, in some cases at least, much of this waste of labor and capital. Such an examination now by individuals in the employment of the State, reporting the results in the execution of a public trust, would effect much in dispelling groundless expectations of this sort hereafter.

Whatever the possession of gold and silver mines may do for individuals, it has not been regarded in modern times as beneficial to a State. A well-known example is appealed to as proof of its baneful influence upon the character and pursuits of a people. It is possible that the change from pros-

[1] Page 77.

perity to poverty and depression, in the case referred to, may be traced to other causes. But, be this as it may, New York may become sufficiently prosperous by cultivating the unquestionable sources of wealth which belong to her. Her agriculture and manufactures, and the more useful minerals which she possesses, with the means she has of transmitting the fruits of her own industry to other States and countries, and conveying their productions to almost every portion of her extended surface by natural or artificial channels of communication, may justly be regarded as the most certain and the purest sources of the prosperity of the State, and the happiness of its citizens.

Peat. — Under the head of minerals, if not strictly belonging to it, may be classed this combustible, which in portions of Europe constitutes the principal fuel in use. As wood becomes scarce it may become valuable here. Extensive beds have been found in Canaan, Columbia county, — sufficient, as is supposed, to supply the town with fuel for a thousand years.[1] In Clinton, Northeast, and Rhinebeck, Dutchess county, it has also been found.[2] This is a section of the State in which such a resource may be acceptable at an earlier period than in any other. The lands along the eastern bank of the Hudson river have recently risen exceedingly in value. The increased price which they bear is probably owing in a considerable degree to a change in the application of the agricultural industry of this section. Formerly it produced large quantities of wheat; but since the construction of the Erie Canal, this grain has been brought in such quantities from the western counties, that its cultivation, excepting for domestic consumption, in the district referred to, has almost ceased. The attention of the farmers is now turned to grazing. This species of husbandry requires a greater area than the cultivation of grains. To procure it, the woods must be gradually cut down, and the supply of fuel diminished. The natural demand for fuel,

[1] Silliman's Journal, Vol. V. p. 9. [2] Ibid. Vol. I. p. 189.

growing out of the increase of inhabitants, is also encroaching upon the forests. A substitute for wood within the limits of this district may be desirable at an earlier day than can now be foreseen, especially to such parts of it as are not in immediate contact with the river. Within the reach of water transportation, coal will doubtless be preferred; but every mile of transportation by land adds greatly to the cost of so heavy a substance. Beds of peat should, therefore, whenever they occur, be examined, their depth ascertained as nearly as possible, and trials should be made to ascertain the quality of the peat, and its comparative economy as a substitute for wood and coal. That which has been discovered in Dutchess and Columbia counties is said to burn with a clear, white flame. If so, it is preferable to the poorer classes of coal consumed in some of our cities; and, indeed, it is considered by a writer in Silliman's Journal, who has tested it, as a good substitute for Liverpool coal.[1]

Mineral Waters, Springs, &c.—The mineral waters of this State are a source of health, as well as profit, to its citizens. Those which are of the greatest celebrity have been carefully analyzed, and their medicinal properties are well known. In the progress of the proposed investigations, others will doubtless be found. In all cases, samples of the water should be taken and preserved for analysis; their temperature should be observed; and, indeed, the nature and temperature of every spring which has anything remarkable in its appearance should be ascertained, together with the mineralogical character of the surrounding localities and the soil or rock from which it issues.

ORGANIC REMAINS, ALLUVIAL DEPOSITS, &c.

It is of the greatest interest, in a scientific point of view, that the remains of animals and plants in a fossil state should be noted, together with the rocks in which they are found. The most remarkable specimens should, of course, be pre-

[1] Silliman's Journal, Vol. I. p. 140.

served, and all remains of the higher orders of animals, should any such be discovered.

It is now well settled among geologists, that the surface of the earth has undergone, at epochs more or less remote, successive alterations of the most extraordinary nature, and that during each intervening period of time it has been the seat of different orders of organic life. With regard to the time and manner in which these changes have taken place, men of science differ. But an examination of the various systems of strata which enter into the superficial structure of the earth has satisfactorily shown that it has been inhabited at successive periods by different races of animals. In the older strata are found the relics of unknown vegetables, and of marine animals, of which scarcely a species exists at the present day. The next superior formation contains reliquia of animals manifestly of a distinct creation, of many of which there are no vestiges in the older strata. It is in the more recent formations only that the bones of terrestrial quadrupeds are found, sometimes in the form of petrifactions, and sometimes preserved amid the traces of diluvial action, in caverns or in alluvial deposits. Of these races many species still exist, while other genera are wholly lost, and are known only by their remains. The amount of the resemblances of these races decreases with the distance, in the order of time, of the different epochs at which they are supposed to have existed;[1] so that between the present day and the most remote period the greatest difference will be found between the existing forms of organized life. As the different periods approach each other, resemblances multiply and differences decrease. Yet each system of strata contains different suites of organic remains, by which it may be distinguished.[2] To so great a degree of certainty has observation in this department of science been carried in Europe, that the nature of the fossil is considered sufficient to determine the character of the stratum in which it is found.

[1] Phillips's Guide to Geology, 2d edition, p. 70, §§ 77, 78.
[2] Parkinson on Organic Remains, p. 334.

GEOLOGICAL REPORT.

Whether strata of the same age in districts geographically remote from each other always contain organic remains of the same species, or how far, as at the present day, different sections of the earth had their peculiar systems of organized life, is one of the most interesting questions in geological science which is to be determined. It can be settled by the observation of facts only, and hence the importance, in a scientific point of view, of examining with the greatest care all the reliquia of ancient periods which may be discovered within our territorial boundaries. Between the organic remains of Europe and America great resemblances have been found, not only with respect to testaceous, but also with respect to several of the higher orders of terrestrial animals. Of the great mastodon, an extinct genus, the remains have been discovered in this State, in France, Italy, and South America.[1] Of existing genera, the remains of a species of the elephant have been found nearly perfect in almost every part of the world.[2] These remains are supposed by Cuvier to be of a species long since extinct, though resembling the living species of Asia.[3]

From the discovery of the remains of animals in sections of the globe characterized by peculiarities of climate essentially different from those of the regions in which living individuals of the same species are now to be found, it is inferred that in the revolutions which have taken place in the structure of the earth and in the character of the animal tribes by which it has been inhabited, changes must also have occurred in the prevailing temperature of particular regions and localities.

In Germany, Great Britain, and other countries, immense quantities of the bones of animals have been found in caverns, embosomed in diluvian earth and gravel. At Kirkdale in Yorkshire, England, remains of the hyena, the elephant, the rhinoceros, the hippopotamus, the horse, several other

[1] Parkinson on Organic Remains, p. 317. [2] Martin on Fossils, p. 42.
[3] Regne Animal, Vol. I. p. 240.

kinds of quadrupeds, and several species of birds,[1] were found in the year 1821, in a cavern, which had been manifestly a den of hyenas. From an examination of the cavern and its contents, no doubt existed that the animals whose remains were contained in it were dragged in, " either entire or piecemeal, by the beasts of prey whose den it was." It was equally apparent that they must have been inhabitants of the region in which they perished, although of several of the existing genera no individuals are now to be found there as natives. In the recent survey of the State of Massachusetts, by Professor Hitchcock,[2] that gentleman discovered a remarkable organic relic, which he considers a Gorgonia of an undescribed species, and from which he infers, with the support of other analogous indications, that the Connecticut valley, in which it was found, " once constituted, and for an immense period, the bottom of a tropical ocean."

The conclusions which are afforded by facts of this description may be confirmed by investigations in this State; and they may enable us to contribute our portion to the discoveries and deductions of science, which have, during the last half-century, done so much towards opening to mankind a knowledge of the internal resources in which the earth abounds, and of its condition during periods characterized by other forms and modifications of animal and vegetable life.

Of local alterations in the surface of the earth, those which result from the formation of valleys and ravines, and from alluvial deposits, will require a critical examination. Whether the former afford indications of having been produced by the elevation of a portion of the earth's surface by the agency of an internal force, whether they have been cut down by the violence of diluvial torrents, or abraded by the action of river waters, are questions which, though difficult of solution, are not void of interest.

The most extensive alluvial formation in the State, and the most important when considered in connection with the great

[1] Parkinson on Organic Remains, p. 329.   [2] Report, p. 237.

deposit of which it is a part, is that of Long Island. This island constitutes the eastern termination of the alluvial formation commencing on the Gulf of Mexico; it has a nucleus of primitive rocks, enclosed in a body of alluvion, which spreads itself out in the direction of the Atlantic ocean, of 130 miles in extent. To the formation of that part of the island which is washed by the Sound, the waters of the rivers emptying into it have doubtless contributed; but the greater part of the island has probably been formed by additions from the sea. On the southeastern shore there is an accumulation of sand of several miles in length, forming a bar above the level of the ocean, and separated by a bay of a mile or more in width from the body of the island. This whole formation is, from its nature and local circumstances, liable to great changes, and it is hardly possible that on such an extended line of alluvion, exposed to the action of powerful winds and marine currents, some interesting observations should not be made.

The alluvial deposits of the interior will require a particular examination. The force and volume of the waters by which such formations have been made are estimated by geologists from an observation of the extent of those formations and the nature of the materials of which they are composed. If they consist of fine silt only, it furnishes reason to believe that the velocity of the stream was not great at the periods of deposition. If they are mixed with coarse sand or gravel, it is an evidence that the stream must have moved with violence, in order to have kept them mechanically suspended in it. Thus the magnitude and force of a current at a given point may often be estimated with tolerable certainty by the nature of the detritus deposited by it.

Many of the considerations which have been last presented are theoretical, or have for their object contributions to the cause of science. As has already been said, these are not the principal motives to the execution of the survey. Its great object is to lay open the mineral resources of the

State, and make them subservient to the prosperity and wealth of its citizens. But in the accomplishment of this object, no opportunities should be lost of making observations which, though merely scientific, may throw new light upon questions connected with the existence of systems known only by the impressions they have left on those by which they have been succeeded.

It would be superfluous to attempt to point out all the objects to be kept in view by those who may be selected to execute the proposed survey, should provision be made for its execution. The magnitude and importance of the undertaking demand that gentlemen of the highest talents and of practical knowledge should be employed in it. If such selections are made, the individuals will find in their familiar acquaintance with the several branches of investigation confided to them the best guide to a successful and creditable discharge of their duty.

There is one topic, however, in reference to which a few suggestions may not be useless. Science is universal. Its laws are everywhere the same; and its language should be so in order that the scientific, wherever they are to be found, may understand each other. In every country there may be peculiarities of geological formation; and yet there are few, perhaps, which may not be brought within some settled rule of generalization. The employment of local terms, or such as are invented to express mere modifications of condition in the substances to which they are applied, is objectionable, because those terms are not understood unless they are accompanied by definitions; and with this accompaniment, science is in danger of becoming confused and complicated by a nomenclature more extended than the differences which it is intended to designate. Certainly nothing is gained, but much may be prejudiced, by an unnecessary multiplication of terms. The scientific of all countries should aim, therefore, to exclude from their researches and investigations everything which can by possibility create confusion in the minds of their co-laborers in the same fields of investigation. In the geological formations of America and Europe great similarity has been found, although some of the characteristic strata of the eastern continent are wanting here. Truth is, unquestionably, the great object to be sought for in all our investigations, and it should be pursued without leaning to either side. But if in our geological examinations any bias is felt, it is likely to be most innocent when it leans to the discovery of resemblances rather than differences; for under the influence of a strong desire to strike out a new path, there is some danger that the beaten track of observation may be unwisely abandoned.

ZOÖLOGY.

In this department it is contemplated by the resolution of the Assembly to furnish a list of the native animals of the State, and procure specimens of them for preservation. The first of these objects may be attained without difficulty; but in some cases the latter will be attended with considerable labor and inconvenience, and some expense, as several species of animals, which were frequently found while the State was comparatively a wilderness, have nearly disappeared as their places of abode have been invaded by the approaches of settlement.

Quadrupeds.— The fiercer species are now almost extinct in this State. The catamount is rarely found, nor has its place in the order of carnivorous animals, as is believed, been fixed beyond dispute. In the catalogue of animals in Massachusetts, appended to Mr. Hitchcock's survey,[1] the cougar, panther, and catamount are found under the species *felis concolor* of Linnæus. In Harlan's *Fauna Americana*,[2] the cougar is found under the species *felis concolor*, and the panther under the species *felis onça*. In a note appended to a description of the species *felis concolor*, the *cougar de Pennsylvanie* of Buffon is considered as a variety. In

[1] Page 526. [2] Page 95.

Godman's American Natural History,[1] it is remarked that a great deal of confusion exists as to the panther, which is decided by Temmink to be the *felis pardus* of Linnæus. But neither in Godman nor Harlan is the term catamount to be found. It is, indeed, a local appellation hardly known excepting in this State and in New England, where but a few years since the animal was often, but is now rarely, seen. The catamount and the panther are by some considered as belonging to the same species; but this opinion is called in question by others.

The panther still exists in this State; and should specimens of both be procured, the question of their identity with each other, or with any known species, may be solved.

The beaver is rarely met with in the northeastern States, and there would be great difficulty in procuring a specimen here. Possibly it may be found in the interior of the northern district. It is in this district only that a specimen of the catamount can be obtained, if it can be found at all.

The moose (*cervus alces* of Linnæus) is as rare as the catamount. If found at all, it will probably be, like the other, in the mountainous region between Lake George and the river St. Lawrence. This animal is supposed to be of the same species as the elk of northern Europe;[2] but this opinion is questioned, and it is only by comparison that it can be determined. A few years since two of these animals were killed in Herkimer county. Their skins were stuffed, and they are still preserved at Fairfield. The elk of Canada (*cervus Canadensis*) is altogether an inferior animal both to the moose and the Scandinavian elk, though sometimes supposed from identity of name to be of the same species as the latter.

It may be necessary to procure a specimen of the beaver beyond the limits of the State. The resolution of the As-

[1] Vol. I. p. 291.
[2] Richardson's *Fauna Boreali Americana*, p. 332, where a description of the animal may be found. See also Godman's American Natural History, Vol. II. p. 274.

sembly requires a specimen to be procured. The animal must be considered as an existing species in the State ; and if specimens of our native animals are preserved at all, those which are credited to us must be included in the number, in order to carry into effect the intention of the Assembly. Whenever it is practicable, the skins should be stuffed at the time the animals to be preserved as specimens are taken. With respect to the smaller quadrupeds, it will almost always be found convenient to do so ; but with respect to the larger kinds, it may be necessary, on account of the inconvenience of transportation, to preserve the skins for stuffing at a future time. In all cases the skeletons of the animals should be prepared, and their comparative anatomy noticed.

Birds. — In ornithology, the United States are in advance of every other country. The investigations of Wilson, Charles Bonaparte, and Audubon have made the list of the birds of America nearly complete. The whole number credited to the United States is about four hundred. Of this number probably about one half are to be found in New York. There are now in the Albany Institute specimens of about one hundred and twenty species of the birds of this State, which have been collected by the unassisted efforts of that association.

In this department of zoölogy there will be no difficulty in making a complete list and procuring a corresponding suite of specimens.

Fishes, Testacea, Zoöphytes, &c. — In these branches of zoölogy, the field to be examined is extensive and almost unexplored. Our fishes especially, both of salt and fresh water, are but little known. There have been some interesting papers published from time to time in philosophical journals in relation to them, and several new species, as is supposed, have been discovered. But there never has been a systematic examination of the inhabitants either of our rivers or lakes, or the waters surrounding Long Island. As far as they go, the articles of Mr. Lesueur, references to which will be found at the end of this report, are of great value.

Our shells, whether of marine, lake, river, or land production, deserve a very critical examination, more especially as the fossil remains of this extensive tribe of animals, both of living and extinct species, are considered as affording the most certain criteria for determining the priority of existing geological formations in the order of time. There is no department of our natural history which, for scientific purposes, requires a more careful investigation. Specimens should be preserved for a systematic classification and arrangement; and it is by no means improbable that these collections, with the fossil specimens which may be found imbedded in our rocks and soils, will be instrumental in showing the identity of formations here and in the old world, which have hitherto been considered entirely different in their geological character.

With the exception of the information contained in a single paper in Silliman's Journal, on the sponges on the shores of Long Island,[1] it is believed that we have nothing in relation to this class of substances, which are considered as having "an animal nature under forms approaching those of vegetables," and constituting, as it were, a connecting link between the animal and vegetable kingdoms. Sponges are found in a fossil state, in some of the early formations,[2] and frequently in the chalk formation of England. Under the generic term, zoöphytes, seven hundred and sixty-one species have been noticed as occurring in a fossil state.[3] At Corlear's Hook, large quantities of fossil milleporites have been discovered.[4] To this order of organic life belongs the relic discovered by Mr. Hitchcock, at West Springfield, in Massachusetts, supposed by him to be a Gorgonia, — a supposition leading, by a natural association, to a train of interesting

[1] Vol. I. p. 149.
[2] Parkinson on Organic Remains, p. 48.
[3] Phillips's Guide to Geology, p. 65.
[4] Silliman's Journal, Vol. II. p. 371.

considerations connected with earlier periods of the geological history of the region in which the relic was found.

This numerous order of animals, like the testaceous, will require a critical examination, — the more so for the reason that little attention has been paid to them. In Silliman's Journal, however, will be found several articles from Mr. Say, in relation to zoöphytes in the United States, principally of such as have been found in a fossil state, and among them several which have been discovered in New York are noticed.

Insects. — Appended to Mr. Hitchcock's report of the geological survey of Massachusetts is a list of the insects found in that State, prepared by Dr. T. W. Harris, amounting to 2350 species; but it is not accompanied with any description of them. The resolution of the Assembly requires nothing more than a complete list with a full series of specimens. Yet in connection with such an account of the entomology of this State, as a part of its natural history, certainly no considerations are of greater importance than those which relate to economical purposes. The destructiveness of many species of insects to vegetation is rarely considered and not often known, perhaps, in its full extent. Yet it is not unusual to see the wheat crop of extensive districts destroyed by the weevil, fruit-trees stripped of their foliage by caterpillars, and whole fields of vegetation cut down by grasshoppers and locusts. That much of this devastation might be guarded against by a better knowledge of their habits, cannot be doubted. By studying these, in connection with their changes, and the periods of their increase, they may be in a great degree counteracted in their invasions, and the cultivator secured in the enjoyment of the fruits of his labor. Such facts as fall under the notice of the observer in completing his list and procuring specimens, should be reduced to writing, and preserved for such future disposition as may be deemed advisable.

BOTANY.

The flora of New York is in a highly advanced state, and all the materials exist for an extensive collection of specimens. To make it complete, some labor and investigation will be necessary. The catalogue of plants appended to Mr. Hitchcock's Report on the Geology of Massachusetts, contains 594 genera and 1737 species; but it is, probably, not complete, and it embraces several exotic plants, which have been introduced or naturalized. The indigenous plants of North America probably equal 3500 species. Of these about 2500 species will no doubt be found in the Northern States. This estimate, however, is exclusive of cryptogamous plants, as ferns, mosses, sea-weeds, &c., which are included in the catalogue of the plants of Massachusetts under the denomination of flowerless plants.

The resolution of the Assembly contemplates nothing more as to the botany of the State than a list of its productions and the preservation of specimens of each. After making the necessary researches to complete the list, classifying the specimens, and arranging them in their proper order in volumes prepared for the purpose, the work will be consummated. The whole number of specimens will require an ordinary bookcase about six feet square.

PLAN OF SURVEY.

When we take into consideration the extended area of the State, the variety of formations which it embraces, and the numerous requirements contained in the resolution, it must be manifest that the contemplated survey could not be executed by a single individual in less than fifteen or twenty years; if indeed a single individual could be found equal to the task. The survey of the State of Massachusetts, by Professor Hitchcock, was completed in two years; but, as he states in his report, he was already familiar with the geology of a large portion of the State, from his own observations or the published accounts of others, and his personal examinations did not extend to its zoölogy or botany. Massachusetts has an area equal to about one sixth of that of New York. Assuming that the survey of Massachusetts was executed in the shortest practicable period of time, a single individual, even with the advantage of some acquaintance with the mineralogical constitution of this State, would require twelve years to examine its geology alone. As the principal object of the survey is to procure information which may be applied to useful purposes, it is desirable to complete the work as soon as possible, in order that the results may be available at the earliest practicable day.

It is proposed, therefore, to divide the State into four districts as to the geological part of the examination, and to assign to each district two geologists and a skilful draughtsman. By associating two observers in each district, it is supposed that an advantage will be attained on the score of accuracy through the suggestions which may be mutually made during their investigation, and that the gain in point of time and expense by a greater subdivision of the State, if the examination of each district were to be conducted by a single individual, would be undeserving of consideration in comparison with the advantage referred to.

In a division of the State for a geological survey, it is manifestly not equal, so far as a distribution of labor is concerned, to adopt a rule which shall regard merely the superficial contents of the different parts. Some districts will embrace a greater variety of formations than others, and present greater facilities for the prosecution of the contemplated investigations. But on the other hand it is not clear that the adoption of a different rule would obviate this inequality, as particular sections, which exhibit few apparent objects of interest, may on a nearer view be found worthy of a very critical examination. It has been thought proper, therefore, to divide the State as equally as possible into districts of the same area, with the exception of the northern primitive district, which, on account of the unsettled condition of a large portion of it, will oppose greater obstacles than cultivated sections to a thorough examination of its mineralogical structure. Thus the county of Hamilton, with an area of seventeen hundred square miles, contains only 1654 inhabitants. In making the division regard has been paid, as far as practicable, to continuity of character in the strata running through the several districts. Thus, the primitive formation along the Hudson river, from Washington and Saratoga counties, and including the Catskill mountains and the Highlands, to the southeastern extremity of the State, has been thrown into the first district; the northern primitive formation from Lake George to the St Lawrence river, including Hamilton county, comprises the second district; the counties including the salt springs have been assigned to the third district; and most of the counties in which a continuation of the coal formation of Pennsylvania may be expected to be found, to the fourth district. From the great variety of formations which enter into the geological constitution of the State, this rule of division is necessarily imperfect, nor is it, indeed, deemed very material; but it may be convenient in some cases, by enabling the observers to run out a particular range of rocks to its termination, without going beyond the limits of the districts assigned to them.

It has been customary, in extensive surveys of this description, to divide the region to be explored according to parallels of latitude or longitude. This is undoubtedly the most scientific mode of proceeding; but as the proposed survey of this State contemplates mainly objects of utility, and as maps of the several counties have already been constructed, exhibiting the minutest municipal divisions of the State with the greatest accuracy, it is deemed preferable to make the districts conform to statistical boundaries, which are well known, and to present the results of the survey in maps constructed on the same principle.

GEOLOGICAL REPORT.

The proposed districts are as follows:—

FIRST DISTRICT.

Counties.	Square miles.
1. Suffolk	973
2. Queens	396
3. Kings	76
4. Richmond	63
5. New York	22
6. Westchester	496
7. Rockland	172
8. Putnam	216
9. Dutchess	765
10. Orange	760
11. Sullivan	919
12. Delaware	1459
13. Ulster	1096
14. Greene	657
15. Columbia	624
16. Rensselaer	626
17. Albany	515
18. Schoharie	621
19. Schenectady	200
20. Saratoga	800
21. Washington	807
	12,263

SECOND DISTRICT.

22. Warren	912
23. Essex	1779
24. Clinton	932
25. Franklin	1652
26. Hamilton	1700
27. St. Lawrence	2717
	9692

THIRD DISTRICT.

28. Montgomery	840
29. Herkimer	1370
30. Oneida	1101
31. Lewis	1127
32. Jefferson	1162
33. Oswego	961

Counties.	Square miles.
34. Madison	582
35. Onondaga	779
36. Cayuga	697
37. Wayne	572
38. Ontario	653
39. Monroe	607
40. Orleans	380
41. Genesee	953
42. Livingston	509
	12,293

FOURTH DISTRICT.

43. Otsego	892
44. Chenango	804
45. Broome	633
46. Tioga	1031
47. Cortland	500
48. Tompkins	580
49. Seneca	304
50. Yates	291
51. Steuben	1518
52. Allegany	1205
53. Cattaraugus	1270
54. Chautauque	1065
55. Erie	1017
56. Niagara	484
	11,594

It is proper to state, that, in giving the geographical contents of each county, round numbers have been employed. This explanation is necessary, as the sum of their respective areas, as above shown, exceeds the actual area of the State, which is 45,658 square miles.

MAPS.

The county maps contained in Burr's atlas may be adopted as a basis for the geological purposes of the survey. They were constructed with the assistance of the late Surveyor-General of the State; and they are, with respect to the statistical divisions existing at the time they were prepared, exceedingly accurate. The scale on which they are constructed gives $2\frac{1}{2}$ miles actual measurement to one inch on the map, or a proportion between the map and the area which it represents of 1 to 158,400. In the atlas, in which it is proposed to exhibit the detailed results of the survey of the State of Maryland, now in progress, the county maps will be on a scale which will make the proportion of each map to the surface represented by it as 1 to 50,000. Taking the scale of the county maps in Burr's atlas as a basis, the results of the proposed survey of this State would be exhibited in maps bearing to the contemplated maps of Maryland a proportion of 1 to 3.16; that is, every actual measurement in this State would be represented on a scale more than two thirds less than every such measurement in Maryland.

There is unquestionably an advantage in exhibiting the results of the survey on the largest scale consistent with convenience; but it is believed that, for almost every practical purpose, the proportion proposed will be sufficient.

The geological formation of the entire State should be exhibited, on a greatly reduced scale, in a single map. The most convenient size will perhaps be a medium between Burr's map of the State, forming a part of his atlas, and his large map published by the Surveyor-General in 1829. The former is on a scale of about eighteen miles to the inch, or, in proportion to actual measurement of the territory represented, as 1 to 1,140,480, and the latter on a scale of seven miles to the inch, or as 1 to 443,520. The latter is about four feet six inches in length, and is inconveniently large for examination. A scale of twelve miles to the inch, or as 1 to 760,320, actual measurement, would give a map of convenient size for examination, and sufficiently so for the purpose of affording a correct view of the principal features of the geological constitution of the State.

Although the municipal divisions of the State are correctly

exhibited in Burr's atlas, it has been suggested that its topography is not always delineated with the same accuracy; that mountains are sometimes not shown at all, and at others, their true direction and extent are mistaken. In executing the proposed geological survey, these defects should be corrected. If every square mile in the State is examined, as it should be, and the observers are accompanied with a draughtsman, there will be no difficulty in ascertaining the elevation and direction of the various mountain ranges and the passes through them, and exhibiting their outlines on the map. For this purpose a second map must be made by the draughtsman, as geological formations cannot always be represented in connection with elevations and depressions of surface on the same sheet. The second map will be of a topographical, rather than a geological character; but as it will add little or nothing to the expense of the survey, it is deemed highly important to cause one of each county to be made. The originals can be deposited in the office of the Surveyor-General, and the Legislature can direct them to be published as a part of the survey, or retained for publication at another time.

EXPENSES.

It is not to be expected that the survey, under the most favorable circumstances, can be executed in less than three years, and it will more probably require four. To execute it properly, men of science and practical knowledge must be chosen. Their services cannot be secured without a compensation in some degree proportioned to the labor to be performed. It is true the work is of great importance, and individuals may be willing to embark in it from other considerations than that of pecuniary profit. But the State ought not to avail itself of such considerations to secure their services for less than a fair remuneration. The estimate, therefore, proceeds upon the supposition that the compensation is to be adequate to the labor. It is proper to add, that the individuals must bear their own expenses, and that no charge against the State should be allowed, excepting that of transporting specimens from distant counties to the general receptacle prepared for them. Their labors in the field will be confined to the milder portions of the year, and they may confidently anticipate from the inhabitants of every section of the State such aids as will alleviate the burden of investigation and lessen their personal expenditures. Under all the circumstances the following is deemed a fair estimate of the expenses which must be incurred in carrying into execution the proposed plan: —

Geology.

Two geologists to each district, at a salary of $1500 per annum each — 4 districts — 8 individuals,	$12,000
One draughtsman to each district, at a salary of $800 per annum — 4 districts — 4 individuals,	3,200

Zoölogy.

One zoölogist for the whole State, at $1500 per annum,	1,500
One draughtsman " " 800 "	800

Botany.

One botanist for the whole State, at $1500 per annum,	1,500
One draughtsman " " 800 "	800
Packing and transporting specimens,	100
Total annual expense of survey,	$19,900

An appropriation of $20,000 per annum for four years will certainly cover the whole expense of making the survey.

The cost of publishing three thousand copies of the report, drawings, and map of the results, will be as follows: —

It is supposed that the entire account of the survey may be contained in three volumes 8vo, of 700 pages each, 3000 copies, 9000 volumes, in boards, at 81 cents each,	$ 7,290
The maps may be lithographed, and, with the necessary drawings of fossil remains, will not exceed $4.33½ per atlas — 3000 copies,	13,000
Coloring the maps will be an additional charge of, say,	3,000
Cost of fitting up cabinet for specimens,	1,000
	$24,290

The amount may, and doubtless will, at first glance seem large; but it cannot, it is believed, be materially reduced without putting at hazard the objects of the survey. It is estimated that the survey of the State of Maryland will cost $20,000 exclusive of the expense of printing the final report, procuring maps, &c. That State has less than one fourth of the superficial extent of New York, and the facilities for ascertaining its geological structure are certainly not inferior to those which are afforded by this State. The relative expense is, therefore, about the same, with the exception that with our geological investigations, researches in botany and zoölogy are proposed to be combined.

If the investigations were confined to geology, and two thousand copies of the report and maps printed, the annual expense of the survey would be reduced to $15,800, and the cost of the publication to $17,500.

The geological examinations will have no connection, according to the plan submitted to the Legislature, with those in zoölogy and botany. With respect to the first, a division of the State is contemplated; whereas, with respect to each of the two latter, a single individual would make the necessary researches for the whole State. Should it be determined to dispense with these two subjects of examination, so far as the appointment of individuals for the special purpose is concerned, the gentlemen making the geological survey could be instructed to extend their researches, as far as practicable, to zoölogy and botany; and in this manner much valuable information might undoubtedly be obtained, and the labor of future investigations would be essentially diminished.

If the survey be made as contemplated by the resolution of the Assembly, the entire cost, including the expense of publication, will be about $104,000.

If the survey be made as contemplated by the resolution, and but 2000 copies of the report, maps, &c. be printed, the entire cost will be about $98,000.

If the examinations are confined to geology alone, and but

2000 copies of the report, maps, &c. be printed, the entire cost will be about $79,000.

The estimates of the expense of printing the report, engraving the maps, &c., were procured, from practical men, and may be considered as accurate as they can be made by the most careful calculation.

As it is proposed to preserve specimens of animals, as well as minerals, a room of some magnitude will be necessary for a cabinet. Such a room may be found in the third story of the capitol, by taking away a partition and throwing two of the apartments, set apart for committee rooms, into one. These rooms are rarely, if ever, used, and there will still be, after thus appropriating two of them, enough remaining for the purpose for which they were originally designed.

It may be proper to state in this place, that a petition was presented to the Legislature in the year 1834, by the Albany Institute, soliciting pecuniary aid for the purpose of making a similar collection. By reference to the petition,[1] it will be perceived that a desire was expressed by that body " to form a grand and comprehensive collection of the natural productions of the State of New York, to exhibit at one view and under one roof its animal, vegetable, and mineral wealth." Should it be deemed desirable, there would be no difficulty, it is presumed, in making an arrangement with the Institute for the custody of the specimens, subject to the pleasure of the Legislature with respect to a different disposition of them at any future time, and subject also to the supervision of any public officer who might be designated for the purpose. This arrangement would be attended with some inconvenience to the Institute, but it would doubtless be acceded to, if it were desired by the Legislature. The Maryland cabinet of minerals is temporarily deposited with St. John's college at Annapolis, the seat of government.

Under all the circumstances, it is submitted whether the

[1] Senate Doc. No. 15, 1834.

arrangement first suggested would not be the most proper. The rooms could be fitted up with little expense, except that of furnishing cases for the security of the specimens. It is supposed, of course, that the Legislature would be desirous of preserving them where they would be at all times accessible to its members and to strangers visiting the seat of government. With respect to the first of these objects, the preservation of the specimens in the capitol would be more convenient than in the Institute, and equally so with respect to the other object referred to.

With regard to the arrangement of the specimens, the plan proposed for the State cabinet of Maryland, so far as respects a geographical distribution,[1] is deemed highly important. On this plan the mineral productions of each county are exhibited separately, so that its representatives can see at a glance those in which their immediate constituents are directly interested. In addition to this arrangement, there is a duplicate series of specimens arranged in their natural order, vith a reference also to their fitness for useful purposes.

The first of these arrangements it would be advisable to adopt. But with respect to the second, it would perhaps be preferable to make it altogether geological; that is, to exhibit the entire suite of specimens in the order in which the rocks are supposed to have been formed, commencing with the lowest or those of earliest formation, and arranging the metallic specimens and organic remains in connection with the beds and strata in which they have respectively been found, thus disregarding in the arrangement of the second series of specimens the economical uses to which the several substances may be applied. This is a suggestion, however, which may more properly be left to the determination of those to whom the duty of arranging the specimens may be intrusted.

In entering upon the execution of the proposed plan, the individuals selected for the purpose should meet at a central

[1] Report on the New Map of Maryland, p. 50.

point and agree, so far as practicable, upon a uniform mode of conducting their examinations. By a comparison of views at the outset, misunderstandings may be obviated and valuable suggestions elicited; and if the survey is not, by means of these preliminary deliberations, accelerated in its progress, they cannot fail to be serviceable in preparing a uniform exhibition of its final results.

Whenever in the examination of a district a sufficient number of specimens shall have been collected, they should be packed with tow or hay, in a strong box or barrel, and sent to the place appointed for their reception. Each specimen should be numbered, and have labelled on it the particular locality in which it was found, and it should be enveloped in thick paper for packing. No specimen should be named; but the observers should of course preserve in a journal of their proceedings a description of the locality, with a memorandum of the different strata, and their order of superposition, assigning each specimen, by a reference to its number, to its proper place.

The number of specimens of each kind must be determined by the Legislature. It would be desirable to deposit an entire suite in each of our colleges. In this case, it would be necessary to preserve eight specimens of each rock, mineral, &c.; and as the number of colleges will probably be increased before many years, it would be well to augment the number to ten.

At the close of the season in which geological examinations may be advantageously carried on, all the parties should repair to the place where their specimens have been sent, and form a Board for examining, analyzing, naming, and arranging them. To name the specimens according to some nomenclature of acknowledged authority, is a duty of the highest importance. The suggestions contained in another part of this report, with respect to the practice of encumbering the science with terms either local or invented to designate unessential differences, apply with great force here. The Board should aim to lessen, as far as possible, the number of local designations, both of American and English origin, and conform to some standard by which they may make themselves understood by the scientific of all countries. If they succeed in this respect, they will render one service, at least, to the cause of science.

In reporting the results of the survey, there may be some little embarrassment in giving to the separate accounts of the different parties of observers that character of uniformity which is indispensable to make the work creditable to the individuals themselves, to the State, and to the cause of science. But it is believed that every difficulty of this sort will be removed by a desire, on the part of the individuals connected with it, to secure for it a high character, and that all other considerations will give place to the influence of this feeling.

For the purpose of laying before the public at the earliest day all the discoveries which may be turned to private account, there should be at the end of every season of examination a report from each district, giving a concise description of the rocks which may be advantageously employed for building, the minerals and ores which shall have been discovered, their qualities, and the uses for which they are fitted, — everything, in short, which may enable the inhabitants in whose neighborhood they occur to understand their value, and to convert them immediately to beneficial purposes. These annual reports will, therefore, embrace one class only of the objects of the survey — those which are practically useful; and the gentlemen who conduct the examination of each district should be left entirely to the exercise of their own discretion in preparing them.

The final report of the results will be of a different character. It will embrace not only the substance of the annual reports already referred to, but it will also present, for the first time, a scientific account of the geological structure of the State, and of all its mineral, animal, and vegetable productions, with such theoretical considerations as occur to the observers in the progress of their investigations. In the character of this report all have an interest, and in preparing it all should have a voice. It must be the result of their united deliberations and receive their united sanction. By whom, and in what manner it shall be prepared, are questions to be decided by the gentlemen themselves. Whether the two individuals intrusted with the examination of a district shall submit to the whole Board a separate report of such district for the approbation of all the others, or whether some one of them shall be chosen to prepare the entire report from the materials collected by all, may cause some deliberation. The latter course would be most likely to secure for the report a character of uniformity, which it is exceedingly desirable to give to it; and in this case the whole State would be exhibited under a single view, instead of being regarded through its subdivisions. Indeed, the entire geological survey would be best conducted through all its stages by a single party of observers, if it were practicable to execute it in this manner within any reasonable period of time. Its division is a matter of necessity, in consequence of its great extent, and is not without inconveniences; but these can be in a great degree, if not wholly, repaired by presenting the results in a continuous detail. Should this course be deemed objectionable, the other may answer the purpose, if each report receives the sanction of all the observers, and is presented to the public with the impress of their united authority. In accomplishing this object, no insuperable difficulty is anticipated. The gentlemen concerned will have too much respect for themselves to allow any minor difference of opinion to separate them in a matter which may so directly affect their own standing, the reputation of the State, and the successful execution of the great work in which they will be embarked. But should any one feel constrained, in any case, to differ from his associates, his dissent might be briefly pointed out in a note to be appended to the work, and in this manner the opportunity of doing justice to his particular views would be afforded to him, without carrying them into the body of the report.

The Secretary of State cannot close this report without adverting briefly to the efforts of other States to effect a systematic examination of the mineralogical constitution of their respective territories. A survey of the entire State of Massachusetts has been executed by Mr. Hitchcock, under the authority of the legislature, and his report bears honorable testimony to his ability, and to the liberal spirit of the State. A similar survey of the State of Tennessee is nearly, if not quite completed, at the public expense, by Dr. Troost. The two Carolinas have caused geological researches to be made within their respective limits, and movements have been made in the States of New Jersey and Virginia with the same object. At the last session of the legislature of Pennsylvania, a report was made in favor of a geological survey of that State; and it is earnestly recommended by Gov. Wolf, in his recent message, as indispensable to a full development of its resources. A geological and topographical survey of the State of Maryland is now in progress, and from the able reports of the gentlemen to whom it has been intrusted it is manifest that it will be executed in a manner in the highest degree creditable to the State and to themselves.

In this enterprise, therefore, New York cannot lead the way; but she may follow the example of her sister States, and do honor to their liberality and wisdom, as they have in many instances done to hers, by imitating her in opening channels of communication through her own territories, thus connecting them with other States, and contributing to strengthen those common bonds of association which unite us to each other. In so doing, it is confidently believed that the work, independently of its contributions to the cause of science, will in a short time add to the productive industry of its citizens an annual profit exceeding the whole amount expended in its execution, — a profit which will be regularly augmented as the resources which it opens to view are brought into operation.

    Respectfully submitted.
        JOHN A. DIX,
         Secretary of State.

PROGRESS OF SCIENCE.

The following Address was delivered before the Alpha Phi Delta and Euglossian Societies of Geneva College, on the 7th of August, 1839.

GENTLEMEN OF THE ALPHA PHI DELTA AND
   EUGLOSSIAN SOCIETIES:

I SHOULD have made but an ungrateful return for the honor you have done me in renewing an invitation which I was compelled on a former occasion to decline, if I had not cheerfully consented to address you. In the performance of the service I have undertaken, I trust I need offer you no apology, if I confine myself to topics which are in strict accordance with the objects of your association, and with the purposes to which this institution is dedicated. I might have chosen a more popular theme. But it is a peculiarity of the present day, that its scientific movements have an intimate connection with all classes of society. The age is distinguished from all that have preceded it by a more direct and successful application of philosophical truth to practical purposes. The moment the investigations of science lead to the discovery of a fact or a principle, art, under the impulse and guidance of self-interest, appropriates and converts it to some profitable use. Thus are all benefited by those triumphs of philosophical research, which, in a less active social state, might for a series of years have had no higher result than to confer honor on the minds by which they have been achieved.

If we consider the advances which science has made since the commencement of the present century, and the comparative freedom of human industry from useless restraints, we shall not be surprised at the changes which have taken place during the same period in the social condition of mankind. All improvements affecting the well-being of our race, whether they relate to government, the external concerns of individuals, or their intellectual and moral state, are comprehended within the general idea of civilization. Yet it has rarely happened that a country has advanced at the same moment in all these respects. Indeed, the highest degrees of intellectual improvement which were attained by the most powerful of ancient, and one of the most distinguished of modern states, were accompanied with great defects of political organization, and a most vicious condition of the social relations.[1] It is our good fortune to live at a period when all the elements of civilization are in progress. The removal, partial though it be, of restrictions upon the enterprise of individuals has opened boundless fields for exertion, and the united labors of science and the arts have been called in to improve the social and intellectual condition of mankind. Indeed, so natural does the connection seem between the several departments of civilization, — so necessary the influence of government upon the social state, and so direct the dependence of the latter upon scientific investigation, — that we can hardly forbear to wonder that one should have advanced while the others remained stationary.

Of the sciences which minister to the wants of mankind, none holds a higher rank than CHEMISTRY; and in none has the progress of experiment, during the last forty years, been attended with more successful results. The distinction and importance which it has attained in its applications to the useful arts are not the less remarkable from the fact that it had its origin in the superstitious belief that it was possible to prepare a substance which should possess the property of transmuting the baser metals into gold, of curing all diseases, and of prolonging human life to an indefinite extent.[2] The discovery of this imaginary substance

---

[1] Rome in the first, and France in the seventeenth, century.
[2] Thomson's History of Chemistry, Vol. I. p. 28.

was the object of almost all the researches of the chemists, (or alchemists, as they were called at a later day,) and of almost all their writings, from the seventh century to the sixteenth, when Paracelsus pointed out the importance of chemical investigations as a branch of the healing art. Although the ancients were acquainted with the principal uses of seven of the metals, and had acquired great skill in working them, the earliest regular treatise on the art of compounding them for medicinal purposes (one of the important practical uses to which chemistry has been applied) is found in the writings of Geber, an Arabian, who lived during the eighth century;[1] and it is worthy of remark, that most of the chemical processes used until nearly the beginning of the nineteenth century were known to this writer.[2] But while it was a prevailing practice to account for chemical phenomena by occult causes, no progress could well be expected in the science, excepting the discovery of new substances, which would naturally grow out of experiments made by experienced workmen. It was by the mixture of different substances, and by subjecting them to the action of heat in confined vessels, that some of the acids were discovered by the alchemists; and these being in their turn made to act upon the metals, metallic salts and preparations were produced. In this manner a multiplicity of facts were collected, to which the subsequent investigations of science assigned their due importance.[3] Although Paracelsus, less than three centuries ago, boasted of possessing the philosopher's stone, yet he insisted that the proper object of chemistry was the preparation of medicines, and not the transmutation of the baser metals into gold; and in this distinction consisted almost exclusively the reformation which he introduced into the science. Pharmacy is at the present day an important department of chemistry, but it is by no means to be ranked among its highest attributes. To trace the progress of the science from these rude beginnings

---

[1] Thomson's History of Chemistry, Vol. I. pp. 14, 16.
[2] Ibid. p. 122.   [3] Ibid. p. 80.

down to the period when its importance in shedding light upon the composition of bodies, and in promoting the cultivation of those arts which are most useful to mankind began to be appreciated, would far exceed the limits of this address, which proposes for its object to take a survey, and from necessity a brief one, of the advancement of science since the commencement of the present century.

Without the aid of analysis, chemistry could never have made any progress. It has been denominated the very essence of chemistry; and it was practised the moment the science began to wear the appearance of a system. About the middle of the last century, the analytical experiments of several distinguished chemists led to very important discoveries. Margraaf, of Prussia, ascertained that gypsum was a compound of sulphuric acid and lime. Scheele, of Sweden, surpassed most of his contemporaries in the number and value of his discoveries. Dr. Black, then of the University of Glasgow, analyzed several of the salts of magnesia, and determined the nature of their constituent parts. His experiments upon gaseous substances, with those of Cavendish and Priestley in England, attracted to the study of chemistry about seventy years ago the celebrated Lavoisier of France, whose researches and labors produced a total revolution in the science, by introducing into it the precision and regularity which belong to the other departments of philosophy.[1] To him and his associates, Berthollet, Morveau, and Fourcroy, and to their united labors, the science is indebted for the new nomenclature which was introduced near the close of the last century. In analytical chemistry, the science owes its highest obligations to Klaproth of Prussia. It was at his instance, and under his direction, that the Academy of Sciences of Berlin, in 1792, undertook a series of experiments with a view to test the respective claims of the phlogistic and anti-phlogistic theories, (the rival systems of the day,) which resulted in the adoption of the latter as estab-

[1] History of Chemistry, Vol. II. p. 75.

lished in France by Lavoisier. Before the adoption of Lavoisier's theory, sulphur, phosphorus, charcoal, and the metals, were considered as compounds, of which phlogiston was one of the constituents, and the other constituents which remained after combustion or calcination, were regarded as acids or calces. But he showed that those bodies were simple substances, and that the acids or calces formed by combustion or calcination were compounds of those substances with oxygen.[1] Klaproth died in 1817, and his labors may be properly considered as belonging to the present century. His great merit consists in the accuracy of the analytical methods which he introduced,[2] and the precision which he attained in the decomposition of bodies. In analyzing a mineral, it is generally found, when its constituent parts are collected, that their weight does not equal that of the mineral before the analysis; on the other hand, it is sometimes found that the weight of the parts exceeds that of the mineral. Before the time of Klaproth, it had been customary to ascribe these differences to errors in the analysis; and in stating the result, to apportion the deficiency or excess among the constituents, so as to make the mineral and its constituents equal. To him the science is indebted for the practice of stating the results accurately, so that the difference is always shown; and to this reform have been attributed most of the subsequent improvements in analytical chemistry;[3] for, whenever the difference was considerable, a repetition of the analysis would naturally be resorted to; and if it had the same result, it would lead to the suspicion that some of the constituents had escaped notice. In this manner potash, soda, water, and various acids, were found to exist in minerals. Vauquelin of France, Stromeyer of Göttingen, Tennant of England, Berzelius of Sweden, and others, improved the methods of Klaproth, and rendered important services to the science. The experiments of Bergman and Gahn of Sweden, near the close of the last century, in the

---

[1] History of Chemistry, Vol. II. p. 267.
[2] Ibid. p. 198. [3] Ibid. p. 199.

application of the blowpipe to the assaying of minerals, and the improvements made by the latter and by Dr. Wollaston of England in the use of this instrument, were also important steps in analytical chemistry, by enabling the operator to discover in a few moments the nature of almost any mineral, and thus to dispense with a preliminary analysis, which in many cases is necessary before an analysis by solution. In the year 1801, a new and extraordinary power was conferred on this instrument by Mr. Hare of Philadelphia, who substituted for atmospheric air a united stream of oxygen and hydrogen gases. By this means the most refractory substances have been readily fused, and a great variety of interesting experiments have been performed in both hemispheres.[1]

But it is to the brilliant discoveries of Sir Humphrey Davy, by the application of galvanism to chemical decompositions, that chemistry owes its greatest obligation. He explained the laws by which this powerful agent is regulated; and by his illustrations he dissipated all the doubts which had enveloped the subject from the period of the discovery by Galvani, and the discussions which took place between Volta and the latter. As early as 1803, eleven salts had been decomposed by Berzelius and Hisinger, by passing a current of electricity through them. Sir Humphrey Davy decomposed, in the same manner, various compounds, on which the efforts of the chemists had been fruitlessly expended. The conclusion which he drew from his experiments, and which is now a familiar principle, was, that all substances which have a chemical affinity for each other, are in different states of electricity, and that the degree of affinity is proportioned to the intensity of these opposite states.[2] Thus, on presenting a compound to the poles of the galvanic battery, the positive pole attracts the constituent which is in the negative state, and the negative the constituent which is positive; each pole repelling, at the same time, the constituent which the other

[1] Silliman's Journal, Vol. I. p. 97.
[2] History of Chemistry, Vol. II. p. 261.

attracts. The force of these attractions and repulsions being proportioned to the strength of the battery, any compound may be decomposed by a sufficiently powerful apparatus. The experiments of Davy on potash and soda were of the greatest value, by leading to the establishment of the fact that the fixed alkalies and alkaline earths are metallic oxides. His experiments on chlorine were not less important. He proved it to be a simple substance, and not, as Berthollet had attempted to show, a compound of oxygen and muriatic acid. He also proved muriatic acid to be a compound of chlorine and hydrogen; and thus the theory of Lavoisier, that oxygen was the universal acidifying principle, was overthrown. Several other acids are now well known to contain no oxygen. The experiments of Gay-Lussac and Thénard in France — of the former on prussic acid and iodine, of the latter on the various combinations of oxygen and hydrogen, and of both on chlorine and muriatic acid — are to be classed among the triumphs of chemical science; and also the facts established by Mr. Faraday, that gases may be condensed into fluids by the united action of pressure and cold, and that chlorine is capable of combining with carbon.[1]

The most recent improvement in the science of chemistry is the atomic theory, first suggested by John Dalton, and almost inseparable from the doctrine that bodies unite with each other in definite proportions; and it has been said that it " has given a degree of accuracy to chemical experiment almost amounting to mathematical precision." [2] According to this theory, " the ultimate particles of bodies are atoms incapable of further division, and chemical combination consists in the union of these atoms with each other." [3] The proportions in which the union takes place are expressed by weight; and hydrogen, being the lightest of all known bodies, is assumed as the unit of atomic weight, and the atomic weights of all other bodies are treated as multiples of

---

[1] History of Chemistry, Vol. II. p. 275.   [2] Ibid. p. 277.
[3] Ibid. p. 294.

it. Chemical analysis has, therefore, a new object of investigation. It formerly aimed almost exclusively to ascertain the nature of the substances which belong to the various departments of organic and inorganic life : it now aims also to determine the relative weights of their different constituents. Although the theory is yet in its infancy, and although differences of opinion exist among chemists as to the mode of settling the combining ratios or atomic weights of bodies, it has led to most important consequences. In the application of chemistry to useful purposes, it teaches the proportions in which different substances should be combined to produce specific effects; and by the economy of material which it has introduced, chemical products have become cheaper and more abundant.[1] It has also led to some remarkable discoveries in regard to the composition of bodies. In the early stages of chemical investigation, a diversity in the properties of bodies was attributed to a difference in their constituents, or in the proportions in which they were combined; but as chemical analysis was improved, bodies similar in their components were found to differ widely in their external characteristics. It is now shown not only that two bodies may have the same constituents, and that the constituents may be combined in the same proportions, and yet the compounds themselves may be different; but it is also demonstrated that two bodies may be unlike, though possessing the same elements, combined in the same proportions, and though having the same atomic weights.[2] To this class of bodies, which are termed *isomeric*, belong the two kinds of phosphuretted hydrogen, one of which ignites when brought into contact with atmospheric air, while the other does not possess this property.[3]

---

[1] History of Chemistry, Vol. II. p. 277.
[2] Reports of the British Association for the Advancement of Science, Vol. I. pp. 434, 456.
[3] The fact was shown by Prof. Rose, of Berlin; but Prof. Graham, of the British Association, ascribes the difference to the presence of an infinitely minute proportion of volatile oxide analogous to nitrous acid in the phosphuretted hydrogen, which inflames by contact with atmospheric air. (Reports of the Association, Vol. I. p. 457, and Vol. III. p. 582).

The applications of chemistry to the useful arts are so numerous that it would be impossible, if it were within the design of this address, to enumerate them. By the use of chlorine in bleaching cotton and linen fabrics, and by the application of tannin to the preparation of leather, tedious and expensive processes have been avoided, and these products of industry have been greatly reduced in price. Numberless other instances of similar improvements might be adduced, in which articles of convenience and necessity have been made cheaper, and thus brought within the reach of additional classes of consumers. Chemistry has not only improved the arts formerly in use, but it has introduced new ones, which are ministering, in a variety of ways, to the health and comfort of the human family. By the extrication of a gas from a substance dug from the bosom of the earth, streets and dwellings are lighted up with new brilliancy. By the action of atmospheric currents artificially produced, and by the application of disinfecting agents, noxious gases and vapors may be dissipated and rendered harmless; and by the light of the safety-lamp, the miner digs fearlessly into the depths of the earth. It has been said, and not perhaps without justice, that chemistry "has contributed as much to the progress of society, and has done as much to augment the comforts and conveniences of life, and to increase the power and resources of mankind, as all the other sciences put together."[1]

Notwithstanding the progress which the science has made, but a small portion of the field of nature has been explored. In the inorganic kingdom, fifty-four elementary substances are recognized, more than half of which have been discovered within the last seventy years. The number of acids known to chemists exceeds one hundred, and the number of alkaline bases exceeds seventy. It has been estimated that every base is capable of uniting with almost every acid in at least three different proportions.[2] Assuming this estimate

[1] History of Chemistry, Vol. I. p. 2.   [2] Ibid. p. 316.

to be true, the whole number of salts which they may form is twenty-one thousand; of these, only about one thousand are yet known. The endless variety exhibited by the animal and vegetable kingdoms opens to chemical investigation boundless fields, of which we have comparatively but little knowledge. In the latter especially a few principles only have been discovered, and most of these by a single chemist,[1] whose attention has been but recently directed to the subject. In the examination of the vegetable kingdom, greater progress has been made than in the animal. Recent investigations have shed much light on the ultimate principles and atomic constitution of vegetable substances. But in the destruction of organic life, and in the decomposition of the substances of which it is the support, the doubt naturally arises whether the results may not be modified by the processes through which they are obtained. Other questions of equal importance have sprung up in the progress of organic chemistry; and this has now become a prolific field of inquiry.

The close approximation, in the character of their constituent parts, of many substances which differ widely in their properties, is one of the most interesting facts which chemistry has furnished. Thus, sugar and starch are composed of the same elementary substances. One is tasteless, the other sweet; one is insoluble, the other soluble. In like manner, some substances which are nutritious are composed of the same constituents as others which are poisonous. Thus are combinations of the same elements, under modifications so slightly varying as to be imperceptible to the most skilful analysis, capable of contributing to the support of human life, and to its destruction. Many of these combinations, as they exist in nature, have been successfully imitated by art; and as chemical analysis makes us familiar with the forms under which various elementary substances are united with each other, the inquiry arises as to the extent of the control which man may acquire over the dominion of nature; how

[1] M. Chevreul.

far the elements he obtains by the artificial decomposition of bodies may be recombined by synthetical processes, and be made to contribute, under various modifications, to the satisfaction of his wants and the prolongation of his life. If, at the threshold of this inquiry, we are, from the imperfection of human reason, compelled to pause, the progress of science is daily carrying us nearer and nearer to its solution; constantly bearing us on, with accelerated steps, to the fulfilment of a destiny, which to attempt to foretell, in the present state of human knowledge, might seem but the wild and visionary dream of speculation.

At the commencement of the present century, GEOLOGY had made far less progress than Chemistry. Indeed, it has been said that it was almost without a name.[1] The great features of the science had been sketched by Steno, Leibnitz, and Hooke, more than a hundred years before; but little had been done to fill up the outline which they had drawn; and in most of the geological discussions anterior to the time of Werner, the true objects of the science were lost by the introduction of hypothetical causes to account for the phenomena of the material world. Of the three grand divisions of geological formations, only one had been carefully examined at the beginning of the present century. It has been mentioned as remarkable, that these three great departments of the science became the subject of investigation in the order according to which the formations belonging to them were produced, — the primitive first, next the secondary, and the tertiary last; and that the leaders of the three schools, by which these departments have been respectively explored, were of three different countries — Germany, England, and France. The researches of the German school under Werner, which had its origin near the close of the eighteenth century, were principally directed to the primitive and transition formations, comprehending the imbedded min-

[1] Buckland's Geology, p. 6.

erals.[1] The English school had been chiefly engaged in the examination of the secondary formations, including the organic remains which give them their distinctive character; and it may be considered as having received its original impulse from William Smith, whose observations were first published in 1799. The French school owes its origin to the investigations of Cuvier and Brongniart, whose work on the mineral geography and organic remains of the neighborhood of Paris was published in 1808;[2] and whose observations on the tertiary formations, and the bones of extinct animals with which those formations abound, have shed so much light on the most recent changes which have taken place in the structure of the earth, and on the history of those animal tribes which were the immediate predecessors of its present inhabitants.

Although geology may yield in utility to some other sciences, there is none with which so many interesting considerations are associated. The physical condition of the earth manifests to the most superficial observer that it has undergone, at periods more or less remote, the most violent and extraordinary revolutions in its structure. Geological investigations have enabled us to form some opinion as to the causes of these revolutions, to determine the order of time in which they have occurred, to ascertain the nature of the systems of organic life by which each successive epoch was distinguished, to estimate the alterations of climate which different regions have undergone, and to comprehend the extent of these changes by comparing the present condition of our planet with the traces which remain of the tremendous physical actions to which it has been subjected. In the progress of these investigations, facts have been developed which are calculated to fill the mind with emotions of amazement. The bones of animals have been found in sections of the earth geographically remote from those in which the same

[1] Reports of the British Association, Vol. I. p. 370.
[2] Lyell's Principles of Geology, Vol. I. p. 104.

animals are now met with as living species, and under circumstances which show conclusively that they were inhabitants of the districts in which their remains have been discovered. The skeletons of other animals of extinct races, and which are now only known by their remains, have also been found in countries distant from each other; some of them of enormous size, and differing in anatomical organization from any existing genus or species. In the regularity which exists in the distribution of organic remains through different systems of strata — from the mollusca of the transition series, to the gigantic saurians of the secondary, and the birds and mammalia of the tertiary, differing from the living inhabitants of the earth in proportions increasing with the distance of the respective periods of deposition of the formations in which they are found — there is a still wider field for contemplation and wonder. Yet all these traces of animal existence in past ages are stamped with evident marks of design, and of a wise adaptation of its forms, so far as they have been disclosed, to the condition of the earth at the periods with which they are connected.[1] The investigations of Cuvier have shown that the whole district of country which includes Paris and its environs has been the theatre of successive inundations from the ocean and from fresh-water lakes, and that it has been frequented by races of animals which have been long extinct. More recent examinations in Great Britain have proved that the rhinoceros, the elephant, the hippopotamus, and the hyena once inhabited that island; and the stems of tropical plants have been found with their roots fastened in beds of limestone, in the positions in which they must have grown.[2] Similar examinations in Germany, and in different parts of this continent, have led to similar conclusions as to the extinct races by which they were formerly occupied. The bones of the great mastodon, and the remains of fossil vegetables of submarine production, have been

---

[1] Buckland's Geology, *passim*.
[2] Reports of the British Association, Vol. I. p. 877.

found in this State; and it requires no effort of the imagination to fancy that the very spot on which we now stand, amid beauties of scenery which few districts of the habitable globe can equal, and still fewer surpass, — amid monuments of science, of art, and of social cultivation, of which older communities might justly be proud, — may have been the abode of gigantic races of animals, and the seat of extinct orders of vegetable production, to which still more ancient forms of organic life may long since have given place.

There is nothing which displays in a more striking manner the power of human intelligence than the knowledge which geological investigations have given us with regard to the condition of the earth in past ages. The geologist breaks off the fragment of a rock, and by a mere inspection of its external appearance he determines what is its mineralogical character, and in what order of superposition the stratum to which it belongs lies in reference to other formations. If he finds impressed upon it the organic remains of animal or vegetable life, he knows to what tribe or class those remains are to be assigned. If the fossil remains of an animal are presented to him, he can tell in what stratum they were found; and, as geological examinations are extended, he will be able to pronounce from what part of the earth they come. When a few of the principal bones of an animal were found by Cuvier, he was able, by his knowledge of comparative osteology, to determine the size and the general character of the remaining parts; and when at a subsequent period an entire skeleton was made up from other discoveries, it differed in no essential particular from that which he had described by the aid of scientific principles alone.

When it is considered that geology, as a science, can hardly be deemed to have had an existence until within the last half century, its progress seems the more remarkable. Let it not be supposed that the extraordinary appearances which the surface of the globe exhibits, had not attracted the attention of more ancient observers. The traces of disturbance which it presents had been examined; distinct successions of strata, and the regular distribution of organic remains, had been recognized at a much earlier period. Indeed, gentlemen, when I refer you to the last book of Ovid's "Metamorphoses," your classical recollections, which are much more fresh than my own, will at once bring to mind a vivid and accurate summary of the principal mutations which the physical condition of the earth has undergone. The object of the science is not to speculate upon these changes, but to collect facts; to compare the geology of one part of the globe with another; to determine whether the same systems of organic life have prevailed at contemporaneous periods of disturbance, or whether, as at the present time, it has been inhabited at the same epoch by different races of animals, and distinguished by different forms and orders of vegetable existence. Important generalizations as to volcanic phenomena have been made, and geologists have ventured to speak with confidence of the periods of elevation of the Alps and Pyrenees. More extended observations may lead to still more important generalizations as to the forces by which disruptions of the surface of the earth have been produced, and the periods at which the elevation of mountains in different countries has taken place. Extraordinary as the disclosures of geological research may seem, we cannot overlook the fact that changes are constantly passing before our eyes, not less violent than those which we can only study through their distant effects.[1] Extensive districts

---

[1] "In the state of tranquil equilibrium, which our planet has attained in the region we inhabit, we are apt to regard the foundation of the solid earth as an emblem of duration and stability. Very different are the feelings of those whose lot is cast near the foci of volcanic eruptions. To them the earth affords no stable resting-place, but during the paroxysms of volcanic activity reels to and fro, and vibrates beneath their feet; overthrowing cities, yawning with dreadful chasms, converting seas into dry lands and dry lands into seas. (See Lyell's Geology, vol. 1, *passim*.) To the inhabitants of such districts we speak a language which they fully comprehend, when we describe the crust of the globe as floating on an internal nucleus of molten elements: They have seen these molten elements burst forth in liquid streams of lava; they have felt the earth beneath them quivering and rolling, as if upon the billows of a subterranean sea; they have seen mountains raised, and valleys depressed, almost in an instant of time; they can duly appreciate from sensible experience the force of the terms in which geologists describe the

are submerged by earthquakes; volcanic fires issue from the summit of mountains, and bury in ruins the villages and habitations at their base; and new lands rise up, as if by enchantment, from the bosom of the ocean. As recently as 1794, the country around Vesuvius was desolated by an eruption, reënacting the scenes so graphically described by the younger Pliny seventeen hundred years before. In 1815, twelve thousand inhabitants were destroyed by an eruption of Tomboro. In 1788, Skaptar Jokul burst forth and dried up the river Skaptâ, filling its bed to the level of the banks, more than six hundred feet in height, with lava. In the Grecian Archipelago, several islands have risen from the sea, the last about a century ago. In 1831, Graham or Hotham Island was formed in the Mediterranean by a subaqueous eruption. In July, it was first observed in the form of a column of water rising to the height of sixty feet. In August, an island had been formed, two hundred feet high, and three miles in circumference, with a crater in the centre. In September, it had sensibly decreased in size; and in 1833, nothing remained but a reef of rocks. More silent, but not less certain, agents are steadily altering the physical condition of the earth. The unceasing flow of river-waters is constantly abrading the lands through which they have worn their way, bearing on their bosom to distant soils the elements of vegetable life, the disintegrated materials of rocks, and the exuviæ of animals; and the perpetual agitation of the ocean, while it frets away, in one place, the rocks and sands by which it is bounded, is, in another, adding mile upon mile to the empire of the land. To the same causes, modified by varying conditions, may doubtless be referred those alterations in the surface of the earth of which we have no other recorded evidence than the traces which they have left upon its geological features.

tremulous throes and convulsive agitations of the earth, during the passage of its strata from the bottom of the seas in which they received their origin, to the plains and mountains in which they find their present place of rest." — *Buckland's Geology*, p. 46.

The connection of geology with objects of utility is not less direct than that of chemistry, though not so extensive and diversified. By an examination of the superficial covering of the earth, it has taught the miner where he may penetrate its interior with the assurance of finding those deposits of coal, the remains of ancient forests,[1] which nature by sudden disturbances has entombed, and thus preserved from decay, to be treasured up as a source of comfort to man, and as the most efficient agent of the mechanical powers which his contrivance and skill have converted to his use. It also informs him, by a similar observation of the superficial strata of a district, what other mineral treasures are likely to be found in those by which they are underlaid. It is constantly adding to the wealth of the human family, by indicating the places where some of the means of creating it exist, and preventing a fruitless dissipation of the stores which industry has accumulated, by turning away capital and labor from localities in which they would be expended in vain. With the aid of chemistry, it ascertains the nature of the ingredients which enter into the composition of the soil of a particular district, and determines not only to what forms of vegetable life it is best adapted, but what artificial aids it requires from the hand of man. In like manner, it ascertains the nature of the various rocks which he appro-

---

[1] "The finest example [of vegetable remains] I have ever witnessed, is that of the coal mines of Bohemia. The most elaborate imitations of living foliage upon the painted ceilings of Italian palaces bear no comparison with the beauteous profusion of extinct vegetable forms with which the galleries of these instructive coal mines are overhung. The roof is covered as with a canopy of gorgeous tapestry, enriched with festoons of most graceful foliage, flung in wild irregular profusion over every portion of its surface. The effect is heightened by the contrast of the coal-black color of these vegetables, with the light groundwork of the rock to which they are attached. The spectator feels himself transported, as if by enchantment, into the forests of another world; he beholds trees of forms and characters now unknown upon the surface of the earth, presented to his senses almost in the vigor and beauty of their primeval life; their scaly stems and bending branches, with their delicate apparatus of foliage, are all spread out before him, little impaired by the lapse of countless ages, and bearing faithful records of extinct systems of vegetation, which began and terminated in times of which these relics are the infallible historians. Such are the grand natural herbaria wherein these most ancient remains of the vegetable kingdom are preserved in a state of integrity little short of their living perfection, under conditions of our planet which exist no more." — *Buckland's Geology*, p. 458.

priates to his use, the purposes for which they are fitted, and foretells, without the tedious process of experiment, whether their disintegration is most likely to be effected by aqueous or atmospheric influences. Thus are investigations, which are constantly adding to our knowledge of the condition of the planet we inhabit in times separated by the lapse of ages from our own, contributing at the same time to multiply the sources and extend the boundaries of human enjoyment.

In the kindred science of MINERALOGY, although it has been the constant subject of persevering and skilful investigation, the results obtained have been far less satisfactory. The attention of Werner and his immediate followers was directed principally to the physical characters of bodies; but it soon became manifest that mineralogy could never be brought to perfection as a system by these alone. Haüy, about the same period, attempted to lay the foundations of a solid system in crystalline form; and from that time to the present his theory has continued to constitute the most important department of the science. Mohs and others have attempted generalizations by a classification of forms in systems of crystallography. But the whole theory of Haüy has received a severe shock by the recent discovery that crystalline angles are not constant in minerals of the same species, and that corresponding angles of the same crystal differ from each other.[1] Chemical analysis has also been called in to determine the connection between the chemical constitution and mineral character of bodies; but so far with little success.[2] Berzelius attempted a general system of classification of minerals, according to their chemical relations; and to this school belongs our countryman Cleaveland, whose work is well known in all parts of Europe, as well as in the United States. But none of the theories which have yet been formed have been found sufficient to unite the scientific world, or to introduce into the science the order and

[1] Reports of the British Association, Vol. II. pp. 351, 486.   [2] Ibid. p. 343.

regularity of a perfect system. Sir David Brewster has, by a variety of interesting experiments, attempted to establish a uniform connection between optical properties and crystalline form; but the infinite variety of forms, and the singular fact that different portions of a crystal, apparently simple, may exhibit different optical relations, render these investigations so complex as to make it doubtful whether they will lead to any satisfactory conclusions.

In OPTICS, the progress of science has been marked by the discovery of several important principles. The rectilinear propagation of light, the equality of the angles of incidence and reflection, and the inclination of a ray of light to the perpendicular in passing from a rare to a denser medium, were observed more than sixteen centuries ago. In the second century, Ptolemy of Alexandria measured the angles of refraction in water and glass, and with singular accuracy. Early in the seventeenth century, Snellius of Leyden discovered the law of refraction, or the constant relation between the sines of incidence and refraction. About the middle of the same century, Bartholinus, a Dane, discovered double refraction, the phenomena of which were explained and the law furnished by Christian Huygens a few years afterwards. About the same period, the latter discovered the polarization of light by double refraction; but neither he nor Sir Isaac Newton, his contemporary, was able to furnish the law by which this property of light is governed. The discovery of the different refrangibility of light by the latter, and that of the dispersive powers of bodies by Hall and Dolland, constitute, with those which have already been enumerated, the most important steps in the progress of physical optics to the end of the seventeenth century; and in this state the science remained for more than a hundred years.

The year 1810 was signalized by the great discovery by Colonel Malus of France, that light reflected at a particular angle from transparent bodies is polarized like one of the rays produced by double refraction. This discovery led to researches on the part of various scientific individuals in Europe, of which it has been said, that "nothing prouder has adorned the annals of physical science since the development of the true system of the universe."[1] Mr. Airy, of the University of Cambridge in England, has more recently discovered elliptical polarization; and M. Cauchy, of the Academy of Sciences in France, the existence of a triple refraction. The latter is also said to have deduced, from the undulatory or wave theory of light, the law of the tangents, which connects the polarizing angle with the refractive power of the body, and to have explained the phenomena of dispersion.[2] If to these steps we add the discovery of dark lines crossing the spectrum formed by the light of the sun, and the presence of all the deficient rays in a spectrum of artificial white flames, the principal acquisitions in this department of natural philosophy will have been enumerated. Many brilliant and interesting experiments have been made by Sir David Brewster and others, on the refractive powers of bodies, and many important facts have been obtained; but the discoveries heretofore made have led to no conclusions in which all coincide, as to the nature of light, or the undeniable truth of either of the two great rival theories of emission and undulation.[3] They serve, nevertheless, to indicate the importance with which the subject is still invested, and may lead the way to more satisfactory investigations of other phenomena which are yet unexplained.

The application, during the eighteenth century, of the discoveries of Galileo, Napier, Descartes, and Newton, to the celestial phenomena, had completed the great outlines of ASTRONOMY, and left apparently but little to be done by the pres-

---

[1] Reports of the British Association, Vol. I. p. 314.
[2] Ibid. p. 317.
[3] The third volume of the Reports of the British Association, page 295, contains a very learned and complete article on the progress and present state of physical optics, by Mr. Humphrey Lloyd, in which the principal phenomena of the science are reconciled with the undulatory theory of Huygens.

ent age, excepting to fill up the details of the science. Herschel had discovered the planet Uranus; various arcs of meridian had been measured, affording bases for extensive calculations; voyages of discovery had been undertaken for the purpose of exploration, and to make observations with a view to determine the dimensions of the solar system;[1] scientific individuals had been sent to high northern latitudes, to the equator, and to the southern hemisphere, to measure the degrees of the meridian and the lengths of the pendulum; and the invention of some of the most important astronomical instruments now in use had given the highest degree of accuracy to observation. The great work of Laplace was in progress, and the principal part of it had been published. He had deduced the motions of the planets from the general principles of the equilibrium and motions of bodies, and the doctrine of universal attraction. The theory of the pertur-

---

[1] Laplace's Mécanique Céleste, translated by Bowditch, Vol. III. pp 12, 13. The merits of this translation are admirably expressed in the following extract from the address of the Duke of Sussex, uncle to Queen Victoria of England, at the last annual meeting of the Royal Society of London, of which he was then president: —

"Every person who is acquainted with the original, must be aware of the great number of steps in the demonstrations which are left unsupplied, in many cases comprehending the entire processes which connect the enunciation of the propositions with the conclusions; and the constant reference which is made, both tacit and expressed, to results and principles, both analytical and mechanical, which are co-extensive with the entire range of known mathematical science. But in Dr. Bowditch's very elaborate translation, every deficient step is supplied, every suppressed demonstration is introduced, every reference explained and illustrated; and a work which the labors of an ordinary life could hardly master is rendered accessible to every reader who is acquainted with the principles of the differential and integral calculus, and in possession of even an elementary knowledge of statical and dynamical principles.

"When we consider the circumstances of Dr. Bowditch's early life, the obstacles which opposed his progress, the steady perseverance with which he overcame them, and the courage with which he ventured to expose the mysterious treasures of that sealed book, which had hitherto only been approached by those whose way had been cleared for them by a systematic and regular mathematical education, we shall be fully justified in pronouncing him to have been a most remarkable example of the pursuit of knowledge under difficulties, and well worthy of the enthusiastic respect and admiration of his countrymen, whose triumphs in the field of practical science have fully equalled, if not surpassed, the noblest works of the ancient world."

This notice of the distinguished mathematician and astronomer of Massachusetts, whose name is known in every part of the civilized world, as well as the compliment paid to the success of our countrymen in the application of scientific principles to practical purposes, cannot fail to be properly appreciated as an evidence of the freedom of science from the prejudices too often to be found in other spheres of human action.

bations of the planets, occasioned by their reciprocal action upon each other, was understood. The two great inequalities of Jupiter and Saturn had been calculated, by subjecting to analysis their mutual perturbations; the aberration of the stars, and the mutation of the earth's axis, had been discovered; and it had also been ascertained, by a comparison of a great number of eclipses, that the moon's mean motion had steadily increased from the earliest period.

At this point the history of astronomy, at the close of the eighteenth century, commences; and its most interesting acquisitions, since the beginning of the nineteenth, are the discovery of four planets before unobserved, and the establishment of some facts in relation to the motion of comets, by means of which their return may be predicted with certainty. Among the most important of these is the retardation of comets in their orbits, and the diminution of their periodic time, by the resistance of the medium through which they pass. The very first day of the nineteenth century was distinguished by the discovery of the planet Ceres, by Piazzi. The introduction of this new member into the celestial family was the cause of no inconsiderable excitement among astronomers, particularly in Germany. Its discovery having been made a few days before its conjunction with the sun, it was lost for several months, when Gauss having determined the elements of its motion, it was readily found again; and he has, on this account, been denominated by Dr. Bowditch,[1] its second discoverer. The satisfaction of the German astronomers was heightened, as has been said,[2] by the fact that, according to a theory suggested by Bode, another of their countrymen, in respect to the distances of the known planets, another was wanting between Mars and Jupiter, where Ceres was discovered; and some of their subsequent dissertations were headed, "On the long expected planet between Mars and Jupiter." In the early part of the ensuing

---

[1] Translation of the Mécanique Céleste, Vol. III. p. 873.
[2] Reports of the British Association, Vol. I. p. 156.

year, the planet Pallas was discovered by Olbers. A comparison of the orbits of these two planets led to the suggestion that they may have been originally parts of the same body, and that other parts might be found, if this hypothesis were true. In consequence of the systematic examinations which were immediately instituted, Juno was discovered in 1804 by Harding, and Vesta in 1807 by Olbers,—and both, like Ceres and Pallas, between Mars and Jupiter. From the smallness of these planetary bodies, the eccentricity of some of their orbits, and their proximity to Jupiter, they are subject to great perturbations, which have been calculated by the German astronomers, by whom three of the four were discovered.

But the present century has been more particularly distinguished for the variety and accuracy of the observations which have been made on the planetary bodies, especially our own, and by the improvement of the instrumental and mathematical powers which have been brought into the field of investigation.[1] At the commencement of the century, the only observatory, as is stated by Professor Airy of Cambridge, England, at which observations were made on any regular system, was at Greenwich. In the year 1833, there were forty public observatories in operation in different parts of the world;[2] not one of which, however, was in America. This reproach has often been noticed in the scientific publications of Europe, though usually accompanied with honorable mention of the distinguished astronomers whom this country contains, and who are so well qualified for conducting such an establishment with honor to themselves and benefit to the interests of science. The theory of astronomical refractions, and the effect of the earth's rotation upon the motion of projectiles, both of which are discussed in the tenth book of Laplace's work, are now among the most interesting investigations of astronomical science ; and as subordinate to the first, the law of the decrease of density in ascending, and the question

[1] Reports of the British Association, Vol. I. p. 126.   [2] Ibid. p. 130.

whether the refractive power of the air is influenced by temperature, or whether it is independent of it as it is of humidity, are among the most important problems to be solved.

While all the other physical sciences relate to the condition of our own planet and the mechanical agencies which are concerned in its government, astronomy directs us also to the examination of spheres at distances from us, which to human calculation seem almost immeasurable, and which no artificial contrivance of man will probably be able so to diminish as to subject them to a closer inspection. But their masses and their motions have been calculated; the paths, which from the beginning of time they have travelled, are known; and superstition is no longer permitted to read, in the phenomena they sometimes present to our eyes, the anger of an offended deity, and the punishment about to be visited upon his disobedient subjects. The wonders which the science has disclosed fill us with amazement; but our feelings are no longer degraded by the stupefaction of ignorance and fear. If we know that the planetary bodies are moving around us with velocities which we can only conceive through the intervention of arithmetical quantities, we know that they are confined to their orbits by agencies too powerful to be overcome. If we know that the globe which we inhabit is projected through space with the same violence, we know also that the shock of elements and the collision of antagonist forces, instead of contributing to the destruction of the system, are the efficient cause of the general harmony and repose.

In several departments of physical science, either subordinate or collateral to those I have referred to, investigations have recently been made, which have led to the observation of a great number of interesting facts. In METEOROLOGY, those which relate to temperature are the most important. Isothermal lines, or lines running through places having the same mean annual temperature, have been drawn from observation, and the causes of their inflection assigned. The increase of the temperature of the earth in descending, which had been suspected for more than a century, has been ascertained; and the point at which radiation from the surface ceases, and the influence of internal heat begins, has been fixed. Above this line, denominated the invariable stratum, which is about one hundred feet below the surface, a successive increase and decrease, from the influence of the solar rays, and from counteracting causes, take place; while below this line there is a regular increase in descending, though the law of increase would seem not to be the same for all parts of the globe.

To the same department belong the observations which have been made on the difference in the quantity of rain which falls at different places, and especially at places of unequal elevation and at small distances from each other. In mountainous regions the fall of rain is greater than in surrounding districts of less elevation, by reason of the clouds and vapors which are attracted by the former. Thus at Geneva in Switzerland, the annual fall of rain is about thirty inches, while at the Grand St. Bernard, about one degree of longitude farther east, it is about sixty. But at different points of elevation in the immediate vicinity of each other, the quantity of rain decreases in a variable ratio with the increase of height. This fact was first noticed at the Observatory in Paris. The observations were made at the top of a tower about ninety feet high, and in the court below; and the result was, that the quantity which fell at the height of the tower was about two inches less per annum than the quantity which fell at its base. In consequence of this discovery, a series of experiments was commenced at York, under the direction of the British Association for the Advancement of Science; the three points of observation having been fixed at the several heights of 29 feet, 72 feet 8 inches, and 241 feet 10 inches, above the level of the River Humber. The observations were continued for three successive years, and the mean quantity for the highest elevation was nearly twelve inches; at the next below, nearly seventeen and a half; and at the lowest, nearly twenty-two inches. This phenomenon has been accounted for by the supposition that the difference in the "quantity of rain at different heights above the surface of the neighboring ground is caused by the continual augmentation of each drop of rain from the commencement to the end of its descent, as it traverses the humid strata of air at a temperature so much lower than that of the surrounding medium as to cause the deposition of moisture upon its surface." In a circular recently addressed by the Regents of the University to the academies of this State, they are requested to make similar observations as to the quantity of rain falling at unequal elevations; and, if the recommendation is acted on, we shall soon be in possession of a mass of interesting facts connected with one of the most recent discoveries in meteorology.

In the attempts of Mr. Redfield of this State, followed by Lieut.-Col. Reid of England, to develop the law of storms, the application of scientific principles to meteorology has led to the most important conclusions. The phenomena of those aërial currents, which often sweep over the sea and the land with destructive violence, have been reduced to general laws. By the investigations of Mr. Redfield, confirmed by the subsequent and more extensive researches of Col. Reid, it is satisfactorily ascertained that violent gales or storms are whirlwinds, of diameters sometimes equal to six hundred miles, having a progressive movement varying in direction at different stages of their course. While the revolving mass of atmosphere may have a rotatory motion equal to a hundred miles an hour, its progress over the surface of the ocean or the land may not exceed twenty, or even a less number. The gyratory motion is always from right to left in the northern, and from left to right in the southern hemisphere; and from the course of the wind in any part of the vortex, the direction which should be taken to escape its fury may always be determined. If the deductions which have been made by these scientific individuals as to the force and direction of storms, do not enable us to disarm the elements of their power, they may be of the greatest value to navigators, by indicating the readiest manner of placing themselves beyond the pale of the prevailing aërial disturbance.

The direction and intensity of the magnetic influence of the earth have been ascertained in different countries by a great variety of careful and persevering investigations; and in opposition to the opinion, which generally prevailed at the commencement of the present century, that the phenomena of attraction could be accounted for by a single magnetic axis, it is now satisfactorily established that there are two, forming two points of convergence in the northern, and two in the southern hemisphere. The lines of variation have also been compared with those which have existed from the earliest period; and the annual changes, which are constantly taking place in the direction of the magnetic force, ascertained by careful observation, though the law of variation remains unknown.

In many instances the action of a general law, which governs a particular class of terrestrial phenomena, is modified by the interference of another law, which it is extremely important to ascertain. Thus, the measurement of heights introduced by Pascal in the seventeenth century, and reduced to great accuracy by the new formula of Laplace,[1] is determined by the diminished pressure of the atmosphere on the mercury of the barometer at increased elevations. Yet it has been ascertained that the atmospheric pressure is subject to horary variation at the same place, and that the variation is not the same in all parts of the globe. The barometer within the tropics attains, at the same elevation, a maximum at nine o'clock in the morning and evening, and a minimum at three or four o'clock in the morning and evening. In like manner, the needle is subject not only to an annual, but to a diurnal variation. It moves to the westward in the morning, and in the afternoon back to the eastward; and the same

[1] Mécanique Céleste, Book X. Chap. 4.

variation takes place again at night, so that its maximum easterly direction is attained at about seven o'clock in the morning. These modifications of the action of general laws render the whole scheme of the terrestrial phenomena extremely complex; and they have contributed to give to scientific investigations a degree of accuracy and minuteness which no preceding age has equalled.

Highly as the age is distinguished by the discovery of scientific principles, it is not less strongly characterized by their successful application to the useful arts. It is, indeed, in this respect that its superiority over preceding ages in improving the social condition of the human family chiefly consists. There is scarcely a branch of industry which has not participated in the triumphs of scientific investigation, by the introduction of new instruments and improved methods in the application of the mechanical powers.[1] In numerous departments of labor, the human arm has given place to machinery; and the substitution of brute force has liberated the intellect from the supervision of the lower processes of manipulation, and left it free to range in more congenial spheres of enterprise. These inventions have multiplied power and economized time to an incalculable extent, and they have opened new sources of wealth by the elaboration of valuable products from matter which would otherwise have been useless. The operations of industry, instead of being, as formerly, chiefly directed and carried on by independent effort, have, by the division of labor, been parcelled out among an infinite number of persons, each class having its appropriate function to perform in perfecting the common product of their toil, but brought from necessity into close contact with

---

[1] " Par une heureuse coincidence, le mouvement scientifique et le mouvement industriel se déclarent à la fois : les hommes de théorie et de pratique, longtemps sans rapport, se rapprochent ; l'industrie recueille les faits, la science les enchaine et les explique. C'est à cet heureux concours que sont dus bien des prodiges."
BRIAVOINNE, Sur les inventions et perfectionnemens dans l'industrie. Mémoires couronnés par l'Académie Royale de Bruxelles. Tome XIII. p. 25.

each other. Under the influence of this new principle, prodigious establishments have been built up, and are carried on with a degree of order and precision which is only equalled by that of the mechanical powers they apply. The establishment of the Messrs. Cockerill near Liege, on the river Meuse in Belgium, comprehending a coal mine and foundry, has an area of about thirty-six acres covered with workshops and edifices. Nine thousand yards of railway connect the various parts of the establishment, and a canal unites it to the Meuse. Sixteen steam-engines, equal to the power of seven hundred horses, are perpetually in operation; and more than two thousand laborers are constantly employed in the mines and in the various forges and workshops. The fires and furnaces consume daily four hundred and fifty tons of coal; and in two cupola furnaces more than forty-five tons of ore are converted into iron. At night, an apparatus of gas lights up this mighty assemblage of human and mechanical power; and by day, the smoke of its numerous chimneys hangs over it in clouds, indicating at the distance of miles the scene of its extensive and diversified operations. Similar establishments, though not often of the same magnitude, are to be found in most of the countries of Europe. Unlike the human frame, which demands its diurnal periods of repose, the machines which the ingenuity of man has contrived and employed in his service, work on, in endless rotation, and cease only when the attrition of continued motion has worn out the matter of which they are composed.

The application of steam, as a motive force, completes the triumph of mechanical skill, and places at the disposal of man a power which is incalculable. The expansive force of steam was not unknown to the ancients. Hero of Alexandria, more than a hundred years before the Christian era, suggested the possibility of its application to produce motion. Brancas and the Marquis of Worcester, in the seventeenth century, made some experiments to test its applicability to machinery. In the early part of the eighteenth century,

Jonathan Hulls obtained a patent for a steam-vessel. But none of the experiments made by these individuals, or the many others who followed or were contemporary with them, were attended with any important results. The great improvements made by Watt at the close of the last century, by substituting steam for atmospheric pressure in moving the piston, by converting the rectilinear into the rotary motion, and by the invention of the double-acting engine, constitute an era in the history of steam. But it was reserved to the present century, and to our own State, to furnish the first instance of the successful application of this great power to navigation. Whatever claims may have been set up in behalf of others, it is now universally conceded that to Fulton belongs the distinction of having carried into effect a plan which others had conceived without being able to execute.[1] In 1807, his labors were crowned with complete success. The first steamboat passed from New York to Albany, a distance of one hundred and fifty miles; in five years afterwards, a boat was put in operation on the river Clyde in Scotland; and there is now scarcely an ocean, a sea, or a navigable river, which does not bear testimony to this great achievement in the annals of science. The more recent invention of railways and locomotive engines, brought to perfection by the skill of English engineers, completes the chain of communication which is henceforth to bring almost into contact the different nations of the earth, and which is destined, as time advances, to become a most efficient instrument in eradicating prejudices arising from a mutual ignorance of their respective characters and conditions. It is the last step in that great social revolution which may, unless the bad passions of mankind shall oppose insuperable obstacles to its progress, convert distant and antagonist communities into friends, and unite the whole family of nations in the common bonds of harmony and peace.

[1] Encyclopædia Metropolitana, Art. Machinery; and Briavoinne, Sur les inventions, &c. p. 39.

In some of the higher departments of political philosophy, the progress of truth has not been less rapid than in physical science. In 1775, Adam Smith published his able work on the wealth of nations; in 1803, it was followed by Say's work on political economy, and at a subsequent period by that of Ricardo. A multitude of other writers have at various times advocated with distinguished ability the principles laid down by Smith; and the truth of those principles is generally admitted. The differences of opinion which exist do not so much concern the foundations of the science as the adoption of its doctrines under all circumstances as a practical rule of conduct. Governments must, of necessity, in regulating their own systems of industry, excepting such as are wholly domestic, have reference to the economical and commercial regulations of others. The great diversity of these regulations in states enjoying commercial intercourse with each other naturally gives rise to numerous questions concerning the applicability of the principles of political economy to the condition of a particular country, when others decline to adopt them. Notwithstanding these embarrassments, the restrictive system has received a severe shock. A more liberal spirit prevails in the commercial regulations of different countries. The question with governments is not, as formerly, how little they can benefit others, but how much they can promote their own interests, in the regulation of their systems of domestic industry, and by a freer intercommunication and exchange of products. In bringing about this change, the policy of our own country, in seeking the greatest possible extension of our commercial intercourse with others, and in liberating individual effort from unnecessary restraints, has had a leading influence. It furnishes evidence not to be impeached, that the spirit of freedom, which lies at the foundation of the social compact, may be safely adopted by all nations in the regulation of their domestic industry and their foreign intercourse. Political economy teaches no more than this; and the social happiness and prosperity of our race are deeply involved in the universal adoption of its axioms.

In the intercourse of nations with each other, there is nothing which more strongly illustrates the progress of liberal principles than the general desire which prevails to ascertain and interchange, for their mutual information and improvement, all facts tending to show their true condition. Statistical inquiries are diligently carried on under the direction of different governments, the results are collected and arranged, and the documents containing them are published and distributed. The veil of secrecy under which, in past ages, it has too often been a rule of policy to conceal all that concerns the internal condition of a state, has, among the most enlightened nations, been drawn aside; and the phenomena of their moral, social, and political development have been laid open for inspection. Statistics may henceforth be ranked among the sciences; and its importance is not likely to be undervalued by those who have noticed the accessions (especially in physical facts) which it has brought to the stores of knowledge, and the generalizations to which it has led with regard to the operation of moral causes, as deduced from the actions of individuals viewed in masses. A comparison of the condition of different countries in Europe as to the number and nature of the crimes committed within them, and a comparison of a country with itself at different periods, have exhibited a series of remarkable facts, and furnish evidence of a uniformity of effects, when the same moral causes operate, hardly exceeded by the regularity of those laws which control the phenomena of the physical world. It seems, and is in fact, extremely difficult to foretell how an individual may act when subjected to the influence of particular motives; but when a great number of individuals are exposed to the action of the same causes, the uncertainty disappears, and the aggregate uniformity becomes almost incredible. In a country like our own, in a course of most active development, receiving fresh stimulants from every new field of enterprise, growing in wealth and population both by intense excitement within and constant accessions from without, the moral like the social phases will be variable. But in comparing two states of full population, long-established institutions, and regular systems of industry, the uniform recurrence in one of certain classes of crimes, which are almost unknown in the other, may often afford the means of determining, with a degree of assurance amounting nearly to certainty, the influence of the particular causes which produce them. In respect to political offences, the practical benefit to be derived from the knowledge thus acquired is much greater than with regard to the violation of those moral obligations which are independent of social regulation. For the question may properly arise, whether a law, not designed to enforce the performance of a moral duty, may not be productive of greater evil than good, if it fails to secure a general obedience. A comparison of the state of crime in two countries leads to an examination of the respective laws which have been violated; and so far as the influence of government is felt in the multiplication of offences through the medium of unjust and oppressive regulations, the examination may afford the means of redressing its own errors and abuses; and thus, by preventing the crimes it has caused, it may give the oppressed a worthier and more appropriate place in the scale of political morality.

While the intellectual world has been so actively and deeply excited, as has been seen, by philosophical investigation, the political has been as profoundly agitated.[1] The revolution in this country and in France in the latter part of the eighteenth century, like those disruptions in the materials of our planet of which we see the traces, constitute eras of new for-

[1] "On ne peut porter ses regards sur les cinquante dernières années, sans qu'à l'instant même mille grands souvenirs ne s'éveillent. C'est qu'aussi les évènemens que cette période embrasse ne s'arrêtent pas seulement à une partie du monde civilisé, ils ne sont pas circonscrits dans un seul résultat. Tous les intérêts, tous les principes, tous les pays, se trouvent en même temps ébranlés: il s'agit à la fois d'une révolution dans la politique, dans la guerre, dans les institutions, dans les sciences, dans l'industrie." — *Briavoinne*, Sur les inventions, etc. p. 5.

mation, and of the recombination of elements under altered conditions of existence; while the silent progress of opinion is carrying on in other countries those slow but not less certain processes of organic change which only become visible at the end of periodic divisions of time. Political authority is asserted with less of the imperiousness which was characteristic of earlier times, and on grounds in better accordance with the deductions of reason. The interests of the subject find a place in the consultations of the sovereign; and plans for the intellectual and social amelioration of the masses show that a new element is in combination with those principles which have, until a very recent day, composed the whole scheme of irresponsible government. The progress of change may be delayed, but it cannot be arrested for a length of time; and it remains for those who imagine their interests concerned in upholding systems at war with the spirit of the age, to determine whether it shall be accomplished by gradual concession, or whether, by closing up all the avenues of improvement through which the radiant heat of popular agitation is passing off, it shall be brought about by sudden explosion and violence.

The influence of CHRISTIANITY upon the political condition of mankind, though silent and almost imperceptible, has doubtless been one of the most powerful instruments of its amelioration. The principles and the practical rules of conduct which it prescribes; the doctrine of the natural equality of men, of a common origin, a common responsibility, and a common fate; the lessons of humility, gentleness, and forbearance which it teaches, are as much at war with political, as they are with all moral, injustice, oppression, and wrong. It has been said, and with justice, that " God's disclosures of himself" are directed not to the intellectual or social, but to the moral improvement of mankind. At the time the Saviour appeared on earth, the grossest political abuses prevailed in the Roman Empire, within the boundaries of which the scene of his mission was laid. But he interfered not with established authorities; to have done so, would have been to put the doctrines which he proclaimed upon the issue of a contest with political institutions. The object of his mission was of far greater importance than to overthrow the evanescent establishments of the day, on which the caprice of men was working perpetual changes. It was to establish principles which, though prescribing only the limits of moral duty, were ultimately to infuse themselves through the whole structure of society and government, and make them both subservient to purposes of beneficence and justice.

During century after century, excepting for brief intervals, the world too often saw the beauty of the system marred by the fiercest intolerance and the grossest depravation. It has been made the confederate of monarchs in carrying out schemes of oppression and fraud. Under its banner, armed multitudes have been banded together, and led on by martial prelates to wars of desolation and revenge. Perpetrators of the blackest crimes have purchased from its chief ministers a mercenary immunity from punishment. It has been made the pretext, by religious sects of almost all denominations, for extirpating differences of opinion by fire and sword; hurling Charity, the first of the virtues, from her throne, and raising up Intolerance, the most odious of the vices, in her place. Such, in the hands of man, have been the abuses of a system which was designed to eradicate from the human breast all " envy, hatred, and uncharitableness!" Nearly two thousand years have passed away, and no trace is left of the millions who, under the influence of bad passions, have dishonored its holy precepts; or of the far smaller number who, in seasons of general depravation, have drunk its current of living water on the solitary mountain or in the hollow rock. But its simple maxims, outliving them all, are silently working out a greater revolution than any which the world has seen; and long as the period may seem since its doctrines were first announced, it is almost imperceptible when regarded as one of the divisions of that time which is of endless duration. To use the language of an eloquent philosophical writer, " The movements of Providence are not restricted to narrow bounds: it is not anxious to deduce to-day the consequence of the premises it laid down yesterday. It may defer this for ages, till the fulness of time shall come. Its logic will not be less conclusive for reasoning slowly. Providence moves through time as the gods of Homer through space ; it makes a step, and years have rolled away. How long a time, how many circumstances intervened before the regeneration of the moral powers of man by Christianity exercised its great, its legitimate function upon his social condition ; yet who can doubt or mistake its power ? "[1]

Amid the advances in science and in social improvement, which have been briefly considered, our own country has sprung into existence — not by slow development, but, as it were, at a single bound. The foundations of her destiny, whatever it shall be, have been laid in an era of intellectual, social, and political agitation unequalled by any other in the history of our race. If she has shared largely in the fruits of the labors of other nations, she has also been a bountiful contributor to their social prosperity and happiness. Her own greatness has been wrought out as much by force of the inventions as by the industry and enterprise of her own citizens. It is true, there are few countries in Europe which have not added something to her wealth and her numbers, or to the scientific principles which her citizens are applying with an assiduity that transcends all precedent and mocks all calculation, on the great theatre of her development. But she has amply repaid the debt, through the genius of a single man,[2] by uniting them in bonds of intercourse, which are gradually eradicating national antipathies, and which are constantly rendering more manifest the great truth, which reason

---

[1] Guizot, General History of Civilization in Europe, p. 28.
[2] Fulton.

and revelation have hitherto taught in vain, that the true policy of nations consists in cultivating the arts of peace.

But whatever may be the issue of the experiments now in progress in government, in science, and in the useful arts, upon the external policy or the internal condition of nations; whatever obstacles may for a time oppose and defeat the triumph of enlightened principles, — whether ancient prejudices shall again revive and ripen into collision, bringing in their train the conquest of provinces, the overthrow of armies, the deposition of monarchs, and the abolition of thrones, — or whether a period of enduring tranquillity has even now begun to dawn upon the inhabitants of the earth, — happily, gentlemen, the cause of Science fears no impediment either from political agitation or discord. Her triumphs, as rapidly as they are achieved, are, by the instrumentality of the press, written down in all languages, and the record treasured up in a thousand places of safety. If any deluge of vandalism shall overwhelm and bury in ruins the stores of knowledge which she has accumulated in one quarter of the globe, the same treasures will be preserved in others. Thus will the point, at which in all future time the researches and discoveries of each generation shall have their termination, become the starting-place of their successors in the career of improvement. Nor has she anything to fear from dissension among her own followers. Her empire is without bounds. Her domains know no geographical demarcations. Her votaries, wherever they are to be found, are citizens of the same great commonwealth; pursuing the same high objects; obeying the same honorable impulses; distracted by no party feuds; ambitious of no other triumphs but to carry the victorious arms of knowledge and truth into the dominions of ignorance and error.

APPORTIONMENT OF MEMBERS OF CONGRESS.

LEGISLATURE OF NEW YORK.

1842.

In the Assembly, the following Resolutions of Protest against the act of Congress "for the apportionment of Representatives among the several States, according to the sixth census," were under consideration : —

" Whereas the Congress of the United States, at its present session, has passed a law entitled " an act for the apportionment of Representatives among the several States according to the sixth census," which act provides that the said Representatives shall be chosen by districts composed of contiguous territory, no one district electing more than one Representative; and whereas the Constitution of the United States declares that the times, places, and manner of holding elections for Senators and Representatives shall be prescribed by the legislatures of the several States, reserving to Congress the power by law to make or alter such regulations, except as to the places of choosing Senators; and whereas the principal ground on which the reservation of this power to Congress was urged when the Constitution was submitted to the States for adoption, was that it was indispensable to enable the general government to provide for its own safety and preservation, in case the States should neglect, refuse, or be unable to provide for the election of Representatives; and whereas a majority of the thirteen original States, by solemn public acts, objected to the provision by which the power was conferred, and declared themselves in favor of such an amendment to the Constitution as should restrain Congress from any interference with the regulations of the States for the election of Representatives, unless the States should neglect, refuse, or be unable to make such regulations; and whereas the States have continued for more than half a century in the undisturbed enjoyment of the right given to them by the Constitution to prescribe the times, places, and manner of choosing their Representatives in Congress, and have faithfully fulfilled that high trust, and no public exigency has arisen to call for the interposition of Congress to overrule them in its exercise : —

" Therefore, *Resolved,* (if the Senate concur,) That, in the opinion of this legislature, the interference of Congress in a matter peculiarly of State concern, under no circumstances of public necessity, is unjustifiable, a violation of the spirit of the provision of the Constitution under which the right of interference is asserted, and at variance with the intention of its framers.

"*Resolved*, (if the Senate concur,) That, in the opinion of this legislature, the act aforesaid is the fruit of an arbitrary and dangerous exercise of power in Congress, and an invasion of the rights of the States, each of which ought to be left, in its own independent judgment, to prescribe such regulations for the choice of its Representatives as may be dictated by the wishes and convenience of its own citizens.

"*Resolved*, (if the Senate concur,) That our Senators in Congress be instructed, and our Representatives requested, to use their influence to procure a repeal of the said act.

"*Resolved*, (if the Senate concur,) That, in the opinion of this legislature, the interference of Congress with the choice of Representatives in the different States, without being justified by any of the circumstances against which the provision of the Constitution authorizing its interposition was particularly designed to guard, can only be viewed as the evidence of an alarming disposition in the Federal legislature to encroach upon the just rights of the States, and that early and efficient measures ought to be taken to provide against the repetition of the evil by an amendment of the Constitution of the United States.

"*Resolved*, (if the Senate concur,) That, in pursuance of the object expressed in the last resolution, the following amendment, which was proposed by the convention of the State of New York when the Constitution of the United States was ratified, ought to be engrafted as a permanent provision upon that instrument, viz:—

"' Congress shall not make or alter any regulation in any State, respecting the times, places, and manner of holding elections for Senators or Representatives, unless the legislature of such State shall neglect or refuse to make laws or regulations for the purpose, or from any circumstance be incapable of making the same, and that in those cases such power shall only be exercised until the legislature of such State shall make provision in the premises: provided that Congress may prescribe the time for the election of Representatives.'

"*Resolved*, (if the Senate concur,) That the Governor of this State be requested to communicate a copy of these resolutions to the Governor of each of the other States of the Union, with the request that they may be laid before the legislatures thereof, respectively.

"*Resolved*, (if the Senate concur,) That the Secretary of State be directed to transmit a certified copy of these resolutions to each of the Senators and Representatives in Congress from this State."

APPORTIONMENT OF MEMBERS OF CONGRESS. 281

The resolutions having been read, Mr. Dix addressed the committee as follows: —

Mr. Chairman: After the repeated embarrassments by which the discussion of this subject has been delayed, I am happy to have it in my power at last to say a few words in support of the resolutions. Having brought them before the legislature, it is incumbent on me to state the general reasonings on which the propositions contained in them are founded. At the same time I desire to forewarn the committee that this duty shall be discharged in the briefest manner possible, — an intimation which I am sure will give pleasure to every gentleman present; for after the lapse of a week consumed with very little progress in the proper business of the session, all must be desirous of bringing our labors to a close.

Mr D. here suggested a verbal amendment to the resolutions, which was assented to. He then continued: —

I consider this subject as one of great importance, involving as it does a question of constitutional power; and it was, therefore, with regret that I noticed a disposition in my friend from Essex,[1] to meet it in a tone of derision. Among other expressions of kindred import, he denounced the resolutions as "a silly protest." Now, sir, there is no one on this floor who entertains a more sincere respect for the talents and character of that gentleman than myself; and he will, therefore, pardon me for reminding him that a few days ago, when a gentleman from New York[2] was making strictures upon the Governor's message, he (the gentleman from Essex) had taken occasion to admonish him that the use of epithets on this floor was out of place, and that questions were to be decided here by fair and intelligent argument. I say, I know he will pardon me for calling this incident to his remembrance, when I assure him that I do it with no feeling of unkindness, nor by way of complaint, but merely to commend his own maxim to his observance.

I repeat, I regard this subject as one of the highest im-

[1] Mr. Simmons.   [2] Mr. Swackhamer.

portance. If the act of Congress is, as is assumed, a violation of the spirit of the provision of the Constitution under which it was passed, then it deserves all the censure which the resolutions cast upon it. On the other hand, if it is in accordance with the provision of the Constitution referred to, both in the letter and the spirit of that instrument, the resolutions are erroneous in their assumptions, and ought not to receive the sanction of the legislature. I believe they are right; that they are fully sustained by facts; and I shall endeavor to make the position apparent to the judgment of the committee. If, as I ought perhaps to infer from the discussion a few days ago, the resolutions do not come quite up to the temper and tone of the House, my task will not be a difficult one to show that they are right as far as they go.

The first question which naturally arises in the discussion of this question is, whether Congress has power under the Constitution to pass a law regulating the times, places, and manner of holding elections for Representatives in Congress. A reference to the 1st clause of the 4th section of the 1st article settles this question. It is in the following terms:—

"The times, places, and manner of holding elections for Senators and Representatives shall be prescribed in each State by the legislature thereof; but the Congress may, at any time, by law, make or alter such regulations, except as to the places of choosing Senators."

It will be observed that the first part of this clause — that which relates to the States — not only confers a power, but enjoins a duty. It is imperative, mandatory. It makes it obligatory on the legislature of each State to prescribe the times, places, and manner of choosing its Senators and Representatives; and a refusal or an intentional omission on the part of a State to perform this duty would be an act of bad faith to the government itself. On the other hand, the second part of the clause — that which relates to Congress — contains no mandate. It confers a power, but does not enjoin the performance of a duty. It is not imperative. It is merely permissive. I advert to this distinction now, because I shall have occasion to point out the reason of it at another stage of my argument.

The next question is, whether Congress, under this provision of the Constitution, has made such regulations as it is authorized to make; or, in other words, is the act of Congress, so far as it prescribes that districts for the election of Representatives in Congress shall be composed of contiguous territory, no one district electing more than one Representative, in accordance with the constitutional provision referred to?

I do not intend to enter into this inquiry in its largest sense. I have concurred with the committee in the propriety of dividing the State into districts for the election of Representatives in Congress in such a manner as not to conflict with the provisions of the act to which the resolutions relate. The resolutions do not go the length of declaring it to be a direct infraction of the Constitution in its letter as well as its spirit. At the same time I desire frankly to state that I do not consider it in any sense such an act as Congress should have passed. When that body interfered with this question at all, and without necessity, as it has done, it should have taken care to make regulations which would have been binding on the people of the State, which could have been enforced and executed under existing State legislation. It should have done so for the plain reason that it has no power to give a direction to the States as to the manner in which Representatives in Congress shall be elected. It can issue no such mandate. Gentlemen will find no warrant for it in the Constitution. Some have chosen to regard this act as advisory. This was the deliberate opinion of the President; and he has gone so far as to put his written exposition of the meaning of the act among the archives of the government. If this be its true construction, it imposes no obligation on the States to act in conformity to it. Others regard it as containing a virtual direction to the States, and therefore void for want of constitutional authority on the part of Congress to give such a direction. A still stronger position has been taken: that it is an open, palpable, deliberate, and dangerous infraction of the Constitution, — such a violation of that instrument as to justify the States in defeating its execution within their own limits. The resolutions do not take this ground. They assert that it is a violation of the spirit of the Constitution and the intention of its framers, and to this point I shall now call the attention of the committee.

Fortunately, in respect to the fair interpretation of this section we have the highest authority, — the evidence of contemporaneous exposition, — the declared opinions of individuals who had a large share in framing the Constitution, — opinions declared while it was before the conventions of the States for their ratification, — opinions put forth for the express purpose of inducing the people of the United States to give their assent to it. That I may not trespass unnecessarily upon the patience of the committee, I shall quote the opinions of gentlemen who were in favor of a strong government, and who would not have been likely to give to the section a construction more favorable to the States than its intention warranted.

The Constitution of the United States, after it had been finally adopted in the Federal convention by which it was framed, was submitted to conventions in the several States for their ratification. These conventions were generally composed of the most distinguished men of that day, men trained and disciplined in the trying school of the Revolution, differing in their views with regard to the nature of the government best suited to the exigencies of the country, but aiming at the same common object, — to build up a system which should be proof, as far as any political organization can be, against external violence and internal agitation. Among the prominent men in the convention of Massachusetts, was Caleb Strong, a member of the convention by which the Constitution was framed, always a distinguished Federalist, and who is well known to the American public as having been engaged while governor of that State, during the war of 1812, in a controversy with the general government in respect to the right of the latter to call the militia into its service for the defence of the country against foreign invasion. In reply to an inquiry addressed to Mr. Strong in reference to the section of the Constitution under consideration, the report of the debates states: —

"The Hon. Mr. Strong followed Mr. Bishop, and pointed out the necessity there is for the 4th section. — The power, says he, to regulate the elections of our Federal Representatives must be lodged somewhere. I know of but two bodies wherein it can be lodged, — *the legislatures of the several States, and the general Congress.* If the legislative bodies of the States, who must be supposed to know at what time, and in what place and manner, the elections can best be held, should so appoint them, it cannot be supposed that Congress, by the power granted by this section, will alter them: but if the legislature of a State should refuse to make such regulations, the consequence will be, that the Representatives will not be chosen, and the general government will be dissolved. In such case, can gentlemen say, that a power to remedy the evil is not necessary to be lodged somewhere? and where can it be lodged but in Congress?" — *Elliot's Debates,* Vol. I. p. 45.

Here it will be perceived that Mr. Strong, himself a member of the Federal convention and familiar with its proceedings and opinions, admitted that the legislatures of the States know at what times, in what places, and in what manner the elections can best be held, and that the great object in giving Congress a controlling power over them was to guard against the dissolution of the general government.

The convention of New York embraced a large number of individuals of high character and eminent abilities. Among them were Geo. and James Clinton, Alexander Hamilton, John Jay, and others who bore a distinguished part in the scenes of the Revolution and in the early operations of the government after the independence of the colonies was established. I shall content myself with quoting the opinion of Mr. Jay in reference to the intention of the Constitution in reserving to Congress an ultimate control over the regulations of the States for the election of Representatives; and I need not add that there was no one in that assembly, full as it was of intellectual power, whose opinion was entitled to greater weight. He had, in conjunction with Hamilton and Madison, written a full exposition of the Constitution in the celebrated numbers of *Publius*, afterwards collected and published in volumes under the title of "The Federalist," the ablest commentary on the Constitution ever written, and indeed one of the most profound works on representative government of any age. He was afterwards, Governor of this State, Chief Justice of the United States, and Minister to Great Britain, and he died at an advanced age without a stain upon the purity of his private life. In answer to some objections to this provision of the Constitution —

"The Hon. Mr. Jay said, that, as far as he understood the ideas of the gentleman, he seemed to have doubts with respect to this paragraph, and feared it might be misconstrued and abused. He said that every government was imperfect unless it had a power of preserving itself. Suppose that by design or accident the States should neglect to appoint Representatives: certainly there should be some constitutional remedy for this evil. The obvious meaning of the paragraph was, that, if this neglect should take place, Congress should have power, by law, to support the government and prevent the dissolution of the Union. He believed this was the design of the Federal convention." — *Elliot's Debates*, Vol. I. p. 289.

The opinion of Mr. Jay fully sustains the opinion of Mr. Strong as to the true intention of the provision — to prevent a dissolution of the Union; and it is hardly necessary to add that, from his talents, his position, and his sincerity, his opinion is entitled to the greatest weight.

The convention of Virginia was not less distinguished for moral purity and high intellectual power than those of other States. It numbered among its members Messrs. Madison and Monroe, afterwards Presidents of the United States; John Marshall, afterwards Chief Justice; Governor Randolph, Patrick Henry, Geo. Mason, George Wythe, Edmund Pendleton, Geo. Nicholas, and many other individuals whose names are connected with the fame and welfare of that great State. I shall now only ask the attention of the committee to the opinion of George Nicholas, then a distinguished citizen of Virginia, but who afterwards removed to Kentucky, and is well known as having introduced into the legislature of the latter the celebrated resolutions of 1798, responding to those of Virginia in relation to the alien and sedition laws. Mr. Nicholas was at that time a powerful coadjutor of Mr. Madison in the Virginia convention, and like him in favor of a strong Federal government. After alluding to objections which had been made to the power vested in Congress to make regulations fixing the time, place, and manner of electing Representatives, and to alter those made by the States, Mr. Nicholas continued : —

"If the State legislature, by accident, design, or any other cause, would not appoint a place for holding elections, then there might be no election till the time was past for which they were to have been chosen ; *and as this would eventually put an end to the Union*, it ought to be guarded against by giving this discretionary power to the Congress of altering the time, place, and manner of holding the elections. *It is absurd* to suppose that Congress will exert this power, or change the time, place, and manner established by the States, if the States will regulate them properly, or so as not to defeat the purposes of the Union."— *Virginia Debates*, (2d edition,) p. 19.

Let me turn to an authority higher, perhaps, than any I have quoted— Alexander Hamilton. I have already alluded to him as having written, in conjunction with James Madison and John Jay, the numbers signed *Publius*, afterwards collected and published under the title of " The Federalist." These numbers were written in the year 1788, while the Constitution of the United States was before the people of the States for their consideration ; and they may be considered as embodying all the arguments in favor of it, and as containing the most authentic interpretation of its provisions and of the intention of its framers. I now quote from the 59th Number, "Concerning the Regulation of Elections," written by Hamilton.

"I am greatly mistaken, notwithstanding, if there be any article in the whole plan more completely defensible than this. Its propriety rests upon the evidence of this plain proposition, that *every government ought to contain in itself the means of its own preservation.*

"It will not be alleged, that an election law could have been framed and inserted in the Constitution, which would have been applicable to every probable change in the situation of the country; and it will, therefore, not be denied, that a discretionary power over elections ought to exist somewhere. It will, I presume, be as readily conceded, that there were only three ways in which this power could have been reasonably organized: that it must either have been lodged wholly in the national legislature, or wholly in the state legislatures, or primarily in the latter, and ultimately in the former. The last mode has with reason been preferred by the convention. They have submitted the regulation of elections for the Federal government, in the first instance, to the local administrations; which, in ordinary cases, and when no improper views prevail, may be both more convenient and more satisfactory; but they have reserved to the national authority a right to interpose, whenever extraordinary circumstances might render that interposition necessary to its safety.

"Nothing can be more evident than that an exclusive power of regulating elections for the national government, in the hands of the state legislatures, would leave the existence of the Union entirely at their mercy. They could at any moment annihilate it, by neglecting to provide for the choice of persons to administer its affairs. It is to little purpose to say, that a neglect or omission of this kind would not be likely to take place. The constitutional possibility of the thing, without an equivalent for the risk, is an unanswerable objection."— *Federalist*, p. 369.

I ask the deliberate attention of the committee to this exposition. They will see that the leading idea which runs through it all is, that the general government should have the power of providing for its own preservation, and that this was the great object in view in reserving to Congress an ultimate control over the election of Representatives.

I quote the opinion of Gen. Hamilton with the more satisfaction, not only on account of his extraordinary abilities, but because he was the author of some of the most high-toned propositions in the Federal convention for abridging the powers of the States, and enlarging those of the general government. I consider his authority of the greater value for this very reason : for it is not to be supposed that he would have given to this provision of the Constitution a construction less favorable to the general government than was consistent with its true intent and meaning.

I consider it settled, therefore, by the high authority of contemporaneous exposition, that the framers of the Constitution never intended that the power of Congress in respect to regulations for the election of Representatives should be exercised unless the States neglected, refused, or were unable to make regulations themselves, or unless, in the discharge of the high trust confided to them, they should enact laws subversive of the objects of the Union.

Let us now see how far the interpretation of the framers of the Constitution and their contemporaries is sustained by commentators of our own times. And here, too, I am happy to have it in my power to quote the opinions of men of high authority as constitutional jurists, whose political views and biases are on the side of those by whose votes this act of Congress was sustained and finally passed. Mr. Justice Story, in his commentaries on the Constitution, devotes a large space to the discussion of this subject; and though I am far from intending to ascribe to him the slightest disposition to carry into his interpretations of the Constitution any other rules than those of fair, enlightened, and impartial construction, there is no injustice to him in saying that from the very decided opinions he holds, he is in no danger of detracting from the authority which the Federal power may reasonably claim to possess. The exposition of this part of the Constitution is so extended that I cannot quote it all without trespassing unreasonably on the patience of the committee. In condensing what he says, I shall endeavor to give a full and accurate view of his positions.

"The Constitution gives to the state legislatures the power to regulate the time, place, and manner of holding elections; and this will be so desirable a boon in their possession, on account of their ability to adapt the regulation, from time to time, to the peculiar local or political convenience of the States, that its representatives in Congress will not be brought to assent to any general system by Congress, *unless from an extreme necessity,* or *a very urgent exigency.* Indeed, the danger rather is, that when such necessity or exigency actually arises, the measures will be postponed, and perhaps defeated, *by the unpopularity of the exercise of the power.* All the States will, under common circumstances, have a local interest and local pride in preventing any interference by Congress; and it is *incredible* that this *influence* should not be felt as well in the Senate as in the House. It is not too much, therefore, to presume that it will not be resorted to by Congress, until there has been some extraordinary abuse or danger in leaving it to the discretion of the States respectively."— *From Vol.* II. pp. 287 *et seq.*

Judge Story then states that it may operate as a check upon undue State legislation.

He then proceeds to cite the reasons in favor of the provision. 1st. To correct any negligence in a State with regard to elections, and to prevent a dissolution of the government by designing and refractory States. 2d. To protect the people against any design of a Federal Senate and their constituents to deprive the people of the State of their right to choose Representatives. 3d. To provide a remedy in case a State by invasion or any other cause cannot appoint a place where the people can safely meet to choose Representatives. And 4th. To secure uniformity in the time, place, and manner of electing Representatives and Senators, so' as to prevent vacancies when there may be calls for extraordinary sessions of Congress.

He then continues:—

" A period of forty years has since passed by, without any *attempt* by Congress to make any regulations or *interfere in the slightest degree* with the elections of members of Congress. If, therefore, experience can demonstrate anything, it is the entire safety of the powers in Congress, which it is *scarcely possible* (reasoning from the past) should be exerted, unless upon very urgent occasions."

After speaking of the want of uniformity in the State regulations and the inconveniences of this system of leaving the regulations to the States, he says: —

" Still, so strong has been the sense of Congress of the importance of leaving these matters to state regulation, that no effort has hitherto been made to cure these evils; and *public opinion* has almost *irresistibly* settled down in favor of the existing system."

Judge Story admits that public opinion is in favor of the system of non-interference on the part of the general government; and in citing the reasons in favor of reserving the power to Congress, he shows clearly that it was intended to be remedial, and to be exercised only in case of abuse or necessity.

The next authority which I shall quote, I refer to with great pleasure, not only because it is as clear and decided as it is brief, but because it emanates from a source which may justly command the highest respect, — I mean Chancellor Kent. Of the great learning, ability, and acuteness of this distinguished jurist I need not speak. There are none within the sound of my voice who are not familiar with his high reputation and the purity of his personal character. I may add, without detracting in the slightest degree from his reputation as an impartial expounder of the law, that his political opinions do not incline him to give to the rights of the States in doubtful questions any weight which they may not justly claim. In his commentaries on American law he says:—

"The legislature of each State prescribes the times, places, and manner of holding elections, subject, however, to the interference and control of Congress, which is *permitted them* for their own *preservation*, but which it is to be presumed they will *never* be disposed to exercise, except when any State shall neglect or refuse to make adequate provision for the purpose." — *Vol. I.* p. 232.

The opinion of Chancellor Kent fully sustains the construction I have put on this provision of the Constitution,— that the authority vested in Congress to make regulations for the election of Representatives, or to alter those of the States, is merely permissive, and that the great object in view was to provide for the preservation of the general government.

May I not then assume, as a position settled alike by

contemporaneous exposition and by the commentaries of our own times, that the power given to Congress by the 1st clause of the 4th section of the Constitution, was designed as a remedial power, to be exercised only when the States neglect, refuse, or are unable to provide for the election of their Representatives, or when their regulations are subversive of the great ends of government? Such was clearly the intention of the Constitution.

Is the act of Congress to which the resolutions relate in accordance with the intention of the Constitution? I answer unhesitatingly, no. It is a direct violation of it. It will not be pretended that the power of Congress was designed to be exercised in a case like this. It is wholly uncalled for. No State has asked for the interposition of Congress. No State has neglected or refused to make proper regulations for the election of its Representatives. Not one of the contingencies, on the occurrence of which this power was designed to be exercised, has happened. It is not necessary for the preservation of the general government, its safety is not endangered by the delinquency or the misfeasance of any State. Sir, if Alexander Hamilton had been a member of the present Congress, he would have voted against this act as a violation of his own construction of the Constitution. This Congress has passed an act which would have been condemned and opposed by men who at the formation of the Constitution were in favor of a Senate of the United States to hold their offices during good behavior, and a President with the same tenure of office and with an absolute negative on bills passed by the two Houses of Congress,—an act condemned by commentators of their own political faith from the foundation of the government down to the present day. Such is the progress of unsound opinion with those who control the two great branches of the Federal legislature! Such is the progress of encroachment on the powers of the States and the just rights of the people!

While the resolutions do not assume that the act of Congress is an open, palpable, deliberate infraction of the Constitution, they do assume that it is a direct violation of its intention and its spirit. The interposition of Congress is justified by no necessity. It is called for by no neglect or refusal on the part of a State to make regulations for the election of Representatives. It is not palliated by any allegation of abuse on the part of the State legislatures in executing the imperative direction which the Constitution gives them to prescribe the times, places, and manner of choosing Representatives in Congress. It is an arbitrary and unwarrantable interference with the legislation of the States,—I will not say for what object,—I have neither the disposition nor the power to look into the motives of others,—but when no circumstances of public necessity call for such a measure, there is no injustice, no harshness in attributing to its authors motives which do them no honor.

When it is said that the single district system is right in itself, I say it is no answer to the charge of interference on the part of Congress in violation of the plain intention of the Constitution. Sir, this is the very class of encroachments against which we should guard with the strictest vigilance—cases in which the propriety of the ostensible object is used to cover up the violation of principle by which it is sought to be accomplished. Open violations of the Constitution, either in its letter or spirit, for objects palpably bad, are never greatly to be feared. The abuse and the danger are so manifest that we need no other stimulants to rouse us to a determined resistance. But when abuse or encroachment puts on the garb of fairness,—when the end it professes to have in view is unexceptionable,—it is then that danger becomes greatest. There is danger that a precedent which may be perverted in after-times to the worst uses, will pass by unresisted and unrebuked. This is precisely such a case. An act violating the acknowledged intention of the Constitution is passed to carry out an arrangement which is in itself sufficiently just,—I mean the single district system, — a system which we ourselves adopted long since, and which we have carried out in practice as far as we could do so consistently with the convenience of the people of the State. The advocates of this act dwell upon the unexceptionable, or, as they call it, the democratic character of the single district system, to cover up, to sanctify, to divert the attention, if possible, from the encroachment on the rights of the States through which it is proposed to be accomplished. And if they succeed, what is to prevent Congress, under the sanction of this precedent, to interpose in a far more dangerous and exceptionable manner, — to establish the general ticket system in all the States, or the single district system in one State, the double district system in another, and election by general ticket in a third? For it has power, under the same warrant of authority, by which it interferes now with the legislation of the States, to act in one or all these modes. It is only by resisting and defeating the exercise of this power that the danger of the precedent may be in some degree diminished.

Sir, this act is not only a violation of the spirit of the Constitution and the intention of its framers, but it is at war with the very genius of our political system. Our government was founded upon a compromise of interests, and in order to preserve it, it must be administered in the spirit in which it was framed, — in a spirit of moderation and forbearance in all its departments. In the exercise of their acknowledged powers, any disposition on the part of the general government to encroach upon the rights of the States, any disposition on the part of the States to resist the legitimate action of the general government within the proper sphere of its authority, cannot fail to create dissension and to produce a feeling of alienation among the States and the people in the highest degree unfriendly to the quietude and stability of the whole system, — a feeling which is calculated to shorten the duration of the government itself.

There is a plain principle involved in this question. Powers in their nature conservative — powers conferred for the express purpose of guarding against anticipated evils — can only be rightfully exercised when those evils occur. To exercise them unnecessarily, or for purposes other than those contemplated in granting them, is unjustifiable on any principle of propriety, and should be resisted as an infringement of the spirit of the fundamental compact. This is such a case. The power reserved to Congress of making regulations in respect to the times, places, and manner of electing Representatives to Congress, or of altering those made by the States, was conferred for the purpose of enabling the general government to provide for its own preservation and to correct abuses tending to defeat the purposes of the Union. It has been exercised without necessity, and for the totally different purpose of controlling, overruling the action of the States on this most important and delicate question. It is a violation of the great principle I have referred to, — a principle inherent in the very nature of our free institutions, — a principle indispensable to the preservation of the government; — for it is not to be expected that a government founded like ours upon mutual forbearance and concession, can ever be successfully administered or peaceably upheld, if its acknowledged powers are exercised in an arbitrary spirit, or with any disposition to encroach upon the just rights of any of those who are subject to its jurisdiction and control. Let this truth be everywhere taught and remembered, — that the general government, if we hope to perpetuate it, must be confined to the exercise of essential powers, and that these powers must be exerted in the spirit in which they were conferred.

In representative governments the legislative body is the great fountain of encroachment; and it is the more dangerous for two reasons : 1st, because its powers are necessarily larger than those lodged with any other department; and 2d, because its members being chosen frequently and from among ourselves, we are not apt to criticise its measures with the same severity with which we scrutinize the acts of the Executive. The State legislatures are the natural guardians of the rights of the States against the encroachments of the Federal legislature: the people are the natural guardians of their own rights against the encroachments of the State legislatures. Standing in this twofold relation between the general government and the people, it is our duty, on all occasions, to resist, to the extent of our ability, the exercise of doubtful powers, or the exertion of acknowledged powers in a manner at variance with the spirit of the instrument which confers them. It is only through this vigilant and unceasing watchfulness over the sources of evil, that our free institutions can be preserved.

I hold it to be our duty, therefore, to resist the exercise of this power in Congress: 1st, because it is at variance with the spirit of the Constitution and the intention of its framers; 2d, because it is unnecessary; and 3d, because it is an unwarrantable and arbitrary exertion of authority, and an encroachment on the rights of the States.

This is the ground taken by the Resolutions. If a majority of the committee are of opinion that it is correctly taken, then the only question is, whether the measures recommended in pursuance of the declaration of principle they contain are the most proper to be adopted. On this point I have no tenacity. If a better course can be suggested, I shall cheerfully concur in it. As at present advised, I consider the one recommended the most judicious. After a brief reference to the considerations in which this provision of the Constitution originated, and the practice of the country under it, with an expression of the opinion of the legislature as to the interposition of Congress, the resolutions instruct the Senators and request the Representatives from this State to use their exertions to procure a repeal of the act. They then recommend an amendment to the Constitution to guard against the repetition of the abuse, — the very amendment which was recommended by the convention of this State when the Constitution of the United States was ratified, for the purpose of securing the State and the people against pre-

APPORTIONMENT OF MEMBERS OF CONGRESS.

cisely such an exertion of the power objected to as has been made by Congress in the act to which the resolutions relate.

On this ground I am content to stand. Certainly a less determined opposition to this act would not comport with the importance of the occasion or with the duty we owe to the people of this State and of the Union. If we were to fail to protest against it, we should be untrue to the principles of the pure and sagacious men who foresaw, through the long perspective of years, that this power would be exercised as it has been, for the purpose of abridging the rights of the States, who raised their voices against it, and who assented to the adoption of the Constitution by this State "in full confidence" that Congress would never exercise it unless the States neglected, refused, or were unable to prescribe the times, places, and manner of choosing their Representatives. We should be unworthy successors of the thirteen original States, a majority of whom protested against the exercise of this power when the evil was remote and contingent, if we were to fail to protest against it now that the evil has been visited upon us. We should be unworthy successors of the democratic members of the convention of this State, who refused to part with that portion of the State sovereignty which was surrendered up for the general good, excepting "on condition" that the general government should never exercise the power so long as the States continued to perform in good faith the duty enjoined on them by the Constitution. After the lapse of more than half a century their fears and predictions have been verified. A power dangerous in itself has been unnecessarily and arbitrarily exercised. Let us take now the ground they took then. Let us protest against it as they protested. And let us, in the very language which they used, appeal to our sister States to aid us in taking from the general government, by the peaceful remedy of an amendment to the Constitution, a power which experience has shown can no longer be deposited in its hands with safety.

In coming to a conclusion to recommend to the House such a division of the State into congress districts as not to conflict with the provisions of the act apportioning Representatives, the committee of sixteen have been actuated by other considerations, which I ought, perhaps, to state frankly. If gentlemen will consider the state of the country under some of its most important aspects, they will, I apprehend, find abundant cause for a prudent and discreet course of conduct on our part. Look at the condition of the general government: the chief magistrate of the Union standing, as it were, alone among the political friends who elevated him to office; the public treasury exhausted; the credit of the government gone; and Congress, perhaps at the very hour I am speaking, breaking up in dissension and ill-blood after a protracted and fruitless session. See Pennsylvania, the next State to us in population and wealth, overwhelmed with debt, bankrupt; her moral influence lost through a course of policy at war with the interests and the prosperity of her honest people, and prosecuted against the deliberate judgment of some of her most distinguished men; without power from her pecuniary embarrassments to take the lead in any great movement to uphold sound principles. Look at Ohio, the third State in the Union in point of population; her credit sinking, her debts unpaid, and her legislature broken up, — the law-making power dissolved by a deliberate act of disorganization, not, I am happy to say, by the political friends of the majority of this House. In more than one other State the greatest disorder and embarrassment prevail, — debts repudiated, financial systems exploded, the regular operations of industry disturbed, suspended. In a general survey of the condition of the country I am constrained to say there is too much resemblance to the condition of some of its parts. Bankrupt institutions, individual insolvency, shaken confidence, financial derangement, predominate in almost any view we can take; and these are social evils which can only be cured by the slow and undisturbed action of the system in obedience to its own laws.

In the midst of all this disorder and confusion, is it not important for her own interest, as well as for the general good, that New York should take a position in which she will be sustained by the judgment of the whole country, — that, while she is firm and determined in the assertion of principles, she should in her action be prudent and even forbearing? When the elements of order are breaking up elsewhere and seeking some point of stability around which they can gather, I should regret that a course on any great question should be taken, which would be calculated to shake the public confidence in the wisdom of her counsels. We have done for finance all that men can do in the system we adopted at our annual session, and in devising and defending which my friend from Herkimer [1] has won so much honor for himself and rendered so noble a service to the State. Let us cling fast to it; resisting all attempts to seduce us into new expenditures, spurning away all propositions, come from whatever quarter they may, to violate the sacred pledges on which it is founded. Sir, this is not the first time New York has been called on to perform high and responsible duties. During the last war with Great Britain, when the general government, by means of its commercial embarrassments, had become nearly powerless, she stood forth in her strength, and sustained, almost unaided, the operations on the Niagara frontier, which led to the brilliant results of the campaign of 1814. At a more recent period, when bank suspensions and insolvencies were universal, she saved, by her prudence and firmness, her own commercial metropolis, and made it the centre of all that was sound in the pecuniary affairs of the country.

She is now called on to perform an equally responsible and delicate duty, — to meet the general government in a conflict of principle, on a great question of constitutional power. I desire that it may be performed as becomes her, that, whatever her course may be, it may not be calculated to impair her

[1] Mr. Hoffman.

standing and influence with her sister States or in the councils of the nation. The committee were unwilling, under the circumstances at which I have glanced, that her full and complete representation in the next Congress should be put at hazard: they deemed it due to herself that she should stand there in her strength, unquestioned and unquestionable, ready to coöperate in restoring to order what is now unsettled and confused. They thought it would best comport with the dignity of the two Houses of the legislature to take at the outset from high considerations the course recommended, if in the end we would consent to take it. While providing for the choice of her Representatives in such a manner as not to conflict with the provisions of the act of Congress, the committee deemed it due to the State and to the Union that she should assert her construction of the Constitution in clear and decided language, that she should instruct her Senators to use their efforts to procure its repeal, and that they should suggest the proper constitutional remedy against a repetition of the abuse. By this course of moderation and forbearance, they believed the great object in view would be best attained; that she would move with the greater influence and effect in accomplishing it; and the friends of our free institutions would be spared the painful spectacle of a direct conflict between the general government and the largest State in the Union, in the execution of a law which, arbitrary, oppressive, and unjustifiable as it is, has been passed by the highest legislative sanctions, and in a country where law and order are the very groundwork of the political fabric.

Such are some of the high considerations which have weighed upon the minds of the committee. The result of their deliberations is submitted to the sober judgment of the legislature. I can sincerely say for myself — and I am sure I may say for every one of them — that we have been actuated by no other desire but to bring forward measures which would have the approbation of our own consciences, which would be supported by the sound sense of the country, and which would stand the test and the scrutiny of time.

At a subsequent stage of the debate, Mr. Dix addressed the committee as follows, in reply to Mr. Simmons.

Mr. Chairman: Wearied as the patience of the committee has been, I shall not undertake to reply in detail to the arguments of the gentleman from Essex.[1] To do so would be to exhaust what has already been sufficiently tried. Besides, the very able and eloquent remarks made by the gentleman from Herkimer,[2] who has just taken his seat, render it unnecessary to do more than to touch on a few points, for the purpose of explaining and enforcing positions I have heretofore taken, and of meeting suggestions thrown out on the other side.

But first, I desire to say a few words by way of preliminary. In his opening some days ago, the gentleman from Essex alluded to a "gentle admonition," which he considered me as having administered, and which he complained that I had not given at the time. If he will recall the circumstances to mind, he will acknowledge that I did notice what he said the first opportunity I had. The subject-matter of the resolutions was dragged into the desultory debate, in which he took part, not only without any agency of mine, but certainly very much to my annoyance; for I was placed in the embarrassing position of being compelled to remain silent, or to rise and address the committee on a subject not before it, and when I supposed I should be entirely out of order. On a call to order from a gentleman from Tompkins,[3] not now in his place, the chairman of the committee decided that the general subject embraced in the resolutions might properly come within the range of the debate. The moment this question was disposed of, I obtained the floor: I expressed a willingness to go on then if the committee would hear me; but the usual hour of adjournment being near at

[1] Mr. Simmons. [2] Mr. Hoffman. [3] Mr. Humphrey.

hand, I gave way for a motion to rise and report progress. The next time the subject came up, I took the floor, and opened the debate on the resolutions; and then, the first opportunity I had, I noticed the remarks, or rather one of the remarks, of the gentleman from Essex. I noticed it without the slightest unkindness of feeling. I intended to say nothing at which he could have taken offence; and I therefore regretted that he should have felt called on to meet my allusion to it with a new and more direct personality. However, I refer to the subject now only to say further, that I desire to let it pass. If his remarks had given me any uneasiness, — they certainly did not, — I ought, perhaps, to have been sufficiently compensated by having been, on Falstaff's principle, the cause of wit in the gentleman from Essex.

And now I desire to correct one or two inaccuracies into which he has fallen, I am sure not intentionally, in stating my positions. The first is, in representing me as having stated that the thirteen original States ratified the Constitution "in full confidence" that the power of interfering with the regulations of the States in the election of Representatives would never be exercised by Congress so long as the States made proper provision for the purpose. Now, sir, though I have no doubt this was the general understanding throughout the country, — an understanding resting upon the declarations of the advocates of the power, — what I said was, that the members of the convention of this State ratified the Constitution "in full confidence" that the power would never be exercised by Congress, unless the States neglected, refused, or were unable to prescribe the times, places, and manner of choosing their Representatives; and in saying this I used their own language.

The next inaccuracy is in representing me as having stated that Alexander Hamilton, if he had been a member of the present Congress, would have voted against the act to which the resolutions refer, because it involved the exercise of so dangerous a power. This was not my position.

I said, if that distinguished man had been a member of the present Congress, he would have been bound to vote against the act on his own construction of the Constitution, which I read to the committee from the 59th Number of the "Federalist." And I might have added that he would have been bound to vote against it on the strength of a still higher obligation, — the obligation arising from a solemn public declaration to which he was a party, — a declaration annexed by the members of the convention of this State to their ratification of the Constitution of the United States, that they assented to it, as I have already said, "in full confidence" that the power of Congress would be exercised only in certain specified cases.

These inaccuracies I did not consider so material as to render it necessary for me to interrupt him in his argument. But I mention them now that he may, if he should put himself on record on this subject, set me right there also.

A large portion of his argument is wholly irrelevant to the subject-matter of the resolutions, that part particularly by which he endeavors to show and maintain the technical existence of the power of interference on the part of Congress. The resolutions do not deny it, nor did I in my argument in support of them. Sir, after a week of wandering in the wide waste into which the gentleman has conducted us, let me call back the attention of the committee to the point from which we started. I ask the clerk to read the first resolution, for it is on this that all the others are dependent.

The resolution was read as follows : —
"*Resolved*, (if the Senate concur,) That, in the opinion of this legislature, the interference of Congress in a matter peculiarly of State concern, under no circumstances of public necessity, is unjustifiable, a violation of the provision of the Constitution, under which the right of interference is asserted, and at variance with the intention of its framers."

To this resolution, then, we return; and I ask the committee to note its import. It assumes that the interference of Congress is a violation of the spirit of the Constitution and at variance with the intention of its framers, because no circumstances of public necessity call for it. To this point I shall confine myself in the few remarks I have to make.

And now I turn to an authority which has been quoted on the other side with great confidence; and if I am compelled to examine it somewhat in detail, I trust I shall be able to make it clear to the judgment of the committee. I mean the authority of Mr. Madison,— a deservedly high and honored authority. I intend to pass over it as rapidly as possible. I will not detain the committee beyond the usual hour of adjournment, and my examination of it must necessarily be hasty and brief. And here I ought to say in justice to myself that I designed to have quoted him on a former occasion; but having no brief of the authorities I intended to refer to,—relying on marks I had put in several volumes of Elliot's Debates, which were most of the time out of my possession,— I unintentionally omitted it. I designed to have referred to it for two reasons : 1st, to acknowledge frankly that gentlemen on the other side would derive more semblance of support from his opinions than from any other quarter; and, 2d, to insist that they contained, when fairly considered, nothing inconsistent with the position taken in the resolution to which the attention of the committee has just been called.

Two opinions given by this distinguished and patriotic man have been quoted: the first in the Federal convention, when it was proposed to reserve this power to Congress; and the second in the Virginia convention, when the provision of the Constitution containing it was under discussion.

The first has already been read by the gentleman from Essex. It is to be found at page 1280, Vol. III. of the "Madison Papers." If gentlemen will examine it, they will find that it proceeds altogether upon the presupposition of abuse, for which this power was intended to provide a remedy. Mr. Madison spoke of the various modes in which elections were and might be held, and the sources of danger they might open; and he maintained the importance of lodging a controlling power in Congress to guard against them in case of necessity. Even in this view of the subject, the interference of Congress is unjustifiable; for it is not warranted by any pretence of abuse or by any neglect on the part of a State to perform the duty enjoined on it by the Constitution to make the necessary provision for the election of its Representatives in Congress.

Let us now look at the opinion given by him in the Virginia convention,— an opinion on which the gentleman from Essex lays so much stress. And here I desire to state it as a rule in the construction of all arguments and opinions, verbal or written, that no detached part is to be taken by itself; but that, in order to gather its fair import, it must be considered as a whole.

Mr. Madison first refers to the election of Senators in Congress, and says it was necessary to give the Federal government a control over the time and manner of choosing them " to prevent its own dissolution,"—the reigning idea which runs through all the arguments and commentaries of that day.

He then says: " With respect to the other point it was thought that the regulation of the time, place, and manner of electing the Representatives should be uniform throughout the continent."

I understand this preliminary proposition as expressing an opinion entertained by himself and others with regard to what was considered a desirable object, and not as intending to assume that this vast power was designed to be exercised under the Constitution unless called for by some public exigency. This could not have been his meaning, for it would have been inconsistent with a subsequent portion of his remarks, in which he says that the power will probably never be exercised by Congress if the States regulate the elections properly.

He then continues: "Some States might regulate the elections on the principles of equality, and others unequally. This diversity would be obviously unjust."

Here, too, he has the correction of abuse in view. There might be inequality or injustice in the regulations of the States, which might be remedied by the exercise of this power. He then shows by an illustration the nature of the inequality to which he refers. "Elections are regulated now unequally in some States, particularly South Carolina, with respect to Charleston, which is represented by thirty members."

This, then, was his first position: if there were any abuses in the regulations of the States, Congress might correct them by the introduction of a uniform rule.

Now let us look at his second position. "Should the people of any State by any means be deprived of the right of suffrage, it was judged proper that it should be remedied by the general government."

Here was another public evil, for which the power would afford a remedy. A preceding provision of the Constitution declares that "the House of Representatives shall be composed of members chosen every second year by the people of the several States." This great constitutional right might be defeated in a variety of modes. A State might refuse, neglect, or be unable to make the regulations necessary to secure it to the people. In this case, the reservation of the power to Congress would furnish the proper remedy.

He then continues: "It was found impossible to fix the time, place, and manner of the election of Representatives in the Constitution. It was found necessary to leave the regulation of these, in the first place, to the State governments, as being best acquainted with the situation of the people, subject to the control of the general government, in order to enable it to produce uniformity, and prevent its own dissolution."

Here, two great objects are presented. The most important is the one so often referred to, — to enable the general government to guard against its own dissolution. The other is to enable it to produce uniformity — not by an unnecessary exercise of the power by Congress, but in case of any of the exigencies before stated; for it will not be denied that this period should be taken in connection with the preceding parts of the same paragraph.

Let us follow him further: — "And considering the State governments and general government as representing distinct bodies, acting in different and independent capacities for the people, it was thought the particular regulations should be submitted to the former, and the general regulations to the latter." What is the fair import of this sentence? Certainly not that the general government should interpose without necessity, and introduce general regulations. This would be inconsistent with another portion of his remarks, to which I shall call the attention of the committee. The only reasonable interpretation to be put upon it is, that, in case of abuse or of inequalities in the regulations of the States subversive of the great ends of government, or the rights of any portion of the people of the several States, Congress might establish general rules to secure both those objects, leaving the minor regulations to the States. I understood the gentleman from Essex to admit that Congress could not, under the view of the subject taken by Mr. Madison, go so far as to regulate elections of Representatives in all their details, excepting where a State had omitted or refused to make the necessary regulations. If he had gone one step further, and admitted that Congress could not make the general regulations, excepting in the cases of exigency before specified, there would be very little difference of opinion between us.

Mr. Madison then adds: — "Were they [the elections] exclusively under the control of the State government, the general government might easily be dissolved. But if they be regulated properly by the State legislatures, the congressional control will very probably never be exercised."

The first of these sentences again brings up the great object, which the reservation of this power to Congress was designed to secure, — the preservation of the general government. The second contains an admission which fully sustains the view I have taken of the subject. It shows clearly that the congressional control was not to be exercised without good cause — without some abuse or improper legislation on the part of the States. It reconciles this opinion with the one given by Mr. Madison in the Federal convention, and makes it consistent with the views presented by his distinguished coadjutors.

He concludes by saying: — "The power appears to me satisfactory, and as unlikely to be abused as any part of the Constitution."

I now submit to the committee whether this opinion, taken as a whole, does not fully support the position taken in the resolutions, and the position taken by every commentator on the Constitution from its formation down to the present day, that the control of Congress over elections of Senators and Representatives was an ultimate, remedial power, to be exercised in case of necessity, and then only. I deny that, on the construction most favorable to the general government, the exercise of the power without necessity is justifiable. I deny that its exercise by Congress now is in accordance with any construction heretofore put on the provision of the Constitution under which the right of interference is claimed. There is no abuse to be corrected, no omission to be supplied, no circumstance of public exigency to call for it, and it is, therefore, a violation of the fair interpretation of the Constitution and the intention of its framers.

That I do not construe the opinion of Mr. Madison too narrowly will be apparent from the opinion of one of his distinguished associates, — George Mason of Virginia. Col. Mason was a member of the Federal convention by which the Constitution was formed, and of the Virginia convention, by which it was ratified. He was present throughout the deliberations in both. He was familiar with the arguments and reasonings of their members, and he bore himself a principal part in the discussion of the great questions before them. He was present on both the days when Mr. Madison gave his opinion in reference to this clause of the Constitution; and in the Virginia convention, on a subsequent day, he made the following remarks in reference to the subject.

" He was of opinion that the control over elections tended to destroy responsibility. He declared he had endeavored to discover whether this power was really necessary, or what was the necessity of vesting it in the government; but that he could find no good reason for giving it. That the reasons suggested were, that in case the States should refuse or neglect to make regulations, or in case they should be prevented from making regulations by rebellion or invasion, then the general government should interpose. [Mr. Mason then proceeded thus.] If there be any other cases, I would be glad to know them; for I know them not."

Thus it appears that Col. Mason understood the reasonings in favor of this provision of the Constitution in a much more limited sense than is now ascribed to them. He did not even understand the argument to be that the general government might interpose for the correction of ordinary abuses, — though he regarded it as a power which, in the hands of Congress, might be perverted to the worst and the most dangerous uses.

But independently of this view of the subject, I insist that, on any fair construction of the Constitution, giving the greatest latitude claimed by the defenders of the act of Congress to contemporaneous exposition, the position taken by the first resolution, which declares the interposition of Congress to be at variance with the intention of the framers of the Constitution, because no public necessity has called for it, cannot be successfully controverted.

Notwithstanding the explanations of Mr. Madison, the Virginia convention was not satisfied that the power should be reserved to Congress without limitation. Mr. Madison was himself one of a committee, of which Mr. Wythe was chairman, to propose amendments to the Constitution, and among them was the following: —

"That Congress shall not alter, modify, or interfere in the times, places, or manner of holding elections for Senators and Representatives, or either of them, except when the legislature of any State shall neglect, refuse, or be disabled by invasion or rebellion to prescribe the same."

Nor was this the only precaution that distinguished body thought it necessary to adopt. It was accompanied with a perpetual instruction to the Representatives in Congress from that State " to exert all their influence, and use all reasonable and legal methods to obtain a ratification" of the proposed amendments, " and in all congressional laws to be passed in the mean time to conform to the spirit of the amendments," as far as the Constitution would admit.

Let us now look at the proceedings of the first Congress on this important question. I understood the gentleman from Essex to say on the first day he addressed the committee, that this amendment was submitted to the thirteen original States and rejected. [Mr. Simmons stated in explanation that he had intended to say it was submitted to Congress and rejected. Mr. Dix resumed.] I understood him to say on a subsequent day that it was submitted to Congress, and that it was abandoned by its own friends. In this he is partly right, and partly wrong. It was submitted to Congress, and rejected; but it was not abandoned by its friends. The gentleman from Essex has created an erroneous impression on this subject. He has created the impression that the whole subject was considered in the only legitimate mode, and finally disposed of. In this he is mistaken. It was never submitted to the States, the parties primarily interested. It was strangled in the first Congress. That body refused to submit it to the consideration of the States at all, for the very natural reason that if adopted it would have curtailed the powers of Congress. It was defeated by the vote of a body interested in preventing its submission to the States. But it did not fall without a struggle. The democratic members from this State, to a man, voted for it in the House. The only votes against it were given by Egbert Benson and John Lawrence, both Federalists, and both representing the city of New York. The republican members from Virginia voted against it, with one or two exceptions. Mr. Madison, Richard Bland Lee, and John Brown separated from their associates on that occasion. It was defeated principally by Federal votes. In the Senate repeated attempts were made to introduce it, but it failed for want of the constitutional majority of two thirds.

I am aware, as the gentleman from Essex stated, that Mr. Madison was on a committee in Congress to submit amendments, and that this was not one of those reported; but, as has been seen, he was decidedly in favor of reserving to Congress an ultimate control over the election of Representatives. It is well known, too, that he was at that time the advocate of a strong Federal government. In the Federal convention he was in favor of giving Congress the general power to grant charters of incorporation, — one of the most fruitful sources of evil in State legislation by which the country has been scourged. He was in favor of taking from the States, and conferring on the general government, the appointment of all officers in the militia above the rank of colonel. Nay, sir, he was in favor of giving Congress a negative on laws passed by the States, thus making the general government the censor of State legislation. But when met by the early encroachments of the Federal government, he saw that in his desire to build up an efficient central government he had not sufficiently appreciated the necessity of guarding the rights of the States. With the decision and honesty of purpose which always distinguished him, he immediately put himself on the ground of strict construction, and labored with his great talents to save the system, which he had so large a share in creating, from the consequences of its own abuses.

An attempt has been made to connect the authority of Mr. Jefferson with the defeat of this amendment to the Constitution. I am happy to say it is an unsuccessful attempt. The gentleman from Essex stated that Mr. Jefferson was at that time at New York, the seat of government, as Secretary of State, that he was the intimate friend of Mr. Madison, and that the latter undoubtedly consulted him on so important a subject. Sir, the gentleman is mistaken in the historical fact. This amendment to the Constitution was disposed of in August, 1789, at the first session of the first Congress. The session terminated on the 29th of September in that year. In Mr. Jefferson's correspondence, a letter will be found addressed by him to John Jay, and dated at Havre, on the 30th September, the day after the adjournment of Congress, stating that he had arrived there from Paris on his way to Cowes, to embark for the United States.

In his "*Ana*" he states that he landed in Virginia in December, 1789, and that he proceeded to New York in March, 1790, (seven months after the amendment to the Constitution was rejected,) to enter on the duties of the office of Secretary of State. I rejoice to have it in my power to exonerate this great friend of popular liberty from all responsibility for defeating this attempt to save to the States a great and essential right.

It will be borne in mind that the Congress by which this amendment was defeated was the same body which, at its third session, incorporated the first Bank of the United States, and which was implicated in the corruptions of the funding-system, so graphically described by Mr. Jefferson, himself an eye-witness of them all. Of the twenty-eight members who voted against this amendment, twenty-three voted for the bank. As the gentleman from Essex has expressed so high a respect for Mr. Jefferson's authority, I will read to the committee an extract from his account of the state of opinion which prevailed at the seat of government at that early day on the subject of our political organization.

"I returned from that mission (France) in the first year of the new government, having landed in Virginia in December, 1789, and proceeded to New York in March, 1790, to enter on the office of Secretary of State. Here, certainly, I found a state of things which, of all I had ever contemplated, I the least expected. I had left France in the first year of her revolution, in the fervor of natural rights, and zeal for reformation. My conscientious devotion to these rights could not be heightened, but it had been aroused and excited by daily exercise. The President received me cordially, and my colleagues and the circle of principal citizens, apparently with welcome. The courtesies of dinner parties given me, as a stranger newly arrived among them, placed me at once in their familiar society. But I cannot describe the wonder and mortification with which the table conversations filled me. Politics were the chief topic, and a preference of kingly over republican government was evidently the favorite sentiment. An apostate I could not be, nor yet a hypocrite; and I found myself, for the most part, the only advocate on the republican side of the question, unless among the guests there chanced to be some member of that party from the legislative Houses."

Under the prevalence of influences like these, this great State right was trodden down!

It was soon afterwards that the great struggle commenced on the part of the democracy of the country against the doctrine of constructive power. The political elements were broken up. New combinations and alliances were formed. Mr. Madison, alarmed at the progress of Federal encroachment, ranged himself on the side of the democracy. He opposed the incorporation of the United States Bank. He became one of the most efficient advocates of the rights of the States, and one of the most firm and unyielding opponents of the attempts of the Federal government to gain by construction powers which the Constitution never designed to confer on it. When the alien and sedition laws were passed, he drew the celebrated Virginia resolutions of 1798, carrying the doctrine of State resistance to Federal encroachment to the very verge of nullification. George Nicholas, his associate in the Virginia convention, and agreeing with him on most questions connected with the organization of the government, introduced into the legislature of Kentucky a series of resolutions, written by Mr. Jefferson,[1] and responding to those of Virginia. This great contest agitated the country for years. It absorbed almost every other question. It was a struggle against the exercise of constructive powers; and the power of Congress to regulate elections remaining unexercised, as its friends predicted, was forgotten. The country settled down into the belief that the assurances which had been given were sincere, and that the power would never be exercised by Congress so long as the States continued in good faith to perform the duty enjoined on them by the Constitution. To use the language of Judge Story, "public opinion almost irresistibly settled down in favor of the existing system," — that of non-interference on the part of Congress.

To show that I have correctly construed Mr. Madison, another fact may be confidently cited. He was eight years President of the United States. During that period of time he made no effort, as far as the public know, to induce Congress to act in this matter. Why did he not recommend the establishment of a uniform rule for elections? Why did he not propose the general regulations to which he referred in the Virginia convention, if he intended to intimate that the control of Congress was to be interposed without some great exigency? His silence goes far to sustain the construction I have put on his opinion. Taken in connection with the practice of the government to the end of his administration, — a period of twenty-eight years, — I consider it conclusive.

Let me now say a few words in relation to the proposed amendment to the Constitution, and I will no longer trespass on the attention of the committee. It proposes to limit the power of Congress to make regulations for the election of Senators and Representatives in Congress or to alter those made by the States to cases in which a State neglects, refuses, or is unable to make such regulations; and the power in such cases is to be exercised only until the legislature of such

[1] Jefferson's Works, Vol. IV. p. 344.

State shall make provision in the premises, with a proviso that Congress may prescribe the time for the election of Representatives. It is in the language of the amendment proposed by the convention of this State in ratifying the Constitution of the United States. It is substantially incorporating into the letter of the Constitution the intention of its framers. It may, however, be considered as narrowing the power of Congress so far as to restrict its interposition in the correction of abuses to such as are subversive of the government itself. The convention of this State did not believe that it was necessary to give Congress a control over the election of Representatives to secure the rights of the people in the exercise of the elective franchise. They believed the central power should have no further control than to provide for its own preservation. They believed the power of regulating elections would be much more likely to be abused by Congress than by the legislatures of the States, linked as the latter are to the great body of the people, in interest as well as feeling, in an infinite variety of forms. The event has proved the correctness of their judgment. For, if in disregard of the common understanding at the time the Constitution was framed and ratified; if without any omission or refusal on the part of a State to perform its duty; if without any pretence of abuse on the part of any State in regulating the election of its Representatives; if in opposition to the general, I may say the uniform, current of contemporaneous exposition and modern commentary; if in defiance of the settled and unvarying practice of the country for more than half a century, Congress has unnecessarily exercised this power; is there not danger, if all this authority is overturned by a silent acquiescence on the part of the States in this unauthorized interposition,—I say, is there not danger that it may be exercised hereafter in a far more exceptionable manner, in a manner fatal perhaps to the rights of the States and the people?

But, sir, I have done. Wearied as the patience of the

committee must be, I will trespass on it no longer. If gentlemen on the other side fancy they see, as has been intimated, any disposition to resist this act of Congress for party purposes, they greatly mistake the motive in which my opposition to it originates. I know the majority of this House is actuated by intentions as free as my own from any improper bias; and certainly no one would be less inclined than myself to bring forward or advocate any measure which would be calculated to detract from the respect which the Federal authority may justly claim from every good citizen so long as it acts within its acknowledged boundaries. But, believing as I do that it has trampled down the barriers which the Constitution designed to set up against its encroachments upon the just rights of the States; believing that it is only by a steady adherence to the conditions of the original compact between the States, both in its letter and spirit, that the general government can move in its appropriate sphere, either with safety to itself or with benefit to the common Union; I hold that we should be guilty of high disloyalty to great principles, to our free institutions, to our constituents, whose rights and interests we are bound to defend, if we were to fail to take the attitude in which the resolutions propose to place us,—an attitude of firm and unyielding resistance to encroachment, asserting our own construction of the Constitution in clear and unequivocal language, but acting with the moderation and forbearance becoming the largest State in the Union.

The gentleman from Essex asks whether we expect that the recommendations contained in these resolutions will be adopted? I say in reply that there is one thing which I do confidently expect: that this act will be repealed; that it will not survive the next Congress; that it will go down to the tomb with the alien and sedition laws, the germs of earlier encroachment, to mingle with the kindred clay of those odious and detestable statutes. Nor, sir, do I despair of seeing the Constitution amended as proposed. I know the difficulty of accomplishing it. I know that the assent of twenty States must be obtained. But with the evidence before us of the tendency of this power in Congress to run into abuse, warned as we have been of our danger by this violation of the Constitution in its clear and indisputable intention, I trust a sufficient number of the States will be aroused to the necessity of applying the remedy we suggest,—that New York, by the course of forbearance recommended, will carry along with her the general judgment of the country, and secure the adoption of the measure proposed. But if we shall be disappointed in this hope, we shall, at least, have the consolation of reflecting that no effort has been spared on our part to arrest the progress of encroachment on the residuary powers of the States; and if she shall be called on hereafter, as I most earnestly trust she never will, to assume a higher attitude in defence of her invaded rights, she may, from her very moderation now, take it with greater confidence of commanding the approbation of the country and of mankind.

RURAL LIFE AND EMBELLISHMENT.

The following Address was delivered on the 2d of October, 1851, at the tenth annual exhibition of the Queens County Agricultural Society, at Jamaica, Long Island.

Mr. President, and Gentlemen: If I had been governed by a consideration of my qualifications for addressing you on the subject of Agriculture, I should certainly not have ventured to accept the invitation of your Committee. I have really very little knowledge of practical husbandry. My occupation until quite recently has not been such as to fit me for making any useful suggestion to you, the farmers of Long Island, known, as you are, throughout the State for your familiar acquaintance with all that concerns a successful cultivation of the soil. But the interest I take in the subject has overruled all other considerations, though in appearing before you I am compelled to throw myself on your indulgence, and to call your attention to topics more remotely connected with agricultural life and occupations than those which are usually discussed on occasions like this. Indeed, gentlemen, I feel that I should justly incur the imputation of presumption if I were to undertake to advise you as to the rotation of crops, the raising of domestic animals, the preparation of manures, or other subjects of a kindred character, — subjects on which you are much better informed than myself. It is under the influence of this conviction that I turn to other topics, collateral to these, and I trust intimately interwoven with the lasting interests of an agricultural community.

Before I proceed to the description of these topics, let me call your attention to some local considerations, which concern you as residents of Long Island. I believe I hazard nothing in saying that few other districts in the State possess higher advantages. As an agricultural district alone, these advantages are inappreciable. Your county lies upon the very confines of a city destined to become one of the most populous in the world, and increasing with rapidity altogether without a parallel. A circle with its centre at Union Square in New York, and with a radius of two miles in extent, will embrace a population of seven hundred and fifty thousand souls. The annual growth of this immense aggregation of people will far outstrip the ability of surrounding districts to supply its wants. Even now it is, by means of railways, reaching into remote counties and States, and drawing forth their agricultural surpluses for consumption. Your proximity to this extended and unfailing market gives you great advantage in the competition. The Sound and the East River afford you a sheltered communication by water. A railroad divides your county in nearly a central course. By one or the other of these channels of intercourse any farmer in this county may reach the city in a few hours with the surplus products of his labor, and always with the certainty of finding a market for all which he can spare from the consumption of his household.

Considered in reference to fertility of soil, your county will bear a favorable comparison with others in the southern portion of the State. From its characteristic qualities it is doubtless destined to be devoted almost exclusively to tillage. There may be exceptions in the northern portion of the county, but I believe I am justified in saying that nature indicates its superior fitness for the cultivation of grains, fruits, and garden products, and that accidental circumstances confirm this application of your agricultural labor.

I remember often to have heard it remarked in former years, that the profits of farming on Long Island were absorbed by the expenses of manuring. But I have become convinced, by personal observation, that the productiveness of your agriculture, labor and manures being both taken into the account, will bear a fair comparison with that of other districts in this part of the State. If much of your soil is light and thin, it is at the same time genial and warm; and the rapidity with which vegetation matures gives you an advantage in the market over districts in which nature is more sluggish in her operations, and tardy in her returns. The variety which your soils possess — from the deep rich loams of your necks to the light sandy formations on the South Bay — gives you the power of a diversified production which is eminently desirable in a district destined to contribute largely to the consumption of a city, demanding from its magnitude a varied supply.

Gentlemen, your county has other advantages which ought not to be overlooked. Placed, as it is, between the waters of the Sound and the Atlantic Ocean, it is alike exempt from the extremes of winter and of summer; you are neither pinched by excessive cold, nor overpowered by enervating heat. I believe I may truly say that there is no region in this hemisphere which possesses in a higher degree the advantages of health and personal comfort, or which admits of a more uninterrupted application of the physical powers. These are all elements of prosperity, and they should be causes of devout thankfulness to the Sovereign Ruler of the universe for having so bountifully endowed you with the capacity of combining individual enjoyment with high social welfare.

Though you have some sources of prosperity peculiar to yourselves, arising out of geographical position and internal advantages, it is gratifying to know that most other portions of the State enjoy like facilities, though not all to the same extent, for improving their condition. Agriculture, under a variety of forms, will, in all probability, be for a long period of time the ruling interest of this State. The modes of its application may be to some extent varied as the western wilderness is filled up, and the thousands of emigrants who come in from the Old World, and the millions of money they bring with them, enter into the great field of production. It is not easy to foresee what may be all the results of these accessions of capital and labor; but I believe they cannot be otherwise than beneficial. I think we may fairly calculate that the standard of agricultural prosperity will be continually advanced, — that the productive industry of the country will from time to time put on new phases, but that under any of its modifications it must of necessity contribute to the advantage of our agriculture.

Under these circumstances, what are the leading objects to which the attention of the agricultural community should be turned, with a view to the improvement of their condition?

First of all is to be ranked the education of children. I have no reference now to the higher aims of intellectual culture, — those which concern the ability of the individual to discharge with intelligence his duties as a citizen, and as an integral part of the political power by which the machinery of government is directed and kept in motion, or those which concern the moral improvement incident to the cultivation of the mental faculties. Nor is it necessary that I should enter into these considerations. We all know that without an intelligent understanding of the nature of our government, some knowledge of its foreign concerns, and its true domestic policy, we cannot do justice to those to whom the political power of the country is intrusted, when they are right, or correct their misconduct when they are in error. So in respect to the influence of education upon the moral condition of a community, I think it cannot be doubted, whatever deductions to the contrary may be drawn from the criminal statistics of particular countries, that crime decreases as knowledge is diffused. Offences of certain classes — those which are conceived and executed in fraud — may increase as the intellect is sharpened by culture. But those which are perpetrated by force, and in general those of great atrocity, are undoubtedly diminished in frequency as the standard of popular intelligence is advanced. But I do not allude to influences or objects like those. I hold education to be one of the highest attainments of an agricultural community as an element of improvement in rural economy. The labor which is most intelligently directed and applied is always the most profitable. An enlightened farmer will always obtain more from an application of equal means than an ignorant one. I do not mean to say that an uneducated man is always ignorant. Knowledge is to be derived from the observation of surrounding objects as well as from the study of books, and a man may become wise in a particular vocation by observation alone. But he would become much wiser if his mind were disciplined by the training of intellectual application. Without this advantage, however high the spirit of inquiry by which he may be moved, however bountiful his mental endowments, his observations will be less critical, and his deductions more tardy and inexact. Education not only leads us to an acquaintance with books, which are the fruits of the observations and reflections of other men, but it gives directness and force to our own, through the influence of intellectual discipline. This is, indeed, one of its highest offices ; it is the great instrument by which obstacles in the path of improvement are overthrown and removed.

The condition of the schools in his immediate neighborhood is, then, an object of leading interest to every farmer. It is of the utmost importance that the teacher should be capable, honest, " and apt to teach." A good teacher is, if possible, of more value than good books. The latter in bad hands are comparatively worthless. To command good teachers, liberal wages must be paid. This has been the great defect in the district schools. There is no reason under the new system why it should exist any longer. The expenses of the schools, after expending the money contributed by the public funds, are paid almost exclusively by taxes upon property. I know there is a serious difference of opinion in respect to the expediency of such a provision ; and I believe the law passed last winter may be regarded as a compromise between those entertaining conflicting views on the subject. I remember, when I was Superintendent of the Common Schools of this State, to have come to the conclusion, and so reported to the Legislature on more than one occasion, that Free Schools, as they are called, though it would be more proper to call them schools in which the expenses are wholly paid by public funds and property, (for our schools were free under the old system,) were indispensable to cities and large villages, and that schools in which the patrons paid a small part of the teacher's wages were preferable as a general rule in purely agricultural districts. But any system of which the tendency is to elevate the standard of instruction in the common schools, is the best; and certainly the school-tax is the one which above all others we ought to pay with most pleasure. In proportion as the condition of the district schools is improved, the necessity for private schools of an elementary character is obviated. For this reason it is of the first importance that the district schools should be liberally supported. Let this be done, let them have teachers who are well qualified to instruct and to maintain order, and private schools will cease to have any advantage over them, and become wholly useless in agricultural districts. I consider such a result eminently to be desired; for where private schools abound, it is nearly an infallible indication that the condition of the district schools is depressed. It should be regarded, then, as one of the first duties of the farming community to cherish the district schools, to elevate their character, and to consider expenditures upon them as the most productive of all investments.

Next to a preparation of his children for the active duties of life, the farmer will naturally regard with most interest the proper use of the soil he cultivates, so as to insure the greatest practicable productiveness. I trust I shall not be considered as sinning against the lights of science, when I say that this must in nearly every case be determined by individual observation and experience. The infinite diversity which is found in the chemical composition of soils, even in contiguous districts and farms, makes the choice of the fertilizing agents best adapted to them a question to be decided mainly by experiment. In almost every great district, the geological formation of which has a distinctive character, an analysis of the principal soils will furnish valuable hints. In this respect the geological survey of the State has rendered an important service to our agriculture, by collecting and analyzing the soils of different counties and towns. But these results can rarely do more in any particular case than to afford suggestions of a general character. For instance, in districts in which the soil derives its distinguishing characteristics from the decomposition of limestone, the analysis will show, as might have been expected, that any manure in which lime is the principal ingredient would be superfluous, if not positively prejudicial. So where the soil depends upon the *débris* of granitic rocks or slate, or some of the later formations, for its mineral agents, a general idea of the particular manures best calculated to render it productive may be obtained from a knowledge of this fact confirmed by chemical analysis. But, as I have already said, only valuable suggestions can be obtained from the results of this analysis. In a district of country varied in its surface as ours is, with alternating valleys and hills, with cultivated fields running up to the summits of mountains and down to the level of the sea, nearly every field may require a specific treatment, and this can only be taught by experiment, for very few farmers have the means of subjecting their farms to a detailed analysis by a practical chemist. In like manner the quantity of land which may be most advantageously devoted to grazing or tillage, the products which from their certainty, or the stability of the prices they bear in market, are likely to yield the greatest average profit, the number of domestic animals which ought to be sustained in reference to the convenience of the farmer and the proper management of the farm, — these are all problems which, from the necessity of the case, every farmer must ultimately decide for himself, and after a few years of observation he will decide them more intelligently than any one can do it for him.

I have already said, gentlemen, that in these matters I have very little practical knowledge, and I am admonished by a consciousness of my deficiency in this respect to abstain from all advice in respect to them.

But there are some points in the economy of rural life on which I venture to throw out a few suggestions. If the positions I have stated in respect to the future condition of this State as an agricultural district are well founded, the farmers of New York may fairly calculate, with a diligent application of their labor, on a more than ordinary prosperity. By far the greater portion may reasonably expect a regular surplus of income after meeting the expenses of their domestic establishments. How shall this surplus be applied? in enlarging their farms, or in rendering the land they already occupy more productive by a more liberal application of labor and of fertilizing agents? I believe experience has satisfactorily proved that our farms are, as a general rule, too large already. This was naturally to be expected in the early settlement of the country when land was cheap. But as prices have advanced, the tendency has been to curtail the dimensions of our farms. Still, the evil continues to exist to some extent. There is no doubt that the same quantity of labor expended upon a diminished surface would be, in most cases, more profitable. This observation is particularly true in respect to farms devoted chiefly to tillage. Very large farms, in nine cases out of ten, will exhibit some traces of slovenly cultivation, — a field here and there overrun with weeds, or some other indication that the surface is too extended for the minute observation of the superintending head. He who has more acres than he can conveniently cultivate had better sell them, and devote the interest of the money to the more thorough cultivation of what he retains. By so doing, his comfort and his pecuniary interest will alike be promoted.

Next to the proper cultivation of the farm should rank the neatness and order of the farmer's residence, the farmhouse. It should be tasteful, comfortable, and, if possible, of durable materials. The best material, undoubtedly, is the one in which your county does not abound — stone. But brick, of which Queens is a large manufacturer, is a good substitute for it. I am aware that there is a strong prejudice against stone dwellings, from the idea that they are damp; but I believe the prejudice to be wholly unfounded. A stone house properly constructed is as warm in winter, as cool in summer, and as dry at all seasons as any other. In many countries in Europe, with climates quite as moist as ours, the dwellings are almost wholly of stone or brick, and they are perfectly free from dampness. They are made so by detaching the plastering from the inner surface of the wall. When a room is plastered directly upon the wall, moisture will show itself in particular states of the atmosphere, and sometimes to such an extent as to run down in streams to the floor. This is not, as is sometimes supposed, because the moisture passes through the body of the wall, but because the wall being a ready conductor of heat, the temperature of the inner surface conforms almost immediately to that of the outer, and in sudden changes from heat to cold, the atmosphere of the room is cooled so rapidly as to deposit on the plastering the moisture it held in solution. This effect is readily obviated by interposing a body of atmospheric air (no matter how thin) between the plastering and the wall. It is only necessary that the one shall not be in contact with the other. The most effectual mode is to fer with studs or scantling; and with this precaution all apprehension of dampness may be discarded.

But whatever material the farmer may choose for the construction of his dwelling, it should be tasteful in design. It costs no more to put materials into a graceful form than it does to throw them together without architectural taste or propriety. The dwelling should be simple, substantial, and unpretending,—a type of the independence and the unobtrusive habits of the occupant. Comfort, not show, should be the leading object in the construction of the American farm-house. Our government is simple in its structure; the same character of simplicity runs through every department of our social and political organization; and it is eminently appropriate and desirable that the agricultural community should preserve in their dwellings, their rural improvements, and their domestic habits, the distinguishing characteristics of their institutions, and set up, if possible, an impassable barrier against the growing waste and extravagance of the great towns.

There is no one thing in the way of domestic improvement, in which we have made so rapid an advance during the last twenty years, as in architecture. Happily the era of Grecian pediments and colonnades for private dwellings has passed away; and it is to be hoped to return no more. The prevailing forms of Italian, Gothic, Norman, and English cottage architecture are far more appropriate for dwellings in external taste, and better adapted to the comfort of the inmates. Of these forms the most simple are the most suitable for farm-houses. There is a little danger that they may run too much into ornament for good taste. All excess of ornamental work is a waste of money, and, what is worse, it impairs the true effect of the edifice of which it is a part.

A still greater error is to build on a more extensive scale than the means of the proprietor warrant. This is perhaps not so much the error of the country as of the town. I doubt whether in any channel of expenditure there has been so much extravagance as in this, and nothing can be more unwise. We have fortunately no system of entails or rule of primogeniture to maintain overgrown establishments. Fortunes dwindle away with us, by the regular operation of law, as rapidly as they are accumulated. I do not remember a large private establishment in the city of New York, twenty-five years old, which has not passed out of the family of him who erected it; and this not so much on account of the changes which have taken place in the currents of fashion and business as because no one of the children could afford to maintain it. In building, the proprietor ought always to ask himself whether any one of his children, with the share of the estate which will be likely to fall to him, will be able to support the establishment, and he should be governed by the answer he can give to this inquiry in determining the dimensions of his dwelling. If he does not, the chances are ten to one that his descendants, before a single generation has passed away, will be compelled to quit the paternal mansion, and do violence to all the endearing associations which, from our very nature, connect themselves with the natal roof and the family fireside. For this reason, it is difficult to see a magnificent mansion rearing itself upon the hill-side, or the bank of a river, overlooking more humble structures and seeming to exercise a manorial supervision over them, without thinking that the unconscious proprietor is in all probability building for strangers, and not for his own children. For the same reason it is always more grateful to contemplate the quiet farm-house, substantial and unobtrusive, standing amid cultivated fields, or the tasteful cottage nestling in the valley, with its rustic improvements about it.

When I speak of the danger of running into excess of ornament, I do not mean that farm-houses should be without embellishment. Far from it. They ought to be highly ornamented; they should be surrounded with the beautiful and graceful in nature: the vine, the flowering shrub, and such other plants as will bear the rigor of our winters. These are the true ornaments for rural dwellings. They are far more appropriate and tasteful than the most elaborate carvings in wood or stone; and nature offers them freely to all who will take pains once a year to bestow on them a few hours of attention. It is in these appendages to rural dwellings that the great charm of the country in England consists. English farm-houses and cottages are not often, I may say very rarely, faultless structures, when tested by a strict application of architectural rules. Nay, they are often ungraceful in design and rude in execution; but with the ivy spreading itself over the gable or covering up the porch, and the woodbine climbing up the casement and enveloping it in foliage, they acquire a beauty and a grace which no work of man's hand can equal.

Such as these I should wish our rural habitations to be. They should be embellished not so much by the hands of the architect as by the taste and care of the occupants. And I trust the fairer portion of my audience will pardon me for reminding them that this is their peculiar province. Let me, Ladies, address myself to you for a single moment as presiding over the household and the family dwelling. Let it be externally a type of the neatness and order which reign within. Ornament it with the vines, plants, and flower-bearing shrubs which are suited to our climate. These require little attention, and many of them carry their foliage and verdure far beyond the season when most others decay. Flowers which require to be housed in winter demand too much care, and, as a general rule, they are in the open air ephemeral in their bloom. The hardier plants, those which come out early and bear their foliage late, are preferable for the decoration of the family dwelling. It is not easy to conceive with how little expenditure of time the most gratifying results may be obtained. A gravelled walk from the entrance-gate to the porch, running through a lawn of well-cropped grass, with here and there a lilac, an althea, or a seringer, a vine trained upon a frame (no matter how rough, for the foliage will cover it), will change the coldest prospect into one of warmth and beauty and grace.

Nor is it to the taste alone that these rural embellishments address themselves; they tend to elevate and refine the moral feelings, and to make us better men. It seems difficult to connect with the homestead the sacred feelings which belong to it, when all around it is bare and cold. But when clothed in rural beauty by kindred hands, the sentiment of home is exalted, and those who have thus embellished it are presented to our minds and hearts under new and more endearing aspects.

I say to you then, Ladies, embellish your dwellings with the beautiful in nature; surround them with verdure and foliage, and give them the highest possible attraction to the eye and the taste. The leading impulses by which men are governed are constantly drawing them out into the world. Ambition, the desire of accumulation, the necessary business of life, are perpetually calling them away from home. Let home, then, be made so attractive in its external as well as its internal aspect, that it shall always be left with regret and regained with eagerness, as the most grateful refuge from the active duties of life. Under these circumstances the minutest work of your hands will have its value. The vine you have trained, the shrub you have planted, will possess an interest in the sight of those who are dear to you which the most elaborate ornament wrought by the hands of the carver can never attain.

I know no works so well calculated to inspire a love for rural beauty, and to teach us how to create it, as those of Mr. Downing of Newburgh. I allude particularly to his works on Landscape Gardening and Rural Architecture. They should be in the hands of every farmer's wife and daughters. Indeed, there is no one in any condition of life who may not be improved by their exquisite taste and sound deductions. They have the great merit of teaching the purest morality without seeming to teach it. I do not know that the intellect can ever be educated too much; but I believe it to be quite possible that the moral feelings may be educated too little; and in this respect Mr. Downing's books supply a lamentable deficiency in all that concerns the embellishment of rural life and the beauties of rustic scenery.

Gentlemen, there is no country on the face of the globe which is susceptible in a higher degree of embellishment than ours, — none which nature has more highly embellished, — though it is painful to admit that we have destroyed much which, if left where she planted it, would have constituted in itself one of the first elements of rural beauty. I allude to the nearly universal destruction of our noble forests in immediate contiguity with our dwellings. When preserved, it is generally for fuel, at a distance from our residences. This error may readily be repaired by planting. Five, six, or seven years are sufficient to provide a house with shade. I do not think a tree should ever be planted within fifty feet of a dwelling, especially if it be of large growth. When it attains so large a size as to spread its branches over the dwelling, they tend to perpetuate dampness, and when in contact with the open windows of sleeping apartments in summer nights, the carbonic acid gas they evolve is often a source of annoyance to sleepers, and sometimes deleterious to the health. A grove five or six rods off, and in such a direction as to shield the house from the bleak winds to which it is most exposed, should be regarded as an indispensable appendage to every farm-house.

I think this grove ought not to consist altogether of mere shade-trees. Economy and comfort both dictate that it should yield fruit as well as shade; and in sections of the country where forests are disappearing, it is desirable, when a tree blows down, or exhibits signs of decay, that the wood may be of such a nature that it may be converted to some practical use. I know few trees more beautiful than the hickory and the chestnut,—one is an excellent fire-wood, and the other is valuable for many farm-purposes. They have an advantage, too, over most others in their long tap-roots, which penetrate deep into the earth, and draw out its secret moisture, so that in the very dryest season their foliage is fresh and green, while that of trees whose roots are superficial is faded and perishing. Such a grove, beside the comfort it affords to a family in hot weather, will, if properly treated, kept free from undergrowth and seeded down, pay the interest on the value of the land in what it produces. The nuts are valuable for home consumption, or the market; and if the leaves are raked up in the fall and thrown into the barn-yard, to be trampled to pieces by the cattle during the winter, they will add to the manure-heap in the spring; and the grove will yield a good crop of grass, though certainly not equal to that of an open meadow. It is only where the leaves are allowed to accumulate in groves, covering the whole surface of the earth with a thick deposit, which the delicate vegetation cannot penetrate, that the grass withers and dies.

There are several other nut-bearing trees which afford excellent shade, and are beautiful in their forms and in their foliage. Of these the black walnut and the butternut, or the white walnut, are among the most valuable and graceful.

Let me not be understood as proscribing mere shade-trees. That is not my intention. There are many of great value, which should be cultivated and preserved. There are the sugar-maple and the locust. There are the elm and the oak, both trees of noble growth, but they are seen to best advantage standing alone; and when they are scattered over an extended landscape, and have attained their full size, they have a fitness as emblems of the majestic stature and growth of our country.

To a country embellished and cultivated as ours may, and I trust will be, we, and those who are to come after us, will cling with new tenacity as time advances and develops in it new capacities for improvement. It is to the country all men turn at last for a refuge from their worldly cares. Born of the earth, our instincts lead us back, as life draws to a close, to scenes in which nature presents herself in her most attractive attire, and under her serenest aspects. No man could endure to pass through his last great trial on earth, amid the confusion and uproar of a large commercial city, unless his native instincts had all been obliterated by a whole life of habits at war with them. Statesmen, warriors, men who leave the impress of their character and actions upon the age in which they live, when their public labors are ended, seek the quietude of the country with that instinctive love for its beauties which seems to be one of the inseparable companions of intellectual greatness. Washington, when his great mission was fulfilled, retired to the shades of Mount Vernon; the elder Adams, at the close of his administration, to Quincy; Jefferson to Monticello; Madison to Montpelier, and Jackson to the Hermitage. Every one of their successors in the administration of the government has found rest from his public toils in the quietude of rural life.

Connecting themselves, as the best and truest impulses of our nature do, with country life, every one should endeavor to do something to embellish it. The first wish of every man is to live in the memory of his descendants. There is something exceedingly unsatisfactory, not to say revolting, in the thought that they are only to be reminded of us by the bare head-stone, lost among a hundred others in the common burial-place, telling in a few words of set phrase when we entered on the theatre of life and when we made our exit from it. A grove judiciously planted, a few trees set out around the family dwelling, will be far better memorials of us with our children. The after-generations who sit down under the refreshing shade will take pleasure in pronouncing the ancestral names, or in acknowledging the parental providence to which their enjoyment is to be referred.

He who builds a farm-house has a still better opportunity of perpetuating himself in the remembrance of his children. Its tastefulness, its fitness for the purpose of its construction, its internal arrangement for comfort and health, will be to the descendants so many mementos of the ancestor in whose good judgment they originated. A well-built and well arranged dwelling is the best mausoleum a man can erect to himself. He may thus perpetuate his taste or his true conception of domestic order and comfort, and leave to his children a memorial of himself, which will enter into the business of their lives and mingle itself with their daily occupations and enjoyments. In this manner we may be truly said to live with our descendants.

He who can add to the attraction of agricultural life by exhibiting it under more interesting aspects will render the country an inestimable service. Most other pursuits present greater allurement to the eyes of the world, in the higher rewards they sometimes afford, and in the broader fields they open for public distinction. But it is with professions as with everything else; those which promise the highest rewards are exposed to the greatest hazards. While one lawyer amasses a fortune, a hundred procure a bare subsistence, and in our cities many go down to early graves with constitutions broken by sedentary habits. While ten merchants become rich, ninety become bankrupt, as our commercial statistics show. Agriculture is the safest of all pursuits, the most independent, the most healthful, and the least laborious. It is true, it affords no examples of sudden elevation from poverty to wealth; it opens no field to speculation or perilous adventure. But its rewards are certain, and with industry and perseverance it is sure to yield the competency which the wise man has said is better than great riches.

More than three quarters of the entire population of the United States are said to be engaged in the pursuits of agriculture; and it will be well for the country if this proportion can be maintained. With our western boundary extended to the Pacific, and with the new stimulants which the riches of California have offered to commercial adventure, it would not be surprising if there should be some diversion of capital and labor from the field of agriculture. But this diminution of the effective force of the agricultural classes cannot be of long duration. The immense forests which are yet to be subdued, beyond the great Lakes, will attract new laborers, and soon repair what agriculture may temporarily lose. It is not probable that for a long course of years there will be a sensible diminution of the numerical proportion which the agricultural classes bear to all others. I consider the perpetuity of our institutions as depending in an eminent degree upon the great preponderance of those who are devoted to the cultivation of the earth. I should regard it as exceedingly unfortunate if either the commercial or manufacturing classes were to acquire a superiority in numbers over the agricultural. They belong to the same great industrious family, but they belong to it in the relation of subordinates. Bound to each other as they are in the general economy of the system by indissoluble ties, it is nevertheless in the steadiness, the quietude, the patient industry of agricultural life and the habits of sobriety it creates, that our greatest security consists. Pursuits which bring men permanently together in large masses have their peculiar dangers. No man can compare the tranquillity which reigns throughout the country with the constant excitement which agitates the great cities, without feeling that it is to the former we must look for safety against any internal shock which shall threaten the social edifice with destruction.

When we contemplate the scenes which some of our commercial towns have enacted within the last ten years, classes and associations warring upon each other, lives sacrificed in attacking property or defending it, multitudes wild with excitement, harnessing themselves, as it were, to the car of youth or beauty, or artistic talent, we cannot but feel that it is to the calmer and purer atmosphere of the country, where men think first and act afterwards, that we must look for the governing power by which the motion of the social machine is to be regulated.

Above all things, gentlemen, let us maintain by every means in our power the dignity of labor, and especially the labor which fertilizes and embellishes the earth. It is the true vocation of our race. It is one of the merciful designs of Providence, that, in carrying out the divine sentence, our prosperity and our happiness should be alike promoted. — Let every man who lives in the country till the earth. No matter how limited the surface on which his toil is expended. If it be but a garden or a grass-plot, let him cultivate it. His health, his feelings, and his character will all be improved.

And, finally, let us remember that, in maintaining the dignity of agricultural labor, enlightening its application and embellishing its abodes, we shall give new importance and stability to the arts of peace. If there were no other reason, agriculture ought to rank first in the order of human occupations because its genius is pacific. Nothing could be more disastrous to us than a spirit of aggression or aggrandizement taking possession of the minds of our people. I know there is much in the extension of empire which appeals to the strongest impulses of our nature, — to the ambition of some, the cupidity of others, and the national pride of all. But if we may trust to the teachings of history, there is nothing in wide-spread dominion which promises either lasting security or strength. The most extended empires are those which have fallen most suddenly and hopelessly into poverty and impotence. Gentlemen, there is a nobler national pride, — one more worthy of our origin and our destiny, — in elevating our internal condition, and developing our resources, in those improved applications of the mechanic arts which have just given us two distinguished triumphs in the face of the assembled world, in presenting to the other nations of the earth an example of order and high civilization at home, and in maintaining in our intercourse with them a sacred regard for all the dictates of truth, honor, and international duty.

GROWTH OF NEW YORK CITY.

The following Lecture, on the Growth, Destinies, and Duties of the City of New York, was delivered before the New York Historical Society, at Metropolitan Hall, on the 6th of January, 1853.

MR. PRESIDENT, LADIES, AND GENTLEMEN: In the opening lecture of the series in which I have been invited to take part, you were addressed with great eloquence and force on the culture of Art, with a special reference to this city. So far as the application is concerned, I propose to follow the example of the distinguished speaker, but in a much more humble sphere. I shall, with your indulgence, devote the hour allotted to me to a brief review of the growth of this city, some glances into the future, to see, if we can, what are its probable destinies, and the discussion of a few topics of domestic interest and social duty.

It is a remarkable circumstance that the Hollanders, who laid the foundations of this city, should have foreseen, more than two centuries ago, the commercial preëminence to which it was destined. In December, 1652, forty-three years after the landing of Henry Hudson, the directors of the West India Company, in a letter to Peter Stuyvesant, the Director-General, urged on him the importance of promoting commerce with the settlers in New England and Virginia, by which means, they say, " must the Manhattans prosper," and their trade and navigation flourish. " For when," the letter adds, " these once become permanently established, — when the ships of New Netherland ride on every part of the ocean, — then numbers, now looking to that coast with eager eyes, will be allured to embark for your island." If these sagacious adventurers could have looked forward to the changes which the lapse of two hundred years has wrought, their language could hardly have been more prophetic or descriptive of the reality. Great discoveries, it is true, have been made in the application of physical powers to the practical uses of mankind, which were not at that day revealed to human foresight. The luxuries which always follow in the train of commerce, the resistless power of our enterprise, the manifestations of industry in an endless variety of forms, — the genius with which architecture has elaborated this hall, — all denote a spirit of development in civilization and in art which no vividness of the imagination would have attributed, even at this day, to the wilderness on the skirts of which that feeble and precarious lodgment had been made.

Indeed, it was not until the United States had thrown off the colonial shackles, by which the spirit of their enterprise was repressed, and the central government had given strong evidence of its ability to sustain the weight of the system it was designed to uphold, that the elements of this city's growth became fully developed. Since that time its progress has had no parallel in the history of modern improvement.

Fifty years ago, Canal Street was entirely beyond the settled precincts of the city. The place of public execution was in Franklin Street, selected, as all such theatres of the vengeance of the law were at that day, on account of its distance from the abodes of the people and the busy haunts of commerce and industry. Thirty years ago, the spot on which I stand was an unoccupied space far from the bustle and the activities of the town. Now at least eight of the twenty-two square miles of surface which the island contains are covered, the population has risen, in half a century, from 60,000 souls to 550,000, and is increasing with augmenting rapidity. A quarter of a century ago, in a pamphlet which I wrote while a student at law on the resources of the city of New York, I expressed the belief that in 1878 twenty-five years hence, the inhabitants would number nearly a million and a half, and that the whole island would be covered with dwellings, and buildings devoted to trade, the mechanic arts, and the various other uses which a large commercial population requires.

The estimate was by most persons thought extravagant at the time it was made, and was by many derided as a wild and unwarrantable speculation. And yet it has been thus far outrun by the progress of the city. All past estimates, however unsupported they may have appeared to be by sober calculations, are mere laggards in the race which we are running against time and the impediments to human progress. It is not probable that I shall live to see my prophecy fulfilled, but there are, no doubt, many within the sound of my voice who will. Setting apart the spaces needed for squares, reservoirs, railway appurtenances, shops, warehouses, manufactories, and public edifices, and the island will not conveniently contain more than a million and a half of people. But this is by no means the limit to its growth. Its population will flow into surrounding spaces. The process has already commenced. It has crossed the East River, the North River, and the Harlem. Brooklyn, Williamsburgh, Jersey City, and Morrisania are all dependencies of the great metropolis, and, for every practical purpose, parts of it. A circle with a radius of four miles in extent, and with its centre at Union Square, will now inclose seven hundred and fifty thousand people. If the population of the city and the surrounding districts referred to increases as rapidly during the next twenty-eight years as it has during the last twenty-five, it will number in 1865 a million and a half of souls, and in 1880 three millions.

If our peaceful relations with other countries continue uninterrupted, I see no reason why there should be any check to this increase. The rapid improvement of the country, the extension of our commerce, the tide of immigration, the numberless lines of communication pointing to this city as to a centre of radiation,— all combine to confirm, and indeed to accelerate its growth. In the pamphlet referred to, published in 1827, I remember to have stated that the inhabitants of the States of New York, Ohio, Indiana, and Illinois, and of the territory of Michigan, whose industry was subservient to the commercial interests of the city, and dependent on it for foreign products, numbered nearly a million and a half of souls; and I estimated that the number would in 1849 amount to nearly three millions, and in 1878 to more than five millions and a half. This estimate also has already been vastly exceeded by the result. Taking the same basis, modified by the railway communications which have been opened to the city, and the population of interior districts now dependent upon us for their commercial supplies cannot number less than five millions and a half, — about equal to the number estimated for the year 1878. We are a quarter of a century in advance of this estimate, and with no apparent limit to the growth of the districts thus connected with us. This extraordinary extension of the internal trade of the city is due, in some degree, to railways, which did not enter into the estimate of its increase twenty-five years ago, because they had not then been introduced into this State. Our communication with Lake Erie and the agricultural supplies it receives from the Northwestern States, is now more speedy and more certain than our intercourse was with Dutchess county fifty years ago. Five hundred miles are now more easily and speedily overcome, both as regards travel and transportation, than fifty miles were at the commencement of the present century. One of the practical effects of these facilities of intercourse is to place the products of the interior of this State and of the States I have referred to at the very outskirts of the city, and to bring the immense variety of the products of other countries, which centre here, into virtual contact with the interior.

Who shall venture to assign limits to this extension? London, with far inferior capacities for commerce, foreign or domestic, has a population of two millions and a half, spread over a surface of forty square miles. With the further advantage which New York possesses as a general mart, to some extent, for the whole Union, there is no reason why she may not go far beyond the British metropolis.

There is another element which is destined to exert a powerful influence on her growth. By means of the warehouse system, yet in its infancy, she is rapidly becoming a mercantile depot for the western hemisphere. The foreign products, which are destined for consumption on this side of the Atlantic, will be deposited here for distribution, and thus put largely in requisition our industry and capital.

This accumulation of men and of commercial wealth must bring with it another consequence of equal significance and efficacy. New York, with all these advantages, cannot fail to become, at no distant day, the centre of the pecuniary, as well as the commercial exchanges for this continent, and perhaps for the world. Such a consequence is almost inseparable from a decided ascendency in commerce. Money, the instrument of commerce, naturally flows into the channels where commercial operations are most extended and active. The precious metals of California will not only insure, but must hasten this result. Like the products of foreign industry, they will come here for distribution, stimulating our enterprise, and facilitating commercial exchanges.

I am sure I speak the sentiments of every person here present when I say, that the great prosperity of our own city has not made us indifferent to that of others. Boston, Philadelphia, Baltimore, Charleston, and New Orleans have their commercial offices to perform in their respective spheres, and there is work enough to be done on this continent to keep us all actively and beneficially employed. When the census of 1850 apprised us that our industrious and energetic neighbor, Philadelphia, numbered over four hundred thousand inhabitants, and was following us closely in enterprise and wealth, I am sure there was no other feeling but of gratification at her prosperity. Between Pennsylvania and New York there must always be a close and familiar association. We border on each other for a distance of more than three hundred miles. Though our interests are not in all respects the same, they are coincident in some remarkable particulars. Indeed, there is, in one respect, so striking an adjustment of her capabilities to our wants, that there never can be, in the commercial relations of the two States, any other rivalry than an honorable and beneficial competition. I refer to the inexhaustible and inestimable wealth of her coal-fields, which are indispensable to the prosperity of our commercial metropolis. Not only the city of New York, but a large number of our counties, with a population of a million and a half of souls, and increasing rapidly, are dependent on her supplies of fuel for their comfort. It is a curious fact, that the instant we reach the northern boundary of Pennsylvania from her interior, the coal-measures disappear! Not a trace of this great article of necessity is to be found on our side of the line. What makes it more singular is, that this boundary is a mere statistical demarcation, not marked out by any great natural division,—not following a watercourse, or a mountain-chain, but traversing both rivers and hills by a line drawn parallel to the equator. May we not regard it as one of those arrangements of Providence, which, in our ignorance or our presumption, we are too apt to ascribe to blind chance? I say, may we not regard it as an arrangement of Providence to bind inseparably to each other these two great States, (constituting, as they do, the heart of the American confederacy,) and to give them the influence they may possibly need, in the progress of events, to maintain the integrity of the Union, by holding together in the same bonds of friendship the other associated States?

Heavy responsibilities, grave questions of social and domestic duty, grow out of our commercial preëminence. Extraordinary aggregations of wealth, unless rightly employed, are never desirable. When they become the ministers of luxury and extravagance, they misdirect industry, pervert the public taste, and endanger the purity of society and the safety of the government. This is the great danger we have to guard against. It is the greater because the chief security of our free institutions has always been deemed to rest essentially upon the maintenance of a simple and economical government. I do not believe it to be possible for such a government to be continued in existence for any length of time, unless the social spirit conforms to it. A luxurious and extravagant people cannot maintain a simple and frugal government. No matter with what safeguards it may be surrounded, they will be silently relaxed until they conform to the social condition of the people. Private profusion comes first, next corporate recklessness and extravagance, and last of all public corruption. This, then, is the great duty which devolves on us, — to make the spirit of the social conform to the political organization, and maintain both in simplicity and economy. I know it is a very difficult duty where wealth abounds, and draws after it the temptations to profuse expenditure with which it is always beset. But let us hope that it is not impossible. Certainly, the most superficial view of our social organization should be sufficient to indicate the folly of all private extravagances which partake of the character of permanent investments. The most common manifestation of lavish expenditure at the present moment is in costly private dwellings. We have, like Genoa, our streets of palaces, but without her apology for them. We have no orders of nobility, no permanent estates to support large establishments. Private fortunes are exceedingly evanescent with us. The regular operation of our laws is to dissolve the accumulations of wealth which are the fruit of successful enterprise. There are very few instances in which property remains in a family beyond the second or third generation. Our forefathers abolished rules of primogeniture, because they considered them inconsistent with the genius of our institutions. The spirit of the community has conformed to this view of social duty, and no man thinks of leaving his property by will (as he may) to one child, for the purpose of keeping up a large establishment. A juster feeling has become universal, and children are endowed equally with the ancestral goods, or at least in proportion to their respective claims or merits, as the ancestor appreciates them. Under these circumstances, nothing can be more unwise than the erection of costly dwellings, which can only be maintained by princely fortunes. At the death of the head of the family, and the division of the ancestral property, no one of the children, as a general rule, has enough to support the establishment, and it passes into other hands. Nothing can be more unjust to children than to bring them up with expectations which cannot be fulfilled, or with habits of life which they are compelled to abandon. The parent, for the sake of a few years of ostentation, invests a large portion of his estate in a splendid dwelling, with the certainty that his death will be the signal for the expulsion of his children from it. Look for the splendid mansions of thirty years ago, and see what has become of them. Scarcely one remains in the family by which it was constructed. They are boarding-houses, places of public exhibition, or the workshops of fashion. The daughter enters the house of which her father was the master, and chaffers for a Parisian mantilla or bonnet in the sacred chamber in which she drew her first breath. In a large commercial city, extending rapidly, the currents of business and fashion sometimes change and bring with them these consequences. But they are more frequently the result of other causes. They are generally the consequence of the inability of any one of the children to maintain the paternal mansion, with the share of the estate which has fallen to him.

Under these social disabilities, no man of fortune should build a house which any one of his children, with the share of the property he is likely to inherit, will not be able to retain. If he does, the chances are ten to one that his descendants, before a single generation shall have passed away, will be compelled to quit the paternal mansion, and do violence to all the endearing associations which connect themselves with the family fireside and the natal roof. Nothing can be more heart-sickening if this necessity is met with sensibility, or more demoralizing to the feelings if it is submitted to with indifference. It has sometimes been said of us reproachfully, that we have no local attachments — no ancestral associations, which endear to us the places occupied by those who have preceded us in the journey of life. In a community like ours, in a state of rapid progression and change, and in which the philosophy of jurisprudence looks to the distribution rather than the accumulation of the proceeds of labor, local ties are unquestionably apt to be loosely worn. This is more especially true in cities, where private residences are often forcibly expelled by the irresistible encroachments of commerce and traffic. In the broader spaces which the country affords, there is happily room left for the sanctity of local attachments, and for the cultivation of those associations which cling to the spots where the bones of our ancestors repose, and where our own eyes, or those of our children, first saw the light.

I consider it as one of the greatest securities of this city, so far as a cultivation of the social affections and virtues is concerned, that it is so closely connected by railways with the rural districts in its vicinity. In one hour, the man of business or the mechanic may pass from the close confinement of his office, his counting-room, or his workshop, into the pure atmosphere of the country. The effect of these facilities is to withdraw from the city, during the genial seasons of the year, a large portion of its inhabitants, — to take men away from the town, where they are busy only with their own works, and place them where they must necessarily become conversant with the works of nature and of nature's God. As the clear atmosphere of the country is the best purifier of the *malaria* of the great cities, so are the quietude and the simple occupations of rural life the most salutary and efficient corrective of their extravagances and luxurious habits. There is nothing so full of hope and of promise for the purity and the invigoration of our social condition as the growing, I might almost say the prevailing, disposition to escape from the bustle, the show, and the ceremoniousness of the city, as soon as the genial season returns, and take refuge from them all in the quietude, the simplicity, and the freedom of the country. Indeed, large numbers of the working classes have made permanent changes in their homes. No one can go from the city on any of the great railroads terminating here, without being struck with the number of villages which have sprung into life within the last three years. They consist, for the most part, of cottages, each with its little garden and grass-plot, with here and there a larger enclosure answering better to the designation of a field. These new creations are the work of the mechanics of the city, who have wisely exchanged close streets and crowded dwellings, where space and pure air are alike unattainable, for rural habitations where they can enjoy both. They have their schools and churches and their quiet neighborhoods, where their children may be brought up without being exposed to the contaminations of the town. What an improvement is this upon the former estate of the industrious man — upon summer evenings in town, when the labors of the day were over, passed in close apartments rarely visited by a breath of pure air, or upon side-walks, with pavements and brick walls sending out in fiery streams the heat they had accumulated while the sun was upon them! Now a railway takes him from his rural home in the morning to his work in town, and after his ten hours of labor he returns to his home again, and passes what remains of daylight in his garden, or sits down with his family at his own porch, with the bosom of his mother earth unveiled before him, and with the shrubs and flowers he has planted sending out freshness and fragrance to soothe and invigorate him for the labors of another day.

The healthy influence of this new life upon the mind, the moral affections, and the physical energies of the industrious classes is beyond all power of appreciation.

To the man of independent circumstances, who can afford to have a house in town, and another in the country, a similar change of life, for a portion of the year at least, would be equally beneficial, under all its moral as well as its physical aspects. It is the love for rural scenes and rural occupations which, above all other causes combined, has given to the higher classes in England an intellectual and corporeal vigor unknown to the same classes in most other countries of Europe. Where the country residence ranks first and the town house second in the scale of the affections, — where the thoughts are, as it were, embalmed in the purifying influences of rural life, — there is no danger that a community will fall into decrepitude on the one hand, or dissoluteness on the other. The most seductive capitals and the most demoralizing, so far as all elevation of thought is concerned, are those which concentrate all the attractions of life in themselves, and where the districts by which they are surrounded are devoid of rural beauty.

A rural residence, if it be simple and unpretending, is one of the best moral teachers to the inhabitant of the town. If it have all the show of the town house, and the " pomp and circumstance " of the winter are maintained in summer, he will gain little by the change. The most friendly wish to the wealthy would be that every family might have its cottage, where the ostentation of equipage, the ceremoniousness of fashionable attendance, and the luxurious habits of the city, might be laid aside for a portion of the year, and where children might be taught the salutary lesson, (a hard one, when necessity is the first to teach it,) that the trappings of artificial life may be thrown off without sacrificing enjoyment or personal dignity. The cost of half a dozen city entertainments would provide such an establishment, and it would be repaid an hundredfold in health and intellectual vigor.

Nature has given us around the city a country singularly varied in its outline, from the quiet shores of the East River and the Sound to the majestic scenery of the Hudson; and with one half the expenditure which is wasted upon frivolous embellishment, it may in twenty-five years be made the most beautiful suburban district on the face of the globe.

In connection with this subject I cannot forbear to congratulate you on the marked improvement which has taken place within the last twenty-five years in our domestic architecture. The era of Grecian pediments and colonnades for private dwellings is happily past, and it is to be hoped to return no more. The substitution of the Norman, Gothic, modern Italian, and English cottage styles is a great gain both as regards convenience and rural embellishment. The most simple of these forms are always in best taste. There is great danger of running too much into ornament, and giving a meretricious cast to our domestic improvements. While in the city the prevailing tendency to overload with ornament literally revels in stucco, and develops itself in the most unmeaning shapes, in the country it runs wild in pinnacles, fantastic vergeboards, and in the endless foliations and efflorescences of the mediæval styles. All this is in the worst taste. A chaste simplicity adapted to our institutions, to the nature of our government, the character of our people, and the equalizing spirit of our laws, is demanded by every consideration of congruity and every dictate of good sense. It were greatly to be desired that some architect would give the rein to his genius, and, rising above the tyranny of rules, would give birth to an American style, — a style suited to our means, our tastes, our wants, and the peculiarities of our climate. The English cottage style, the most picturesque of all for rural architecture, would not be suited to us without essential modifications. We must have deep verandas and protected attics to shelter us from the scorching heat of our summer sun. Our interior arrangements must have their modifications also, to meet peculiarities in our social condition. No man is equal to the work who is not thoroughly imbued with the spirit of our system, and who has not the strength to burst away from all the bonds with which the Delilahs of fashion will strive to fetter his genius and his independence of thought.

There is one sphere of embellishment in which there can be no excess: in the cultivation of trees and plants, and in the enrichment by artificial culture of the numberless forms under which exuberant nature manifests herself in the realms of vegetable life. The simplest dwelling, surrounded by shade and verdure, is always attractive. It is in these accessories to rural architecture that the great charm of the country in England consists. Her country houses are very rarely faultless when brought to the test of strict architectural rules. Indeed, they are often ungraceful in design and rude in execution. But with the woodbine covering up the porch, and the ivy climbing up the gable and the oriel, and enveloping them in verdure and in shade, they have a charm which no others possess. Such as these I should wish our rural habitations to be. Let the wealthy go forth from their luxurious city dwellings, and make themselves familiar with the beauties of nature, while there is time left to enjoy them. Let them busy themselves in planting trees around their rustic abodes, let them teach the vine where to entwine itself, and the shrub where to grow and to flower. Let their children mingle with them in these primeval occupations, the purest and the most grateful which life affords, and they shall be stronger, happier, and better men. Their children will grow up with juster views of their responsibilities and duties, with more vigorous frames and purer affections, and with stouter hearts for the battle of life.

No man can look out upon the living forms which are gathering beauty and strength from his fostering care, without feeling his thoughts elevated and purified. He knows that his own hand is laboring with the hand of God, and that he himself, though but a created being with limited capacities, is giving to the works of the Almighty a beauty and a grace which but for his care they would never have possessed. Thoughts like these diminish the distance between him and the Author of his existence, and strengthen the hope that there may be, when the fulness of time shall come, a higher, a closer, and a holier coöperation.

But, ladies and gentlemen, I fear I am dwelling too long upon this branch of my subject. Before I resign it, I cannot forbear to direct your attention to a series of works on rural embellishment, which by a painful dispensation of Providence has been suddenly brought to a close. I mean the writings of the late Mr. Downing, of Newburgh. I know no works so well calculated to give elevated conceptions of the dignity and the charm of rural occupations, — none which have done and are doing so much for the embellishment of our glorious country. Nor do I know any which teach a purer morality. It is now understood that another of the series, more extended, and far surpassing its predecessors in its eloquence and the beauty of its illustrations, was in a course of preparation. Under any circumstances, the death of such a man is a public bereavement. Coming as it did, it was still more deplorable. It is an irreparable loss. The country could better have spared more than one of its most distinguished statesmen, or jurists, or divines. Their places might have been supplied, but his is not likely to be in our day. It is only once in an age that a man rises up so thoroughly imbued with the spirit of his profession, and with the sacred flame of art kindled in his bosom by the breath of Heaven.

There is one subject of great interest, which was briefly referred to by the distinguished gentleman who delivered the opening lecture, and which I am sure my auditors will pardon me for presenting to them with greater particularity. It is a subject on which I have bestowed some thought, and in respect to which I made, a few years ago, an attempt (I am sorry to say an unsuccessful one) to enlist the coöperation of some of our wealthy citizens. I mean the establishment in this city of an American Academy of Art, the foundation of which shall be a collection of pictures and statuary open to the public, furnished with all the facilities which artists require for study and improvement in their professions, and with schools of design for the gratuitous instruction of young persons without pecuniary means. With the exception of a public park of proper extent, I consider this nearly the only great want of the city which can be supplied by ourselves. Popular education is amply provided for by public law. The preaching of the gospel is extended, by the unassisted operation of the voluntary system, to every portion of the city. The sick are healed, the hungry fed, and the naked clothed, by munificent public charities. A noble library, already the most valuable in the world in proportion to the number of volumes it contains, is about to be opened to the public, and will give to the name of Astor a duration as lasting as the city itself. Another popular institution, designed for the special benefit of the industrious classes, and endowed with the same princely liberality, will insure to the name of Cooper an undying life. These institutions are, in some degree, local, though they are to be open to the whole American public. But an Academy of Art, containing specimens of the best schools of painting, ancient and modern, casts of ancient statues, and modern statuary of the most eminent masters, would become immediately a national institution. It would make New York the emporium of Art for the western hemisphere. Artists would flock to it from all sections of the Union, and from every portion of this continent, and return to the study of nature with a full knowledge of all that the genius of man has done for the perfection of the processes by which she may be most faithfully and feelingly copied. I believe I may safely say that no country, which has had so short a life as ours, has done more for art. But it is all the work of artists themselves, and the private encouragement by which they have been sustained. Neither the public nor the private wealth of the country has come forward with any great or permanent scheme of endowment for the encouragement of American art. It has struggled on unaided, battling dauntlessly with all the discouragements which have beset its path, — discouragements arising from the want of elementary instruction at home and the rivalry of better disciplined competitors abroad, — and yet it has gained for some of its votaries an immortal name.

It was thought that such an institution as I have described might be founded upon an extended individual subscription. I have abandoned all such hope. It must be the work of some one man — some one of our wealthy and enlightened citizens, like Astor and Cooper, who, under the influence of a good inspiration, shall see in the accomplishment of a great public work for the benefit of present and future generations a better motive and a higher fame than the brief possession of the few hundred thousand dollars which are necessary for it. I would not have him underrate the cost of such an institution. I do not think less than four hundred thousand dollars would suitably accomplish it, — one hundred and fifty thousand for the ground and the building, an equal amount for the purchase of pictures and statuary, and a hundred thousand more to be invested to meet its annual wants. There are men enough in this city whose fortunes would not be inconveniently diminished by such a contribution, who may, in a year, or a month, in the order of human life, be summoned to surrender all they possess into the hands of those who do not need it, or by whom it may be uselessly employed. I believe no higher niche remains to be filled in the temple of our city's fame than this, — no work by which a man may more certainly inscribe his name upon its loftiest pediment, — there to stand until the last column which sustains it shall crumble into dust.

It is in establishments and institutions like these that the munificence of republics and republicans is best displayed. While all individual profusion is at war with the spirit of the system under which we live, and can only bring with it unmixed evil, public institutions for the elevation of industry and the perfection of art — institutions in which all can meet on the footing of equality inherent in our political organization — are at once the conservative agencies and the glory of free governments.

But it is time for me to return to a topic to which I briefly alluded at the commencement of my remarks. I mean the necessity of a practical conformity of the social movement to the principles on which the political organization is founded. I believe there is only one condition to be fulfilled in order to insure for our system of government all the stability of which human institutions are capable. It must be carried out in the spirit in which it was created. Society must not set up distinctions unknown to the system itself, and give them, by habit or conventional sanctions, an influence at war with it. We must not weaken what was designed to be secure, or introduce what was designed to be excluded.

And, 1st, let it be distinctly understood, that the law must be inflexibly maintained. I use the term law in its largest sense, not only as including what has been specifically decreed, but as comprehending the general order, on the preservation of which the inviolability of all public authority depends. The law is the will of the people constitutionally expressed. Whoever arrays himself against it, excepting to procure its repeal in the mode prescribed by the fundamental compact, commits an act of treachery to the people themselves. The law is the basis of all popular supremacy. It is the very feature by which free government is distinguished from despotism. To uphold it is one of the highest duties which is devolved on us as freemen. It is always possible that those who are intrusted with its execution may err in the performance of their duty. They may employ unnecessary, arbitrary, or even wanton severity in enforcing it. For all this they may be held to a rigid account. But no error in the execution can impair the obligation to uphold it. It must be understood, and without reservation, that the law is to be inflexibly maintained.

2d. Kindred to the inviolability of the law, is the inviolability of rights of property. Under our system of government, life is always secure, except from private passion, hatred, and revenge, and these the law visits with a retribution which many regard as incompatible with the humanity of the age. The inviolability of private property rests upon the same basis as security to life. It is one of the leading objects of all social compacts. Life, liberty, property, — security to those is the great end for which men enter into society. We believe it to be prejudicial to the general interest that property shall be kept in masses by the operation of law. We have declared that children, in cases of intestacy, shall inherit equally. We believe that accumulations of wealth should not be made permanent. We have abolished entails. We believe that the distribution of property should not be unduly restricted. We have provided that the absolute power of alienation shall not be suspended beyond the period of two lives in being at the creation of the state. All these provisions are designed to distribute, as soon as possible without discouraging individual enterprise and industry, accumulations of property which superior sagacity, good fortune, or accident has created. None of these restrictions are invasions of the rights which social compacts are designed to secure. We may go farther, and assign limits to future accumulation or to the investment of the proceeds of industry in particular objects. These are questions of practical wisdom and policy which may be fairly settled by reference to their probable influence upon the general interest and prosperity. But any regulation which has the effect of rendering an existing tenure insecure or worthless is a direct violation of one of the great purposes for which we entered into society, and must weaken the security of liberty and life, by impairing the fundamental obligations by which all are supported. This is a question in which the many have a far deeper interest than the few. The tens of millions which are held by large proprietors are as nothing in comparison with the hundreds of millions distributed in smaller portions among the great body of people. The security of all must stand or fall together.

3d. The different members of the general society must understand and be willing to do justice to each other. External forms of organization, rules of political conduct, do much. But the internal spirit which animates the system and imparts its vital powers must be in harmony with its formal constitution, in order that its movements may meet with no interruption or shock from the antagonism of the elements of which it is composed. One of the theories of our government is, that all are politically equal. We have reduced the theory to practice by making suffrage universal, and public employments and honors accessible to all. Let us forbear to set up social distinctions, which may practically affect, though certainly to a limited extent, what political distinctions produce in other countries. Let us avoid, as far as in us lies, all which tends to divide society into classes; for all such divisions imply diversity of interests, and almost always produce isolation. Social distinctions must of necessity be, in the highest degree, evanescent with us. We have neither orders of nobility nor permanent estates to sustain or perpetuate them. They rest almost exclusively upon commercial wealth, and they partake of its vicissitudes and its instability. To seek to found distinctions upon wealth alone, where accumulations of property are so transient, is not only vainly attempting what is unattainable, but its tendency is to make wealth the object of pernicious jealousies, and thus to inflict upon society a great public evil. Absolute equality in the possession of property, as a practical condition of life, is but the dream of the enthusiast. Nature has so pronounced it by endowing her children unequally. But in the enjoyment of all the comforts of life, and in the means of satisfying all our necessary wants, the condition of men approaches much nearer to equality than is generally supposed. We rarely consider how little is needed where there are no artificial wants to disquiet us,—how much is required in circles where conventional exactions are the rule of expenditure. Misunderstanding on this subject,—ignorance on the part of one portion of the community, of the objects, desires, and wants of other portions, lie at the foundation of all the jealousies which exist between those whose condition is unequal. This misunderstanding should be corrected—these jealousies removed; and he who, instead of contributing to objects of such vital importance, shall attempt to excite in one portion of society prejudices against another, should be ranked among the most dangerous enemies of the republic.

I have already spoken of divisions into classes as undesirable and pernicious in their tendency. They carry with them the idea of opposite interests. Dissociation, separate action, alienation, jealousy, unkindness, opposition, hatred, collision; these are the steps by which their progress to maturity is to be traced in other countries. Let us, then, regard each other as members of a single association, standing in the same relation to the system of which we are a part, and having none but common interests. Let him who has little property consider that those who possess it take with it burdens and responsibilities from which he himself is exempt,—that they contribute, in proportion to their possessions, to the public expenditure; that their anxieties are increased, and that great wealth, as the experience of all ages attests, does not contribute to augment the sum of human happiness. On the other hand, let those who have much consider that much is required of them,—that their possessions are a sacred trust which will be best fulfilled by a liberal and confiding regard for those whom fortune has less highly favored. In a word, gentlemen, sympathy and fraternal feeling must take the place of indifference and distrust in the intercourse of those whose condition is unequal. Organize society as you will, however correct your formulas, or however wisely adjusted the different parts of the system, you cannot make it independent of the passions and affections of men. It is by enlightening and purifying these that the great ends of society are to be wrought out.

And finally, fellow-citizens, let us bear ever in remembrance, as a motive to the fulfilment of our social obligations, that we stand before the world as the chief representatives of free institutions. The great features of this continent seem to mark it out for the accomplishment of labors and destinies of corresponding magnitude,—the Mississippi pouring into the ocean the majestic current it has accumulated in its course of three thousand miles,—the Niagara, collecting the waters of an inland sea, and precipitating them into another in a cataract of gigantic volume and Herculean power,—the Rocky-Mountain chain, pushing up its snowy summits to the heavens, with its deep indentation cut down to its base, and indicating a design as palpable as if the Omniscient Power that created it had said, "Through this pass thousands of years hence, the railway which is to unite the Columbia river with the Hudson shall bear the burdens of associated continents and oceans." A country thus strongly marked in its physical lineaments is a fit theatre for the great experiment we are making of the competency of mankind to self-government, and for the social developments which are in progress here on so vast a scale.

This city, as the metropolis of such a country, should correspond with it in the magnitude of its improvements. Though yet in its infancy, it has proved itself, in all it has done, not unworthy of the distinction. Père La Chaise sinks into insignificance when contrasted with the sylvan grandeur of Greenwood. The aqueduct which conveys the Croton river across the Harlem compares well in the solidity and beauty of its architecture with the kindred work spanning the Valley of Alcantara, or with those magnificent structures which, after the lapse of two thousand years, though now falling into ruins, still stretch across the Campagna, and by the agency of which imperial Rome was perpetually refreshed by the pure waters of her distant hills.

For what remains to be done,—for popular institutions, on a scale so broad as to embrace her whole population, and to endow all with the capacities necessary for the discharge of their social and political duties,—for the facilities which her industrious classes require to prepare them for the exercise of their various avocations,—for the depositories of art, and the elementary training which are needed to call out genius and to refine the public taste,—she must look to her commercial wealth. Her mercantile men have a reputation as wide as the world itself for their activity, the grasp of their enterprise, and their fidelity to their pecuniary engagements. Under their influence, aided by the unrivalled energy and skill of her ship-builders, her commerce has been pushed to the very confines of the habitable globe. Neither equatorial heat, nor polar frosts, nor barbarism, nor the conflicts of civilized races, have constituted an impediment to the execution of their commercial adventures. In the beauty, the speed, and the internal arrangements of their ships they have left all rivals at an immeasurable distance behind. They have accomplished all this by their own unassisted energies. They have not, like the mercantile classes of England, been aided by a direct trade with extensive colonial dependencies, from which, until a very recent day, other nations were shut out. They have cast themselves upon the ocean, self-reliant and fearless, and entered into triumphant competition with the whole commercial world. Their boldness, their perseverance, and their success have contributed, in an eminent degree, to the practical vindication of the great element of freedom, as the true basis of international communications and exchanges, and have had a powerful agency in compelling other nations to relax the rigor of their commercial systems. One more great truth remains to be asserted and verified by a stern adherence to the fundamental principles of our institutions in their social as well as their political requirements, — a truth to which we should cling with undying faith, — that extended commerce, social refinement, and accumulated wealth are perfectly compatible with public order, domestic purity, and national strength.

AGRICULTURE OF NEW YORK.

The following Address was delivered before the New York State Agricultural Society, at Albany, on the 7th of October, 1859.

MR. PRESIDENT, LADIES, GENTLEMEN OF THE
SOCIETY, FELLOW-CITIZENS:

TWELVE years ago I had the honor to appear before this Society at one of its annual exhibitions in a neighboring county, under circumstances of a peculiar character. I did not come then, as I do now, to present any views or state any conclusions of my own in regard to the great interest to which your labors are devoted; but to perform the vicarious service of reading to you the address prepared for the occasion by Silas Wright. Most of you, I do not doubt, remember well that the address was written by its distinguished author during the intervals of agricultural labor through the summer harvest, — not the mere labor of superintendence, but earnest and thorough field-work, with the scythe, the rake, and the hay-fork, standing side by side with his laborers, and measuring his own strength with theirs. A few hours after the closing lines of the address were written, he died suddenly of an affection of the heart. They were, probably, the last lines traced by his pen; and there is no doubt that the sudden termination of his life is to be ascribed to the equally sudden change of his habits, — from the sedentary occupations of twenty years in court-rooms, executive bureaus, and legislative halls, to the hard labor of a farm. It might, at first glance, seem more in harmony with the tenor of his public career, if he had fallen in the Senate chamber — the theatre on which his distinction was chiefly earned. But those who know how little he prized public office and its honors, how much more he loved the quietude of the country and the occupations of rural life, cannot but regard the closing scenes of his earthly pilgrimage as peculiarly in accordance with the tone of his thoughts, the simplicity of his character, and his devotion, throughout his whole official career, to the cause of productive industry.

It is no small distinction to the agriculture of the country and the State to have numbered among its followers a man of so much talent and purity. If it had been in the order of Providence that he should have lived to attain the highest political honors of the republic, his incorruptible integrity, his conscientiousness, his firmness, and his thorough acquaintance with the details of public business must have told with great effect upon the administration of our national affairs, by checking extravagant expenditure, correcting abuses, and giving steadiness to the movement of the government in critical emergencies; and at the close of his labors he would have returned with the same simplicity and unaffected zeal to the cultivation of his farm.

I have not alluded to this subject for the mere purpose of paying a tribute of respect to the memory of a departed statesman, peculiarly connected as he was with the cause of agriculture, and with the proceedings of this Society; but as an appropriate introduction also to the principal subject of his address — the importance of the foreign grain and provision market to the farmers of the United States.

Twelve years ago this subject was scarcely deemed worthy of a place in our schemes of domestic economy; and it is one of the strong evidences of Governor Wright's sagacity and forecast that he should have made it the leading topic of discussion in his address. Indeed, it had acquired, at the time he was discussing it, an importance of which he himself was not aware. Our exports of breadstuffs and provisions in 1846 were a little less than $28,000,000. In 1847, they rose to nearly $79,000,000; but at the time he was preparing his address the statistics of the year had not been collected and published.

During the last fifteen years these exports of our agriculture have made a great though not a steady advance, and it may be safely assumed by agriculturists that there will be a constant demand in the European markets for the products of their industry, — a demand as uniform as the varying productiveness of different years abroad will admit. I think it may be stated as a proposition from which the farmers of the country may draw conclusions, and by which they may be guided in their practical operations, that Europe cannot raise a sufficient amount of food for the consumption of its increasing population, and that even with the most abundant harvests there will be an annual deficiency, which can only be supplied by the United States.

This whole subject has been treated with great ability by Mr. John Jay, of the city of New York, in an address on the Statistics of American Agriculture before the American Geographical and Statistical Society; and I shall draw largely from the materials collected by him in support of the proposition I have stated.

It is well known that in most of the principal states of Europe, and nearly all the minor, the increase of population, though small in proportion to the rate of increase in the United States, is greater than that of the means of subsistence. In old and thickly settled countries, it must of necessity be so. The best lands having been long under cultivation, poorer soils must be resorted to as population increases, and with it the demand for food; and the difficult question always arises, (a question only to be settled by experiment,) whether the products of these soils will be equal to the increased demand for them; or, in other words, whether the whole labor of the additional population can extract from them a supply of food sufficient for its subsistence? This question may be considered settled, not only in Great Britain, but in most of the countries of central and southern Europe. The conclusion has been manifesting itself for years in practical, and not always the wisest measures, to remedy an inconvenience felt, rather than accounted for by any rational investigation of its causes, — sometimes by the prohibition of the exportation of breadstuffs, and at others by the imposition of duties on foreign grains to protect and stimulate domestic production. In the mean time the deficiency has been continually increasing, and large masses of people have been supported by constantly diminishing amounts of food. France, as a nation, has not enough to eat. It is estimated that four millions of her inhabitants do not eat bread. The vine, an exhausting crop, which gives back to the earth none of the nutriment extracted from it, takes an immense extent of surface from the production of grain, and in central and southern Europe, as well as in France, is annually increasing the necessity for supplies of foreign breadstuffs. In the last-named country, too, the cultivation of the beet-root for the sugar manufacture has reduced the surface for the production of grain; and, on a recent occasion, the Emperor found it necessary to allow its free importation from other countries. In England, the deficiency of breadstuffs has become still more apparent; and though she exported largely a century ago, she is now a large importer, and her inhabitants cannot be subsisted on what she produces. She may be considered, from the density of her population, as having nearly, if not quite, reached her maximum capacity for production; and the one thousand people added every day in the year to the number of her inhabitants must be subsisted by imported food.

This increasing demand for food in Europe has been largely supplied by us. During the last eleven years our exports of breadstuffs and provisions have averaged over $47,000,000 per annum; and of the exports of 1847, over $55,000,000 went to Europe. Their increase will be better understood by comparing the last seven years with the preceding seven. During the former period they averaged a little over $31,000,000, and during the latter nearly

$50,000,000. The average of 1856 and 1857 was over $75,000,000. In 1858, we had, in some of the large wheat-producing States, a short crop, and the exports of the year may show a diminution. Fluctuations in the amount of agricultural exports are unavoidable. A deficient crop in any country necessarily limits its ability to export, as it can only part with the surplus which remains after supplying its own people. This inability in the countries of Europe to supply their own inhabitants with food, the certainty that it must become greater as population increases, and the assurance that it can only be met by the products of our own agricultural industry, make the subject one of the most interesting and important that can engage the attention of the American farmer and statesman. It concerns the prosperity and the progress of the country for centuries to come, and its exemption from any serious or lasting disturbance of our friendly relations with European powers. No country can afford to quarrel with another, from which it derives the means of subsistence. Nor can the country which furnishes the supply afford to part with its valuable customer. There is every reason, therefore, to expect that questions of dispute will be discussed and adjusted in a spirit of mutual forbearance; and where such a spirit exists, there can be no long-continued alienation.

To you, gentlemen, as a part of the agricultural interest of the country, the question presents itself under a variety of the most important aspects. Can the production of food in this country be made to keep pace with the European demand for it? In other words, can the additions to be annually made to the population of Europe be sustained by the export of our agricultural products? This is a great question of political economy, which may be elucidated by theory, but the answer to which the farming interest of the country must work out in practice.

There is certainly no country better adapted than ours to become the granary of the world. It occupies the most favorable portion of the North American continent for production, neither running up to the regions of severe cold on the one hand, nor to those of excessive heat on the other. It is the great temperate district of the western hemisphere, and yet so extensive as to embrace every variety of vegetation, which does not require the stimulus of intertropical heat. Navigable rivers, almost unequalled in the surfaces which they water, are so many great natural channels for conveying our products to the Atlantic Ocean, which has within our limits a coast of nearly seven thousand miles in extent, affording extraordinary facilities for commerce. A few hundred miles back from the coast a range of mountains, with a mean altitude of 2500 feet, runs from north to south, and in the more heated districts furnishes on its slopes the mitigated temperature which arises from elevation. Our territorial area, including California and Oregon, is nearly 3,000,000 of square miles, — a larger surface than that of Russia in Europe. British America has a little over 3,000,000, but a large portion is locked up in hyperborean frost. Taking the Atlantic district, from the Gulf of Mexico to the Lakes, with the vast territory drained by the Mississippi and its tributaries, embracing altogether a surface of nearly 2,200,000 square miles, and I believe it may be safely said that there is no region on earth of the same magnitude, which has an equal capacity for production. With the exception of New England and the Middle States, there are in every portion of this extended district large quantities of the most fertile land, which the hand of agriculture has not yet touched; and I believe it may also be said that there is no portion, of any considerable extent, which is absolutely unproductive. Of the Pacific district we know little, except from the constant tide of treasure which for ten years has been setting into our Atlantic cities. Enough, however, has been gleaned from the hasty and imperfect explorations which have been made, to assure us that over this great district the richest fields of grain are hereafter to wave, and that numberless herds of cattle are to range through meadows and over mountain-slopes clad with grasses unsurpassed in luxuriance. There is a great district, spreading out from the eastern slope of the Rocky Mountains, which nature, it is said, has consigned to perpetual barrenness. Scientific observations seem to warrant this conclusion. But let us not decide too hastily. I remember when it was asserted, on the basis of actual exploration, that there was only fertile territory enough between the Mississippi and the Rocky Mountains for four States of the size of New York; and yet a surface vastly more extended is now occupied under State or territorial governments, and promises to rival in productiveness the richest soils in the Union. We all remember the attempt to demonstrate on principles of natural science that the Atlantic Ocean could not be navigated by steam. And yet, in a few years afterwards, steamers were regularly crossing it, with voyages averaging from ten to fifteen days, and they are now so multiplied that they threaten to supersede sailing-vessels in carrying on the commerce of America with Europe. Science never fails to give the true solution of a problem, if it is in possession of all the elements which belong to it. It may be that there are elements of production in the region referred to which have escaped observation, and that it may at least be found, as I believe it will, to be much less extended than is supposed.

I have thus briefly alluded, gentlemen, to the physical characteristics of the immense region over which dominion has been, in the order of Providence, given to you and your fellow-countrymen. It is the noblest inheritance ever bestowed by the Sovereign Ruler of the Universe on any race of men that has inhabited the earth. We possess it, too, under advantages which no other people ever enjoyed. Our independence as a nation was almost coeval with the new impulse given to the natural sciences by the genius of the old world. They have in our own day reached a point from which there seems to be little left to be accomplished in the future, except through the application of established principles. We know the elementary substances which enter into the composition of organized and unorganized bodies. There is nothing we deal with of which we do not know the nature and the characteristic properties. We understand, in all its intricacies, the marvellous mechanism of the human constitution, all but the ethereal spirit which animates it, and the knowledge of which alone, as an emanation of the Divine essence, the great Creator reserves to himself till the fulness of our time shall come. During the last few years, natural science, which had expended its labors on astronomy, chemistry, geology, and the mechanic arts, has been turned to the great field of agriculture. It has analyzed soils and disclosed their constituents; it has taught us the composition of plants, the nature of the food they require, and the degree in which they extract from the earth its principles of fertility and impair its capacity for their reproduction.

It is thus armed that we are entering on the great work of subduing the untamed soils of the western hemisphere, and making them yield what is needed for our own sustenance and for the unfed multitudes of the old world. I say we are just entering on this work, for only about one thirteenth part of our vastly extended territory is under cultivation. Small as this portion is, I fear but little of it is improved as it should be. Our whole system of agriculture has been one of gradual spoliation. The soil, which we should have at least preserved unimpaired in fertility, has been rapidly deteriorating in our hands. The Southern planter has been in the habit of extracting crop after crop of tobacco and corn from his lands, and when they had lost all capacity for production, of abandoning them, and emigrating with his negroes to new soils. The Northern farmer has done the same thing, not without some feeble attempts, perhaps, in most cases, to keep up, by rotation of crops, the average fertility of his land; and multitudes who have emigrated from the east are carrying on the same process of exhaustion on the prairies of Illinois, Wisconsin, and Iowa. I was last spring in a city in one of these States, on the Mississippi, and found the inhabitants throwing their manure into the river. I inquired the cause of this extraordinary practice, and was told, in reply, that their lands were naturally fertile enough without artificial aid. A few years will bring with them, as time has everywhere else, the penalties of wastefulness, in diminished crops and lighter grains. The annual loss in the United States, from the abuse of the soil, is to be computed not by millions of dollars, but by hundreds of millions. We know from statistical facts that the average production per acre has greatly diminished. In this State, less than a century ago, the average wheat crop was over twenty-five bushels per acre. It is now about twelve. In Ohio, one of the most fertile States in the Union, and but little more than half a century old, the average is about the same as in New York. The virgin soil is already half worn out. In some of the Southern States the deterioration has been more rapid, and the average production is still less. These are the legitimate fruits of careless systems of husbandry. They are not merely careless, they are systems of the most wasteful and culpable extravagance. The man who extracts from his land all it is capable of producing, without giving back to it an equivalent in fertilizing substances, is in fact selling his farm in his crops. It is precisely the system of the prodigal, who spends his money capital, instead of living by a prudent economy on the interest. It was the same system of spoliation which exhausted the grain-fields of imperial Rome. Cato, more than two thousand years ago, and Columella, Varro, and Virgil, at a later day, wrote learnedly, and some of them gracefully, on the subject of agriculture. They laid down the most unexceptionable rules in regard to rotation of crops, the cultivation of plants, the treatment of the soil, and all the leading subjects of practical husbandry. But the agriculture of Rome died out under their precepts, and the desolation of the Campagna, once the prolific mother of nations, and now to a great extent overrun with noxious vegetation, and made uninhabitable by pestilential exhalations, attests the insufficiency of their systems. The Maremma, in ancient Etruria, was exhausted by the same process of spoliation; it became nearly uninhabitable, and, like the Campagna, exhaled an atmosphere of pestilence and death. But by the persevering efforts of Leopold the First, of Tuscany, against great physical impediments, a large portion of it has been reclaimed and made healthful and productive. The ancients labored under disadvantages which time has removed. They had no knowledge of the natural sciences, which are the offspring almost of our own generation. Analytical chemistry has taught us the component parts of the soil, and of the plants and grains which it produces. We know precisely the amount of each organic and inorganic element, which is lost to the earth in bringing a certain quantity of grain to perfection. We know that unless these elements are restored, the earth is robbed of so much of its vegetative power, and gradually becomes worn out and unproductive.

I have dwelt upon this subject, gentlemen, because it is the great danger which threatens our agriculture, and which we must guard against by timely reform, if we would fulfil our destined work of supplying the increasing wants of the eastern hemisphere. I desire to give it prominence, because I believe there has been no instance in the history of our race in which the fertility of the earth has been so rapidly wasted. It would have been otherwise, no doubt, if we had not been able to resort to boundless tracts of fertile land in the West, which were open to emigrants at prices almost nominal. It was thought easier to wear out old lands and remove to new than it was to keep up the fertility of the old by manuring. It was a fatal error, as the condition of our agriculture shows. But for the extraordinary productiveness of the western States and territories, the old States would, at this very moment, have been dependent on other countries for their supplies of food. The remedy for all this evil is in our own hands. It is to restore to our lands, by manuring, what we take from them in crops. We all know that this process of restoration has been going on for nearly a quarter of a century in Virginia, and that lands which had been worn out by successive crops of tobacco, corn, and wheat, have been reclaimed and made to produce abundantly. It is estimated that thirty millions of dollars were added in value to the agricultural capital of that State in twelve years from the commencement of this process of reform. The same results would follow the same measures in all cases in which the powers of the soil have been overtasked; and it is not doubted by those who have closely investigated the subject, that the crop of Indian corn might be trebled without enlarging the surface on which it is now cultivated, and that millions of dollars might be added to the annual value of that crop alone. Nor can it be doubted that the production of the other great staple articles of food might be augmented in a like proportion, increasing enormously the wealth of the country, and furnishing larger surpluses for exportation.

But it is time, gentlemen, that I should dismiss this general topic, and turn to others which more directly concern the agricultural interest of New York. Let me, before leaving it, return to the proposition with which I commenced, and make a single additional observation in support of the concluding part of it, — that the increasing deficiency in the production of food in Europe can only be supplied by the United States. The remark I wish to make is this, that, while labor is more abundant and cheaper in Europe than it is in the United States, we have three advantages which give us, and will give us for years to come, a decided superiority over the countries of the eastern hemisphere.

1st. An immense region, unsurpassed in fertility, yet to be occupied.

2d. A more intelligent laboring community, constantly improving through the influence of a free and cheap press, and a social organization which not only secures to every citizen the enjoyment of the fruits of his industry, but gives him a direct voice in the choice of his own rulers; and

3d. The great extent to which machinery is employed in agriculture as a substitute for men, counterbalancing largely the advantage of cheap labor in Europe.

I do not venture to make an estimate of the extent to which mowing-machines, reapers, and other substitutes for manual labor have superseded the latter in the cultivation of the soil in this country; but I believe I am within bounds when I say that it is equivalent to five millions of men. These advantages must give us, in the competition for the European grain and provision market, a superiority over all other countries, and will make us, if we husband our natural resources with ordinary prudence, the granary of the world.

In leaving the general topic which I have discussed, and limiting our view to the State of New York, we cannot fail to be struck with the advantages which our farmers and agriculturists possess. First of all, we have, within our own boundaries, the emporium of the country, — not only destined, in all probability, to remain for centuries the principal commercial city of the Union, for export, import, and distribution, but also to become the grain-market of the world. It is a matter of the highest importance to our farmers to be so near the chief point of export and import, not merely because the expense of transportation is usually in an inverse ratio of distance, but because great marts are always cash markets, and from the magnitude of their operations, and the accumulation of supplies for all the wants of men, they furnish readily, and at the lowest prices, all that the agricultural classes demand, in return for the products of their labor. Thus, the agriculturist is always sure of selling for cash his surplus produce, and of buying what he needs at rates which an extended and active competition is certain to reduce to the lowest standard. Artificial communication has greatly added to the value of this privilege. With the exception of a few sequestered localities, and these of very inconsiderable importance, the city of New York may be reached in twenty hours from the remotest district in the State.

The capacities of the State for agricultural production, arising from variety of soil, unequal elevations of surface, and diversity in the geological formation of different districts, may be favorably compared with those of any other State in the Union. A geographical district having throughout the same geological formation, and relying almost exclusively on a single class of productions, is much more in danger of suffering from unfavorable seasons than one which, from the diversity of its surface, is enabled to apply its labor to a variety of products. In the former the failure of a crop may produce general distress, while in the other it would only be the cause of a partial inconvenience.

In the final report of the geological survey of the State, it was divided, with reference to its physical constitution and agricultural capacities, into six great districts; but, in a comparison of soils, on the basis of productiveness, they were reduced to five. Let us glance hastily at some of these divisions.

The western and central district, extending from the Mohawk to Lake Erie, and embracing all the intermediate counties, is in reference to the great staple production, wheat, the first in importance. Though the average product is much lower than it was when the soil was first reduced to culture, it is still over fifteen bushels per acre, and in this respect has maintained its productiveness better than any other portion of the State. One reason unquestionably is, that it is the most recently settled. But there is probably another cause to be found in the geological constitution of this district. It is underlaid in some portions by the Medina sandstone, rich in marls, and in others by shales and limestones, which, for the most part, disintegrate rapidly under the influence of atmospheric agents, and re-supply to the soil the mineral elements removed by the cultivation of wheat. It is in this point of view that the western and central district of New York may be regarded as one of the most reliable wheat-growing regions in the United States, and likely, with proper treatment, to remain so in all future time.

The great wheat-growing districts of the Union consist, for the most part, of prairies in the western States and territories, some of which have been for centuries denuded of trees, and have yielded little else than grasses, by the decaying remains of which the soil has been constantly enriched. But whether with or without timber, the surface soil of these great plains is much the same. It is composed of the carbonaceous remains of decayed and decaying vegetation, and is usually of a depth which, to persons unacquainted with the principles of vegetation, and their influence on the soil, would seem to give it an exhaustless fertility. It is for this reason that the first cultivators have gone on, year after year, carrying away the produce of the land without giving anything back to it in compensation for the organic and inorganic elements which have constituted the food of the plants they have removed. The result has been everywhere the same. The crops have steadily deteriorated in quantity and quality. Experience has shown the expectation of undiminishing productiveness in new soils, no matter how fertile, to be a gross delusion. Science explains the cause of the deterioration. Vegetables, like animals, are developed by means of the food they consume. The former draw their sustenance directly from the earth. Every crop reduces the quantity of food the earth contains, and diminishes the conditions of its fertility; and, after a certain period, the capacity of the earth to produce the same crop ceases. In other words, the supply of food which the crop requires for its production becomes exhausted. There is but one mode of guarding against this result, and that is by restoring to the earth the same amount of organic and inorganic matters which have entered into the organization of the crops removed. This is the universal law of compensation in every department of physical life. Chemical analysis shows that plants contain the same principal ingredients in very different proportions. It shows, also, that soils, apparently similar, vary essentially in their chemical components, and that while one is better adapted to wheat, another contains in more suitable proportions the mineral substances required by other grains. If the cause of the deterioration of the wheat-crop in this State could be ascertained, it is probable it would be found that the soil on which it has been cultivated possesses, in a reduced proportion, one or more of the mineral substances essential to the growth of that grain, and that if the deficiency were supplied the soil would possess the original fitness for its production. It is not probable that the counties on the North River and its vicinity will, for a long course of years, if ever, return to the cultivation of wheat to any great extent. The wants of New York, and of the large number of populous cities and towns which have sprung up in that portion of the State, call for an immense quantity of agricultural productions, many of which cannot be transported to great distances, and must, therefore, be produced near at hand. The question of remuneration will enter largely into the solution of every problem of this sort. A farmer who can raise two hundred bushels of potatoes on an acre of land, with a ready market for them at a moderate price, will find it more profitable than to raise thirty bushels of wheat on the same acre, at the highest market-rate in times even of scarcity. Milk, fresh butter, green vegetables of all kinds, and animals for the slaughter-house, are among the daily necessities of great towns, and most of them must be raised or prepared for the market in the immediate neighborhood. Their production will absorb most of the geographical area of Long Island and the river counties. But the western and central portions of New York are beyond the influence of these daily wants, and the only question as to the continued cultivation of wheat will be, whether with the advantage of a market near at hand, they can compete with the wheat districts of the West, and sell at remunerating prices. I had occasion, some five years ago, to settle an account on the basis of the price of wheat at Albany, in May, for the twenty preceding years, and it was adjusted at the average of $1.32 per bushel. I doubt whether, in any twenty consecutive years hereafter, it will average less. At this price, a crop of twenty bushels the acre will pay liberally. There is reason to believe that the soil of the wheat-growing district of this State is as well fitted for the permanent cultivation of wheat as that of the western prairies; for though the latter are so rich in humus, or the remains of organic life, they are less liberally supplied with the mineral substances which wheat requires, and which are, to some extent, furnished by the constant disintegration of the rocks on which the soil of the former district rests. In other words, if this supposition is correct, the former will, with the same treatment, produce in a long succession of years equally remunerative crops; and if the cultivation of wheat shall decline in this district, it will probably be from the growth of large towns in the western part of the State, demanding, like the city of New York, a different class of agricultural products.

Though the other great districts of the State are less adapted to the growth of wheat, they have a peculiar fitness for other productions. The counties on the east of the Hudson, which were denominated in the final report of the geological survey of the State, the maize district, are, from the geological character of the underlying rocks, admirably adapted to the cultivation of Indian corn. The district constituting the southern tier of counties, while it is productive in corn and coarse grains, is more particularly fitted for grazing. And the same remark is applicable to the counties which skirt the western bank of the Hudson. Our mountains, with the exception of a few granitic ridges and peaks, in the northern and southern highland districts, are susceptible of cultivation to their very summits. The eastern range particularly, running as it does from north to south, is warmed on both sides either by the morning or the evening sun.

There are two great districts which have been considered nearly worthless, but which, I think, are destined to contribute largely to the agricultural production of the State. The first of these lies between the upper waters of the Hudson and Lake Ontario. It abounds in minerals and in timber; the valleys are filled with a rich vegetable mould, and the sides of the sharp peaks, which rise to the maximum height of five thousand feet, are capable of producing the most luxuriant grasses. It is a cold region, and on its greatest elevation the snow, in backward seasons, lies unmelted even into midsummer; but beneficent Nature seems to have distributed throughout all portions of her vast dominion, even the most inhospitable in their aspect, the substances which support vegetable life. The Swiss, leaving the valleys when the summer returns, ascend the Alps, almost to the elevation of perpetual snow, and building their châlets on the mountain-sides, pasture their flocks and herds on narrow plateaus, which, from below, seem inaccessible. Here, indeed, as in our knowledge of the spiritual life, there is a limit to our progress upward. Man must not rise, even in the physical world, above his prescribed level. As we go up into the loftiest mountains on our globe, above the clouds, which God sends down to veil their summits from our sight, Nature locks up her treasures of organic life in chambers of frost, and warns us by signs as significant as that which scattered the presumptuous builders of Babel, that our mission here lies nearer the lower surface of the earth. But within our appointed limits everything is mercifully made to minister to our wants. Even the most refractory rocks are instinct with the principles of organic life, and are slowly but steadily yielding them up to the silent agencies of nature. The granite ridges of our highland districts, which seem so unchangeable, are undergoing perpetual alterations. Felspar and other constituents of granitic rocks contain, in large proportions, the substances necessary for the nutrition of plants. Frost, and heat, and rains, acting on their surfaces, are constantly breaking them up, and thus these huge masses are forever distilling like dew into the valleys beneath, the elementary principles of vegetable life. The cattle, if left to themselves, would turn away from the rank vegetation of the meadows and plains, and gather around the bases of the mountains to feed upon the sweet grasses that spring up from the disintegration of their rocky breasts. It needs no prophet's vision to foresee that the valleys of this neglected district are to teem with waving grains, and that its mountains are to be covered, far up from their bases, with flocks and herds.

The other district to which I refer was called in the geological survey of the State the Atlantic district. It consists of Long Island, stretching out from New York harbor 130 miles into the Atlantic ocean. A most extraordinary delusion has prevailed in regard to the productiveness of the central portion of this district, a delusion natural enough with those who only know it by description; for one of the historians of the Island pronounced it "a vast barren plain," with a soil " so thin and gravelly that it cannot be cultivated by any known process." And yet the surface soil of this whole region, with some inconsiderable exceptions, consists of a rich loam, from twenty to thirty inches in depth, easily cultivated, and made highly productive without immoderate manuring. Some of the best farms in the southern part of the State have, during the last five years, been made in this condemned region; and it is shown by the agricultural survey of the State that the Island produces fourteen bushels of wheat to the acre, considerably beyond the average of the State, and very little less than that of the western district. In a few places the gravel, with which the surface soil is underlaid, crops out, but these localities are believed not to exceed two per cent. of the whole Island. I have been in the habit of visiting it in summer for twenty-five years, and have had the best opportunity of noting its productiveness. There are farms which have been two centuries under cultivation, and which, by good management, continue to yield abundant crops. Fields of corn, and of the most luxuriant grasses, run down to the very sand-hills which the ocean throws up, as it were, to bound its own encroachments. Here, too, as on mountains of granitic rock, nature is busy with her ceaseless transformations. The sand-hills are no sooner thrown up by the sea than they begin to perform their office as a part of the solid earth by ministering to the sustenance of its inhabitants. Some weeks ago, while strolling over them, I was struck with the variety of the vegetation with which they were covered, and in a few minutes I gathered specimens of twenty-one plants, some of them in bloom, with colors as rich and delicate as any to be found in cultivated fields, and all within a stone's throw of the breakers.

> "From these bleak sands spontaneous shoot
> Fresh forms of re-created life, —
> The spear-shaped grass, the clustering fruit,
> Born of the elemental strife."

The seeds, borne down by rivers, or carried on the wings of the winds to the ocean, lie for a while buried in the depths of the ungenial waters; but when, in the progress of time, they are thrown out upon the sands into the warmth of the sunlight, and are fed by the liquid streams of ammonia, which are distilled from heaven in summer showers, they burst into life, and clothe the naked strand in verdure and beauty.

Of all the districts of the State, this has the finest summer climate, and the winters are mitigated and made temperate by the surrounding waters. Closer observation and successful experiment have dissipated misapprehension in regard to its fertility: they have shown that its soil is warm, genial, and productive; and there is little hazard in predicting that it will, at no distant time, become the garden of the city of New York.

Whether the agriculture of this State shall become what the natural capacities of the soil fit it to be, or whether the fertility of our lands shall be worn out by overtasking them, and we become the dependants of other communities for our daily bread, depends on ourselves. I believe our duty may be comprehended in a single precept. Let us give back to the earth in manures and fertilizing substances as much as the earth gives to us in food. Nothing less will fulfil the universal law. Nature, which has decreed that no atom of matter shall be destroyed, has decreed also that nothing can be taken with impunity from any one of her great kingdoms without making compensation for it. The elements, of which the earth, the air, the sea, their inhabitants, and the vegetable world are composed, disappear and appear again under new forms: the substances which enter into the organization of plants are consumed, and are converted into the flesh of animals, and when these decay, are given back to the earth to begin anew the same process of transformation; but not the minutest particle shall perish until the end of all created things shall come. To preserve the productiveness of the earth, nature only prescribes to us a conformity to her own law. Nothing is to be wasted or thrown away. The remains of all we consume, and of the food of our cattle, the portions of vegetable or animal matter which we reject as unfit for our use, are to be restored to the fields from which we have drawn our sustenance. The distinguishing characteristic of our husbandry is wastefulness. Every great town draws largely on the fertility of the country for its subsistence, and gives back little in return. The offal and the remains of all the animal and farinaceous substances which are consumed by the city of New York, given back to the soil from which they are derived, would be worth millions of dollars a year in the productive power they would create. The time will come when a thorough reform will be made in this respect; when our great cities, instead of draining into the ocean and into rivers the remains of what they consume, will gather them up and restore them to the earth, the fertility of which they are gradually wasting.

In the mean time, let those whose high vocation it is to cultivate the soil, to preside over the sources of production, from which all classes of men derive their sustenance, bear in mind a few great truths. The farmer who stints his fields is as unwise and improvident as he who starves his working-cattle; in both cases he is diminishing the ability of a faithful servant to be useful to him. The man who obtains from a field, not properly fertilized, ten bushels of wheat, when by manuring he might have obtained twenty, is selling his labor at half its value. He who does not give back to his fields as much as he takes from them, sells their fertility in his crops; and the fertility of the soil is the farmer's capital. He who permits the remains of animal or vegetable substances to decay around him, instead of incorporating them with the soil, impairs the comfort and healthfulness of his home, and by a slow but unfailing process prepares the destruction of his farm, and the impoverishment of his posterity. The farmer who will keep these truths in view, and act in accordance with the rules they suggest, will find his compensation in the increasing products of his farm, in the augmentation of his wealth, and in the promotion of the general prosperity.

An admirable work, by Baron Liebig, entitled "Letters on Modern Agriculture," has just been published by Wiley, in New York, and it would be well if it were in the hands of every agriculturist in the State. It enters largely into the subjects on which I have briefly touched; and it shows that practical agriculture and scientific chemistry, instead of being in conflict, as some matter-of-fact men suppose, are, in truth, mutually dependent on each other in the great work of reforming prevailing errors. It is the province of science to seek out and disclose principles and causes, and it is the business of practice to use the knowledge thus acquired to the greatest advantage for the common purposes of life.

Agricultural chemistry has rendered no greater service to the public than in showing the necessity of scientific training for the cultivation of the earth. It was a common opinion a few years ago, that any man who could hold a plough, or use a hay-fork with dexterity, was fit to be a farmer. And yet his vocation is one of the most difficult, when considered in its numerous relations to the chemical properties of his fields, the influences of wind, moisture, and temperature varying in different localities, and the numberless causes which promote or obstruct the growth of plants. If there is any pursuit, which more than all others requires training, with some knowledge of the great principles which concern the fruitfulness of soils and the support of vegetable life, it is this. And yet, while we have for years had training-schools for medicine, and law, and theology, we have, until recently, had none for agriculture, the basis of all human industry. This is a great social wrong, which we have only just begun to reform by the institution of a school in the western district.

But, gentlemen, I have already outrun the time which I had allotted to the performance of the duty with which you have honored me, and will hasten to a conclusion. I cannot do so without bearing testimony to the great service which this Society has rendered to the cause of American agriculture by its steady and its disinterested labors. The valuable information it has circulated through its annual publications for nearly twenty years, on all the great subjects of practical husbandry, has given them new interest and importance, and the noble display of the last four days, in the products of the earth, in animals, and in agricultural machinery, attests its eminent success, and the strong hold it has gained on the confidence of the community.

In conclusion, gentlemen, let me repeat my conviction that no State in the Union possesses in a higher degree than ours the elements of a varied and abundant production. On such an occasion as this I could do no more than glance hastily at the leading characteristics of some of the larger divisions of our territory, in their relations to certain classes of agricultural products. Half a century more will, I do not doubt, develop the peculiar fitness of each for the productions for which they are respectively best adapted by climate and physical constitution. Those who are to come after us, if we do our duty as faithful custodians of the productive powers of that portion of the earth which has been confided to us, will see the western district yielding, in undiminished abundance, its annual contributions of wheat; the eastern equally bountiful in corn and the coarser grains ; the valleys everywhere teeming with varied productions; the elevated portions of the southern tier of counties, and the mountain-slopes of the northern and southern highlands, covered with flocks and herds, and the Atlantic district pouring its daily supplies into the vegetable and fruit markets of the great city. Before the nineteenth century shall have ended, the island of New York will be covered with warehouses, and workshops, and dwellings, with a population so full as to be incapable of further condensation. He who shall live to that day, and shall stand on the heights of Fort Washington, — an elevation worthy of the immortal name it bears, the future central point of the wealth and taste of the great commercial capital,— will look down on a fairer scene than that which bursts on the sight from the plain of Sorrento, or the classical crest of Pausilippo. For he will look out, not over the sites of buried cities, or living cities abased by inaction and sloth, and on waters scarcely stirred by the keels of commerce, but on rivers bearing on their bosom the mighty traffic of continents, and on cities and shores instinct with life, and liberty, and industry, and intellectual power.

WAR WITH TRIPOLI.

This Lecture was prepared for the General Society of Mechanics and Tradesmen of the City of New York, in 1859. It was repeated before the Historical Society of New York in the same year, and is now published for the first time.

THE subject I have chosen for the lecture which you have invited me to deliver before your Society, is the war of the United States with Tripoli, one of the Barbary States occupying the northern portion of the African continent between Egypt and the Atlantic Ocean. My object in making the selection was to revive the remembrance of some of the most brilliant achievements in our early history, and I may say also one of the most important enterprises of the times, when considered in connection with the circumstances under which the contest was commenced, and its consequences not only to ourselves, but to the cause of humanity and civilization. It is now more than half a century since these events occurred; and if I may judge others by myself, the memory may be refreshed, not only in regard to details, but to the strong impulse which was given by our example to the older nations of the Eastern hemisphere.

Before I enter upon the narrative, it may not be uninteresting to take a brief survey of the geographical position of the Barbary States, and of the past and present condition of the country they possess.

I believe I hazard nothing in saying that the portion of Africa bounded on the north by the Mediterranean, west by the Atlantic Ocean, east by Egypt and the Desert of Barca, and south by Mount Atlas and the Great Desert, or Sahara, comprising the whole surface occupied by the empire of Morocco and the regencies of Algiers, Tunis, and Tripoli, is physically one of the most beautiful regions in the world, and that it has in the progress of human society undergone more extraordinary revolutions than almost any other country on the face of the globe. The whole southern line of this district is flanked by Mount Atlas, taking its rise on the Atlantic coast, and terminating at the Desert of Barca, which separates Egypt from the territories of Tripoli, the most eastern of the Barbary States. South of Mount Atlas and along its whole extent lies the Sahara, or Great Desert. Barbary is thus completely insulated by seas and sands. Indeed, the Great Desert is believed to have been part of the Atlantic Ocean, and Barbary the Island of Atlantis, which was described to Plato by the priests of Egypt 400 years before the Christian era.

The lower declivities of Mount Atlas are covered by the most luxuriant vegetation, — trees and plants of the most graceful forms bending under the burden of their fruit, and flowers of the richest colors exhaling delicious fragrance. In the midst of this gorgeous display of vegetable life innumerable tribes of animals luxuriate in undisturbed repose. Although Mount Atlas traverses a continent with which we are accustomed to associate nothing but intolerable heat, it rises to the elevation of perpetual frost; and in the very middle of summer, when the sirocco is most fierce, the mountain-peaks are seen, through the steaming mists of the valleys, pushing their snowy crests far up into the heavens.

North of the Atlas range, the country to the very shores of the Mediterranean is extremely fertile and beautiful. Sugar, coffee, grains, vegetables, and fruits of all kinds are produced in the greatest abundance. It was at one time the chief granary of the Roman empire. South of the mountains the country runs into the Desert. The portion nearest to them is known as the date Region, from the great profusion of that fruit. As it approaches the Desert, it becomes sterile and is productive only where water is found.

This is all that time will allow me to say of its physical characteristics. Let us glance with the same rapidity at its ancient history.

The earliest authentic records are of the city of Carthage, about 500 years before the Christian era. It was founded some four centuries earlier; and at the time of its greatest prosperity, when engaged in the wars, which terminated in its destruction, with the Roman republic, it had a population of 700,000 souls. Razed to its foundations by Scipio 146 years before Christ, it was rebuilt under the Roman emperors, and became the great City of Africa. Seven hundred and fifty years later it was again destroyed by the Saracens; and its site is still marked by a ruined aqueduct, a broken wall, and a few other fragments of architecture, which are to be seen twelve miles from Tunis.

Farther east lay the five great cities of Cyrenaica or Pentapolis, of which Cyrene was the principal. The remains of this flourishing and luxurious town, which attained its greatest splendor under the Ptolemies, are on the declivity of a range of hills opening upon views of surpassing beauty and grandeur. It fell, like Carthage, under the scimitars of the Saracens; and the possession of its ruins is shared by jackals and hyenas, and by wandering Arabs, occupying it alternately with the variation of the seasons. Over all this vast region, from the Desert of Barca to the Pillars of Hercules, or the mountains which flank the Strait of Gibraltar, lie the scattered fragments of ancient art, — in the Pentapolis the remains of Doric temples denoting the perfection of Grecian architecture, — on the sites of later cities the Corinthian column and other tokens of the decline of the purer taste of earlier epochs. Ages wide apart impressed on this beautiful region the seals of their peculiar developments in art, to be obliterated by the barbarism of later eras in the history of our race. Among these relics of an extinct civilization the Bedouin Arabs, the Ishmaelites of our day, pitch their tents and elaborate their schemes of traffic, knowing little of the mighty struggles, with which their predecessors two thousand years ago disputed with the Roman people the dominion of the world.

ADDRESSES AND REPORTS.

For more than 1150 years Barbary has been governed by the followers of Mahomet. They gained possession of it at the close of the seventh century, after it had been devastated and depopulated by the sanguinary contests of the Vandals and the Romans. In the reign of Justinian alone it is estimated that nearly five millions of inhabitants perished by famine and the sword.

It was from Barbary that the Saracenic race passed into Spain, and held it for eight centuries, making it the centre of European learning, refinement, and splendor. Under Ferdinand and Isabella, at the close of the fifteenth century, they were driven back into Africa, where they soon relapsed into their primeval barbarism.

This brief review brings us down to the period connecting the history of Barbary with the events which form the subject of this lecture. For the three hundred years preceding the commencement of the present century, the states of Algiers, Tunis, and Tripoli were the scourge of the commerce of the Mediterranean. The cities along their coasts were nests of pirates subsisting by depredation on the property and subjects of Christian states. The submission of the kingdoms of Europe to this organized system of plunder is one of the marvels of modern history. The piratical States of Barbary never possessed respectable navies; and yet their armed vessels or corsairs, generally small in size and rarely commanded by skilful seamen, were the terror of the minor, and sometimes of the most powerful, nations of Europe, — seizing their ships, appropriating vessels and cargoes, reducing their subjects to slavery, and liberating them only on the payment of heavy ransoms. The boldness and enormity of these depredations roused the larger states from time to time to resistance, and their vengeance was visited on the depredators by signal acts of retaliation. The most memorable of these was the invasion of Tunis by the Emperor Charles the Fifth, in the early part of the sixteenth century. He defeated the Tunisian army, captured the city, liberated 20,000 Christian captives belonging to different countries, and thus gained a reputation in Europe which no other sovereign possessed as the vindicator of its wrongs.

Immediately after the establishment of our independence we entered upon the negotiation of treaties with foreign powers; first with the nations of Europe, and next with the States of Barbary. In 1787 a treaty was concluded with Morocco, in 1795 with Algiers, in 1796 with Tripoli, and in 1799 with Tunis. In the treaties with Algiers and Tripoli the payment of tribute is expressly acknowledged. In the treaty with Algiers we agreed to pay an annual tribute of 12,000 sequins, — about $21,000. In the treaty with Tripoli, one of the articles alludes to the receipt of the money and presents demanded by the Bey of Tripoli " as a full and satisfactory consideration on his part and on the part of his subjects for this treaty of perpetual peace and friendship." In all cases similar contributions were made under private agreements as preliminaries to the conclusion of treaties. Some of these contributions were enormous, as we shall see.

The exposed condition of our commerce in the Mediterranean was one of the subjects of General Washington's annual message to Congress in 1790. On its reference by the House of Representatives to the Secretary of State, Mr. Jefferson reported, that Algiers had already captured two of our merchant-vessels, and reduced their crews to slavery; that the Dey refused to treat of peace on any terms, and demanded $59,496 for the ransom of the captives, twenty-one in number. About the same period an ambassador from Tripoli called on the Minister Plenipotentiary of the United States in London, and demanded for peace with that state $150,000. It was thought that a treaty with Algiers might cost us $1,000,000, including the ransom of captives. It was known that a treaty with that power had cost Spain over $3,000,000. In 1788 France purchased a renewal of a treaty with the same power for fifty years by the payment of an annual tribute of $100,000. Notwithstanding this arrangement, the Algerines in less than two years afterwards, availing themselves of the disturbed condition of France, seized six of her merchant-vessels, and reduced the crews, forty-four in number, to slavery. The Dutch, Danes, Swedes, and Venetians paid from twenty-four to thirty thousand dollars annually to Algiers in money or naval stores. It was believed that peace with all the Barbary States cost Great Britain two hundred and eighty thousand dollars a year. Mr. Jefferson did not state these facts as authentically shown, because, to use his own words, " from a principle of self-condemnation the governments keep them from the public eye as much as possible." Of their general accuracy there are abundant proofs.

Such were the relations of the European states with the Barbary Powers when our treaties with them were negotiated. Our government was not in condition to adopt a more manly policy, and, therefore, submitted to the universal custom of bribing these marauders to abstain from depredating on our commerce. I have not been able to ascertain what all these treaties cost us. In December, 1798, our contributions to Algiers, in consideration of our treaty with her, went out under convoy of the United States brig-of-war Sophia, Captain Henry Geddes commander. There was a shipload of naval stores, a frigate, and three small armed vessels. The three latter may have been purchased. The frigate was a present to the Dey of Algiers. The cost of this treaty is shown, in a confidential letter of the Secretary of the Treasury of the 4th January, 1797, at the close of Washington's administration, to have been $992,463.25, of which $525,000 was for the redemption of captives. In addition to this enormous sum, our contribution of naval stores for the two preceding years cost over $140,000.

On board the Sophia was the newly appointed consul to Tunis, General William Eaton, who bore a conspicuous part in our hostilities with Tripoli. He had been a captain in the army of the United States, and had served with distinction under General Wayne. He was a man of great resource and energy, bold, fearless, frank, and impatient of all subterfuge and insincerity. He had a strong sense of national honor and dignity, and was in favor of meeting the depredations of the Barbary States by war instead of purchasing a pusillanimous peace by tribute. On his arrival at Algiers in February, 1799, on his way to Tunis, he was presented to the Dey. The following extract from his journal is not only characteristic of the man, but it illustrates in a striking manner the humiliating submission of the civilized world to the caprices, the lawlessness, and the impudent exactions of these barbarians.

"Consuls O'Brien, Cathcart, and myself, Captains Geddes, Smith, Penrose, and Maley, proceeded from the American house to the court-yard of the palace, uncovered our heads, entered the area of the hall, ascended a winding maze of five flights of stairs to a narrow dark entry, leading to a contracted apartment of about twelve by eight feet, the private audience-room. Here we took off our shoes, and entering the cave (for so it seemed), with small apertures for light and with iron grates, we were shown to a huge shaggy beast sitting upon a low bench covered with a cushion of embroidered velvet, with his legs gathered up like a bear. On our approach he reached out his forepaw as if to receive something to eat. Our guide exclaimed, 'Kiss the Dey's hand.' The Consul-General bowed very elegantly and kissed it, and we followed his example in succession." Having, as he says, stood a few moments "in silent agony" under this humiliation, they had leave to take their shoes and depart. He adds, "Can any man believe that this brute has seven kings of Europe, two republics, and a continent tributary to him, when his whole naval force is not equal to two line-of-battle ships! Yet it is so."

General Eaton was associated with Mr. James Leander Cathcart, our consul to Tripoli, to conclude a treaty with Tunis, which had been signed by the Bey and his chief ministers in 1797, but objected to by the Senate of the United States on account of one of its stipulations. On the 2d of March, after having been delayed nearly a month in Algiers, they sailed for Tunis, and arrived on the twelfth. After a good deal of difficulty the treaty was amended and ratified by both parties. During the discussions the Bey of Tunis exhibited great irritation on account of the superior value of the tribute paid to Algiers. He said the United States ought to be equally liberal to him, and demanded that they should make him a present of a frigate. It transpired, in the progress of these discussions, that we had already paid him $50,000 in cash, and that a valuable tribute in naval stores and merchandise was to follow the conclusion of the treaty.

General Eaton assumed a bold and independent tone with the Tunisian government from the commencement of his diplomatic career. In his despatches to the home government he contended that the United States had begun wrong; that we had made too many concessions to Algiers; that there was but one language to be held to the Barbary States, — the language of defiance, — and that a naval force should be sent to the Mediterranean to protect our commerce and avenge insult and aggression.

The treaty with Tunis having been concluded, Mr. Cathcart proceeded to Tripoli to assume his duties as consul, — a treaty with that power having been signed more than two years before.

Before leaving General Eaton, it is proper to say here that he was perpetually in controversy with the Tunisian government on account of its exorbitant demands and exactions, which he resisted with unwavering tenacity. In June, 1801, he wrote to the Secretary of State, that on the night of the 18th a fire broke out in the Bey's palace, which in its progress consumed 50,000 stand of arms. The second day after he received a message to wait on the Bey, who demanded 10,000 stand of arms from the United States. The Bey said, "I have apportioned my loss among my friends, and this falls to you to furnish. Tell your government to send them without delay." Eaton refused even to communicate the demand to his government. He said to the minister who took up the controversy: "Has not the Bey within eighteen months received two large ship-cargoes in regalia? Have we not now another ship laden for him on its passage? Has he not within sixty days demanded cannon extraordinary from the United States? At this rate, when are our payments to have an end?" The minister replied, "They will never have an end." He added, that the ships were but part-payment for peace, and that "the other claims were such as were granted by all friendly nations once in two or three years." General Eaton rejoined that they might abandon all idea of such claims, that the United States would never grant them, and that he would take the responsibility of breaking the peace if they were insisted on.

In October, 1802, General Eaton wrote to the government that the indignities he had suffered were intolerable, that, if further concessions were to be made, he did not wish to be the medium of presenting them, and that he preferred to be displaced. In March, 1803, he was dismissed by the Bey; and he received, on his departure, from the consuls of Great Britain, France, Spain, Holland, and Denmark, a letter bearing testimony to the dignity and integrity with which he had supported the rights of his nation.

Let us now turn to Tripoli. On the 1st of April, 1799, Mr. Cathcart embarked at Tunis for his post. From the very commencement of his official service, he was involved in an angry contention with the Tripolitan government. The reigning Bashaw had been advised of the enormous sum paid to Algiers as a consideration for peace, — or rather a bribe to abstain from depredation and plunder, — and was dissatisfied with the comparatively small amount paid to him for a like immunity from piratical aggressions on our commerce. We had made a present of a frigate to the Dey of Algiers, built in the United States, and completely armed and equipped at a cost of about $100,000, and the Bashaw insisted that he should be treated with the same liberality and consideration. Not satisfied with the reasons assigned by Mr. Cathcart for making a distinction between the two regencies, the Bashaw in 1800, about a year after Mr. Cathcart's arrival, wrote to the President of the United States, demanding that his regency should be placed on the same footing of friendship and importance as those of Algiers and Tunis. He said he wished the President's expressions of friendship were followed by deeds and not by empty words. He added: "You will, therefore, endeavor to satisfy us by a good manner of proceeding. We on our part will correspond with you with equal friendship as well in words as deeds. But if only flattering words are meant without performance, every one will act as he finds convenient. We beg a speedy answer, without neglect of time, as a delay on your part cannot but be prejudicial to your interests."

The purport of this impudent letter was perfectly understood to be, that, if the President did not send a tribute in ships and naval stores corresponding in value with that received by Algiers, he would send out his corsairs to plunder our vessels and reduce their crews to slavery. When it is considered that he had entered into a solemn treaty of peace with us two years before, and had received a large amount in money and naval stores as a consideration for his friendship, the perfidy of these piratical states and the utter uselessness of all arrangements with them not backed up by a constant exhibition of force, will be better understood.

In an interview with Mr. Cathcart on the subject of these exactions, the Bashaw said: "Consul, there is no nation I wish more to be at peace with than yours; but all nations pay me, and so must the Americans." Mr. Cathcart answered: "We have already paid you all we owe you, and are nothing in arrear." The Bashaw replied, that for making the peace we had paid him, it was true, but that for keeping it we had paid him nothing. Mr. Cathcart rejoined, that by the terms of the treaty we were to pay him the stipulated "cash, stores, &c., in full of all demands forever." The Bashaw was not at all satisfied with this explanation. He said we had given a great deal to Algiers and Tunis, and he terminated the discussion as follows : " Let your government give me a sum of money and I will be content ; but paid I will be one way or another. I now desire you to inform your government that I will wait six months for an answer to my letter to the President; that, if it do not arrive in that period, and is not satisfactory if it do arrive, I will declare war in form against the United States. Inform your government," said he, " how I have served the Swedes, who concluded their treaty since yours; let them know the French, English, and Spaniards have always sent me presents from time to time to preserve peace with them ; and if you do not do the same, I will order my cruisers to bring your vessels in wherever they can find them."

Soon after this interview (in October, 1800) Mr. Cathcart made a formal protest against the acts of the Bashaw and his officers as a violation of the treaty of peace and friendship between Tripoli and the United States. While the Bashaw is waiting for an answer to his impudent letter to the President of the United States, let us look at the state of things in Algiers, to which we had just paid a million of dollars as the price of its friendship.

Early in September, 1800, nearly two months before Mr. Cathcart made his protest against the acts of the Tripolitan government, the United States ship George Washington, an armed transport, under the command of Capt. Bainbridge, arrived at Algiers with naval stores for the Dey, who immediately took a fancy to use her for the transportation of his ambassador to the Grand Signior at Constantinople, and to return with another cargo to Algiers. It was in vain that Capt. Bainbridge and Mr. O'Brien, the United States consul, protested against such a compulsory use of the ship as an indignity to the United States. The Dey answered that other nations had done Algiers like favors; but he consented to release her, if the British consul would furnish a ship-of-war for the purpose. This was agreed to, and a British ship was prepared accordingly. When all seemed settled, the Dey changed his mind, and in great fury (according to consul O'Brien) said the American ship should go, or he would not hold to his treaty of peace, which, as we have stated, was just purchased at the price of a million of dollars. On the renewal of their protests he told Capt. Bainbridge that the ship should go perforce, and he ordered the Algerine flag to be hoisted at the maintop-gallant masthead. When this was objected to as an indignity to a national ship, and they asked that it might be hoisted at the foremast, the General of Marine flew "into a great passion," to use the words of the consul, and as there was no alternative, this additional indignity was submitted to, and the ship proceeded on her voyage, with the following crew and mixed cargo: 1. Crew of the ship, 131; 2. Ambassador and suite, 100; 3. Negro women and children, 100;—331 souls. 4 horses, 150 sheep, 25 horned cattle, 4 lions, 4 tigers, 4 antelopes, 12 parrots. Funds and regalia, or presents, according to consul O'Brien, amounted to nearly $1,000,000.

Mr. O'Brien, in a letter to the Secretary of State, giving an account of this humiliating transaction, says: "I am convinced, if an accident should happen to the Washington in being captured by any nation or by being driven on shore, that as soon as this news should reach Algiers, they would immediately send out their corsairs and send in all American vessels they should meet with in order to repay themselves for the Algerine property on board the Washington. We submitted to it in the affair of the ship Fortune, and if the amount in reality was $600,000, the regency would take to the amount of a million of dollars. It is their custom. Is it not a hard case for us to risk the ship and crew of the United States, and Algiers to force said ship, and if any accident [occurs] to be liable to [the] difficulties and calamities I have described!"

These piratical states had certainly very original methods of providing for themselves. After compelling a government to pay enormous sums for their friendship and for a treaty of peace, they immediately threatened new depredations, unless they were paid additional sums for keeping the peace, or abstaining from a violation of the treaty they had just made. The custom of seizing ships and compelling them to go on voyages and carry cargoes for them, and in case of capture or shipwreck, indemnifying themselves for the loss by depredating on the commerce of the country to which the ship belonged, is as ingenious as it is original. And it is one of the wonders of modern history that the great naval powers of Europe,—England, Holland, Spain, and France,—with their magnificent fleets and armadas, should have submitted for centuries to such enormities.

On the receipt of the intelligence of the indignity offered to the George Washington, the government wrote General Eaton in the following cautious language: "The sending to Constantinople the national ship-of-war, the George Washington, by force under the Algerine flag, and for such a purpose, has deeply affected the sensibility not only of the President but of the people of the United States. Whatever temporary effects it may have had favorable to our interests, the indignity is of so serious a nature that it is not impossible it may be deemed necessary, on a fit occasion, to revive the subject."

Let us see how the sensitive and fiery Eaton received the intelligence at Tunis.

"Genius of my country," said he, "how art thou prostrate! Hast thou not one son whose soul revolts, whose nerves convulse, and heart indignant swells at [the] thought of such abasement! This," he adds, "is the price of peace. But if we will have peace at such a price, recall me and send a slave accustomed to abasement to represent the nation. I frankly own I would have lost the peace, and have been myself impaled rather than [have] yielded this concession. Will nothing rouse my country!"

The country was roused. The despatches of Messrs. Eaton, O'Brien, and Cathcart produced at last their proper effect. Mr. Jefferson, as we know, was strongly averse to war. But these indignities and exactions were too much for the man of peace. In May, 1801, less than three months after his inauguration, he sent Commodore Dale, with a squadron of three frigates and a sloop-of-war, to the Mediterranean, to protect our commerce. It is a curious fact that the letter of instructions from the Secretary of the Navy to the Commodore shows that the latter had on board thirty thousand dollars, which it was hoped Algiers would consent to receive as our tribute for one year ; that a ship was preparing to sail with stores for the regency of Tunis, and that the Commodore had ten thousand dollars as a present to the Bashaw of Tripoli if he had conducted himself peaceably towards the United States. In case, however, Algiers had declared war, the Commodore was instructed to cruise off the port, and burn, sink, or otherwise destroy their ships and vessels wherever he could find them ; and he was further instructed to chastise the regencies of Tunis and Tripoli in the same manner, if they had been faithless to their treaties.

It may seem strange to us at this day that the outrages of these piratical states were not resented by the administrations of General Washington and John Adams. But there are reasons enough in the condition of the country to account for their acquiescence in the universal practice of Europe. We were then a comparatively feeble state. We had but recently come out of the war of the Revolution and taken our rank among the independent nations of the earth. Under General Washington we were organizing a new government on the basis of the Federal constitution ; our finances were disordered; we had irritating and unsettled questions with Great Britain extending far into Washington's second term of office ; and France was pressing us to perform certain stipulations under treaties executed with her in 1778, which would have involved us in hostilities with her great rival. Under Mr. Adams we were, without any formal declaration of war, actually engaged in hostile encounters with France on the ocean, and our navy was fully employed. Under these circumstances it was thought best, and it was doubtless indispensable, to imitate the example of the European states, even the most powerful, and purchase peace and friendship of the Barbary States by tribute, precarious as all treaty arrangements with them were known to be.

When Mr. Jefferson came into power, our foreign and domestic relations were both on a better footing; and he lost no time in vindicating the national honor and maintaining the cause of justice, humanity, and good faith against the presumption and perfidiousness of these barbarians. It is due to him to state in this place, that, when he was minister to France in 1787, fourteen years before, he made an effort to induce the European powers to join the United States in a special confederation against the Barbary States, beginning, as he says in his journal, with the Algerines, to put an end to this whole system of piracy on the one hand and tribute on the other, and he would probably have succeeded but for the unsettled condition of our affairs before the establishment of the Federal government.

Before the squadron under Commodore Dale sailed from the United States, the Bashaw of Tripoli had carried out his threat of war. He had, as appears by the despatches of Mr. Cathcart, in the three years and a half preceding the treaty of peace, received over $100,000 in money and presents. He now demanded $250,000 cash to make peace, and $25,000 a year to keep it after it was made. Mr. Cathcart refused to give assurances of any kind, and the Bashaw declared war. Among other original and facetious practices to which the Bashaw was addicted, was that of ordering the consular flag-staff to be cut down when he intended to break with a government. Each consul had in front of his house a flag-staff, on which the colors of his nation were hoisted. Whenever the Bashaw went to war, the flag-staff of the nation against which it was declared was cut away. When peace was made, a new one was put up. On one occasion, when a peace had been made with Sweden, and it was reported to the Bashaw, in Mr. Cathcart's presence, that a piece of timber was not to be found in the whole regency large enough to make a new flag-staff for the Swedes, the United States and other nations were made the subject of a number of jocular remarks by the Bashaw. "It is a difficult thing," said he, "to get a flag-staff up when it once comes down; when the American flag-staff comes down, it will take a great deal of grease (meaning money) to get it up again. The Danish flag is broke, I hear, and wants mending with a new one." The consul adds: "He then smiled a ghastly grin, and said, "After all, what is $20,000 a year for a Christian nation that has such vast resources."

Not long after this interview, on the fourteenth of May, 1801, the Bashaw sent a message to Mr. Cathcart, that he declared war against the United States, and that orders had been given to cut away his flag-staff. Mr. Cathcart says: "At a quarter past two they effected the grand achievement, and our flag-staff was chopped down six feet from the ground, and left reclining on the terrace." In a few days after, Mr. Cathcart departed from Tripoli.

Commodore Dale arrived at Gibraltar in June, 1801, and soon afterwards appeared at Tunis and Tripoli, to the great dismay of both regencies. On the first of August, the schooner Enterprise, commanded by Lieutenant Andrew Sterrett, fell in with a Tripolitan polacre ship mounting fourteen guns, and with a crew of eighty men, commanded by Rais Mahomet Sous, one of the Bashaw's most distinguished officers. An action immediately commenced, and continued three hours. The two vessels were within pistol-shot of each other. The Tripolitans fought desperately, but were horribly cut to pieces. Their ship suffered severely. Her mizzenmast went over the side. Of her crew of eighty men twenty were killed and thirty wounded. Among the latter were the commander and his first lieutenant. The Enterprise had not a single man killed or wounded, and sustained no material damage in her hull or rigging. Twice during the action the Tripolitan commander had hauled down his flag, and then hoisted it and reopened his fire, thinking to take his adversary unprepared. Lieutenant Sterrett then determined to sink his enemy, and would have done so had not the Tripolitan hauled down his ensign and thrown it overboard, presenting himself in the waist of his ship in the attitude of a suppliant.

The result of this action affords the best possible proof of the unskilfulness of the Tripolitan commanders and crews. Their corsairs were generally sharp, swift-sailing vessels, and their commanders relied on boarding and hand-to-hand encounters. But for naval combats, requiring skilful seamanship and gunnery, they were wretchedly inefficient.

Commodore Dale, not being authorized to make prizes, dismantled the captured ship, and suffered her to return to Tripoli, with a message to the Dey, that this was all the tribute he would ever receive from the United States.

This brilliant and decisive action filled the Tripolitans with consternation. The Bashaw, in his rage and mortification, accused the unfortunate commander, who had fought with great gallantry and had been wounded in the action, of cowardice; and after exposing him to insult in the public streets mounted on an ass, ordered him to receive 500 strokes of the bastinado. His other commanders, fearing similar treatment, and feeling their inferiority to the Americans, refused to go to sea, and those who were out cruising, on hearing of this act of injustice and cruelty, took refuge among the islands of the Archipelago and in friendly ports.

Through these events the American commerce in the Mediterranean was freed from all danger. After cruising off the port of Tripoli for some time, and finding its commercial communications completely suspended, Commodore Dale drew off his squadron, and part of the vessels returned to the United Sates. Those left were reinforced in 1802 by other vessels, but nothing was done in that year, except to afford protection to our commerce. The frigate Constitution, during the summer, had a rencounter with a large number of gunboats, and seven of them were said to have been destroyed.

The early part of the year 1803 passed away much like the preceding year. Our naval force in the Mediterranean kept Algiers and Tunis quiet; and Tripoli being invested by our cruisers, the commerce of that regency was annihilated. In June, one of the Bashaw's largest corsairs, mounting twenty-two guns, made an attempt to get to sea. She was discovered by the Enterprise, then commanded by Lieut. Hull, who made signals to the John Adams, a twenty-eight gun ship, under the command of Capt. Rodgers. The corsair had run into a bay about twenty miles from Tripoli, and come to anchor close to the land. In this position she was attacked by the John Adams, and in forty-five minutes she was abandoned by her crew, many of whom leaped overboard and swam ashore. Before the boats of the John Adams could be manned to take possession of her, she blew up, but whether by accident or design has never been ascertained.

The government and people of the United States had now become completely aroused, and great dissatisfaction existed in regard to the comparative inactivity of the American squadron in 1802. The commander, on his return home, was brought before a court of inquiry, and the court having found that he had not shown due diligence and activity in annoying the enemy, the President dismissed him from the service.

Early in 1803 Commodore Preble was appointed to the command of the squadron, but being delayed at Tangier to settle a difficulty with the Emperor of Morocco, he did not reach Tripoli until the end of the year. In the mean time a most unfortunate accident had befallen the United States. On the 31st of October, while the frigate Philadelphia, commanded by Capt. Bainbridge, was cruising off Tripoli, with no other vessel in company, Commodore Preble having been detained at Tangier, and the rest of the squadron being engaged in other services, a vessel was descried near the land, standing in for the harbor. The Philadelphia immediately gave chase, and had opened her fire, when she struck a reef of rocks while running at the rate of eight knots an hour. Every effort was made to get her off, first by throwing most of her guns overboard, starting her water-casks, and pumping the water out, and at last by cutting away the foremast. She was then about a league from Tripoli, and her condition having been ascertained, she was surrounded by gunboats, which, by taking positions where they could not be reached, had the unfortunate ship entirely at their mercy. All attempts to get her off having failed, Capt. Bainbridge was compelled to surrender to his enemies, who plundered the ship of everything valuable she contained, and stripped the officers and crew of all they possessed, even their clothing. In the course of the ensuing week the ship was got off, carried into port, and moored under the guns of the Bashaw's castle.

Near the end of December, Commodore Preble, in the frigate Constitution, forty-four guns, reached Tripoli in company with the Enterprise, commanded by Lieut. Decatur, who on the twenty-third of that month captured the Mastico, a ketch of about fifty tons burden, with a crew of seventy men.

The capture of the Philadelphia had changed the whole aspect of things in Tripoli. The Bashaw, annoyed by the interruption of his commerce and the destruction of his corsairs, was talking of peace. He now determined to continue the war, having added the crew of the Philadelphia, 315 souls, among them twenty-two quarter-deck officers, to the number of his captives, and having gained a frigate, which he forthwith commenced repairing and fitting for sea.

Capt. Bainbridge, having found means to communicate with Commodore Preble, suggested the possibility of destroying the Philadelphia. The Commodore consulted Lieut. Decatur in regard to the project, which was precisely such an enterprise as suited the ardent and adventurous spirit of the latter. It was accordingly organized under his direction. The Mastico, recently captured by him, had been a French gun-vessel, and having been taken by the British had passed into the hands of the Tripolitans. She was taken into the service of the American squadron as a tender, and named the Intrepid. Lieut. Decatur, with sixty-two of the crew of the Enterprise, and six midshipmen from the Constitution, went on board of her, and the Siren, a sixteen-gun brig, commanded by Lieut. Stewart, was sent with her to cover the retreat of the attacking party in case of necessity. It was the ninth of February, 1804, when the two vessels approached the Tripolitan coast and anchored. In the night a gale came on and drove them to sea; and it was not until the fifteenth that the storm subsided and enabled them again to approach Tripoli. On the sixteenth the attacking party in the Intrepid was reinforced from the Siren, increasing their numbers to eighty-two; and the vessels approached the harbor, the Intrepid leading, and the Siren, disguised, following at a distance, so as not to be taken for a consort.

As the Intrepid drew near the port, the Philadelphia became visible, lying about a mile within it, abreast of the town, with two corsairs, a few gunboats, and a galley or two just inside of her. The evening was one which can only be realized by those who are familiar with the southern shores of the Mediterranean, — mild and beautiful, and fresh with the balmy breath of returning spring. The storm had blown over, and the bay and even the sea had all the smoothness of summer. As the shadows of night fell over the face of the land and the water, a young moon lighted them up sufficiently to make all objects visible. It was ten at night before the Intrepid reached the entrance of the harbor. The breeze had nearly died away, and her motion was scarcely perceptible. She steered directly for the frigate. All was tranquil, and without the slightest sign of mistrust. The officers and crew of the Intrepid, with the exception of a few men to handle her, were lying flat on the deck, concealed by the low bulwarks. As she drew near, the frigate hailed. The pilot, who was also the interpreter, answered that she was a ketch from Malta, on a trading-voyage, and having lost her anchors in the late gale, she asked leave to lay alongside the frigate till morning. The Turks were completely deceived, and sent a boat with a fast to secure her. It was passed into the Intrepid, and being put into the hands of the men lying on deck, they slowly drew her alongside of the frigate without rising. As she came near, the Turks discovered her anchors, and perceiving that they had been duped, they ordered her to keep off. It was too late. By a strong pull she was brought alongside; and as the cry of "Amerikanos" burst from the astonished Mussulmans, Decatur gave the signal, and his officers and men, leaping to their feet, poured into the frigate like a torrent and drove their adversaries over her side. In two minutes the spar-deck was cleared; in eight more the ship was in complete possession of her gallant captors. Express orders had been given by Preble to destroy her. He had foreseen that she could not be brought off. Not a sail was bent or a yard crossed; nor had her foremast been replaced. Combustibles were immediately brought from the Intrepid; the ship, which in that latitude had become perfectly dry, burnt like tinder; and in less than twenty-five minutes the captors were driven out by the flames. There was some danger that the Intrepid could not be cast off in time to escape them. The fasts were cut by the crew with their swords, and by a vigorous effort she was extricated from her perilous position. "As she swung clear of the frigate," to use the words of the eloquent historian of the Navy of the United States, "the flames reached the rigging, up which they went hissing like a rocket." The sweeps of the Intrepid were hastily manned, and when a few strokes had sent her out of the reach of danger, the men ceased rowing and sent up three cheers for victory. The triumphant shout from the little vessel seemed to awaken the Tripolitans from the stupor of their amazement. The batteries and corsairs opened their fire on her; but in a few minutes she was out of their reach, and a single shot, which passed through her top-gallant sail, was the only one that struck her. The scene presented by the harbor as the Intrepid passed out of it, is said to have been inconceivably beautiful and impressive,— the burning frigate now completely enveloped in flame, the picturesque town, fortifications, and surrounding country illuminated by the conflagration, the perpetual roar of cannon, the clamor of the Turks as they gave vent to their astonishment and execration, and the little vessel, which had caused all this commotion, sweeping triumphantly out of the reach of her enemies. As the frigate became heated, the guns, which were loaded, were discharged, some of them in the direction of the town; and the flames having reached her tops, are represented as falling over and giving to the whole "the appearance of glowing columns and fiery capitals."

Thus terminated one of the most daring and successful feats in our naval history. The enterprise could not have been better contrived, organized, or executed. It was full of danger. The Philadelphia was moored under cover of the fortifications and batteries, which were very strong, and she was defended by the enemy's corsairs and gunboats. If the attack had not succeeded, the Intrepid and her crew must inevitably have been destroyed. The very temerity of the achievement contributed to its success; and the admirable arrangement and discipline with which it was carried out, bold as it was, seemed to insure its execution. The Turks, taken by surprise, and not even comprehending the nature of the attack when it was discovered, were completely bewildered, and it was ended before they had so regained their self-possession as to understand how it was to be met. It blotted out the painful and disheartening impression caused by the capture of the ill-fated ship, and infused into the officers and seamen of the squadron a spirit of confidence and determination which was irresistible. Its effect on the Tripolitans was inconceivably depressing. They began to regard the Americans as invincible,—devils, as they called them,—and the Bashaw began to talk again of peace.

On the 3d of August, Commodore Preble, having obtained some gunboats and bomb-vessels from Naples, attacked the town. He captured three gunboats and sank three others, and the city, shipping, and fortifications were much damaged. On the 2d and 28th of August and the 3d of September, the attacks were renewed; several gunboats were destroyed and the town very much injured. On the 4th of September, another daring enterprise was undertaken. The Intrepid was filled with powder and combustibles, and went in at night with three lieutenants and ten seamen, with the intention of setting fire to the Tripolitan fleet. As she approached, a terrific explosion took place, and she was shivered to atoms. Her fate will be forever shrouded in mystery. Whether the explosion was accidental, or whether, as has been supposed, she was assailed by the enemy's galleys and was involved by her own gallant and devoted crew in a common destruction with her adversaries, can never be known. Cooper, in his "Naval History," obviously leans to the conclusion that it was an accident, although one of the enemy's gunboats was missing from the same night.

With this lamentable occurrence the operations of the squadron in 1804 may be said to have ended. I have not time to enter into the detail of the acts of gallantry which signalized the successive attacks on Tripoli. The gunboats which were captured and destroyed came into our possession, in most cases, by boarding, after the most desperate contests with the crews. Though the Tripolitans, after the first naval engagement of ship with ship, acknowledged their inferiority in gunnery and seamanship, they still hoped to contend with us successfully in personal conflict, man to man. In this they were doomed to the same disappointment. In every instance they were overpowered by the superior activity, strength, and resolution of our officers and men. Some of these personal conflicts seem to partake more of the apocryphal legends of romance than of authentic history. The capitals of the Barbary States contained the representatives of all the great powers of Europe, and their men-of-war and merchant-vessels were looking with the deepest interest on this struggle against piracy and plunder. Through them the knowledge of these rencounters was spread over all Europe, exciting not only admiration of the chivalrous bearing of our officers and seamen, but astonishment that a nation then almost unheard of should have the boldness to defy a power to which the nations of the old world, great and small, were paying tribute.

The narrative of the war with Tripoli would not be complete without a brief sketch of a movement by land under General Eaton, our consul at Tunis. After his dismission, he returned to the United States, and endeavored to engage the government in the cause of Hamet, the elder brother of Yusuf, the reigning Bashaw of Tripoli. Hamet had been deposed, driven out of the regency, and taken refuge in Egypt. It was the opinion of Eaton, that, if he should go back, aided by a respectable force, the people of Tripoli would rise against the usurper and restore the legitimate sovereign, and that this would be the most effectual mode of terminating the war and insuring friendly treatment in the future. The government, without committing itself fully to the scheme, appointed Eaton Navy Agent of the United States for the Barbary powers, and he sailed in June, 1803. He was commended to the commander of the squadron, and a coöperation with Hamet Bashaw was suggested. Eaton repaired to Egypt, found the deposed Bashaw, organized a force of five hundred men, one hundred of whom were Christians recruited in Egypt, and only nine of whom were Americans. With this force he commenced his march across the desert of Barca, from the neighborhood of Alexandria, on the 5th of March, 1805, and arrived at Derne, the capital of one of the finest provinces of Tripoli, on the 25th of April. The passage of the desert was accomplished after incredible hardships and difficulties. The Arabs, who constituted four fifths of his force, frequently mutinied, and as the only resource Eaton surrounded himself and his provisions with his Christian followers, and reduced them to obedience by the fear of starvation. By his energy and decision he at length reached his destination, and attacking the city with his slender and exhausted force, five hundred men against four or five thousand, he carried it, and for several weeks defended himself against repeated attacks. His *protégé*, Hamet, did not prove to be a man of energy or resource, nor did the people of the province manifest a general disposition to take up arms in his behalf against the usurper. The movement, however, gave great uneasiness to the latter, and he renewed his efforts to make peace, which was finally concluded between him and Mr. Lear, the American commissioner, who had been sent out as consul-general for the Barbary States, with authority to treat with Tripoli. The treaty was signed on the 4th of June, 1805. Captives were ransomed on both sides at a fixed price, and the Bashaw, having the largest number, received $60,000 for the difference. All tribute and the enslavement of captives were abolished; and for the first time since the reign of the Emperor Charles the Fifth the organized system of piracy practised by the States of Barbary was discountenanced and disowned. In every other instance friendly arrangements with these outlaws were perpetuated by the payment of tribute. So strong was the impression of our successes on the public mind of Europe, that the Pope is said to have declared that the United States had done more for the cause of humanity than all the rest of Christendom.

A few years later, Algiers and Tunis availed themselves of the war in which we were engaged with Great Britain, to renew their schemes of pillage against us; but at its close, in 1815, a naval force was sent out under Decatur, who imposed on both those regencies the terms prescribed to Tripoli ten years before. In the mean time the old system of tribute was enforced against the nations of Europe, until Great Britain, shamed by our example, sent Lord Exmouth the following year on that expedition against Algiers, in which he immortalized himself by his gallantry, and the whole Barbary system of piracy and tribute was abolished forever. The "London Annual Register" for that year thus mildly confesses the truth: The spirited exertions of the United States, "in the last year, to enforce redress for the injuries they had sustained, were calculated to excite invidious comparisons with respect to this country; and either a feeling of glory or some unexplained motives at length inspired a resolution in the British government to engage in earnest in that task which the general expectation seems to assign to it."

After the abolition of the system of plunder, by which the States of Barbary were supported, they sank rapidly into poverty and significance. Tunis has become one of the most wretched of communities — the abode of unmitigated squalor and misery. Tripoli is somewhat more elevated in the social scale. Algiers has fallen under the dominion of France, and to the farthest limit of the Upper Atlas the country is gradually rising from its abasement under the auspices of its new masters. The empire of Morocco is invaded by the armies of Spain. The same races, which were struggling four centuries ago for the dominion of Andalusia and Grenada, are now fighting for the mastery on the plains of Barbary. In the fifteenth century the Saracen, in sullen despondence, but facing his adversary and contending at every step, retired from Spain before the new-born chivalry by which he was defied and overthrown. In the nineteenth he will fall under the resistless power of European improvement. When the wave of modern civilization shall have passed over the fabled Atlantis, overwhelming its barbarism, restoring its neglected fields to their pristine luxuriance and glory, and embellishing it again with the treasures of art, it will become one of the most attractive regions of the earth, and will dispute with Italy the possession of the multitudes who flee from the icy blasts of northern winters in quest of southern flowers and sunshine.

And finally, gentlemen, if the history of the Barbary States for the eighteenth and nineteenth centuries shall be impartially written, our children's children shall read with swelling hearts, that, when all Christendom was submitting, in ignominious subserviency, to predatory attacks on its commerce and its subjects, a distant people, who had just fought their way through adversity and peril to independence, — feeble in numbers, but strong in courage and the sense of right, — sent their little fleet 5000 miles across the Atlantic to vindicate the cause of justice and humanity, — that they did not hesitate to beard the African tiger in his den, while the surrounding nations of the old world were crouching before him, — and that, while the tricolor of France, the cross of Saint George, the proud ensign of the Mistress of the Ocean, and even the sacred standard of the Vatican, bearing on its folds the keys of Saint Peter, could only float on the waters of the Mediterranean by sufferance of the piratical children of the Prophet, the star-spangled banner was sent out from the Western hemisphere to defy them, and was boldly upreared in the presence of subservient nations, — the sole emblem of the freedom of the seas.

THE REBELLION IN LOUISIANA.

Letter from the Secretary of the Treasury, in response to a resolution of the House calling for information as to whether duties on imports continue to be collected in the ports of entry in certain Southern States, &c.

TREASURY DEPARTMENT, *February* 21, 1861.

SIR: On the 11th instant the following resolution was adopted by the House of Representatives: —

Resolved, That the Secretary of the Treasury be requested to inform this House whether the duties on imports continue to be collected in the ports of entry established by law in the States of South Carolina, Georgia, Alabama, Louisiana, and Florida; and whether any hindrances exist to the law of entry and clearing of vessels therein. Also, the present condition of the light-houses, beacons, and buoys, in the said harbors and adjacent waters. Also, what measures, if any, have been taken to secure the revenue-vessels in the service of the department from seizure, or to recover possession of such as have been seized. Also, what measures have been adopted for the security of the public moneys in the hands of depositaries in the aforesaid States, and whether they are available to the Treasury. Also, whether the use and control of any of the marine hospitals, permanent or temporary, have been interfered with, and what proceedings have been adopted with reference thereto.

In obedience to the foregoing resolution, I have the honor to submit the following report in relation to the matters of inquiry embraced therein.

I. THE COLLECTION OF DUTIES ON IMPORTS.

It is believed that the duties on imports continue to be collected in the ports of entry established by law in the States of South Carolina, Georgia, Alabama, Louisiana, and Florida, and that vessels are entered and cleared in the usual manner. But, so far as this department is advised, the collectors assume to perform their duties under the authority of the States in which they reside, and hold the moneys they receive subject to the same authority.

The Collector at Savannah, Georgia. — On the 4th instant the following letter was received from John Boston, Esq., collector of the customs for the port of Savannah, whose resignation, dated January 31, was subsequently tendered:

CUSTOM-HOUSE, COLLECTOR'S OFFICE,
Savannah, January, 30, 1861.

SIR: I to-day received the following despatch from his Excellency Joseph E. Brown, Governor of Georgia.

"You will pay no more money from the custom-house to any government or person without my order."

Respectfully, your obedient servant,
JOHN BOSTON, *Collector.*

Hon. JOHN A. DIX,
  Secretary of the Treasury, Washington.

The following answer was immediately despatched by mail: —

TREASURY DEPARTMENT, *February* 4, 1861.

SIR: Your letter of the 30th ultimo, containing a copy of a despatch from the governor of Georgia, directing you to pay "no more money from the custom-house to any government or person, without his order," is received.

You will please to advise me, by return of mail, whether it is your purpose to obey his direction, or whether you will conform to the instructions of this department and perform your duty under the laws of the United States.

Very respectfully,   JOHN A. DIX,
Secretary of the Treasury.

JOHN BOSTON, Esq.,
  Collector of the Customs, Savannah, Georgia.

On the 12th instant the following reply was received: —

SAVANNAH, *February* 8, 1861.

SIR: Your letter, under date of the 4th instant, asking me whether it is my purpose to obey the direction of the government of Georgia to pay no more money from the custom-house to any government or person, without his order, or whether I will conform to the instructions of this [your] department, and perform your [my] duty under the laws of the

United States, is this moment received; and, in reply, I beg to say, that I will, as a good and loyal citizen, as I hope I am, obey the authority of my State.

Very respectfully, your obedient servant,

JOHN BOSTON.

Hon. JOHN A. DIX,
Secretary of the Treasury, Washington.

This declaration was carried out at a later day by refusing to pay a draft for the compensation of a revenue officer in his own State.

Surveyor of the Port of Augusta, Georgia. — Augusta is a port of delivery for goods entered at Savannah, and the surveyor, who is the chief officer of the revenue, performs the duties of collector.

On the 21st of January he tendered his resignation, expressing the desire that he might continue to perform his duties until the 4th of March.

It was naturally supposed that he would, while acting in his usual relations to the government, at his own request, consider himself bound by his official oath to discharge his duties faithfully; and, especially, to pay over to the United States all moneys received by him. But by the monthly statement for January, recently made, he credits his account with the sum of $2,490.78, paid over by him to "the State of Georgia, to their credit, by order of Governor Joseph E. Brown, dated the 2d instant."

In rendering his account, as if conscious of the official dereliction it disclosed, he says: "I am well aware the account is not made out as required; still, you must consider me as an honest man, and if you do, pass it." The department did not pass it, but advised him that he would be held responsible under his bond for the payment of the amount to the United States.

About half of the officers of the customs in the States of South Carolina, Florida, Alabama, Georgia, and Louisiana, have resigned their commissions, while others appear to have entered on their duties to the governments of those States, without considering it necessary to perform this official ceremony. So greatly has the moral tone of some of these Federal officers been impaired by the example of disloyalty to the Union presented to them by the States in which their duties were discharged, that a resignation seems to have been regarded by them as a mere formality, and not as indispensable to their release from high official obligations.

Custom-House and Collector at New Orleans. — On the 2d instant it was publicly announced that the custom-house at New Orleans had been taken possession of by the State of Louisiana, and that the collector of the customs had taken the oath of allegiance.

On the receipt of this intelligence the following despatch was sent by telegraph : —

TREASURY DEPARTMENT, *February* 2, 1861.

Have the authorities of the State of Louisiana taken possession of the custom-house?

Have you taken the oath of allegiance to that State?

JOHN A. DIX,
Secretary of the Treasury.

F. H. HATCH,
Collector of Customs, New Orleans.

No answer was received until the 6th instant, when the following despatch came to hand: —

NEW ORLEANS, *February* 6, 1861.

SIR: Your despatch of the 2d was received this day. The authorities of the State of Louisiana took possession of this custom-house on the 31st ultimo. I mailed my resignation on that day, and advised you of the same by letter of that date, to which please refer.

F. H. HATCH.

Hon. JOHN A. DIX,
Secretary of the Treasury.

It may be proper to state in this place, that, while despatches by telegraph from New Orleans to this department have come in their regular course, when sent by persons in the interest of the State authorities, those sent from the department have, since the first instant, been from four to five days on the way, indicating that they were intercepted and scrutinized at some intervening point, and perhaps forwarded thence, through a different channel, to the persons to whom they were addressed. Between this city and New Orleans despatches are rewritten at Augusta, Ga., and Montgomery and Mobile, Ala., affording the opportunity of enforcing, against the wishes of the telegraph company, at each of these places, a system of *espionage* known only to the despotic governments of the Old World.

On the 5th instant the following despatch was received by telegraph: —

LOUISVILLE, *February* 4, 1861.

Collector at New Orleans declines to pass goods on bonds given here, unless cancelling certificates are given in name of Louisiana or duties are paid there. What shall I do about the matter? Will parties having goods for which they have given bonds for payment of duties here be held released by government if, to get them without delay, they pay duties at New Orleans? W. N. HALDEMAN,

Hon. JOHN A. DIX. *Surveyor of Customs.*

The following was immediately transmitted: —

TREASURY DEPARTMENT, *February* 5, 1861.

Telegraph despatches received; too indefinite; particulars in full by mail. JOHN A DIX,
Secretary of the Treasury.

W. N. HALDEMAN,
Surveyor, &c., Louisville, Ky.

On the ensuing day the following was transmitted: —

TREASURY DEPARTMENT, *February* 6, 1861.

What evidence have you that the collector of customs at New Orleans has acted as you stated in your despatch of yesterday?
JOHN A. DIX,
Secretary of the Treasury.

WALTER N. HALDEMAN,
Surveyor, &c., Louisville, Ky.

The following reply was received on the same day: —

LOUISVILLE, *February* 6, 1861.

Casseday & Sons, importers here, were so advised by Clarke, Mosby & Co., their agents at New Orleans. Wrote you fully yesterday.

W. N. HALDEMAN,
Hon. JOHN A. DIX, *Surveyor of Customs.*
Secretary of the Treasury.

On the same day the mail brought the following letter, alluded to in the foregoing despatch : —

UNITED STATES CUSTOM-HOUSE,
Louisville, February 4, 1861.

SIR: Messrs. S. Casseday & Sons, china merchants, of this city, received the following telegraphic despatch this morning, from their agents at New Orleans:

"NEW ORLEANS, *February* 1, 1861. Custom-house in possession of Louisiana. Kentucky bonds refused. Will your surveyor grant cancelling certificates for goods bonded in name of Louisiana? Otherwise, must pay duty. CLARKE, MOSBY & Co.
"Messrs. S. CASSEDAY & SON."

At the urgent request of the Messrs Casseday, I at once telegraphed you for instructions. They are anxious to get their goods, without delay, from New Orleans, and had arranged to bond here and withdraw them as their sales required.

Having given bond, however, for the payment of duties here, the question has occurred to them if they are not still liable for the duties to the United States, even if they pay them now, at the custom-house at New Orleans?

Of course I declined to give a cancelling certificate, as requested; but, as other like cases will arise, and as nearly all the goods brought to this port are received *via* New Orleans, I respectfully request full instructions in the premises.

I am, very respectfully, your obedient servant,
W. N. HALDEMAN,
Hon. JOHN A. DIX, *Surveyor of Customs.*
Secretary of U. S. Treasury, Washington, D. C.

On the 8th the following was received from the surveyor of the port of Cincinnati : —

CUSTOM-HOUSE, *Cincinnati, February* 8.

The following despatch received here: "New Orleans, February 6, 1861. — Hunneywell, Hill & Co., Cincinnati. Carlyle arrived; can't enter in bond ; shall pay duties here. Remit six hundred and thirty-two dollars. Voorhees, Griggs & Co. Several cases here of same kind. Merchants wish advice and instructions."

T. JEFFERSON SHERLOCK,
Surveyor of Customs.

Hon. JOHN A. DIX,
Secretary of the Treasury, Washington.

On the same day the following was sent, by telegraph, in reply to the surveyors of the ports of Louisville and Cincinnati: —

TREASURY DEPARTMENT, *February* 8, 1861.

Department cannot recognize the payment of duties to the State collector at New Orleans.

The goods will be liable to the United States for duties, notwithstanding such payments.

JOHN A. DIX,
Secretary of the Treasury.

On the 9th the following was received from the surveyor of the port of Cincinnati: —

CUSTOM-HOUSE, *Cincinnati, February* 9, 1861.

The following despatch received here this morning : " New Orleans, February 8, 1861. — Hunneywell, Hill & Co., Cincinnati. Convention decided goods can be transported in bond, as heretofore. Certificates only required. Publish telegraph. Voorhees, Griggs & Co."

Your despatch received.   T. JEFFERSON SHERLOCK.

Hon JOHN A. DIX,
Secretary of the Treasury.

It will be seen hereafter that this despatch was founded on a misapprehension, or that the oppressive and illegal practice supposed to have been abandoned was speedily resumed.

From these communications by letter and by telegraph from mercantile houses, and from the chief revenue officers at the ports of Cincinnati and Louisville, it appears that the collector of the customs at New Orleans, after assuming to act under the authorities of the State of Louisiana, refused to pass goods entered at that port for transportation to, and delivery at, Louisville, Kentucky, and other ports of delivery, unless the surveyors of the latter ports, holding their commissions from the United States and performing their duties

THE REBELLION IN LOUISIANA. 417

within a State loyal to the Union, would acknowledge the authority of the State of Louisiana by cancelling transportation bonds given in her name to secure the payment of duties on goods imported by sea. This they could not do without violating their oaths of office; and in default of such an act of official turpitude, in any case, the duties were to be exacted at New Orleans. No doubt this was the alternative designed to be secured. The declaration of an intention to execute a particular purpose, except on a condition impossible to be performed, can only be regarded as an absolute determination to carry out the purpose without condition.

Under existing laws the importer of goods by sea to be delivered at Louisville, a port of delivery, may make entry at New Orleans, and give a bond for their transportation to the former port, where the duties are paid.

On their arrival at Louisville the importer may place them in a warehouse, and pay the duties when he withdraws them for consumption. On payment of the duties the bond is cancelled. The interior ports of delivery above New Orleans are twenty in number, and among them are Nashville and Memphis, Tennessee; Louisville, Kentucky; Cincinnati, Ohio; Evansville, Indiana; St. Louis, Missouri; Wheeling, Virginia; Pittsburg, Pennsylvania; and Cairo and Alton, Illinois. The duties collected at these twenty ports of delivery have, during the last five years, averaged over $500,000 per annum. For the year ending June 30, 1857, they exceeded $700,000.

The refusal of the collector at New Orleans to pass goods in bond for transportation to the ports of delivery above, and the exaction of duties at the former port, (for such was the effect of his requirements during the first seven days of this month,) not only subjected importers to the onerous obligation of paying the impost before the goods were needed for consumption, and thus deprived them of a privilege secured by the revenue laws, but it forced them either to resort to other channels of communication or pay double duties; for the department cannot recognize the collector at New Orleans, who has resigned his commission and assumes to act under the authority of the State of Louisiana; and therefore the payment of duties to him does not exonerate them from the payment to the United States.

But there is a larger view of the subject, which is of far graver importance.

The revenue derived from merchandise imported for consumption, by way of New Orleans, into the great States bordering on the rivers which have their outlet to the Gulf of Mexico through the territories of Louisiana, has been monopolized by her. In so doing she has struck a fatal blow at the free navigation of the Mississippi, by making the inward commerce of the west by sea subject to her authority and tributary to her treasury.

Whatever may be the practice in regard to goods received from our own cities by sea and destined to the upper ports, there can be no doubt that merchandise imported from foreign countries is required to be entered at New Orleans; and if the duties are not exacted, they must be bonded in the name of the State of Louisiana for transportation; for, notwithstanding the assurance contained in the despatch of the surveyor of the port of Cincinnati of the 9th of February, communicating one from Voorhees, Griggs & Co., of the 8th, goods are not "transported in bond as heretofore." On the contrary, it appears that bonds executed at the twenty ports of delivery above New Orleans in the name of the United States, as they may be under existing laws, are not recognized by the collector of the latter port, but that he requires them to be executed at New Orleans, and in the name of the State of Louisiana.

On the 14th instant the following letter was received at the department: —

CINCINNATI, *February* 12, 1861.

DEAR SIR: We notice to-day that the collector at New Orleans has decided that duties on all goods passing through New Orleans, destined for inland ports, must be paid at that port, on account of the treasury of Louisiana.

We have about 200 crates earthen-ware due at New Orleans in the ships Wurtemburg and Oroöndates, and will thank you to inform us, on receipt of this, what course we shall pursue in regard to payment of duties.

Will the department protect us, or must we pay duties at New Orleans? The invoices are all sworn to here and sent forward for shipment to this port in bond.

Very respectfully, BARE & WEST.

Hon. J. A. Dix,
    Secretary of the Treasury.

Two days before the receipt of this letter a despatch had been transmitted to the surveyor of the port of Louisville to ascertain what rule was then enforced by the collector at New Orleans in regard to bonds for duties and transportation. On the 14th the following reply was received:—

LOUISVILLE, KY., *February* 14, 1861.

Bonds for the goods were given here, not at New Orleans, and our importers inform me that the collector there still declines to recognize them. Have telegraphed him to know definitely, and will advise you immediately after his reply comes. W. N. HALDEMAN, *Surveyor.*

Hon. JOHN A. DIX, *Secretary of the Treasury.*

At a later hour on the same day the following despatch was received:—

LOUISVILLE, *February* 14, 1861.

Collector Hatch telegraphs me that transportations are continued as usual, but bonds must be to the State of Louisiana, and executed at New Orleans. W. N. HALDEMAN, *Surveyor, &c.*

Hon. JOHN A. DIX, *Secretary of the Treasury.*

As this despatch was founded on one received on that day from the collector at New Orleans, it must be regarded not only as authentic but official; and it shows that no bonds are received unless executed at that port, and in the name of the State of Louisiana.

That the department has not misinterpreted the meaning of this despatch, or misapprehended the effect of the practice adopted in New Orleans in regard to the payment of duties and the nature of the bonds required of importers residing at the upper ports, is also manifest from the letters of complaint received almost every day, asking the protection of the government against these exactions. The following is one of these letters: —

LOUISVILLE, *February* 14, 1861.

DEAR SIR: We are just in receipt of a letter from the custom-house at New Orleans, informing us that a lot of queensware for us had arrived, but that it would be impossible for us to get it unless it would be paid for (the customs). We have given a bond for it here, and we would not like to pay for it twice. You would confer upon us a great favor by answering us immediately what to do.

Yours, truly,   GODSHAW & FLEXNER,
Per LYONS.

Hon. J. A. DIX.

It is not distinctly understood whether the duties are, by the condition of these bonds, to be paid at New Orleans, or whether the obligors may be discharged by payment at the port of delivery. In either case the authority of the Federal government is overthrown, and the free navigation of the Mississippi abrogated. If Louisiana is, as she assumes to be, a foreign power in reference to the nine Sates above her, which have ports of delivery where duties on goods imported by way of New Orleans may be paid, the exercise of the right of requiring such goods to be entered and bonded for transportation to those ports is in violation of the principle always asserted by the United States in regard to the free commercial use of navigable streams by States bordering on them.

The question is not varied in principle if she has become, or shall hereafter become, a confederate of the five other States which have assumed to throw off their allegiance to the Union. While this right was exercised by the United States, Louisiana and the States above in which there are ports of delivery, being subject to the same government, it was merely for the institution of revenue regulations common to all. But if Louisiana has become a foreign power in reference to them, it rises into an international question of the very highest delicacy and importance.

The United States have uniformly placed the free navigation of rivers on the ground of natural right. The Congress of Vienna, in 1815, recognized the same principle by declaring the navigation of the rivers separating or crossing the territories of the great powers to be entirely free. The vindication of this right, in regard to the Mississippi river, at various epochs in our correspondence with foreign powers when they were in possession of territories bordering on it, has produced some of the ablest State papers in the archives of the government.

One of the chief objects in view, in the purchase of the territory of Louisiana, was to secure this right to the people of the United States. The possession of the country at and near the mouth of the Mississippi, by Spain and France, had given rise to embarrassments and contentions which threatened at different periods to involve us in hostilities with both those powers; and it was in order to put an end to these dissensions forever, and especially to protect the people of the States on the higher portions of the river in the free use of its waters for commercial purposes, that the territory was purchased of France by Mr. Jefferson, after a protracted negotiation, and at a heavy expense to the national treasury; thus securing to the United States and their inhabitants, to use his own language, the " uncontrolled navigation of that river in its whole course." Louisiana was created a State out of a portion of the territory thus acquired, on the express and fundamental condition " that the river Mississippi and the navigable rivers and waters leading into the same and into the Gulf of Mexico [should] be common highways, and forever free, as well to the inhabitants of the said State as to the inhabitants of other States and the territories of the United States, without any tax, duty, impost, or toll therefor imposed by the said State."

In violation of this condition, and in open defiance of a great natural right, written, to use the language of our diplomacy, in deep characters on the heart of man, the State of Louisiana, after declaring herself separated from the other States of the Union, and in the exercise of a sovereignty wholly independent of them, assumes to arrest the free passage of goods from the ocean to the States above her, to estimate their value by her own officers, to assess imposts on them, and to exact from the importers, not her own citizens, bonds for the payment of the duties, and for their transportation to the places out of her own territory to which they are destined.

The control thus assumed over the commerce of the Mississippi goes far beyond the pretensions set up in the old world on the basis of ancient prescription, — pretensions which have been, in times past, a fruitful source of dissension and bloodshed, but are now condemned by the general judgment of mankind.

In its bearing on the revenue system of the United States, this subject assumes an importance peculiar to itself. The usurpation in question practically abolishes the twenty ports of delivery above New Orleans, at any one of which, under existing laws, goods may be received by sea, and the duties on them paid. It diverts the customs revenue, ordinarily collected on such goods at these ports, from the treasury of the United States into that of Louisiana. It abrogates the whole revenue system of the United States in the valley of the Mississippi above New Orleans, so far as it is applicable to the importation of merchandise by sea.

This subversion of the authority of the United States is sustained and enforced through the military occupation by Louisiana of the fortresses erected at the mouth of the Mississippi, at the common expense of the States of the Union for the protection of the vast commerce of that river and its tributaries. The vessels placed there by the Federal government, to enforce the execution of the revenue laws, have fallen into her hands. It matters not whether the officers to whom they were confided were corrupted through the agency of others, or whether their treachery to the government to which they had sworn allegiance and fidelity was the fruit of a spontaneous dereliction of high moral and official obligations. The State, by receiving them and the vessels they commanded into her service, has given her countenance and sanction to the most odious of political offences. She has completed a series of unresisted usurpations without a parellel in our history, by seizing the public treasure in the branch-mint at New Orleans, (placed there by a confiding government, with the assurance that under the ægis of her honor it would be secure from violation,) and appropriating it under circumstances showing either that there was a criminal complicity on the part of the officer to whom it was intrusted, or that he yielded to the coercive power of superior physical force. As aids to a forcible assumption of the revenue authority of the government, these successive acts have an importance too obvious to be overlooked. That this pretension will be speedily renounced can hardly be doubted. It concerns the interests of nine States which are loyal to the Union, and which have an aggregate population of more than fourteen millions of souls. If persisted in, it must soon become a source of the most embittered strife. Its assertion, as an exponent of the independent attitude Louisiana has assumed, shows that the safety of the riparian States on the Mississippi and its tributaries must depend on the regulation of the revenue system on these waters by a common government, in the administration of which all have a voice, and that the possession of the fortresses which command the entrance into this great natural channel of internal communication, cannot for any length of time remain under a less restricted military control without danger of the most serious disturbances. And it behooves the whole country, especially that great portion of it which is penetrated by the currents of the Mississippi and its confluents, to consider where the commercial ascendency thus assumed by the State of Louisiana will be likely to have its termination, if any just conception of its magnitude and arbitrary control may be inferred from these, its incipient developments.

Throughout this whole course of encroachment and aggression the Federal government has borne itself with a spirit of paternal forbearance of which there is no example in the history of political society; waiting in patient hope that the empire of reason would resume its sway over those whom the excitement of passion had thus blinded, and trusting that the friends of good order, wearied with submission to proceedings which they disapproved, would at no distant day rally under the banner of the Union, and assert themselves with vigor and success against the prevailing recklessness and violence.

II. LIGHT-HOUSES, BEACONS, AND BUOYS.

South Carolina. — On the 30th of December last, Commander T. T. Hunter, United States light-house inspector at Charleston, reported to the Light-House Board that the governor of South Carolina had requested him to leave the State, authorizing him to take the light-house tender, but prohibiting him from removing any property belonging to the United States in the buoy-shed. On the 1st of January the governor forbade the removal of the vessels belonging to the light-house establishment from Charleston; but the inspector, Commander Hunter, was allowed to leave by land. On the 8th, the removal of the light-vessel at Rattlesnake Shoals, off the harbor of Charleston, was reported to the Light-House Board, and the Board was informed that the three tenders in the harbor of Charleston had been seized by the authorities of South Carolina.

Official information having also been received of the removal of buoys, the extinction of lights, and the obstruction of the principal channel of the harbor of Charleston, the following notice was published:—

NOTICE TO MARINERS. — No. 106.
TREASURY DEPARTMENT, OFFICE LIGHT-HOUSE BOARD,
Washington, D. C., January 26, 1861.

Information has been received at this office that the light-vessel at Rattlesnake Shoals has been withdrawn; that the lights on Morris Island at the entrance into the port of Charleston, South Carolina, have been discontinued; the buoys removed, and the main ship-channel so obstructed as to be unsafe for navigation.

By order, R. SEMMES, *Secretary.*

Georgia. — On the 6th of February the keeper of St. Simon's Light, near Darien, reported that his light had been obscured by a party of persons claiming authority from the State, but the light was not extinguished.

On the 8th, Captain W. H. C. Whiting, of the United States Engineers, reported that possession had been taken of his office, furniture, &c., in Savannah, by the authorities of the State.

Alabama. — On the 20th of January, Commander E. L. Handy, light-house inspector, reported that the tender Alert, belonging to the light-house establishment, was seized at Mobile by order of the commanding officer of the State troops at Fort Morgan. On the 21st, T. Sanford, collector of the customs at Mobile, notified Commander Handy that he, "in the name of the sovereign State of Alabama, takes possession of the several light-houses within the State, and all appurtenances pertaining to the same." Mr. Sanford had resigned his commission as collector on the 12th of the same month.

On the 1st of February, Commander Handy transmitted a copy of a letter addressed to R. T. Chapman, Esq., late of the United States Navy, by T. Sanford, collector, appointing him light-house inspector in place of Commander Handy, to whom the appointment was tendered by the authorities of Alabama, but who refused to accept it.

Commander Handy having no force at his disposal to resist these assumptions of authority, was, at his own request, relieved from the embarrassing position in which they had placed him.

Louisiana and Florida. — Several keepers of lights in these two States have tendered their resignations, alleging as a reason that their States had seceded from the Union. No successors have been appointed.

Florida Reef. — A special agent has been despatched to provide for the safety of the lights on this reef by arming the keepers. They are at a distance from the main coast of Florida, and no apprehension is entertained that they will be interfered with by the State authorities. But it was thought not impossible, in the present disordered state of the country, and with the relaxation of moral and political ties involved in it, that they might be extinguished by evil-minded persons for the purpose of causing shipwrecks.

It is not known that any lights on the Southern coast, except those in South Carolina, have been extinguished. The lights and all other aids to navigation on that coast were amply supplied with all necessaries, and in good condition when they were seized.

III. THE BRANCH-MINT AT NEW ORLEANS.

The treasurer of the branch-mint at New Orleans is *ex officio* assistant treasurer of the United States at that place.

On the 21st of January, six days after I took charge of the Treasury Department, I caused a draft on him, as treasurer of the branch-mint, to be issued for $350,000, payable to Adams's Express Company, for transfer to the mint at Philadelphia. At the time this draft was given there were in his hands the following sums: —

As treasurer of the mint..........................	$389,267.46
As assistant treasurer, to the credit of the Treasurer of the United States........................	265,445.14
As assistant treasurer, to the credit of disbursing officers	225,374.80
	$880,087.40

In view of the unscrupulousness with which the public property had been seized in other quarters, I did not think it right to leave so large an amount in a State which, from all indications, was about to pass an ordinance of secession. A draft was accordingly drawn for $350,000, as above stated, with a view to transfer the coin and bullion to a safe place of deposit. The Treasurer of the United States was also instructed to draw rapidly for disbursement on the balance standing to his credit. As the deposit to the credit of disbursing officers was in a regular course of reduction by their payments, and as the retransfer of these moneys to the treasury would have been attended with some embarrassment, they were not disturbed. In pursuance of my instructions to the Treasurer of the United States, the deposit to his credit was reduced by his drafts from $265,445.14 to $18,149.20. It has been ascertained that about $76,000 were paid on these drafts before the 31st of January, when, as will be seen hereafter, the branch-mint and its contents were seized by the authorities of the State of Louisiana. If all the drafts drawn by this department had been paid, the first two items in the above statement, amounting to $654,712.60, would have been reduced to $57,416.66.

By some irregularity of the mail, which cannot be accounted for, the draft for $350,000 to the order of Adams's Express Company, though transmitted from this department on the 21st of January, was not received at Baltimore till the 24th, on which day a duplicate was issued, with a request that no time should be lost in presenting it. In answer to an inquiry made by the department on the 26th, the following telegraphic despatch was received: —

BALTIMORE, *January* 26, 1861.

Your telegram received. Instructions went forward two days since to execute your order. S. M. SHOEMAKER,
Superintendent of Adams's Express Company.

Hon. JOHN A. DIX, *Secretary of the Treasury.*

On the 30th of January the following despatch came to hand : —

OFFICE OF ADAMS'S EXPRESS COMPANY,
Baltimore, Md., January 30, 1861.

Our advices in cipher, by telegraph from New Orleans, are that the assistant treasurer has not sufficient funds in hand to pay your draft; that three or four days will elapse before the mint will turn over sufficient to meet this demand. The assistant treasurer declines paying until he is able to pay the whole. I deem it my duty to inform you of these facts. We have nothing which would indicate an intention on the part of the United States officers or others to throw any difficulties in the way of our receiving the bullion.

  Respectfully and truly,   S. M. SHOEMAKER,
    Superintendent Adams's Express Company.

Hon. JOHN A. DIX,
 Secretary of the Treasury, Washington, D. C.

This department did not put on the conduct of the treasurer the charitable construction expressed in the last paragraph of the foregoing despatch. On the contrary, it was regarded as indicating a design to gain time, and a predetermination to place the government of Louisiana in possession of the branch-mint and its treasure. There was no ground for the pretext assigned for not paying a portion of the draft. There were gold and silver coins amounting to over $280,000, which might have been delivered on its presentation. A large part of the coin and bullion was in silver. It weighed several tons. It could not all have been taken for remittance by the express company on the same day. Nor was there any foundation for the excuse that there was not a sufficient amount on hand to pay the whole draft. This pretence had been anticipated. There was more than $389,000, and the draft was purposely drawn for $350,000 only, leaving a balance of nearly $40,000. The despatch was received on the night of the 30th, and early the next day the following was sent by telegraph:—

      TREASURY DEPARTMENT,
       January 31, 1861.

You are requested to pay as much as you can on the transfer draft in favor of Adams's Express Company at once.

       JOHN A. DIX,
A. J. GUIROT, Esq.,   *Secretary of the Treasury.*
 Treasurer of the Branch-Mint, New Orleans.

No further advices were received until the 2d instant, when the following despatch came to hand: —

BALTIMORE, *February* 2, 1861.

United States treasury notified on yesterday your transfer draft would not be paid, as the State convention had taken charge. I am unable to give you the precise language, but this is the purport of it. We await your instructions in the premises. S. M. SHOEMAKER,
Superintendent Adams's Express.

Hon. JOHN A. DIX,
Secretary of the Treasury.

On the same day the following despatch was sent: —

TREASURY DEPARTMENT,
February 2, 1861.

Have the authorities of the State of Louisiana taken possession of the branch-mint? Have you taken the oath of allegiance to that State? Have you paid over to Adams's Express Company any part of the coin or bullion in your custody on the draft of the United States Treasurer, and in obedience to my order? JOHN A. DIX,
Secretary of the Treasury.

A. J. GUIROT,
Treasurer of the Branch-Mint, New Orleans.

On the evening of the 6th instant the following was received: —

NEW ORLEANS, *February* 6, 1861.

Your telegram of the second instant has been received to-day. The State of Louisiana took possession of the branch-mint on the thirty-first ultimo, at half-past nine o'clock A. M. The agent of the Adams's Express came to the mint the same day, at two o'clock P. M., and asked me whether the report of the taking of the mint was correct? I answered in the affirmative. He then said, if so, there is no use to present the transfer draft of three hundred and fifty thousand dollars for payment. I told him to apply to the convention. Whether he did so or not, I cannot say. I transmitted the same day my resignation to the President, under your cover, and I have since taken the oath of allegiance to the State of Louisiana.

Respectfully, A. J. GUIROT.

Hon. JOHN A. DIX,
Secretary of the Treasury.

In this despatch the treasurer of the branch-mint wholly omits to acknowledge the first presentation of the draft, or to refer to and explain the attending circumstances, which were regarded as the evidence of a predetermination on his part to violate his duty to his government. The facility with which his official obligations were thrown off, as shown by his own statement, justifies the interpretation put on his conduct six days before. In his official oath, on file in this department, he solemnly swore that he would "faithfully and diligently perform the duties of his appointment" as treasurer of the branch-mint and assistant treasurer of the United States at New Orleans "according to law." The law required that he should keep safely all public money in his possession and custody, and when orders for transfer or payment were made by the proper department or officer of the government, and such orders for transfer or payment were received, "faithfully and promptly to make the same as directed." These duties were violated before he took the oath of allegiance to the State of Louisiana; for no officer can by a mere resignation, without a discharge by the government to which he is accountable, release himself from the engagements he has assumed. Even if the seizure of the mint by the authorities of Louisiana was an act of coercion which he could not resist, he might have protected himself from imputations derogatory to his official character by protesting against it instead of yielding to it the tacit consent which his communication to the department implies. The assistant treasurer at Charleston, Benjamin C. Presly, Esq., in honorable contrast, has promptly paid all drafts on presentation to him, and has applied to this department to draw for the balance in his hands in order that he may be released from his official liabilities.

The precise amount of coin and bullion thus appropriated by the State of Louisiana in entering on her assumed career of independence cannot be ascertained until the drafts issued by the treasurer of the United States shall be returned for non-payment, or until she shall deem it due to herself to restore the treasure confided to one of her own citizens with no other protection from public rapacity than the generous trust reposed in her. An opportunity will be speedily furnished by the presentation of other drafts for payments due her own citizens and the citizens of neighboring States.

By the enclosed copy of a letter, marked A, from the director of the mint at Philadelphia, it will be seen that the weekly returns required to be made by the treasurer of the branch-mint at New Orleans have not been furnished since the first instant, and that if money is coined at the latter, the government has no means, under existing circumstances, of securing a conformity to the established standards of value.

DEPOSITARIES OF THE PUBLIC MONEY.

At an early day after taking charge of this department, I directed the treasurer to issue his drafts for disbursement on the depositaries of the public moneys in all the States (including those specified by the resolution of the House of Representatives) in which there were any decided manifestations of an intention to follow the example of South Carolina in throwing off their allegiance to the Union. These drafts were, as a general rule, paid, and the balances in the hands of the depositaries referred to were reduced to very small sums.

IV. THE MARINE HOSPITAL.

In the month of June, 1858, the marine hospital opposite New Orleans became seriously injured by the overflow of the waters of the Mississippi river. Its foundations were so disturbed by the flood that it was deemed unsafe for occupation. The barracks, two miles below the city, being untenanted, and not needed for troops, they were, with the consent of the War Department, appropriated to the use of the sick, who were removed to them, and have occupied them ever since.

On the 26th day of January, ultimo, I received the following letter from the collector of the customs at New Orleans:

CUSTOM-HOUSE, NEW ORLEANS,
Collector's Office, January 14, 1861.

SIR: I have the honor to inform you that the United States barracks below the city have been taken possession of in the name of the State of Louisiana, as will appear by the enclosed communication from "C. M. Bradford, captain Louisiana infantry." I shall take steps to remove these invalids, if necessary, at an early date, and with due regard to economy.

Very respectfully, your obedient servant,

F. H. HATCH, *Collector.*

Hon. P. F. THOMAS,
   Secretary of the Treasury, Washington.

In this letter was enclosed one from Captain Bradford, to which it alluded, and which is as follows: —

BARRACKS NEAR NEW ORLEANS,
January 13, (*Sunday,*) 1861.

SIR: On the 11th instant I took possession of these barracks in the name of the State of Louisiana, and they will hereafter be held by the same authority. I find herein some two hundred and sixteen invalids and convalescent patients, who were removed here some months ago, by your authority, from the marine hospital on the opposite bank of the river during the recent overflow.

As these quarters will all be required for the Louisiana troops now being enlisted, I have to request that you will immediately remove those patients who are convalescent, and, as soon as, in the opinion of the resident surgeon, it may be practicable and humane, those also who are now confined to their beds.

I beg leave further to add that the quarters now occupied by the surgeon and his assistants, nurses, stewards, &c., will remain at their use and disposal as long as may, in the surgeon's opinion, be necessary.

Very respectfully, your obedient servant,

C. M. BRADFORD,
Captain 1*st Louisiana Infantry.*

F. H. HATCH, Esq.,
   Collector U. S. Customs, New Orleans.

On the following day I sent to the collector the following despatch, by telegraph: —

TREASURY DEPARTMENT, *January* 27, 1861.

Apply to the governor of Louisiana to revoke Captain Bradford's order. Remonstrate with the governor against the inhumanity of turning the sick out of the hospital. If he refuses to interfere, have them

removed under the care of the resident surgeon, and do all in your power to provide for their comfort. JOHN A. DIX,
Secretary of the Treasury.
F. H. HATCH,
Collector of Customs, New Orleans.

On the 28th I addressed the following letter to the collector:—

TREASURY DEPARTMENT, *January* 28, 1861.

SIR: I did not receive until the 26th instant yours of the 14th, informing me that the United States barracks below the city of New Orleans, which have for several months been occupied as a marine hospital, had "been taken possession of in the name of the State of Louisiana." I found enclosed a copy of the letter of Captain C. M. Bradford, of the First Louisiana Infantry, advising you that he had taken possession of the barracks, that they would "be required for the Louisiana troops now being enlisted," and requesting you to "immediately remove those patients who are convalescent, and, as soon as in the opinion of the resident surgeon it may be practicable and humane, those also who are now confined to their beds." He also states that the barracks contained "two hundred and sixteen invalids and convalescent patients."

On this transaction, as an outrage to the public authority, I have no comment to make. But I cannot believe that a proceeding so discordant with the character of the people of the United States, and so revolting to the civilization of the age, has had the sanction of the governor of the State of Louisiana. I sent a telegraphic despatch to you yesterday, desiring you to remonstrate with him against the inhumanity of Captain Bradford's order, and ask him to revoke it. But if he should decline to interfere, I instructed you in regard to the removal and treatment of the sick; and in that event, I trust you will carry out my direction, not merely with "economy," but with a careful regard to their helpless condition.

The barracks, it seems, were taken possession of on the 11th instant. Captain Bradford's letter is dated the 13th, and yours the 14th, though I had no information on the subject until the 26th. I infer from the newspaper paragraph you enclosed, which telegraphic advices in regard to the subject-matter show to be of a later date than your letter, that the latter was not despatched until the 21st or 22d instant. I hope I am mistaken, and that the cause of the delay is to be found in some unexplained interruption of the mail. I should otherwise have great reason to be dissatisfied that the information was not more promptly communicated.

From the tone of the newspaper paragraph you enclosed, and from the seizure of the barracks, in violation of a usage of humanity, which in open war between contending nations, and even in the most revengeful civil conflicts between kindred races, has always held sacred from disturbance edifices dedicated to the care and comfort of the sick, I fear that no public property is likely to be respected. You will therefore have no more money expended on the revenue-cutter Washington, now hauled up for repairs, until I can have the assurance that she will not be seized as soon as she is refitted, and taken into the service of those who are seeking to break up the Union and overthrow the authority of the Federal government.

I am, respectfully, yours,   JOHN A. DIX,
Secretary of the Treasury.

F. H. HATCH, Esq.,
Collector of the Customs, New Orleans.

In order to understand the last paragraph, it is proper to say that in the letter of the collector of the 14th January was enclosed a newspaper article correcting the statement that the revenue-cutter Washington had been seized by irresponsible parties. It added, "We hope that no attempt will be made by illegal and unauthorized bodies to make any seizure or commit any violence against the Federal or any other property. Whatever the defence or necessities of the State may require to be done in these matters should be done by the executive of the State alone." That the precaution of the department in ordering expenditures for repairs on the Washington to be discontinued was not premature is apparent from the fact that she was seized by the State within three days afterwards, the public necessities alluded to having, it would seem, become so urgent in that brief period of time as to demand this exercise of sovereignty.

On the succeeding day the following letter from the collector was received: —

CUSTOM-HOUSE, NEW ORLEANS,
Collector's Office, January 21, 1861.

SIR: Referring to my letter of the 14th instant, I have the honor to inform you that by proper representations and remonstrances I have been able to retain the United States barracks for the use of the United

States marine hospital, and will probably continue to do so without further molestation.

Very respectfully, your obedient servant,
F. H. HATCH, *Collector.*

Hon. PHILIP F. THOMAS,
Secretary of the Treasury, Washington.

To this letter the department deemed it due to the collector immediately to return the following reply: —

TREASURY DEPARTMENT, *January* 29, 1861.

SIR: I have received your letter of the 21st instant, and cannot withhold the prompt expression of my acknowledgment of the service you have done to the cause of humanity by preventing, through your representations and remonstrances, all interference with the invalids at the barracks occupied as a marine hospital.

I cannot imagine why your letters are so long in reaching me. The delay of the last shows that the fault is with the mails, as I supposed.

I am, respectfully, yours, JOHN A. DIX,
Secretary of the Treasury.

F. H. HATCH, Esq.,
Collector of Customs, New Orleans, La.

On the evening of the 28th the department also received the following despatch by telegraph: —

NEW ORLEANS, *January* 28, 1861.

Marine hospital affair satisfactorily arranged. Barracks retained. See my letter of 21st instant. F. H. HATCH, *Collector.*

Hon. JOHN A. DIX,
Secretary of the Treasury.

On the 19th instant the following letter was received from the late United States collector at New Orleans: —

CUSTOM-HOUSE, NEW ORLEANS,
Collector's Office, February 9, 1861.

SIR: I have the honor to acknowledge receipt of your letter of the 29th ultimo, expressing your acknowledgments of what you are pleased to regard " the service I have done the cause of humanity by preventing, through my representations and remonstrances, all interference with the invalids at the barracks occupied as a marine hospital."

While your prompt withdrawal of the imputations of inhumanity on the part of the authorities of Louisiana is but an act of simple justice, I feel I cannot justly appropriate the merit you are pleased to attribute to my agency. The authorities would never have exercised the least inhumanity towards these patients; for, if the barracks had been required for the use of the troops Louisiana has been compelled to raise for her protection and defence, her Charity Hospital, justly the glory and pride of her munificence, into whose portals the afflicted of all nations can enter, without money and without price, would have amply provided for their wants.

In closing this communication I am constrained to observe, in reply to the remark in your letter of the 28th, that you "fear no public property is likely to be respected," that, in compliance with the ordinance of the convention of the people of Louisiana, the State took possession of the public property in trust to prevent any abuse of the same by the Federal government, which it was believed would pervert that which the Constitution intended for defence to the purposes of destruction. This property she will be ready to render a just and true account of at the proper time.

I have the honor to be, very respectfully, your obedient servant,

F. H. HATCH, *Collector.*

Hon. JOHN A. DIX,
    Secretary of the Treasury, Washington.

On this letter a few brief comments seem essential to a correct appreciation of the subject.

1. No imputation of inhumanity against the authorities of Louisiana was withdrawn; none was made. On the contrary, in the first letter from this department the belief was expressed that the seizure of the hospital was without the sanction of the governor.

2. Though Mr. Hatch, in the foregoing letter, declines to appropriate the merit attributed to him by the department in saving the United States barracks and their invalid inmates from disturbance, he claims, in his letter of the 21st of January, that, by "proper representations and remonstrances, he [had] been able to retain" them for use as a marine hospital; and it was in response to this claim that the merit he now disowns was promptly and cheerfully acknowledged.

3. When Mr. Hatch advised the department that the two hundred and sixteen invalids and convalescent patients had been ordered out of the barracks used as a marine hospital, no allusion was made to the Charity Hospital of Louisiana, where it now appears they could have been received "with-

out money and without price." On the contrary, he informed the department that he should, if necessary, take steps to remove them " with due regard to economy," leaving it to be inferred that they were to be provided for at the expense of the United States.

4. The government has received from the State of Louisiana no acknowledgment that the property it has seized, including the branch-mint and the revenue-cutters, is held in trust; and it is one of the first instances on record in which such an estate has been created by forcibly wresting national property from the possession of the lawful owner.

5. On what explicable theory the branch-mint, a part of the property seized in trust, could have been perverted to purposes of destruction is not readily perceived. If the treasurer had, as was his duty, paid the drafts drawn on him by this department, the moneys in his custody would have been disbursed long ago for the private benefit and relief of the public creditors. Nor is it perceived how the revenue-cutter Robert McClelland could have been used for the destruction of the State of Louisiana if she had been allowed to proceed to New York, more than a thousand miles distant, in obedience to the orders of this department.

6. Mr. Hatch, as will be seen hereafter, was engaged, more than a week before the convention of Louisiana met to consider the question of secession, in a conspiracy, unfortunately a successful one, to surrender the revenue-cutter Robert McClelland to the State authorities, while he held a commission from the United States, and was acting under an oath of fidelity to the government. It is under these circumstances, and with this stain on his official character, that he comes forward to respond for the good faith of the State of Louisiana in seizing the public property, including the treasure in the branch-mint.

V. REVENUE–CUTTERS.

On the 18th of January ultimo, three days after I took

charge of this department, I decided to despatch a special agent to New Orleans and Mobile to save, if possible, the revenue-cutters on those stations. Mr. Wm. Hemphill Jones, chief clerk in the First Comptroller's office, was selected for the purpose; and on the 19th he left this city with instructions to provision the vessels, and give the commanding officers verbal orders to take them to New York. This mode of conveying the directions to them was chosen, because no confidence was felt that the mails or the telegraph could be relied on as a safe medium of communication. That the authority of Mr. Jones to communicate to these officers the directions intrusted to him might not be questioned, he was furnished with the following letter, addressed to the commanders of the cutters Lewis Cass, at Mobile, and the Robert McClelland, at New Orleans: —

TREASURY DEPARTMENT,
January 19, 1861.

SIR: This letter will be presented to you by Wm. Hemphill Jones, a special agent of this department.

You are required to obey such directions as may be given you, either verbally or in writing, by Mr. Jones, with regard to the vessel under your command.

I am, respectfully, JOHN A. DIX,
Secretary of the Treasury.

It was deemed prudent to detach Captain Morrison, who was from the State of Georgia, from the Lewis Cass, then at Mobile; and he was accordingly ordered to Galveston, to take command of the Henry Dodge, which was without a captain. The precaution was too late. Before Mr. Jones reached Mobile, Captain Morrison, regardless of the obligation of his oath, had surrendered his vessel to the authorities of Alabama. His resignation was subsequently received; but it was not accepted, and the following order was issued, dismissing him from the revenue-service: —

ORDER.

Treasury Department,
February 11, 1861.

J. J. Morrison, of Georgia, a captain in the revenue-cutter service of the United States, late in command of the Lewis Cass, having, in violation of his official oath, and of his duty to the government, surrendered his vessel to the State of Alabama, it is hereby directed that his name be stricken from the rolls of said service.

By order of the President of the United States.

JOHN A. DIX,
Secretary of the Treasury.

The circumstances under which Captain Morrison surrendered his vessel, and which constitute the justification for his dismissal, are detailed in the annexed report of Mr. Jones, marked B.

The revenue-cutter Robert McClelland, one of the largest and finest in the service, and recently refitted, was on duty in the Mississippi river, below New Orleans; and it was this vessel which the department was particularly desirous of saving, on account of her value. The failure of the attempt is fully detailed in Mr. Jones's report, hereto annexed. It discloses an act of official infidelity on the part of the collector at New Orleans, F. H. Hatch, which cannot fail to receive the condemnation of all right-thinking men. The service to be performed by the McClelland was between the forts, seventy-two miles below the city of New Orleans, and the mouth of the river. On the 15th of January, eight days before the convention of Louisiana met, and eleven days before the ordinance of secession was passed, Mr. Hatch, in a letter secured by Mr. Jones, and now on file in the department, ordered Captain Breshwood to bring his vessel up the river, and anchor her opposite the city, for the purpose, afterwards avowed to Mr. Jones, of getting her into the possession of the State of Louisiana. Mr. Hatch, at the time he was engaged in this conspiracy against the United States, held a commission in its service, and did not hesitate to violate his official oath, and to prostitute the authority with which his government had clothed him to accomplish an act of the grossest infidelity. Captain Breshwood, as events subsequently disclosed, was a party to this treachery. On his refusal to obey the order of the department, Mr. Jones sent the following despatch: —

NEW ORLEANS, *January* 29, 1861.

Captain Breshwood has refused positively, in writing, to obey any instructions of the department; in this I am sure he is sustained by the collector, and I believe acts by his advice. What must I do?

W. H. JONES, *Special Agent.*

Hon. J. A. DIX,
    Secretary of the Treasury.

It was supposed, when this despatch was received, that the McClelland was at her station at the mouth of the river; and the following was telegraphed in reply. It was intercepted by the governor of Alabama, and forwarded to the authorities of Louisiana, only reaching Mr. Jones through the newspapers: —

TREASURY DEPARTMENT, *January* 29, 1861.

Tell Lieutenant Caldwell to arrest Captain Breshwood, assume command of the cutter, and obey the order I gave through you. If Captain Breshwood, after arrest, undertakes to interfere with the command of the cutter, tell Lieutenant Caldwell to consider him as a mutineer, and treat him accordingly. If any one attempts to haul down the American flag, shoot him on the spot.

JOHN A. DIX,
Secretary of the Treasury.

WM. HEMPHILL JONES, *New Orleans.*

The officers of the revenue service are placed by law under the direction of the Secretary of the Treasury, and are required to obey his instructions. The refusal on the part of Captain Breshwood to act as directed was regarded not as a mere act of disobedience for which he would, under ordinary circumstances, have been promptly dismissed from the service, but it was also considered as a prelude to the graver act of infidelity he was believed to be meditating. The only chance of anticipating and preventing it was through an order bearing some relation in severity to the enormity of the offence he was about to commit. Had the despatch not been intercepted by the governor of Alabama, who did not deem it beneath his dignity to violate the sanctity of a system of confidential communication for the purpose of scrutinizing the correspondence of a department of the government with one of its special agents in a matter relating exclusively to its own interests, the vessel might have been saved and the State of Louisiana spared the reproach of consenting to an act which all civilized communities hold in merited detestation.

It may be proper to add, in reference to the closing period of the foregoing despatch, that, as the flag of the Union, since 1777, when it was devised and adopted by the founders of the Republic, had never until a recent day been hauled down, except by honorable hands in manly conflict, no hesitation was felt in attempting to uphold it at any cost against an act of treachery, as the ensign of the public authority, and the emblem of unnumbered victories by land and sea.

The revenue-cutter Henry Dodge, at Galveston, Texas, was understood to be so much out of repair as to render it very questionable whether she could be safely taken to New York. Under these circumstances, the following order was sent to her commanding officer: —

TREASURY DEPARTMENT, *January* 22, 1861.

SIR: If the revenue-cutter Henry Dodge, to the command of which you were assigned by an order of the 19th instant, should on examination prove to be seaworthy, you will immediately provision her for six weeks and sail for New York, reporting yourself on your arrival to the collector of the port. While making your preparations for sailing, you will exercise the utmost vigilance in guarding your vessel against attack from any quarter. If any hostile movement should be made against you, you will defend yourself to the last extremity. The national flag must not be dishonored. If you are in danger of being overpowered by superior numbers, you will put to sea and proceed to Key West to provision; or if intercepted so that you cannot go to sea, and are unable to keep possession of your vessel, you will run her ashore, and if possible blow her up, so that she may not be used against the United States.

I am, very respectfully, JOHN A. DIX,
Secretary of the Treasury.

Captain J. J. MORRISON,
Commanding Revenue-Cutter Henry Dodge, *Galveston, Texas.*

It was the determination of this department to adopt such measures as to prevent, if possible, the revenue-vessels, for which it was responsible, from being taken by force, and used for the purpose of overthrowing the public authority. Any attempt to gain possession of them by military coercion could not be regarded in any other light than as an act of war, proper to be resisted by force of arms; and it was deemed far more creditable to the country that they should be blown into fragments than that they should be pusillanimously or treacherously surrendered and employed against the government which they were constructed and commissioned to support.

At the last accounts the Dodge, in consequence of her unfitness to proceed to New York, was to be placed at the disposal of the coast-survey in the vicinity of Galveston for temporary service, in case of any hostile demonstration against her. Captain Morrison, who was ordered to take charge of her before his fidelity to the government was questioned, having been dismissed from the service, the command has devolved on Lieutenant William F. Rogers, in whose good faith and firmness entire confidence is reposed.

It only remains to state, under this branch of the inquiries addressed to this department, that Captain John G. Breshwood and Lieutenants S. B. Caldwell and Thomas D. Fister, who voluntarily surrendered the revenue-cutter Robert McClelland to the State of Louisiana, have been dismissed from the revenue service.

I am, very respectfully, your obedient servant,
JOHN A. DIX,
Secretary of the Treasury.

Hon. WM. PENNINGTON,
Speaker of the House of Representatives.

A.

Mint of the United States,
Philadelphia, February 18, 1861.

Sir: I send you enclosed a copy of a letter I have recently received from Mr. Elmore, the superintendent of the branch-mint at New Orleans.

It appears from this communication that a committee, acting under the order of a convention, has taken possession of the branch-mint in the name of the State of Louisiana. The right to coin money — one of the highest acts of sovereignty — being expressly granted to the United States,[1] and withheld from the States,[2] the action of the Louisiana convention cannot but be regarded as revolutionary in its character, and destructive of the rights of the people and government of the United States.

By the law establishing branches of the mint of the United States,[3] "the general direction of the business of the said branches is under the control and regulation of the director of the mint at Philadelphia, subject to the approbation of the Secretary of the Treasury; and for that purpose it shall be the duty of the said director to prescribe such regulations, and require such returns periodically and occasionally, as shall appear to him to be necessary for the purpose of carrying into effect the intention of this act in establishing said branches; also for the purpose of discriminating the coin which shall be stamped at each branch and at the mint itself; also for the purpose of preserving uniformity of weight, form, and fineness in the coin stamped at each place; and for that purpose to require the transmission and delivery to him at the mint, from time to time, of such parcels of the coinage of each branch as he shall think proper, to be subjected to such assays and tests as he shall direct."

My instructions require weekly reports of its operations from the branch-mint at New Orleans, and monthly returns of parcels of coinage taken from each delivery of coin from the carrier to the treasurer. These reports and coins for the

---

[1] Constitution U. S. art. 1, sec. 8. [2] Ibid. sec. 10.
[3] Act of March 3, 1835.

month of January have been received, but the weekly returns since the close of the month have been omitted to be sent to me.

It thus appears that the institution in question is not conducting its operations in a lawful manner, and although it is still a branch of the mint of the United States, (for no action of the State of Louisiana can legally alter its relation to the general government,) yet, as its coinage from the close of the month of January will not be subject to the tests required by law, it has practically ceased to be a branch of the mint. The coinage of that branch is designated by the letter O on the reverse side of each piece. The coins struck in January are legal coins of the United States; but as these pieces cannot be distinguished from others coined since that time, having the date of 1861, the whole coinage of this year ought to be discredited by the government. The announcement should be made, either by the proclamation of the President, or by act of Congress, if the former should not be deemed proper, that the coins of the branch-mint at New Orleans of the year 1861 are not of the coinage of the United States, and are therefore not a legal tender in the payment of debts; said coins are designated by the letter O on the reverse of each piece.

I may here state that the coins stamped at San Francisco are designated by the letter S; those of Dahlonega, Georgia, by the letter D; and of Charlotte, North Carolina, by the letter C. The coinage of the mint at Philadelphia may be known by the absence of any letter or a mint-mark.

The coining-dies are prepared at the mint in Philadelphia for the branches. I furnished, at the close of the last year, the New Orleans branch the following number of working-dies for 1861: double eagles, 3 obverses and 3 reverses; eagles, 2 obverses; half eagles, 2 obverses; three dollar, 2 obverses (the date is on the reverse of this piece); quarter eagle, 4 obverses; gold dollar, 2 reverses (same as three-dollar piece); silver dollar, 2 obverses; half dollar, 12 obverses; quarter dollar, 4 obverses; dime, 2 obverses, 2 reverses; half dime, 2 obverses, 2 reverses.

In reference to these dies, I suggest that it is desirable that the agent of the department should be requested to call at the branch-mint and ask to have them delivered to him for the purpose of returning them to the mint at Philadelphia. The person in charge of that institution may, perhaps, be willing to comply with this request. If so, it will relieve us from the embarrassment of having coins issued purporting to be the coins of the United States, but which are not subjected to the assays and trials required by law.

I may add, as appropriate to this communication, that the building of the branch-mint at New Orleans, including the rendering of it fire-proof in 1855–'56, cost the United States the sum of $591,514.05. The amount of bullion in that institution at the present time, the property of the United States, is $389,267.46; to which must be added the balance to the credit of the United States on the coinage-charge, and for purchases of silver, (profit,) $12,413.62.

The ground upon which the branch-mint is erected, known as "Jackson Square," was conveyed to the United States by the authorities of the city of New Orleans on the 19th day of June, 1835. It was a donation by the city to the United States.

I have the honor to be, with great respect, your faithful servant,

JAMES ROSS SNOWDEN,
Director of the Mint.

Hon. JOHN A. DIX,
Secretary of the Treasury, Washington City.

UNITED STATES BRANCH MINT,
New Orleans, January 31, 1861.

SIR: This morning a committee of the convention, acting under an ordinance passed by that body, took possession of this institution in the name of the State of Louisiana.

As soon as I can get a copy of the ordinance I will forward it to you.

Yours, very truly, WM. A. ELMORE,
Superintendent.

Hon. JAMES ROSS SNOWDEN,
Director of the Mint, Philadelphia.

B.

WASHINGTON CITY, *February* 15, 1861.

SIR: In accordance with your instructions of the 19th ultimo, directing me to repair to New Orleans and Mobile for the purpose of securing to the United States the revenue-cutters Robert McClelland and Lewis Cass, I left Washington in the next mail-train for those cities respectively.

Owing to numerous derangements on the railroads, produced by land-slides covering the tracks, I did not reach New Orleans until Saturday, the 26th January, — one day, however, in advance of the mail.

Supposing, of course, that the McClelland was on her station at the mouth of the Mississippi river, or at the head of the passes, I made arrangements on the next day with the captain of a tug-boat, which was to leave New Orleans on Monday evening, to take me down the river and place me on board the cutter. At the time appointed for her departure, while on the levee and about to join the steamer, I was much astonished to learn that the cutter had just anchored immediately below the city. I at once hired a skiff, and boarded her about dusk. On inquiring for Captain Breshwood, I was informed that he had gone ashore. A boat was despatched with an officer to find him, if possible, and about 10 o'clock he returned on board.

I exhibited to him my own instructions, handed him your letter, placing him and his vessel under my orders, and directed him to get under weigh and proceed to sea.

He declined doing so at that late hour, and both his officers united with the captain in his objections. No positive disobedience, however, was manifested, but an evident reluctance to comply at that time. The next morning I was introduced to F. H. Hatch, Esq., collector of customs, by Captain Breshwood. These gentlemen had a private interview, and I was soon convinced that the collector could not be depended on to assist in getting the cutter out of the waters of Louisiana, but did not then know the full extent of his action in the premises.

I then handed Captain Breshwood the following letter: —

NEW ORLEANS, *January* 29, 1861.

SIR: You are hereby directed to get the United States revenue-cutter Robert McClelland, now lying here, under weigh immediately, and proceed with her to New York, where you will await the further instructions of the Secretary of the Treasury.

For my authority to make this order you are referred to the letter of the Secretary dated the 19th instant, and handed you personally by me.

Very respectfully, WM. HEMPHILL JONES,
Special Agent.

Captain J. G. BRESHWOOD,
Comm'g U. S. Revenue-Cutter Robert McClelland.

Another conference was held between Captain Breshwood and Collector Hatch, and finally I received from the former the following reply: —

U. S. REVENUE-CUTTER ROBERT MCCLELLAND,
New Orleans, January 29, 1861.

SIR: Your letter, with the one of the 19th of January, from the Hon. Secretary of the Treasury, I have duly received, and, in reply, refuse to obey the order.

I am, sir, your obedient servant,
JOHN G. BRESHWOOD, *Captain.*

WM. HEMPHILL JONES, Esq., *Special Agent.*

Believing that Captain Breshwood would not have ventured upon this most positive act of insubordination and disobedience of his own volition, I waited upon the collector at the custom-house, and had with him a full and free conversation upon the whole subject. In the course of it Mr. Hatch admitted to me that he had caused the cutter to be brought to the city of New Orleans by an order of his own, dated January 15, so that she might be secured to the State of Louisiana, although at that time the State had not only not seceded, but the convention had not met, and in fact did not meet until eight days afterwards.

This, I must confess, seemed to me a singular confession for one who at that very time had sworn to do his duty faithfully as an officer of the United States; and on intimating as much to Mr. Hatch, he excused himself on the ground that " in these revolutions all other things must give way to the force of circumstances."

Mr. Hatch likewise informed me that the officers of the cutter had long since determined to abandon their allegiance to the United States, and cast their fortunes with the independent State of Louisiana. In order to test the correctness of this statement, I addressed another communication to Captain Breshwood, of the following tenor:—

NEW ORLEANS, *January* 29, 1861.

SIR: By your note of this date I am informed that you refuse to obey the orders of the honorable Secretary of the Treasury.

As on accepting your commission you took and subscribed an oath faithfully to discharge your duties to the government, and as you well know the law has placed the revenue-cutters and their officers under the entire control of the Secretary of the Treasury, I request you to advise me whether you consider yourself at this time an officer in the service of the United States.

Very respectfully,   WM. HEMPHILL JONES,
Captain BRESHWOOD.   *Special Agent.*

To this letter I never received any reply. I then repaired again on board the cutter, and asked for the order of the collector bringing them to New Orleans. The original was placed in my possession, of which the following is a copy; and here it may be proper to observe that the order is written and signed by the collector himself:—

CUSTOM-HOUSE, NEW ORLEANS,
Collector's Office, January 15, 1861.

SIR: You are hereby directed to proceed forthwith under sail to this city, and anchor the vessel under your command opposite the United States marine hospital, above Algiers.

Very respectfully, your obedient servant,
F. H. HATCH, *Collector.*

Captain J. G. BRESHWOOD,
U. S. Revenue-Cutter McClelland, *S. W. Pass, Louisiana.*

The effect of this order may readily be foreseen by you. While on her station at the passes the vessel was measurably under the control of the government, and could be easily got to sea from that point. While lying at New Orleans, however, and any hostile power in possession of the forts St. Philip and Jackson, seventy-two miles below, it is evident that any vessel is completely at the mercy of such power so far as respects her passing down the river.

The State of Louisiana is now, and has been for several weeks, in full possession of these forts; and Mr. Hatch of course intended that the government should be deprived of any chance of keeping the McClelland, even if her officers remained faithful to their trust. If these latter, as was the case, proved derelict, I had made ample arrangements to seize the vessel, and carry her to sea in defiance of any ordinary contingency to the contrary, could I have either found her or got her below the fortifications. As it was, however, this was impossible. She lay in the river, watched from shore, a distance of seventy-two miles above the forts, with a telegraphic line in working order, communicating directly between the city and garrison; and as I was subsequently informed by the commander of Fort St. Philip, he was determined to blow her out of the water rather than let her pass to sea.

I was therefore under the necessity of witnessing the transfer of this fine vessel, her stores and armament, to the State of Louisiana, and report to you that she is no longer in the United States revenue service. Her officers have likewise taken an oath of allegiance to the State, and have received and accepted commissions in her service.

I then, in further pursuance of your directions, proceeded to the port of Mobile to look after the cutter Lewis Cass, stationed in that harbor.

I found her at anchor opposite the city, within about one hundred yards of the wharves, and apparently deserted. On going to the custom-house, I fell in with Lieutenant Lawrence, and subsequently found Lieutenants Rogers and Shoemaker. I was informed by them that Captain Morrison had received your orders for him to repair to Galveston, but that he had refused to obey them, and had given up his vessel to the authorities of the State of Alabama.

On going on board the Lewis Cass I found her to be in very bad condition, — no one on board but the men, and no order or discipline observed. Captain Morrison could not be met with; but in the letter-book of the vessel, which was lying in the cabin, I found the following letter from Collector Sandford, which will fully explain the manner in which that officer thought proper to perform his duty to the government of the United States: —

STATE OF ALABAMA,
Collector's Office, Mobile, January 30, 1861.

SIR: In obedience to an ordinance recently adopted by a convention of the people of Alabama, I have to require you to surrender into my hands, for the use of the State, the revenue-cutter Lewis Cass, now under your command, together with her armaments, properties, and provisions on board the same.

I am instructed also to notify you that you have the option to continue in command of the said revenue-cutter under the authority of the State of Alabama, in the exercise of the same duties that you have hitherto rendered to the United States, and at the same compensation, reporting to this office and to the governor of the State.

In surrendering the vessel to the State you will furnish me with a detailed inventory of its armaments, provisions, and properties of every description.

You will receive special instructions from this office in regard to the duties you will be required to perform. I wait your immediate reply.

Very respectfully, your obedient servant,
T. SANDFORD, *Collector.*

J. J. MORRISON, Esq.,
Captain Revenue-Cutter Lewis Cass, *Mobile, Ala.*

Captain Morrison thereupon transferred his vessel, with her equipments, to the State of Alabama, and took an oath of allegiance to that State.

It is proper here to remark that the other officers of the Lewis Cass, viz: First Lieutenant Rogers and Lieutenants Lawrence and Shoemaker, remained faithful to their government, and rendered me much assistance at Mobile. They unanimously and cheerfully volunteered their services, in case an opportunity might be afforded, to recapture the McClelland, and this would undoubtedly have been effected if any chance could have been found to take her to sea.

I gave Mr. Rogers written orders to return to New London, his place of residence, and await there your instructions. In like manner Mr. Shoemaker was directed to repair to Baltimore, while Mr. Lawrence preferred to remain with his family on the shore of Mobile Bay.

The Lewis Cass, in her present condition, is entirely unseaworthy. Her seams are open, causing her to leak badly, and in fact she came very near foundering while beating up Mobile harbor, with but a whole-sail breeze.

Her late officers inform me that she will require extensive repairs to put her in any condition to do service to her present holders.

I then returned to New Orleans and made a final effort with the junior officers of the McClelland to induce them at least to consent for me to carry the vessel under sail as far as the forts, as I was desirous to test the question of the determination of the State of Louisiana to use force in retaining her, but they refused positively to have her removed from her anchorage.

Finding that nothing further could be effected by me — that the two vessels were entirely lost to the United States, and no possible benefit could arise from my remaining any longer in New Orleans, I left that city, *via* the river-route, and reached here on Thursday evening, the 14th instant.

I propose to make the conduct of the officers of the telegraph company, with reference to official despatches, the subject of a special communication.

Very respectfully, your obedient servant,
WM. HEMPHILL JONES,
Special Agent.

Hon. JOHN A. DIX,
Secretary of the Treasury.

PROCLAMATION OF MAJOR-GENERAL DIX TO THE PEOPLE.

About the middle of July, 1863, a riot of a very serious character broke out in the city of New York and continued for three or four days, when it was quelled by military force. The immediate cause was the dissatisfaction with the draft for the army, the first attack having been made on the office of one of the provost-marshals. The number of killed and wounded is believed to have been about one thousand. The dissatisfaction, in which the outbreak originated, was created to a considerable extent by the opposition of newspaper presses and politicians to the act of Congress providing for the draft. It was opposed as arbitrary, oppressive, and inconsistent with the Constitution of the United States. Gen. Dix was at this juncture assigned to the command of the Eastern Department, of which the State of New York is a part. The draft, having been temporarily suspended on account of the riot, was resumed and carried into execution in August ensuing, and it was on this occasion that the following proclamation was published.

HEADQUARTERS, DEPARTMENT OF THE EAST,
NEW YORK CITY, *August* 17, 1863.

TO THE CITIZENS OF NEW YORK:—

THE draft of men in this city to replenish the ranks of the army, in order to complete more speedily the suppression of the insurrection in the South, having, in consequence of forcible resistance to the execution of the law, been placed under my direction as commanding officer of the forces of the United States in this military department, I have thought it not out of place to present to you some suggestions for your consideration as friends of the Union and of the good order of society.

The law under which the draft is to be made is for enrolling and calling out the national forces. It is founded on the principle that every citizen, who enjoys the protection of the government and looks to it for the security of his property and his life, may be called on in seasons of great public danger to take up arms for the common defence. No political society can be held together unless this principle is acknowledged as one to which the government may have recourse when its existence is in peril. There is no civilized country in which it is not recognized.

The law authorizing the draft has been persistently called a conscription law by those who desire to make it odious and defeat its execution. It is in no just sense a conscription like that which was put in force in the sixth year of the French republic, and abandoned on the restoration of the Bourbons, on account of its oppressive exactions. It is a simple law for enrolling and calling into the service the arms-bearing population of certain ages, and differs in no essential principle from the law authorizing the militia to be called out, excepting that in the latter case complete organizations are brought into the field. The object of the very provisions of the law which are most beneficial to individuals has been most grossly perverted. If a drafted man finds it inconvenient to serve, he is allowed to furnish a substitute, or to purchase his exemption from service by paying the smallest sum of money for which substitutes are ordinarily obtained. Both these provisions have the same purpose — to provide, for cases of hardship; and if either were stricken out, these cases would be proportionably increased in number.

The draft about to be made is for one fifth part of all persons between twenty and thirty-five years of age, and of the unmarried between thirty-five and forty-five. The entire class between eighteen and thirty-five was long since drafted in the seceded States, and the draft has recently been extended to embrace nearly the whole arms-bearing population. Compared with the burden they are sustaining, ours is as nothing. The contest on our part is to defend our nationality, to uphold the institutions under the protection of which we have lived and prospered, and to preserve untarnished the proud memories of our history, brief, it is true, but full of high achievements in science, in art, and in arms. Shall we, in such a cause, shrink from labors and sacrifices which our misguided brethren in the seceded States are sustaining in the cause of treason and social disorganization? For the honor of New York let us take care that the history of this rebellion, more vast than any which has ever convulsed a nation, shall contain nothing to make our children blush for the patriotism of their fathers.

Whatever objection there may be to the law authorizing the draft, whatever defects it may have, it is the law of the land, and resistance to it is revolt against the constituted authorities of the country. If one law can be set at defiance, any other may be, and the foundations of all government may be broken up. Those who, in the history of political societies, have been the first to set themselves up against the law, have been the surest victims of the disorder which they have created. The poor have a far deeper interest in maintaining the inviolability of the law than the rich. Property, through the means it can command, is power. But the only security for those who have little more than life and the labor of their own hands to protect lies in the supremacy of the law. On them, and on those who are dependent on them, social disorder falls with fatal effect.

The constitutionality of the law authorizing the draft has been disputed. Near the close of the year 1814, when the country was engaged in war with Great Britain, a similar law was recommended to Congress by the government, to draft men to fill the ranks of the army, which was gallantly battling, as our armies are now, for the nation's honor and life. Madison, one of the great expounders of the Constitution, which he took a prominent part in framing, was President. Monroe, his successor, then acting both as Secretary of State and Secretary of War, addressed to the House of Representatives a lucid argument in support of the right of

Congress to pass such a law. Alexander J. Dallas was Secretary of the Treasury ; Wm. Jones, Secretary of the Navy; Return J. Meigs, Postmaster-General, and Richard Rush, Attorney-General. The measure could not well have received a higher party sanction. All laws passed with the established legislative forms are valid until declared otherwise by judicial tribunals of competent jurisdiction. What would become of a people in critical emergencies if no law could be carried into effect until it had passed the ordeal of the courts? or if State or municipal authorities could arrest its execution by calling in question its conformity to the provisions of the Constitution? The President has promptly consented to have it tested by judicial interpretation ; but while the car of victory is moving on, and treason is flying before it, God forbid that the State of New York or its constituted authorities should attempt to stay its progress until the judicial process can be consummated.

The accuracy of the enrolment in the city districts having been impeached, a revision was immediately ordered by the President, on a representation from the Governor of the State. But as the men are needed for immediate service, and as the correction of the returns requires time, the quota was ordered to be reduced in all the districts — in some more than half the whole amount — leaving the account for future adjustment. The reduction in the quota exceeds in proportion the alleged excess of the enrolment; so that no personal injustice can possibly occur.

Under these circumstances, no good citizen will array himself, either by word or deed, against the draft. Submission to the law in seasons of tranquillity is always the highest of political duties. But when the existence of the government is in peril, he who resists its authority commits a crime of the deepest turpitude. He is the voluntary instrument of those who are seeking to overthrow it, and becomes himself a public enemy. Moreover, resistance to the government by those who are living under its protection, and are indebted to it for the daily tenure of their property and their lives, has not even the palliation under which those who lead the insurrection at the South seek to shelter themselves, — that they are acting under color of authority derived from legislatures or conventions of the people in their respective States. With us resistance to the constituted authorities is both treason and lawless violence; and if there are any who thus combine to reënact the scenes of cruelty and devastation by which this city has recently been dishonored, and to defeat by force of arms the execution of the paramount law of Congress, they will be treated as enemies of the country and of mankind.

Returning among you from a distance, fellow-citizens, after more than two years of military service in the cause of the Union, to uphold which this city has, in all emergencies, stood forth with a manly patriotism worthy of her high position, — having no feeling but to see her good name preserved without blemish, no wish but that she may continue, as she has ever been, the most orderly of the great commercial towns of the age, — I have ventured to address to you these suggestions, to exhort you to the maintenance of order, to obedience to the laws, and to the quiet pursuit of your accustomed avocations, while the draft is in progress.

Should these suggestions be disregarded by any among you, and renewed attempts be made to disturb the public peace, to break down the barriers which have been set up for the security of property and life, and to defeat the execution of a law which it is my duty to enforce, I warn all such persons that ample preparation has been made to vindicate the authority of the government, and that the first exhibitions of disorder or violence will be met by the most prompt and vigorous measures for their repression.

END OF VOL. II.

INDEX.

ACADEMY OF ART, recommended in New York, ii. 351; probable cost of, 352.
Adams, C. F., i. 357, 360.
Adams, John, frigate, fight of, with corsair, ii. 400.
Adams, J. Q., extracts from diary of, i. 357; opinion of, on Missouri Compromise, 357, 360.
Adet, letter of, i. 88.
Africa, condition of, ii. 52.
African colonization, ii. 41; success of, 42; societies to promote, 43; advantages of, 44, 50; origin of, 45; objects of, 51.
Agriculture, effect of slave-labor on, ii. 46, 49; character of pursuit of, 334; dignity of, 336; of New York, address on, 360; Silas Wright's address on, 360; statistics of exports of, 361–364; wasteful system of, in America, 367, 368; in ancient Rome, 369; reform in, 370; Liebig on, 380.
Akerly, Dr., on granite in the Highlands, ii. 186.
Alabama, violent measures in, ii. 425; governor of, intercepts despatch, 440, 441.
Algiers, corsairs of, ii. 386; tribute paid to, 387; captures by, 387; French tribute to, 387; tribute to, from other Powers, 388; renews attacks on United States, 408; present state of, 408.
Alienism, opinion concerning, ii. 56. See *Naturalization*.
Aliens, enrolment of, ii. 57; exemption of, 59. See *Naturalization*.
Allen, Mr., views on Oregon question, i. 2.
Alluvial formations of New York, ii. 219.
Apportionment of members of Congress, resolutions concerning, ii. 279, 280; speech on, 281; power of Congress over, 283; constitutionality of act to regulate, 292; mischiefs of, 294; second speech on, 301; Hamilton on, 302; action of Congress on, 310; vote on, 311.

Architecture, of farm-houses, ii. 327; progress of domestic, 327, 348; Downing on rural, 330, 350; of Croton Aqueduct, 357; rural, in England, 349.
Arithmetic, course of study of, ii. 89; importance of, 90.
Army, regular, prejudice against, ii. 119; of Europe, 120; evils of, 120; organization of, reformed, 130; operations of, in Mexico, i. 163, ii. 36; command of, i. 164; organization of, 165, 166; achievements of, in Mexico, 202, 203; number of, in Mexico, 235.
Art, academy of, recommended, ii. 351; probable cost of, 352.
Ashes, import of, from Canada, i. 392.
Astor, John Jacob, founded Astoria, i. 46; sold to British, 47.
Astor Library, ii. 351.
Astoria, restored under treaty of Ghent, 47.
Astronomy, study of, ii. 95; progress of, 261; history of, 263.
Atlas, Mount, description of, ii. 384.
Atomic theory discovered, ii. 248; value of, 249.
Augusta, surveyor of, resigns, ii. 412; account of, rejected, 412.
Ausable Valley, iron of, ii. 208.

Bainbridge, Captain, arrives at Algiers, ii. 393; protest of, 393; loses Philadelphia, 401.
Balize, British, encroachments in, i. 271; British settlement in, 296.
Barbary States, physical character of, ii. 383; history of, 385; Mohammedan government of, 386; wars in, 386; corsairs of, 386; treaties with, 387; relations of Europe with, 388.
Barracks, at New Orleans, seized, ii. 432.
Bartholinus, discovery of, ii. 260.
Bashaw of Tripoli, joke of, on flag-staff, ii. 398; message of, to Mr. Cathcart, 398; punishes commander of corsair, 399.
Beck, Dr., on salt springs of New York, ii. 202; on gypsum, 207.

Bell, James S., statement of, regarding Mosquitoes, i. 268.
Berkeley, sees Strait of Juan de Fuca, i. 11.
Berrien, Mr., on Guerrero's decree, i. 437.
Berzelius, researches of, ii. 259.
Bey of Tunis, demands of, ii. 390; palace of, burned, 390.
Blowpipe, experiments with, ii. 247.
Black, analyses of, ii. 245.
Book-keeping, instruction in, ii. 91.
Boston, John, despatch from, ii. 411; resignation of, 411.
Boundaries, natural, i. 426.
Bradford, Captain, letter of, ii. 432.
Brancas, experiments of, ii. 270.
Breshwood, Captain, misconduct of, ii. 439, 440, 447; arrest of, ordered, 440; dismissed the service, 442.
Brewster, Sir David experiments of, ii. 260, 261.
Bristol, the, wreck of, ii. 3.
Butler, Senator, reply to, i. 347–350.
Butler, Col., death of, 350.

Calhoun, Mr., on Missouri Compromise, i. 356, 358, 359 ; on extension of slavery, 362.
California, coast of, surveyed by Vizcaino, i. 8; Irish colonies for, 275; British schemes in, 278, 280, 282; Macnamara's schemes in, 275–277, 281; Great Basin of, 379; maritime valley of, 380, 438 ; admission of, to the Union, 413; proposition for government of, 415; objections to admission of, 420; character of population of, 420; condition of, 424; dismemberment of, 426.
California claims, speech on, i. 262.
Campagna, Roman, i. 257; Mercantidi, 257; owners of, 257.
Campbell v. Gordon, doctrine of, ii. 66.
Canada, trade with, speech on, i. 383; population of, 389; political system of, 390; carrier of wheat, 391; tariff of, 391; exports of, to United States, 392; export of flour through United States, 395; advantages of, from trade with, 394, 396; imports of flour by, 397; value of exports to United States, 401; value of imports from United States, 401; statistics of trade with, 403; quasi annexation of, 405; anti-liberal party of, 407.
Cardinals, Roman, i. 248.
Carthage, population of, ii. 385; fate of, 385.
Cass, Lewis, revenue-cutter, seizure of, ii. 450; condition of, 451.
Catamounts, of New York, ii. 221; character of, 222.

Cathcart, J. L., consul at Tripoli, ii. 389; negotiations of, 391, 392; protest by, 393.
Ceres, planet discovered, ii. 263.
Charles V., invades Tunis, ii. 386.
Chatfield, Frederick, letter of, on Mosquito question, 301.
Chemistry, study of, ii. 95; value of, 243; history of, 244–249; Geber's writings on, 244; Paracelsus on, 244; Margraaf's discoveries in, 245; Scheele's discoveries, 245; Black's discoveries, 245; Cavendish and Priestley's discoveries, 245; Lavoisier's researches, 245; Klaproth's researches, 245; Hare's discoveries, 247; galvanism applied to, 247; Davy's experiments in, 248; Gay-Lussac's experiments, 248; atomic theory of, 248; Dalton's discovery, 248; uses of, 250.
Christianity, influence of, ii. 275.
Civil war, evils of, i. 196, 197.
Clayton, J. M., views on Oregon question, i. 2; remarks of, 41, 43; propositions of, 373, 376.
Cleaveland, researches of, ii. 259.
Coal, connection of, with salt, ii. 204; formations of, in England, 204; in New York, 205.
Coal mines of Bohemia, description of, ii. 258.
Cockerill, Messrs., works of, described, ii. 270.
Coins, American, how stamped, ii. 444.
Colonization, British, i. 273; Grecian, 273; Roman, 274. See *African Colonization.*
Columbia River, discovered by Haceta, i. 9; by Gray, 26.
Commerce, Chamber of, pilot regulations of, ii. 16.
Compromise act of 1842, i. 111.
Constitution of United States, compromises of, i. 354; proposed amendment of, concerning elections, 314; method of study of, ii. 97.
Constitution, frigate, encounter of, with corsairs, ii. 400.
Contest with the rebels, what, 453.
Cook, Captain, voyage to northwest coast, i. 10; lands at Nootka Sound, 10.
Cooper Institute, ii. 351.
Cortez, operations of, in Mexico, ii. 36.
Courts-martial, penalties imposed by, ii. 136–140.
Croton Aqueduct, beauty of, ii. 357.
Cyrene, ruins of, ii. 385; conquest of, 385.

Dale, Commodore, sent to Mediterranean, ii. 396; arrives at Gibraltar, 398.

INDEX. 459

Dalton, John, discovers atomic theory, ii. 248.
Danes, tribute paid by, to Algiers, ii. 388.
Davis, Mr., statements of, in regard to pilots, ii. 23, 26, 27, 28.
Davy, Sir Humphrey, discoveries by, ii. 247.
Decatur, destroys frigate Philadelphia, ii. 402–404.
Dey of Algiers, appearance of, ii. 389; seizes American frigate, 394.
Discovery, title by, i. 5.
Dodge, Henry, revenue-cutter, order concerning, ii. 441.
Downing, Mr., on rural architecture, ii. 330, 350; death of, 350.
Draft, forcible resistance to, 452; principle of, 453; not conscription, 453; extent of, 453; constitutionality of, 454; Madison, Monroe, and others on, 454.
Drake, Sir Francis, visits northwest coast, i. 7; expedition of, discussed, i. 33.
Drawing, method of teaching, ii. 89.
Dutch, tribute paid to Algiers, ii. 388.

Eaton, Mr., on salt springs of New York, ii. 202, 203; on gypsum, 206.
Eaton, General, character of, ii. 389; arrives at Algiers, 389; interview of, with Dey, 389; negotiates with Tunis, 390; firmness of, 391; dismissed by Bey, 391; indignation of, 395; expedition of, 406; energy of, 407.
Education of teachers, ii. 72; Prussian system of, 73, 107; act to promote, 75; New York system of, 76; departments for, 77, 78; selection of academies for, 81; scheme of 84–105; time of study for, 107; apparatus needful for, 110; importance of, 321.
Election of members of Congress, power of Congress over, ii. 284; Caleb Strong on, 285; John Jay on, 286; George Nicolas on, 287; Hamilton on, 288; Story on, 289, 290; Kent on, 291; Madison on, 304–307, 811; Mason on, 309; proposed amendment of constitution concerning, 314.
Emancipation, progress of, ii. 49; by Southern States, 51.
English Language, method of study of, ii. 87; course of instruction in, 88.
Enrolling Act, ii. 452.
Enrolment in the city of New York, ii. 455.
Enterprise, schooner, fight of, with corsair, ii. 398.
Europe, imports of breadstuffs into, ii. 363; lack of subsistence in, 364.

Exports of provisions, statistics of, ii. 361–364.

Farms, of New York, too large, ii. 325; evils of large, 325.
Farm-houses, ii. 326; material of, 826; architecture of, 327; size of, 328; embellishment of, 328–330.
Farming, profits of, on Long Island, ii. 319.
Federalist, the authority of, ii. 287.
Fenelon, on intervention, i. 210.
Ferrelo, discovers northwest coast, i. 6.
Fire companies, exemption of, from military duty, ii. 160; from jury duty, 160.
Flag, American, order concerning, ii. 440, 441.
Florida, territorial government of, i. 416; admission of, 422; light-house keepers in, resign, ii. 426.
Flour, trade in, with Canada, i. 393.
Foote, Mr., on Mr. Adams, i. 360; inquiry by, 438, 440.
Foreigners, imports by, i. 147, 149.
France, treaties with, i. 65–68, 89–92; negotiations with, in 1777, 66; treaty of alliance with, 69; declares war against England, 69; authorizes spoliation of American commerce, 70; repudiates treaty of 1778, 71, 79, 81; claims of, under treaty of 1778, 72, 73; refuses to receive Mr. Pinckney, 76; captures American ships, 76; decree of directory of, 76; conduct towards envoys, 83; negotiations of, with United States, 84, 85, 87; loses West India Islands, 87; treaty of 1800 with, 91; questions under that treaty, 92 – 94; abandons claims against the United States, 99; intervention of, proposed in Mexico, 207, 208, 214; relations with, 226; scarcity of food in, ii. 363; cultivation of beet-root in, 363; tribute paid by, to Algiers, 387.
Frazer, establishment of, at Frazer Lake, i. 16.
Frazer River, discovered by Spaniards, i. 51; by Great Britain, 51.
Freestone, in New York, ii. 192.
Frémont, Col., services of, i. 262, 283; affidavit of, on Macnamara, 277; breaks up Macnamara's plans, 278.
Fuca, Juan de, visits northwest coast, i. 7.
Fugitive slaves, surrender of, i. 347; in New York, 348.
Fulton, invention of, ii. 271.

Galvanism, applied to chemical decompositions, ii. 247.
Genet, fits out privateers, i. 71; complaints of, 74; letter of, 86.

460 INDEX.

Geology, schools of, ii. 252; progress of, 253; object of, 256; uses of, 258.

Geography, method of study of, ii. 91; physical importance of, 92; topics of, 92.

Geological survey of New York, plan of, ii. 181, 226–241; objects of, 183; districts for, 227–230; maps for, 231; expense of, 232–235; reports of, 238; of Massachusetts, 240; of Tennessee, 240; of two Carolinas, 240.

George Washington, frigate, seized by Dey, ii. 393; cargo of, 394.

Georgia, order by governor of, ii. 411; light-house in, seized, 425.

Germany, American commerce with, i. 387.

Gneiss, value of, ii. 186; where found in New York, 187.

Gold mines, delusions concerning, ii. 213; value of, to the state, 213.

Graham's Island, formation of, ii. 257.

Granite in New York, ii. 185; uses of, 185, 186; in the Highlands, 186; in Saratoga county, 186; of New England, 186; cost of, 186.

Gray, Captain, visits the Strait of Juan de Fuca, i. 23; meets Vancouver, 24; discovers Bulfinch Harbor, 26; and the Columbia River, 26; Vancouver's account of his discoveries, 25, 26, notes; the true discoverer of the Columbia, 27; his discovery discussed by Lord John Russell, 36, 37; ascends the Columbia, 45.

Great Britain, claim to Oregon, i. 2, 4, 8, 10; doctrine of, concerning title by discovery, 5; power of, for war, 58; her warehouse system, 114, 127, 129–131, 134–144; anti-commercial policy of, 131; commercial treaties of, 132–134; commercial maxim of, 134; statistical returns of, 140, 151; tonnage of, in her foreign commerce, 151; encroachments of, 218, 263; protection by, of Mosquitoes, 218, 220, 263; proposed intervention in Mexico, 221, 222; progress of, 225; trade of, with Italy, 259; intervention of, in Argentine Republic, 265; encroachments of, in Central America, 267; grant of Mosquito territory to, 268; purpose of that grant, 268; encroachments in Honduras, 270; and Nicaragua, 270; purpose of encroachments, 270; establishment of, at Balize, 271; arms savages, 271; system of encroachment of, 272; services of, 274; intrigues of agents of, in California, 278, 280; squadron of, off California, 280; designs of, in California, 282; conduct of subjects of, in Yucatan, 295; claims of, to Nicaragua, 298; guarantees Mosquito territory, 299; claims of, to Mosquito territory, 300; policy of, toward Canada, 390; want of breadstuffs in, ii. 368; increase of population of, 368; tribute paid by, to Barbary States, ii. 388.

Greenwood Cemetery described, ii. 82; beauty of, 357.

Grotius, on intervention, i. 210.

Groves, advantages of, ii. 331, 333; proper composition of, 332.

Guerrero abolishes slavery in Mexico, i. 184; abolishes slavery, 436; character of his decree, 436; decree of, 448; appropriate powers conferred on, 450, 451.

Guirot, A. T., despatch of, ii. 429; resignation of, 429.

Guizot, on intervention in American affairs, i. 207, 208, 214.

Gypsum, connection of, with rock-salt, ii. 206, 207; in New York, 208.

Haldeman, W. N., despatches of, ii. 414, 415, 419.

Hamet, Bashaw, expedition of, ii. 407.

Hamilton, on election of members of Congress, ii. 288.

Handy, Commander, report of, ii. 425.

Hannegan, Mr., remarks of, i. 43.

Hare, Mr., improvements of the blowpipe by, ii. 247.

Hatch, F. H., despatches of, ii. 413, 432, 434, 435; misconduct of, 439, 447; order of, to Capt. Breshwood, 449; letter of, 436.

Haüy, theory of, ii. 259.

Heceta, visits northwest coast, i. 9; discovers Columbia River, 9.

Hensley, Capt., testimony of, i. 280.

Hero, of Alexandria, suggests use of steam, ii. 270.

History, study of, ii. 92; of the United States, 93.

Hollanders found New York, ii. 337.

Hudson's Bay Company, nature of possession by, i. 52.

Hulls, Jonathan, patent of, ii. 271.

Humboldt, Baron, on rights of riparian states, i. 411.

Hunter, Mr., remarks of, on trade with Canada, i. 405.

Huntington, Mr., objections of, to warehouse system, i. 124–128, 144; errors of, regarding British system, 135–141.

Importations, number of foreigners engaged in, i. 149; value of, in New York in 1845, 149.

Indemnities, whether promised by France, i. 93; whether released by United States, 93; whether due to American citizens, 98.

INDEX. 461

Indiana territory, act to create, i. 321.
Institutions, public, in republics, ii. 353.
Intervention, Guizot on, i. 207; doctrine of, 209; history of, 209; authorities on, 210; true limits of, 211; abuses of, 212; of France in Mexico, 214; of Spain in Mexico, 214; Olozoga on, 214, note; French, proposed by de Mofras, 215; British, proposed in Mexico, 221, 222; British, in Argentine Republic, 265, 266; of France, 265; British, in Central America, 271; character of British intervention, 271; in Yucatan, proposed, 284; origin of right of, 306.
Intrepid, the, attacks the Philadelphia, ii. 403; blown up, 405.
Iron in New York, ii. 208; value of, in Ausable valley, 208; sulphuret of, at Canton, 209.
Isothermal lines, ii. 266.
Italy, trade of Great Britain with, i. 259; railroads in, 260.

Jay's treaty, adoption of, i. 75; complaint of France concerning, 75.
Jay, John, character of, ii. 286; on election of members of Congress, 286.
Jefferson, views of, on French treaty, i. 73; circular letter of, 77, 78; letter to Mr. Madison, 88; his construction of treaty of 1800, 95; letter to Mr. Smith, 100; on the slave-trade, 368; return of, to United States, ii. 312; on public opinion in 1790, 313; report of, on tribute paid Barbary States, 397; attitude of, toward Algiers, 396; proposes confederation against Barbary States, 397.
Jefferson's plan, i. 431, 443, App.; vote on anti-slavery clause of, 431; proposed by Rufus King, 432; vote on, 445.
Jervis, Sir John, conquers West India Islands, i. 87.
Jones, W. H., sent to New Orleans, ii. 438; despatch of, 440; despatch to, 440; report of, 446; order of, to Capt. Breshwood, 447; conference of, with Mr. Hatch, 448; letter to Capt. Breshwood, 448; report on cutter Lewis Cass, 450.
Juno, discovery of, ii. 264.

Kent, Chancellor, on military duty of aliens, ii. 57; on construction of alien act, 67, 68; on election of members of Congress, ii. 291; character of, 291.
King, Rufus, proposes Jefferson's plan, i. 432; vote on his proposition, 446, App.
Klaproth, analyses of, ii. 245, 246.

Lavoisier, researches of, ii. 245.
Law, submission to, 455; resistance to, what, 455.
Lawrence, Lieut., fidelity of, ii. 451.
Lead in New York, ii. 211.
Lear, Commissioner, negotiates peace with Tripoli, ii. 407.
Lewis and Clark, voyage of, i. 45, 46; explore the Columbia, 45.
Lewis, Dixon H., remarks on death of, ii. 31; funeral ceremonies of, 32.
Liberia, progress of, ii. 42.
Liebig, on agriculture, ii. 380.
Lieutenant-General of the army, i. 163; grade of, created in 1798, 167; conferred on Washington, 167; essential part of military organization, 168, 177.
Limestone, value of, ii. 188; where found in New York, 188–194; water, 189; for burning, 189; gray, 190; at Sing-Sing, 190.
Literature fund, distribution of, ii. 75, 76; income of, 77, 83.
Livingston, Mr., his construction of treaty of 1800, i. 95, 96.
Long Island, shipwrecks on, ii. 2; advantages of, 319; profits of farming on, 319, 377; soil of, 320, 377; sandhills of, 378; climate of, 378.
Lotteries in Papal States, i. 254.
Louisiana, territory divided, i. 321; territorial government of, 417; admission of, 421; rebellion in, ii. 410; seizes custom-house, 413; exacts bonds for duties, 414, 415, 419; secession of, 421; purchase of, 421; condition of admission to the Union, 421; impedes free commerce on the Mississippi, 422; occupies United States fortresses, 422, 449; violent measures in, 423; light-house keepers in, resign, 426; seizure of branch-mint in, 429, 443.
Lowndes, Mr., on Missouri Compromise, i. 359.
Lumber, import of, from Canada, i. 392.

Mackenzie, explorations of, i. 44.
Macnamara, memorial of, i. 275–277; grant to, 277; connection of, with Great Britain, 277, 281; plans of, 278; lands at St. Barbara, 279; in Mexico city, 280.
Madison, Mr., instructions to Pinckney, i. 97, 98; propositions in Federal convention, 312; on the ordinance of 1787, 314–317; on slavery, 362; on election of members of Congress, ii. 304–307, 311, 314; joins democratic party, 313; draws Virginia resolutions, 313.

Marble quarries at Sing-Sing, character of, ii. 185, 190.
Margraaf, discoveries of, ii. 245.
Martens on intervention, i. 210.
Martinez arrives at Nootka, i. 13, 16; seizes the Iphigenia, 13; and the Argonaut and Princess Royal, 14; takes possession, 21.
Mason, Col., on slavery, i. 363; on election of members of Congress, ii. 309.
Maurelle visits the northwest coast, i. 9.
McCulloch on inconveniences of warehouse system, i. 130.
McLelland, Robert, revenue-cutter, seizure of, ii. 439, 451.
Meares, transactions of, on northwest coast, i. 11; lands at Nootka Sound, 11; treaty of, with Maquinna, 12; his memorial to Parliament, 13; twofold character of, 13.
Measurement of heights, ii. 268.
Mediterranean Sea, American commerce in, ii. 387.
Mercanti di Campagna, i. 257.
Merry v. Chexnaider, cited i. 320.
Meteorology, investigations in, ii. 265.
Mexican war, speech on, i. 198; conduct of, 169, 170, 205, 206; character of, 170; policy of, 198; successes in, 202.
Mexico, army operations in, i. 163, 164, 167; Indian hostilities in, 171; manifesto of Republican party of, 172; purchase of territory from, 183, 193; slavery prohibited in, 184, 186, 436; peonage in, 184; political condition of, 186, 204; parties in, 205; intervention in, proposed by Guizot, 207; indemnity from, 228; occupation of, 234, 236, 238; hostilities with Yucatan, 287; campaign in, ii. 36.
Mexico, the, wreck of, ii. 3.
Militia, power of Congress over, ii. 58; report on system of, 116; attacks upon, 116; origin of, 117; theory of, 117; uses of, 118; relation of, to defence, 120; efficiency of, 121; Washington on, 121; advantages of, 121; exercises of, 123, 126, 146–153; instruction of, 123, 127; law of United States concerning, 124, 152; constitutional provision concerning, 124; regimental parades of, 127; rendezvous of, 128; officers of, 129, 130; inspection of, 131, 133–135; non-commissioned officers of, 132, 164; penalties, 136; exemptions in, 142; students, 143; training of, regulated by Congress, 147–149; purpose of training, 152; volunteer corps, 153; parade of, in New York city, 157; firemen exempt from duty in, 160; parades of, in country, 162; term of duty in, 162, 164; expense of, 163; meetings of, 165; commutation in, 167, 168; law of 1792, 170, 176; enrolment of, 171, 172; minors exempted, 173; equipment of, 176; defects of system, 178.
Mineralogy, ii. 96; investigations in, 259.
Minerals of New York, ii. 198–215.
Minor, Lieutenant, testimony of, i. 279.
Mint, branch at New Orleans, draft on, ii. 426; deposit at, 427; payment of draft refused, 428; coinage, how stamped, 444; cost of, 445; taken possession of by Louisiana, 445.
Mississippi, free navigation of, impeded, ii. 416, 418, 420, 421; free navigation of, stipulated, 421.
Mississippi Territory, act establishing, i. 320; slaves prohibited in, 321.
Missouri Compromise, i. 355; Mr. Monroe's inquiry concerning, 355; Mr. Calhoun on, 356–358; Mr. Adams on, 357; Mr. Lowndes on, 359; extension of line of, 378–380.
Mofras, de, book of, on Mexico, i. 214; advocates intervention in, 215.
Mohs, system of, ii. 259.
Monroe, Mr., memorandum of, on Missouri Compromise, i. 355; letter of, to General Jackson, 358.
Monroe doctrine, i. 217, 264; violated by Great Britain, 265; not enforced by United States, 266; reiterated, 267.
Moose, of New York, ii. 222.
Morocco, treaty with, ii. 387; invaded by Spain, 408.
Morrison, J. J., dismissed the service of the United States, ii. 439.
Mosquitoes, British protection of, i. 218; limits of, 218; character of, 219, 268; king of, 220, 268, 270, 297; government of, 268; territory of, granted to England, 268; value of territory, 268; explorations of, 268; British claims in, 269, 300; navy of, 270; British encroachment on, 297; differences of, with Central America, 299; extent of territory of, 301.
Murray, Mr., his views on indemnities from France, i. 96.

Napoleon, maxim of, i. 166.
Natural philosophy, study of, ii. 94.
Naturalization, of minor child, ii. 59; legislation concerning, 60; act of March 26, 1790, 60; repealed, 61; act of January 29, 1795, 61; act of June 18, 1798, 62; unconstitutionality of act, 63; act of July 14, 1806, construction of, 64; construction of

INDEX. 463

4th section of, 65; retroactive effect of, 66; decision of United States Supreme Court concerning, 66; Kent on, 67, 70; Supreme Court of New York on, 68; British statute of, 69.
Negroes, free, do not increase, i. 332; prejudice against, 333; condition of, in the North, ii. 44.
Neutrality, proclamation of, by Washington, i. 71.
New Grenada, claims of, in Mosquito Territory, i. 301.
New Mexico, i. 427; government of, 428; character of, 438.
New Orleans, collector at, resigns, ii. 413; misconduct of collector at, 414, 416, 417; seizure of branch-mint at, 427.
New York, interest of, in French spoliation claims, i. 61; on slavery question, 345, 442; resolution of legislature on slave-stealing, 348; specie payments maintained in, 349; protects the frontier, 349; institutions of, 350; soldiers of, in Mexico, 350; lumber interests of, 393; pilot laws of, ii. 1, 4; pilot system of, 3; pilot question of, 12; military force of, in 1830, 175; duty of, in 1814, 299; services of, in 1814, 299; agriculture of, 360; advantages of agriculturists of, 371; agricultural capacity of, 372; agricultural districts of, 372, 377; cultivation of wheat in, 372, 374, 375; of maize, 375; productiveness of, 381.
New York city, defences of, i. 59; militia of, ii. 131, 157, 158; dangers of, 159; lecture on growth of, 337; foundation of, 337; progress of, 338, increase of population of, 338; future growth of, 339, 340, 382; luxury of, 343; environs of, 345, 346; mercantile men of, 358; accessibility of, 362; future grain-market of the world, 371.
Nicaragua, protest of, against British occupation, i. 219.
Nicolas, George, character of, ii. 287; on election of members of Congress, 287; resolutions introduced by, 313.
Nootka Sound, discovered by Perez, i. 9; visited by Cook, 10; Meares, 11; by Martinez, 13, 21; by the Argonaut and Princess Royal, 14; by Captain Broughton, 17; relinquished by Great Britain, 18; Vancouver's visit, 21; Spanish possession of, 22. Convention of, 14; discussed by Colonel Benton, 15, note; by Mr. Fox, 15, note; by Mr. Pitt, 16, note; De Koch's account of, 17; practical execution of, 17-19; construction of, third article of, 20; terminated by war, 23.

North, alleged aggressions of, i. 352; concessions of, 353.
Northwest Company, explorations of, i. 35.

O'Brien, Consul, visits Dey, ii. 389; protest of, 393; letter of, 394.
Observatories, ii. 264.
Officers of customs, misconduct of, ii. 412.
Officers in Mexico, memorial of, ii. 35, 39.
Ohio, wheat-crop of, i. 402; condition of, ii. 298.
O'Leary, D. F., letter of, to government of New Grenada, i. 269.
Olozoga, on intervention in Mexico, i. 214.
Optics, progress of, ii. 260.
Ordinance of 1787, Madison on, i. 314-317; recognized by first Congress, 318; Virginia concurred in passing, 320; Supreme Court of Louisiana on, 320; provisions of, 422; vote on, 447, App.; proposed by Jefferson, 188; vote on, 188, 433.
Oregon, title to, i. 2; question stated, 2; discovery of, 3, 6; claim of Russia to, 4; exploration of, 7-14; by Ferrelo, 6; by Drake, 7; by Fuca, 7; by Vizcaino, 8; by Perez, 8; by Heceta, 9; by Quadra and Maurelle, 9; by Cook, 10; by Berkeley, 11; by Meares, 11; by Martinez, 13; by Gray, 23; by Vancouver, 24-32. Nookta, convention concerning, 14-16; controversy between Vancouver and Quadra, 17; surrender by Spain, 17-19; extent of Spanish occupation, 20-22; discussion in Parliament, 32; Lord Clarendon's views, 33-35; Lord John Russell's views, 36-39; Lord Aberdeen's views, 41; Sir Robert Peel's views, 41; Mackenzie's discoveries, 44; Lewis and Clark's discoveries, 44, 45; Mr. Astor's settlement of, 46; occupation by Captain Biddle, 47; convention of 1818, 48; convention of 1827, 48; Spanish title maintained, 52-54; Canadian jurisdiction extended over, 55; speech on territorial government in, 309; climate of, unfit for blacks, 336; prohibition of slavery in, 343.
Organic remains, ii. 215-218.
Oribe, flight of, i. 266; besieges Montevideo, 266.
Orleans, Territory of, act concerning, i. 322; discussion on, 338.

Pacific Fur Company, founded, i. 46; sells to Northwest Company, 47.
Pallas, discovered, ii. 264.

Papal States, minister to, speech on, i. 247; government of, 249; political divisions of, 250; justice in, 251; finances of, 254; lotteries in, 254; area of, 255; population of, 255; commerce of, 255; harbors of, 255; exports of, 257; marine of, 257; agriculture of, 257; monopolies in, 258.
Peat, in New York, ii. 214.
Pennsylvania, condition of, ii. 298.
Peonage, in Mexico, i. 184; origin of word, 184; nature of, 185.
Perez, explores northwest coast, i. 8.
Philadelphia, frigate, loss of, ii. 401; burning of, 402–404.
Philosophy, study of, ii. 99; importance of, 99; political, progress of, 272.
Pierce, on granite in the Highlands, ii. 186.
Pilots, how regulated before the constitution, ii. 1; of New York, 1, 3, 4, 12, 19; of New Jersey, 3, 4; power to regulate, 6–9; New York, agreement of, 12; New York, appeal of, 15.
Pilot laws, speeches on, ii. 1, 12; act of 1789, 2; act of 1837, 3; defects of, 8–10; of New York, 13; of 1837, 14; of New York, repealed, 15; consequences of act of 1837, 17–21; injustice of, 21; working of, before 1837, 22; system of, suggested, 29.
Pinckney, Mr., speech of, in Federal convention, i. 418.
Polarization, discovered, ii. 260.
Poor, interest of, in maintaining good order, 454.
Pope, character of, i. 247; territorial possessions of, 247; government of, 248, 249; reforms by present, 252–254, 260.
Population, ratio of increase of, ii. 362.
Preble, Commodore, sent to Mediterranean, ii. 400; arrives at Tripoli, 401; attacks Tripoli, 405.
Presly, B. C., honorable conduct of, ii. 430.
Proclamation in regard to draft, ii. 452.
Property, inviolability of, ii. 354.
Prussia, education of teachers in, ii. 73; efficiency of, 79.
Purvis, Admiral, intervention of, in Uruguay, i. 266; declaration of, 281.

Quadra, y Bodega, visits northwest coast, i. 9; discussion with Vancouver, 17, 18, 19; refuses to surrender Nootka, 19; his construction of Nootka Sound convention, 22.
Queen's county, advantages of, ii. 319, 320; fertility of, 319.

Rain, observations on fall of, ii. 266.
Randolph, Mr., report of, i. 340; on slavery, 361; speech of, in Federal convention, i. 417.
Reciprocity treaties, construction of, i. 385; character of, 386.
Redfield, on storms, ii. 267.
Refraction, observed, ii. 260; double, 260; triple, 261.
Reid, on storms, ii. 267.
Revolutionary War, account of, in 1777, i. 67.
Rioters, warning to, ii. 456.
Riparian states, rights of, in watercourses, i. 411.
Riveria, succeeds Oribe, i. 266.
Rivers, free navigation of, ii. 421.
Rochester Aqueduct, building of, ii. 193.
Rocks of New York, 184–194.
Rogers, Lieutenant, fidelity of, ii. 451.
Rome, agriculture of, ii. 369.
Russell, Sir John, on Oregon question, i. 36–39.
Russia, claims of, to Oregon, i. 4.

Sahara, Desert of, origin of, ii. 384.
Saliferous rock, ii. 202–204.
Salt, springs of, in Onondaga county, ii. 198; manufactories of, 198; production of, 199; excise on, 199; export of, 200; rock, 202; extent of district, 203; connection of, with coal, 204.
Sandford, T., order of concerning cutter Lewis Cass, ii. 451.
Santa Ana, rule of, i. 174; manifesto of his party, 175.
Santa Barbara, junta of, i. 279.
Saracens, destroy Carthage, ii. 385; destroy Cyrene, 385; invade Spain, 386; history of, 408.
Science, progress of, ii. 242; application of, to the arts, ii. 269.
Shell-mar, value of, ii. 197.
Sherlock, J. T., despatch of, ii. 416.
Shoemaker, S. A., despatches of, ii. 428, 429; fidelity of, 451.
Sing-Sing, quarries at, ii. 185, 190.
Slavery, under the constitution, i. 180; admission of new states with, 181–183; prohibited in Mexico, 184; history of, in Mexico, 184, 185; New York, resolutions concerning, 186; views of non-slaveholding States concerning, 187, 191, 195; ordinance of 1787 concerning, 188; ordinance proposed by Mr. Jefferson, 188; vote on ordinance, 188; course of Northern States concerning, 189; Southern view of, 190; demands of the South concerning, 192; power to prohibit in territories, 194; prohibited in Mis-

INDEX. 465

sissippi Territory, 320; effect of extension of, 328, 329; prohibition of, in Oregon, 343; settlement of question of, 344; views of New York on question of, 345; opposition to extension of, 351; resolutions concerning, 351; Mr. Randolph on, 361; Mr. Butler on, 361; Mr. Madison on, 362; Mr. Mason on, 363; in Virginia, 365; Tucker on, 366; action of Virginia concerning, 367; origin of, 430; abolition of, proposed by Jefferson's ordinance, 431; power of Federal government over, 435; abolished in Mexico, 436; in California, 435; Trist on exclusion of, 441; effect of, on agriculture, ii. 45–47; injurious effects of, 50.

Slaves, importation of, prohibited, i. 321; increase of, 329; debate on importation of, 362; traffic in, 431. See *Fugitive Slaves.*

Soapstone in New York, ii. 192.
Society, organization of, ii. 355.
Soil, proper care of, ii. 324; of New York, 194, 198, 372; of prairies, 373; varieties of, 374; of Long Island, 377.
South Carolina, light-houses extinguished in, ii. 425.
Spain, title of, to Oregon, i. 3, 6, 8, 9.
States, admission of new, i. 418, 419, 421–428.
Statistics, science of, ii. 273.
St. Lawrence, free navigation of, i. 408; value of, to American commerce, 409.
Steam, uses of, ii. 270; history of, 271.
Storms, law of, ii. 267; movement of, 267.
Story, Judge, on election of members of Congress, ii. 289, 290.
Strong, Caleb, character of, ii. 284; on election of members of Congress, 285.
Students, exemption of, from military duty, ii. 143.
Sutliffe *v.* Forgey, ii. 68.
Swedes, tribute paid by, to Algiers, ii. 388.

Tallmadge, Mr., resolution of, concerning pilots, ii. 14.
Teachers, how selected, ii. 78; compensation of, 79, 106; course of study of, 84–86; responsibility of, 104; evidence of qualification of, 111; diplomas of, 112.
Teaching, principles of, ii. 101; true method of, 102; inductive method of, 103; business of, 106.
Territories, power of Congress over, i. 311–327; clause in constitution concerning, 313; speech on government in, 346.

Territories acquired from Mexico, speech on, i. 413.
Texas, admission of, i. 181; no slavery in above 36° 30', 181; cost of annexation of, 370.
Three million bill, i. 179.
Tiber, description of, i. 256.
Titcomb, James, case of, ii. 56–59.
Tonnage, foreign, in American commerce, i. 150, 152–157; American, 150, 153; increase of, 151; British, in British foreign commerce, 151.
Tripoli, war with, ii. 383; corsairs of, 386; treaty with, 387; demands of, 387, 392, 397; cuts down flag-staff, 398; invested by fleet, 400; attacked by Preble, 405; peace with, 407; present condition of, 408.
Trist, Mr., negotiation of, i. 440; letter to Mr. Buchanan, 441.
Tucker, St. George, on slavery, i. 366, 367.
Tunis, corsairs of, ii. 386; invaded by Charles V., 386; treaty with United States, 389; renews hostilities, 408; present condition of, 408.

Underwriters, action of, concerning pilots, ii. 16; influence of, 16; remonstrance of, 19; notice of, to ship-masters, 26.
United States, measures of, against France, i. 80; at war with France, 82; demands of, against France, 83; negotiations of, with France, 84, 85; rights of, under treaty of 1800, 92; liabilities of, under that treaty, 93, 94, 98–100, 102; destiny of, 238–245, 330, 331; reciprocity treaties of, 384; trade of, with Germany, 387; imports of, from Canada, 392, 393; value of imports from Canada, 401; value of exports to Canada, 401; militia law of, ii. 124; productiveness of, 365; area of, 365; agricultural advantages over Europe, 370; wheat-growing regions of, 373; treaties of, with Barbary States, 387; commerce of, in Mediterranean, 387; contributions of, to Algiers, 388; treaty of, with Tripoli, 407.
Uranus, discovery of, ii. 262.
Uruguay, dissensions in, i. 266.

Valley Forge, American army at, i. 67.
Vancouver, discussion with Quadra, 17; his claim under Nootka Sound convention, 20; his arrival at Nootka Sound, 21 and note; explores northwest coast, 24; meets Capt. Gray, 24; recognizes Gray as discoverer of the Columbia, 27; his discov-

VOL. II. 59

eries discussed by Mr. Pakenham, 28; surveys the coast, 29; extent of, his survey, 30; correspondence with Spanish officials, 31; his discoveries discussed by Lord Clarendon, 32; by Lord John Russell, 36; extract from journal of, 51.
Vattel, on intervention, i. 210.
Venetians, tribute paid by, to Algiers, ii. 388.
Virginia, cession of territory by, i. 319; vote for ordinance of 1787, 320; slavery in, 365; action of, concerning slavery, 367; opposition of, to slave-trade, 434; author of African colonization, ii. 45; resolution of 1798, 287, 313; reply of Kentucky to, 314.
Vizcaino visits northwest coast, i. 8.
Volcanoes, eruptions of, ii. 257.

Walpole introduces warehouse system, i. 142.
War, influence of, i. 230; with Tripoli, lecture on, ii. 383.
Warehouse system, i. 104; state of, before 1846, 105-110; proposed amendment of, 113; time of storage, 114; remission of interest, 115, 117; withdrawal for reëxportation, 116; sale of warehoused goods, 119; advantages of, 121-123; second speech on, 124; objections to, 125-128; inconveniences of, by McCulloch, 130; British system of, 114, 127, 129-131, 134-144; what goods may be warehoused under, 135; statute of William IV. concerning, 136-138; prohibition under, 136; powers of commissioners under, 137-139; warehousing of silks, 139; introduced by Walpole, 142; opposition to, 143; effect of proposed system, 145; on domestic production, 145; on business of importation, 147-149; estimated increase of revenue from, 146; benefit of, to New York, 160; compared with other cities, 160-162.
Washington, Gen., issues proclamation of neutrality, i. 71; responsible for conduct toward France, 77; on the militia, ii. 121.
Washington's Island, named by Captain Gray, i. 9; visited by Perez, 9.
Watt, his steam-engine, ii. 271.
Werner, researches of, in mineralogy, ii. 259.
Westcott, Mr., on Mr. Monroe's letter to Gen. Jackson, i. 358.
West India Company, letter of directors of, to Stuyvesant, ii. 337.
Wheat, importation of, i. 388; into England, through Canada, 391; export of, 394; Canadian, crops of, 396, 397; Canadian, exports of, 397-399; crop of, in Ohio, 402.
Worcester, Marquis of, his experiments, ii. 270.
Wright, Silas, address of, on agriculture, ii. 360; death of, 361; character of, 361.
Writing, method of teaching, ii. 89.

Yucatan, British encroachments in, i. 271; hostilities in, 271; bill to take possession of, 284; dissension in, 285; history of, 286; gains independence, 286; united to Mexico, 286; regains independence, 286; subdued by Santa Ana, 286; hostilities with Mexico, 287; neutrality of, 287; relation of, to United States, 288; internal condition of, 308.

Zule, case of, ii. 59.

www.ingramcontent.com/pod-product-compliance
Lightning Source LLC
Chambersburg PA
CBHW022104300426
44117CB00007B/577